Property, Paternalism and Power

Property, Paternalism and Power

Class and Control in Rural England

Howard Newby
Colin Bell
David Rose
Peter Saunders

Hutchinson of London

Hutchinson & Co. (Publishers) Ltd
3 Fitzroy Square, London W1P 6JD

London Melbourne Sydney Auckland
Wellington Johannesburg and agencies
throughout the world

First published 1978

© Howard Newby, Colin Bell, David Rose and Peter Saunders 1978

Set in Monotype Times New Roman
Printed in Great Britain by The Anchor Press Ltd
and bound by Wm Brendon & Son Ltd
both of Tiptree, Essex

British Library CIP data

Property, paternalism and power.
   1. Social classes – England – East Anglia
   2. Land – England – East Anglia
   3. East Anglia – Rural conditions
   I. Newby, Howard
   301.35′2′09426   HN400.56

ISBN 0 09 133670 8

Contents

6 *Contents*

Tables

Figures

Figures

Preface

This book is part of an ongoing research process which began with a study of Suffolk farm workers and will continue with a study of property. It was made possible by a grant from the Social Science Research Council and we are grateful to that body, particularly Stella Shaw, Gill Townend and Linda Park, for their help and cooperation. The Ministry of Agriculture eased our task considerably and we are also grateful to successive Academic Liaison Officers at the Ministry for allowing us to base our samples upon unpublished agricultural data; in addition the Ministry's Census and Survey Branch at Guildford dealt with our numerous queries with much patience. The Ministry has also allowed us to reproduce some of their data in Chapters 2 and 3 which were previously unpublished and are Crown copyright.

We have been fortunate in receiving the cooperation of many farming organizations at both the national and the local level. In the NFU Mr Richard Butler smoothed our path at a very early stage; and Brigadier J. Fishbourne and Mr Roger Paul performed the same duties on behalf of the CLA. We are pleased to acknowledge their help and that of other local and national officials of the two organizations. We must also offer our thanks to the many local councillors and council officials throughout East Anglia, but particularly in Suffolk, who provided us with information but who perforce must remain anonymous. And more than anyone else we must thank all those farmers and farm managers whom we interviewed as part of our survey and who generally received us with more friendliness and good humour than we had a right to expect. We used Peter Wormell and Anthony Rosen as sounding boards for many of our ideas and we are indebted to them for their hospitality and for sparing so much of their time to talk to us. Susan Miller and Sharon and David Bashaw provided hospitable bases for our sorties into the East Anglian countryside.

In the academic world we have obviously gained a great deal from discussions with our colleagues at the University of Essex, as well as from the members of the SSRC Stratification Seminars held periodically in Edinburgh and Cambridge. In particular we would like to thank Ada Cavazzoni, Ruth Gasson, Alan Harrison and Ray Pahl for their help.

Phil Holden and Bill Fitzgerald provided invaluable computing assistance; Geoff Norris and Susan Saunders assisted with the coding of questionnaires; and Linda Peachey and Nadia Massoud typed the manuscript with their customary efficiency.

This research was a genuinely cooperative effort and we were all involved in all aspects of it. Nevertheless writing this book involved a division of labour so that the responsibility of producing the first draft was as follows: Chapter 1 by Howard Newby; Chapter 2 by David Rose and Howard Newby; Chapter 3 by David Rose; Chapter 4 by Howard Newby; Chapter 5 by Colin Bell; Chapters 6 and 7 by Peter Saunders; and Chapter 8 by Howard Newby, David Rose and Peter Saunders. Howard Newby was responsible for pulling these drafts together and producing the published manuscript.

H.N., C.B., D.R., P.S.
Colchester, Sydney, Cambridge, Brighton

1 Introduction

Among the 97 per cent of the British population who do not work on the land, the farmer is stereotyped in varied and often contradictory ways. He is viewed as solid and dependable, a source of down-to-earth wisdom and a haven of continuity and stability in an ever-changing modern world. He is also regarded as a ruddy-complexioned John Bull, bluff and forthright in the expression of his opinions. Less flatteringly, the farmer is sometimes looked upon as the archetypal moaner, feather-bedded by the taxpayer's money, but forever pleading poverty while riding around in a large new car. In times of war or a world food crisis the urban population is reassured by his presence and the security which an indigenous agriculture allows; but otherwise the farmer is apt to be ignored or taken for granted, and even, as when he demands further cash support, resented. More recently with the rise of a trendy environmentalism the farmer has been branded as the destroyer of the nation's heritage, promoting the rape of the rural landscape and poisoning its flora and fauna in the pursuit of Mammon. To all this the farmer has had one stock response: no one understands the farmer except farmers themselves. Any sociological inquiry which attempts to delve behind the stereotypes is therefore fraught with difficulties.

These difficulties are not eased by the fact that even among themselves farmers are not entirely consistent in how they view agriculture as an occupation. On the one hand farming is a *business* – and very big business at that. Indeed, in terms of the value of its output it is the biggest business in the United Kingdom, larger than either the motor industry or the steel industry, more productive than the agriculture of Canada and as large as that of Australia and New Zealand put together (Plumb, 1971). But farming is also, to repeat a well-worn cliché, a *way of life*, much more, as any farmer will affirm, than a mere job, but a highly distinctive and unique life's experience. It is this belief in the unique qualities of the rural way of life which allows the farmer to set himself at a distance, socially as well as geographically, from the urban mass, and it is this social distance which produces the stereotyping. The farmer believes that these stereotypes reflect the misunderstanding and incomprehension of agriculture which so characterize prevailing urban attitudes. Thus farming to the farmer is also a constant battle against the meddling of an ignorant, but intimidatingly large, urban majority of the population. We are aware of the risk that this book may be regarded by them as yet another example of uninformed criticism. We hope, though, that what follows, will, if nothing else, lead to a more informed understanding of the social situation of the modern farmer.

Farmers in the British class structure

In Britain little sociological attention has been directed towards agriculture, a consequence, at least in part, of the dominance of the view that British society is rapidly becoming totally urbanized and industrialized. Almost inevitably scarce sociological resources have been directed towards towns and factories as locales for research, but this is not to say that there is nothing of sociological interest in the British countryside. For although the proportion of the population engaged in agriculture is such an extraordinarily low one in comparison with other countries, the influence of farmers and landowners extends far beyond the scope indicated by their numbers.

Farmers and farming in Britain have, indeed, been studied by sociologists, but almost entirely in areas of 'family' farming in upland pastoral areas (Newby, 1972b; Bell and Newby, 1974). These studies (for example, Arensberg and Kimball, 1968; Rees, 1950; Williams, 1956, 1964; Nalson, 1968; Jenkins, 1971) have, with one notable exception (Littlejohn, 1963), emphasized the *gemeinschaftlich* qualities of the local social structures (see Bell and Newby, 1971, Chapter 5). By and large the lack of occupational differentiation, the absence of hired agricultural workers and the existence of extensive kinship ties among the local population produced analyses of local stratification systems based upon status rather than class (Day and Fitton, 1975). These monographs also concentrated upon that section of the farming population which maintains what might be called, for the sake of convenience, expressive rather than instrumental ties with the land. Hence we know much more about the mechanisms by which 'the name is kept on the land' than we do about rates of return on capital invested. In addition, the sociology of farming, such as it is, tells us little about agricultural workers and about rural employer–employee relationships (again Littlejohn [1963] is an exception to this).

There are no sociological accounts of farming outside these areas of subsistence agriculture. In the predominantly lowland arable areas of southern and eastern England, where farming is big business and a very different social structure predominates, sociologists have directed their attention more towards the 'adventitious' population of ex-urbanites (Pahl, 1965; Ambrose, 1974). Farming in such areas is characterized by much greater economic differentiation, the presence of large numbers of hired workers unconnected by kinship ties with their employers and thus a much more class-based and (comparatively) class-conscious social structure (see Newby, 1977). Farmers in these areas are much more thoroughgoing capitalists than the subsistence farmers of the upland areas (Poulantzas, 1973a, p. 37; Bell and Newby, 1974), since they hire wage labour and extract a surplus value from this labour directly. They are also more capitalist in a looser sense – more sensitive to and oriented towards production for the market, more economically instrumental and less concerned with the affective aspects of farming. It is now some time since Frankenberg lamented that there was no account of social life in 'the capitalist organized business farming areas' of lowland England, an omission which he viewed as 'one of the most glaring gaps in the literature' (Frankenberg, 1965, p. 252). It is one of the purposes of this book to isolate some of the key theoretical issues to which we believe a study of capitalist farmers may contribute, and to describe and analyse the location of capitalist farmers in the class structure.

In addition to providing a sociological description of a hitherto unexamined section of the British population we are also concerned to examine a related set of theoretical problems which lie beyond the narrow confines of the sociology of agriculture. We wish to argue that farmers occupy a dominant position in the rural social structure and we will eventually want to explore the consequences of this in terms of their relationships with other sections of contemporary rural society. At its simplest this will involve an addition to the some-what meagre sociological knowledge about the English middle class, and it is worth emphasizing at the outset that we consider this study to be as much a contribution to research on social stratification in modern Britain as a piece of occupational, or even rural, sociology.

However, we inevitably encounter difficulties when it comes to placing our study in the context of other sociological investigations of the middle class. Not only has the English middle class received far less attention than its working-class counterparts, but even within the middle class sociological investigation has been directed disproportionately towards certain specific occupational groups and organizations. For example, if we divide the middle class according to an admittedly somewhat dubious division of labour into entrepreneurial, professional, managerial and 'white-collar' groupings, then the bulk of research attention has been devoted to the latter group, for reasons of both theoretical importance (especially in relation to orthodox Marxist class analysis) and accessibility. Thus otherwise admirable discussions of the class structure in modern Britain and other Western societies may begin a discussion of the middle class *in toto*, but soon descend into a detailed consideration of clerical and other lower-level non-manual employees and the significance of the growth of this sector in re-shaping the class structure (see Giddens, 1973, Chapters 9, 10; Roberts *et al.*, 1977, Chapters 6, 7). Since such discussions must perforce follow the available literature and evidence this is hardly surprising, for what is available is all too often the investigation of bureaucratic work situations (e.g. Lockwood, 1958; Prandy, 1965) and/or the scope and nature of white-collar trade unionism (e.g. Blackburn, 1967; Bain, 1970). The enterprise structure of agriculture in this country, as we shall see, precludes any systematic comparison with this literature.

Similarly the somewhat scanty literature on the professional and managerial sections of the middle class is only tangentially relevant to a discussion of farmers. Farmers are not conventionally regarded as members of the 'professions'. Their education and training, methods of entry into their occupation and the kinds of restricted access which operate are not those which are to be found in the 'classic' professions like law and medicine (see Johnson, 1972). Neither does the notion of 'professionalization' mean the same to a farmer as it does to, say, a schoolteacher or a social worker. Certainly farmers are by no means immune to the connotations of status which the term 'profession' evokes, but professionalism in agriculture is interpreted as an unremitting economic rationality which makes comparisons with the literature on professionalization (e.g. Carr-Saunders and Wilson, 1964; Jackson, 1970) somewhat hazardous. In other words, professionalism in agriculture cannot be divorced from the entrepreneurial role of the farmer and this restricts any comparison with other professions where entrepreneurialism is either totally absent or constitutes a relatively minor aspect of achieving professional status.

When we move to a consideration of the managerial middle class, however, we move into an area which is of much more direct relevance to our own concerns in this study. The managerial function is obviously an important part of the entrepreneurial role and indeed one of the main areas of academic interest has been to assess the significance of the division between ownership and managerial control in modern joint-stock companies. Proponents of the 'managerial revolution' thesis (e.g. Burnham, 1941; for a summary see Child, 1969, Chapter 3) have argued that the division of ownership and control within large-scale industry has prompted the rise of a new managerial élite with a different set of values and interests to those of the profit-maximizing business owner. However, the widespread absence of any division between ownership and control in agriculture, because of the prevailing number of small-scale, family-owned businesses, again limits any direct comparison between agriculture and industry. Nevertheless, the very largest agricultural companies share a management structure not entirely dissimilar to many industrial companies and, moreover, the emergence of large-scale 'company farming' is a trend in agriculture to which we shall pay particular attention. Furthermore the lengthy debate on the significance of the division between ownership and control in modern industry directs our attention towards a number of issues which have received relatively little attention from sociologists. For example, to what extent are the interests of predominantly non-propertied managers coincident with those of owner-entrepreneurs? Only Nichols (1969) and Pahl and Winkler (1973) have directly addressed themselves to this question in an empirical manner. Nichols found that the ideologies and activities of managers were such that they perceived few differences between themselves and the owners of capital. Pahl and Winkler, on the other hand, emphasized the distinction between those managers who pursue a rationally calculated policy of profit maximization and those who accept that they have additional social responsibilities which may lead them to temper their instrumentalism with more humanistic concerns. What limits both these and other discussions of managerial ideology, however (cf. Child, 1969; Crouch, 1974), is the absence of any standard entrepreneurial ideology with which to make a comparison. This also applies to studies of managerial middle-class life-styles (Watson, 1964; Bell, 1968; Pahl and Pahl, 1972) centring on the interaction between career and family.

It is, therefore, the entrepreneurial section of the middle class –

within which most farmers are firmly located – which has received least sociological attention. While there are scattered references in the literature on élites (e.g. Guttsman, 1969; Crewe, 1974; Stanworth and Giddens, 1973) and on the state in capitalist societies (e.g. Miliband, 1969; Poulantzas, 1973*b*, 1975), they are mostly concerned with the 'positional power' of certain élite or ruling-class groupings and the social backgrounds of their members. While there is an awareness of the need to observe such groupings 'in action' (see Stanworth and Giddens, 1975; Pahl and Winkler, 1973), the formidable problems of accessibility have made such empirical analyses few and far between (see e.g. Finer, 1955/56; Hewitt, 1973; Winkler, 1976). Consequently that section of the middle class which is widely recognized as being of considerable theoretical interest remains largely unexamined and our overall perception of the middle class has become distorted as a result. As it currently stands, the literature concentrates on the problems of middle-class *employees*, especially on the social accoutrements of managerialism and mobility, rather than on business owners and entrepreneurs. This has led to an emphasis in stratification theory upon the distribution of income rather than *wealth* and upon authority relationships in the work situation rather than *property* relationships more broadly defined. Yet any empirical investigation of the entrepreneurial middle class is immediately confronted with the issue of property relationships – as recent studies of shopkeepers and petty landlords have shown (Bechhofer and Elliott, 1968; Bechhofer *et al.*, 1974; Elliott and McCrone, 1975).

A sociological investigation of farmers can therefore contribute significantly to our understanding of property and the entrepreneurial activity for which it forms a basis. It is a premise of this study that property is *at least* as important a feature of the stratification system of modern Britain as the distribution of income and authority. For many, no doubt, this is a truism, yet the fact remains that while the centrality of property as an institution is often referred to, it has largely been ignored as an object of study. Indeed, much the same could be stated about entrepreneurial activity in general. Here the only consistent theme to have emerged – mainly from the study of *petit-bourgeois* groups like shopkeepers and small-scale landlords – has been the threat of 'proletarianization': the reduction of the entrepreneur to the status of an employee. This threat is believed to colour much of their values and their politics and accounts for the emphasis which they lay upon independence and thrift, a populist distrust of any state intervention in their own affairs, and an increasing willingness to engage, however reluctantly, in political action to secure their own continued existence. The danger of proletarianization is, moreover, far from notional, since the number of self-employed people in Britain has nearly halved during this century and currently stands at a little over 3 per cent. Even a superficial examination of agriculture shows that farmers are subject to the same economic pressures. Farms are becoming larger and more capital-intensive; the marginal producer is being squeezed out and the number of farmers has fallen, slowly but consistently, since the war. However, when analysing agriculture we are also dealing with one of the most important concentrations of wealth – land – which serves as a reminder that, while the entrepreneurial middle class may be a small and decreasing section of the population, its significance in terms of the ownership of wealth (Atkinson, 1974) makes its members a far from negligible factor in the class structure. In addition, the analysis of landownership takes us at one extreme into the traditional landed upper class – almost unchartered sociological territory.

Property and property relationships

The precise role of property and property relationships in British society have, then, by no means been systematically investigated. As we have indicated, while there is no lack of agreement that property represents a crucial aspect of the British, and indeed any other, capitalist class structure, there has been a surprising lack of emphasis on the institution of property in recent empirical studies (see, for example, Westergaard and Resler, 1975). Perhaps this has been because, with one or two significant exceptions, property rights have appeared to be largely uncontested in contemporary British society. Yet such appearances can be deceptive: as Moorhouse and Chamberlain (1974) have demonstrated, the extent of lower-class adherence to the dominant ideology of property rights cannot be taken for granted. Nevertheless, apart from the limited political issue of nationalization of this or that industry, there are few signs of a vigorously contested public – or indeed academic – debate on the nature and distribution of property in British society as there is on, say, income. This state of affairs contrasts markedly with the long and continuous historical debate on the nature of property that has exercised political philosophers since the time of the ancient Greeks.

While it lies beyond the scope of this book comprehensively to examine the various themes that have occurred in the lengthy history of writings about property (see Schlatter, 1951, for a useful summary; also Rose *et al.*, 1976), it is necessary briefly to draw attention to some of the more important theories of property which have some significance for our argument.

We may begin by outlining one of the most influential explanations of the origins of private property: Locke's 'natural rights' theory. Locke argued that property ownership rested upon the 'natural rights' of man – the right to use whatever in the natural environment men deem necessary for their needs, and the right to take as one's own whatever one has expended labour upon, provided it is not then wasted:

> Though the earth and all inferior creatures be common to all men, yet every man has a 'property' in his own 'person'. This nobody has any right to but himself. The 'labour' of his body and 'work' of his hands, we may say, are properly his. Whatsoever, then, he removes out of the state that Nature hath provided and left it in, he hath mixed his labour with it, and joined to it something that is his own, and thereby makes it his property. ... As much as anyone can make use of to any advantage of life before it spoils, so much he may by his labour fix a property in. ... As much land as a man tills, plants, improves, cultivates, and can use the product of, so much is his property. [Locke, 1960, pp. 306, 308.]

Locke is, then, justifying only that property which one man can produce by his own labour, and use for his own purposes. It is a theory more applicable to a society where property is widely distributed. The three criteria of a 'naturally-just' distribution of property – need (which could be interpreted as desire), expenditure of labour (which could be interpreted as creative entrepreneurship), and use (which could be interpreted as exploitation and accumulation) – provided a neat 'elective affinity' with the economic realities of Locke's generation (see Macpherson, 1973, pp. 128–31). But, as with all justifications couched in universalistic terms, Locke's theory was open to diverse interpretations. In particular, his insistence on mixing the sweat of one's brow with the object of 'need' provoked what today would be an immediately-anticipated radical attack on the very *status quo* which Locke was himself concerned to defend. For, if property was that which man has 'mixed his labour with', then how can it be either natural or just for the privileged few to expropriate the surplus created by the labour of the many?

Utilitarianism attempted to provide an answer to this question. As expounded by Hume, utilitarianism became an antithesis to Locke's 'natural rights' theory:

Against all theories of formal right, Hume urged the principle of utility – the rules of justice are conventions which experience has shown to be useful for the promotion of happiness. . . . Applying this general principle to property, Hume argued that private ownership and its laws had no other origin or justification than utility. . . . The true system of property, he concluded, is that which the theorists of natural rights have defended, for the wrong reasons. [Schlatter, 1951, pp. 241–2.]

Hume set out what he considered the principal rules establishing title to property – namely, present possession, first possession, long possession, accession and succession – and argued that the origins and justice of such rules derived from conventions which in turn arose out of the history of man's social experience. The distribution of property was as it was because that was the system which had evolved in response to men's needs. It was the 'right' system because it alone was the product of men's history, and it alone best 'fitted' men's present situation. As developed by other utilitarians, such as Bentham and James Mill, this presented not only an 'explanation' of property and a justification of its contemporary distribution, but was the centrepiece of the classical liberal creed observed by the new industrialists of the nineteenth century.

It was the landed interest who had most to fear from a philosophy of property based upon utility, but in Edmund Burke they found a spokesman who opposed the principle of 'mere' utility with others of experience and tradition. Burke therefore conceived of landed property in terms of stewardship – that in the context of the historical 'process of nature' man's transitory and fleeting existence reduced him to the status of a steward serving and caring for the landed estate which transcended the generations. This led Burke in his *Reflections on the French Revolution* to venerate 'the partnership . . . between those who are living, those who are dead, and those who are to be born', sanctified by the Constitution and epitomized by the continuity of the landed estate. The 'steward' therefore served rather than owned his property. Consequently Burke emphasized the obligations as much as the rights of property ownership. He feared the transfer of political power from land to the new industrial capitalists, since their utilitarian denial of moral obligation and duty as guides to action represented a threat to the continuation of a stable social order. As Nisbet (1966, p. 27) points out: 'In the new economic order he could see the fragmentation, the atomisation of property, and its conversion into impersonal shares that would never inspire allegiance or lead to stability. And Burke, of course, was right.' This philosophy is by no means an anachronism in the view of many landowners today. As we shall see in Chapter 3, the current debate over the future of private landownership is conducted in precisely these terms.

However, it was only with the Scottish political economists – Millar, Ferguson and Smith – that the analysis of property ownership was extended to take account of the relationship between access to property, and the basis of class formation. They, of course, in turn led Marx to develop the first truly sociological account of the importance of property, stressing its significance as the basis of economic and political domination, and the relationship between property ownership and ideological formations. Thus: 'Property is a kind of power. For instance capital is called by the economists, "the power over the labour of others". We are faced therefore with two kinds of power: the power of property, that is of property owners, on the one hand, and political power, the might of the state, on the other' (Marx, in Jordan (ed.), 1972, p. 145); and: 'Upon the different forms of property, upon the social conditions of existence, rises an entire superstructure of distinct and peculiarly formed sentiments, illusions, modes of thought, and views of life' (Marx, in Jordan (ed.), 1972, p. 272).

Weber, too, recognized the economic and political significance of the fundamental cleavage in society between owners and non-owners of property. He, however, also pointed to the divisions and variations which existed within the class situations of property-owners themselves, arguing that different sections of the propertied stratum in society may conceive of the use of their property in different ways:

It is the most elemental economic fact that the way in which the disposition over material property is distributed among a plurality of people, meeting competitively in the market for the purpose of exchange, in itself creates specific life chances. . . . 'Property' and 'lack of property' are therefore the basic characteristics of all class situations. . . . Within these categories, however, class situations are further differentiated . . . [numerous] distinctions differentiate the class situations of the propertied, just as does the 'meaning' which they can and do give to the utilization of property. . . . Accordingly, the propertied, for instance, may belong to the class of rentiers or to the class of entrepreneurs. [Gerth and Mills, 1948, p. 182.]

We shall have cause to return to these different 'meanings' in Chapter 8 when we consider the various types of ideologies of property ownership held by farmers. However, it should by now be apparent that the concept of property refers not to the inherent quality of external objects *per se*, but to the socially and legally defined rights which attach to such objects. It is in this sense that various conceptions of property ownership become highly relevant to the consideration of social inequality in contemporary rural society. This is not only in the obvious sense that the distribution of material resources will in large part determine the character of that society's economic and political life, but also in the sense that such conceptions serve as important legitimating ideologies buttressing the stability of social life. For example, those who have never heard of Locke, Burke or Hume nevertheless pay such philosophers tribute when unknowingly they resurrect such centuries-old theories to 'explain' modern situations which these writers could never have envisaged. One of our concerns will be to illustrate how various justificatory theories concerned with the legitimacy and domain of the distribution of property, once they have entered our stock of knowledge and vocabulary of understanding, retain their essence and are transmitted down the generations and across classes, to reappear as unthinking 'statements of fact'. Decontextualized from the initial situation in which they originated these ideologies of property ownership have served to create a sense of immutability and inevitability to the distribution of property, particularly in the ownership of land which is surrounded by a varied set of cultural symbols emphasizing continuity (Williams, 1973). In other words, such ideologies of property ownership contribute to a system of 'natural' inequality in the countryside which can remain an extraordinarily prevalent feature of the taken-for-granted perception of rural society.

One of the themes of this book is therefore to explore the ramifications of a property-based system of rural social stratification. We shall be addressing this theme most explicitly in Chapter 3, where we shall discuss the changing nature of agricultural landownership and the various threats to the continuity of private capital in agriculture, and in Chapter 8, where we shall return to a detailed discussion of the ideologies of property ownership and their implications for stabilizing the rural class structure. However, the institution of private property is something which forms a basis for all the activities of the farmers which we describe in the following pages, whether we are concerned with inter-generational continuity (Chapter 2), relationships with hired workers (Chapter 4), issues of public access to the countryside and environmental conservation (Chapter 5) or the engagement of farmers in local political activity (Chapter 6). The importance of land as a factor of production in agriculture, and the significance of agriculture in rural society, make property a far more important feature of the stratification system than either occupation or income *per se* (cf. Stinchcombe, 1962). Thus agriculture is a not altogether inappropriate area in which to begin an examination of property relationships in British society generally.

Paternalism and power

This book has another important and parallel theme. We are also concerned to analyse the normative and relational aspects of contemporary class relationships in rural England. More specifically we shall be concerned with East Anglia, since this book follows on very closely from an earlier study by Newby (1977) of agricultural workers in Suffolk. At the conclusion of his study Newby argued strongly that in order fully to appreciate the social behaviour of the agricultural worker in a highly stratified rural class structure it was necessary to consider this structure as a totality, rather than devote attention solely to the agricultural workers themselves (Newby, 1977, Chapter VIII). In other words, in order to understand how this social system is perceived and 'explained' from below we must also understand how it is perceived and 'explained' from above. Moreover this imposition of certain definitions of the situations has to be seen as a continuous social process, occurring both on the farm while the work goes on and outside through the possession of important authority roles in the local community by farmers and landowners. Any complete explanation of rural inter-class relationships must, therefore, take account of both of these arenas.

The basis of Newby's argument was that in a highly stratified, but also highly particularistic, face-to-face social structure, farmers and landowners attempt to enforce a necessary degree of stability to their domination by operating a complex web of traditional authority relationships – what is customarily referred to as 'paternalism' (for detailed discussion, see Newby, 1976; 1977, Chapter VIII).[1] There is a good deal of historical evidence (summarized in Newby, 1975; 1977, Chapter I) to suggest that farmers and landowners have recognized that a labour force that *identified* with the system that subordinated it was in the long run more reliable and more efficient than a group of workers who gave their grudging consent under the threat of sanctions. Employers therefore often set about cultivating this identification since it confers the necessary stability in the organization of rural society that is essential, not only for general social order, but successfully to perform the many arduous and complex farming operations which span the agricultural year. Typically this legitimation has been carried out on the basis of tradition, which as Weber (1964, pp. 341–2) recognized, was the most stable form of authority since it applied both to 'the sanctity of age-old rules' and to the *person* embodying these rules, who could on occasions act on the basis of personal prerogative without jeopardizing his claims to legitimacy.

In rural England the idiom in which this traditional authority has been expressed has been the ethic of the gentleman (Wilkinson, 1970; Coleman, 1973; Newby, 1975). 'Real' gentlemen were distinguished by a strict code of what was 'done' and 'not done' and part of the rules of gentlemanly behaviour was a benevolent concern for the 'lower orders' in rural society. This concern was summarized as follows by John Stuart Mill:

. . . the lot of the poor, in all things which affect them collectively, should be regulated *for* them, not *by* them. They should not be required or encouraged to think for themselves, or give to their own reflection or forecast an influential voice in the determination of their destiny. It is the duty of the higher classes to think for them, and to take responsibility for their lot, as the Commander and Officers of an army take that of the soldiers composing it. This function the higher classes should prepare themselves to perform conscientiously, and their whole demeanour should impress the poor with a reliance on it in order that, while yielding passive and active obedience to the rules prescribed for them, they may resign themselves in all other respects to a trustful *insouciance*, and repose under the shadow of their protectors. The relation between rich and poor should be only partially authoritative; it should be amiable, moral, and sentimental; affectionate tutelage on the one side, respectful and grateful deference on the other. The rich should be *in loco parentis* to the poor, guiding and restraining them like children. Of spontaneous action on their part there should be no need. They should be called on for nothing but to do their day's work, and to be moral and religious. Their morality and religion should be provided for them by their superiors, who should see them properly taught it, and should do all that is necessary to ensure their being, in return for labour and attachment, properly fed, clothed, housed, spiritually edified and innocently amused. [Mill, 1848, pp. 318–20.]

It should be emphasized that this is a normative prescription: how many rural villages ever corresponded to such a smoothly run paternalistic system must remain a subject for considerable conjecture if not scepticism. Nevertheless Mill is expressing what many nineteenth-century employers naturally felt – that the sedative effects of paternalism were of a kind that would bring about stability and order and an identification of the workers with their 'betters'.

Paternalism therefore enabled power relationships to become moral ones, and embedded in the very concept of paternalism is the notion of dependence upon the moral judgements of others and how they define the prevailing social situation. It is because of this that Mill placed so much emphasis upon ideological control as well as fulfilling material needs. Ideologically 'correct' evaluations and moral attitudes would be inculcated, legitimating the existing social hierarchy and defining the limits and possibilities of the behaviour of those in subordinate situations. Such a complete hegemony over beliefs and values is, of course, extremely difficult to achieve. It is approached most closely in a context whereby an institutional framework is created for a self-contained and total social situation. Perhaps the most extensive analysis of this process has been carried out by Coser, who has dubbed such small-scale and total social structures 'greedy institutions' (Coser, 1974). Certainly the occurrence of stable paternalist rule seems to accord with the presence of conditions conducive to the construction of such greedy institutions – i.e. somewhat isolated and/or self-contained work and community situations. Empirical examples from nineteenth- and twentieth-century England include nineteenth-century Glossop (Birch, 1960, Chapter 2) and St Helens (Lane and Roberts, 1971), Banbury before the arrival of the aluminium factory (Stacey, 1960; Stacey *et al.*, 1975), 'Casterton Mills' (Martin and Fryer, 1973) and domestic service (Davidoff, 1974). Most importantly for our present perspective, there seems to be a good deal of evidence to suggest that such paternalism is particularly common in certain configurations of agrarian social structures (Genovese, 1971, 1974; Scott, 1974; Newby, 1977).

At this point it is necessary to emphasize once again that paternalism does not exist in a social vacuum – it is derived from and embedded in a particular system of social stratification, the source of which is basically economic and objectified through property. Paternalism is therefore a method by which class relationships become defined, and grows out of the necessity to stabilize and hence morally justify a fundamentally inegalitarian system. Paternalism – and its obverse, deference – must therefore be regarded as a *relationship* rather than an attribute of the parties involved (for extended discussion see Newby, 1975, 1976). Indeed it is tempting to regard such a system of traditional authority as involving no more than an exchange relationship, between paternalism on the one hand and deference on the other, yet this is to overlook the inherently hegemonic nature of traditional authority which defines the prevailing 'rate of exchange' as legitimate. It is precisely by defining the relationship as a free and fair exchange that it is stabilized. The exercise of traditional authority thus involves not so much an exchange as the management of the social hierarchy. Moreover, this management involves the superordinate class being drawn into an inherently contradictory relationship with its subordinates. On the one hand its interest is to maintain a degree of hierarchical *differentiation* from those over whom it rules; on the other hand it wishes to cultivate their *identification* by defining the relationship as an organic partnership in a cooperative enterprise (Newby, 1975).

Paternalism contains this contradiction at every level. At one and the same time paternalism may be exemplified by autocracy and obligation, cruelty and kindness, oppression and benevolence, exploitation and protection. Each facet derives from the necessity simultaneously to maintain both social differentiation and social identification within a hierarchical social structure. Paternalism therefore creates a tendency to identify with a particular institution and its strength lies in the fact that as the subordinates come to accept these relationships as legitimate so the prevailing ethos increases in strength. Kindness and affection may develop as the appropriate definitions of mutual obligations are accepted. It thus tends to disguise, however imperfectly, fundamental conflicts of interest and to mediate, however unjustly, between one class and another (see Genovese, 1974, Part One and Appendix). In doing so, however, it grants to subordinate individuals certain prerogatives which, while supposedly in the gift of those in power, tend over time to be appropriated as 'rights'. It is therefore necessary to take account of paternalism and deference as an ongoing social process, for while custom may sanction claims upon those exercising traditional authority, this can frequently lead to the relationship being redefined from below, acting as a basis from which to project rights and demands. Hence the importance of what Newby has called 'tension-management' in the successful exercise of traditional authority, i.e.

the manner in which the contradictions in the relationship may be successfully contained, controlled or dissipated (see Newby, 1975, for details).

We are engaged, therefore, in a case study of a much broader structural phenomenon, which Newby (1975) has termed the 'deferential dialectic' (for a further case study, see Bell and Newby, 1976). The successful management of the contradictions inherent in the deferential dialectic forms the key to stable traditional authority in rural society and we shall be exploring such 'tension-management' in action. As Williams (1973, p. 182) has pointed out, 'there was always a contradiction in English agrarian capitalism: its economics were those of a market order; its politics were those of a self-styled aristocracy and squirearchy, exerting quite different and "traditional" disciplines and controls'. Much of the analysis of the rural class structure in this book will be concerned with how far farmers continue to maintain a stable hegemony over other groups in contemporary rural society. In this case we shall be specifically engaged in a comparative analysis with Newby's study of the same situation 'from below'. We have information about rural inter-class relationships from data gathered from farm workers, but this will only take us so far; now we wish to explore it further by examining the situation of farmers. Newby, however, more or less took it for granted that farmers, both in the work situation and in the local community, were engaged in the exercise of traditional authority. While as a generalization (especially in comparison with the majority of industrial employers) this may be allowed to stand, in a study of farmers themselves this assumption must be examined more closely. Certainly it needs to be regarded as an hypothesis suitable for empirical investigation rather than as a fully-attested 'fact'. It is a commonplace to observe that the industrialization of British society has been accompanied by an increasing division of labour and a growth of specialization. This in turn has wrought a general cultural change – 'rationalization' in Weberian terms – away from justifying authority in terms of tradition towards legitimation in terms of knowledge and expertise. The cult of the gentlemanly amateur has been replaced by that of the professional expert. It seems plausible to suppose that farmers, too, have been caught up – more so than agricultural workers – in this general cultural shift. If farming as a business has, since the Second World War, become more emphasized at the expense of farming as a way of life, then one might suppose that farmers today are increasingly adopting a professional ethic rather than a gentlemanly one. In any case this whole issue will need to be explored empirically rather than taken for granted.

Similarly, we shall find it necessary to develop much more finely-discriminating typologies of the farmers themselves according to sociologically relevant variables. These problems have already been alluded to in a previously published paper (Bell and Newby, 1974) and will be developed further in succeeding chapters. However, as should be apparent from the issues raised already in this chapter, we shall be concerned primarily (although not exclusively) with farmers who are *owners* of property; who are *employers* of hired labour; and who are actively engaged in risk-bearing decision-making as *entrepreneurs*. In addition, it is in the logic of our analysis to return to East Anglia, where Newby carried out his study of agricultural workers, for the empirical investigation of these issues. Thus, we recognize in advance that the farmers whom we studied are far from being typical of farmers in England as a whole and no claims for typicality are made. Rather we have selected them on the basis of the particular *theoretical* interests of a sociological nature that we have introduced above.

It is also apparent that we shall not be solely concerned with the role of farmers *qua* farmers. The village as a 'greedy institution' has recently come under considerable attack, mainly due to the influx of urbanite newcomers. The traditional dominance of farmers and landowners in the wider community can no longer be assumed as axiomatic and we shall need to investigate carefully their changing role in the wider community, particularly the mechanisms whereby their dominance of local government in rural areas may be maintained. A substantial proportion of our analysis (see Chapters 5 and 6 below) has been concerned with assessing the strength of the 'agricultural interest' in local politics (including the changes that followed local government reorganization) and the extent to which the policies pursued by local government continue to reflect their interests, despite the influx of newcomers to rural areas. Hence we have been engaged in a study of what has become known as 'community power' which has involved not only interviewing farmers, but councillors, local government officers, pressure-group activists and other interested parties in the area.

Change and continuity in the rural class structure

Finally, in this introductory chapter, we need to consider the historical development of the contemporary rural class structure. It would be easy, though somewhat mistaken, to regard the continuing influence of farmers and landowners in the social, political and economic affairs of British society as merely an historical lag. Historically it is of course true that the ownership of land conferred enormous economic and political power, as well as social prestige, upon the tiny minority of the population fortunate enough to take advantage of it. Thus, until the nineteenth century the British ruling class was a landowning class, and even though, since the Industrial Revolution, the main sources of wealth have shifted elsewhere, landowning has continued to represent an important basis of power within a predominantly industrial plutocracy (see Perkin, 1969). Until the First World War the principal institution of landownership was the large landed estate, owned privately by a family which belonged to a small, aristocratic élite group, a ruling class which, despite its declining importance as a source of the country's wealth, still controlled most of the levers of political power. For much of the nineteenth century, therefore, the landed interest was the government, though it did not always rule in its own interest. Each successive Reform Act from 1832 onwards cut inroads into the power of the landowners, gradually reducing their political influence, especially in the form of the effective control of seats in the House of Commons. Nevertheless it was not until 1885 that representatives of the landed interest were outnumbered in the House of Commons and not until 1906 that they were a minority in the Cabinet.

Of course, owning land was then quite distinct from farming land and this distinction was made manifest in the so-called 'natural orders' of rural society, the great tripartite distinction of landowners, tenant farmers and landless agricultural labourers which was the mainstay of Victorian rural England. As one parliamentarian is reported to have said in an anti-Corn Law debate, 'A landowner is no more a farmer than a shipowner is a sailor.' The overall picture of a landowning class with specific functions quite separate from farming was firmly entrenched. These functions were outlined by *The Economist* in 1857 as follows:

The business of a landowner – the management of land as property in the best manner – is something quite distinct from farming. It consists in rendering the land attractive to the best class of farmers, the men of skill and capital, by means of permanent outlays combined with conditions of lettings which are consistent with profitable farming. [Cited in Guttsman, 1969, pp. 104–5.]

By 1878 Caird was also able to offer a somewhat idealized view of a
natural system of landed social stratification. According to Caird,

The landowners are the capitalists to whom the land belongs. Their
property comprises the soil and all that is beneath it, and the buildings
and other permanent works upon it. . . . In nearly all permanent improvements arising from the progress of agriculture the landowner is also
expected to share the cost. And he is necessarily concerned in the general
prosperity and good management of his estate, and in the welfare of those
who live upon it, with which his own is so closely involved. He takes a lead
in the business of his parish and from his class the magistrates who
administer the criminal affairs of the country, and superintend its roads,
the public buildings, and charitable institutions are selected. Nor do his
duties end here, for the landowner, from his position, is expected to be at
the head of all objects of public utility, to subscribe to, and, if so inclined,
to ride with the hounds, showing at once an example to the farmers and
tradesmen, and meeting them on terms of neighbourly friendship and
acquaintance. The same example is carried out in his intercourse with the
clergy and schoolmaster, and his influence, where wisely exercised, is felt
in the church, the farm and the cottage.

This class in the United Kingdom comprises a body of about 180,000,
who possess among them the whole of the agricultural land from ten acres
upwards. . . . There is no other body of men who administer so large a
capital on their own account, and whose influence is so widely extended
and universally present. From them the learned professions, the church,
the army, and the public services are largely recruited. [Caird, 1878,
pp. 58–9.]

Farming, however, was the responsibility of the tenants:

The tenant farmers are the second class, and a much more numerous one.
Their business is the cultivation of the land, with a capital quite independent of that of the owner. . . . A spirit of emulation exists among them,
elicited by county, provincial and national exhibitions of agricultural
stock, and by a natural desire, in a country where everything is open to
comment, not to be behind their neighbours in the neatness, style, and
success of their cultivation, or in the symmetry and condition of their
livestock. They are brought into the closest relation with their labourers,
and, although, occasionally, feelings of keen antagonism have arisen, there
is generally a very friendly understanding between them. The farmer knows
that it is for his interest that the labourers should find their position made
so comfortable as to value it.

To the farmer is committed the management of the details of the parish,
as those of the county to the landowner. His intimate knowledge of the
condition of the labourer, and constant residence in the parish, fit him best
for the duty of Overseer of the Poor, member of the Board of Guardians,

Churchwarden and Surveyor of the Roads. He is frank and hospitable to strangers as a rule; in favour of the established political institutions of the country; loyal as a subject; often available in case of need as mounted yeoman; and constantly in requisition as a juryman in the courts of law.

The farmers are six times as numerous as the landowners. . . . [*ibid.*, pp. 104–6.]

Caird was writing during the onset of the Great Depression in British agriculture which began in 1873 and lasted, interrupted briefly by the Great War, until 1939. His portrait reflects the 'Golden Age' of high farming in mid-Victorian England when this tripartite class structure seemed one of the eternal verities of rural life along with the changing of the seasons. Behind the glittering façade, however, there were, as Thompson (1963) makes clear, a number of factors contributing towards an underlying deterioration in the economic basis of the landowners' power. As the nineteenth century progressed and England became more urbanized and more industrialized, so the standard of living of the majority of the population increased and the proportion of income spent on food declined. Increasingly any extra money was being used to purchase manufactured goods. Consequently, returns to agriculture began to fall further and further behind returns to capital invested in manufacture or trade. Despite the prosperity of the 'Golden Age' it was becoming increasingly difficult for the great landed estates to maintain the degree of fixed capital investment *and* the grandiose life-style to which their incumbents had become accustomed. The Great Depression accelerated this process, particularly among those landowners in the arable south and east (the hardest-hit areas) and those with no industrial investment to act as a buffer (Thompson, 1963, Chapters X, XI; Perry, 1974). The landowning interest, which had long been on the defensive politically, was now thrown on the defensive economically by the acute and persistent depressed conditions. Moreover, this cost them the social deference of many of their tenant farmers, who, throughout the final quarter of the nineteenth century, campaigned with some success for tenant rights and an associated set of legislative constraints which would tip the economic and political balance in their favour (Perkin, 1973).

From the 1870s onwards, therefore, it is possible to discern the disintegration, slowly at first but very rapidly later on, of the traditional rural class structure. The ownership of land began to pass from the hands of the 7000 men which, so the New Domesday Survey revealed in 1873, owned 80 per cent of the United Kingdom.

The survey was an embarrassment to the landed interest, especially to Lord Derby, who had persuaded Parliament to compile *The Return of Owners of Land* in order to scotch the arguments of reformists who had attacked the landowning monopoly in Britain. Instead, as Caird pointed out:

When we come more closely to analyse the purely landowning class, the aggregation of land among small numbers becomes very conspicuous. One fourth of the whole territory, excluding those under one acre, is held by 1,200 persons, at an average of 16,200 acres; another fourth by 6,200 persons at an average for each of 3,150 acres; another fourth by 50,770 persons at an average of each of 380 acres; whilst the remaining fourth is held by 261,830 persons at an average each of 70 acres. An interesting compilation by the *Scotsman* newspaper shows that the peerage of the United Kingdom, about 600 in number, possess among them rather more than a fifth of all the land, and between a tenth and an eleventh of its annual income. [Caird, 1878, p. 44.][2]

Even as Caird was writing, however, the great landed estates were slipping into decline. The Depression was to have a paradoxical effect on the extent of owner-occupation. As tenancies fell in and tenants felt unable to continue under the depressed conditions, so many landowners were forced to take more land 'in hand', i.e. farm it themselves. However, because rents were falling, landowners faced an often acute cash shortage and so, where possible, were inclined to sell off small parcels of land, usually to sitting tenants. Thus, during the 1880s owner-occupation became more widespread, but in the 1890s, with the worst of the Depression over, more tenants could be found and the overall effect was a decline in owner-occupation (see Fig. 1). But this apparent revival of the landlord–tenant system hid underlying changes. In 1888 14·5 per cent of holdings were owner-occupied, but 15·4 per cent of the area of crops and grass. By 1908 the proportion of holdings owner-occupied had dropped to 12·8 per cent but the area owner-occupied had declined much further – to 12·3 per cent. One can infer, therefore, that by 1908, while tenants had been found for larger farms, smaller holdings were still being sold – mostly to sitting tenants. Hence as Sturmey (1955) has pointed out, the changes in the class structure of rural society were beginning rather earlier than inferences from the gross trends in land tenure might indicate.

The dismantling of the landed estates – the aristocratic diaspora from the land – although usually dated from the period immediately

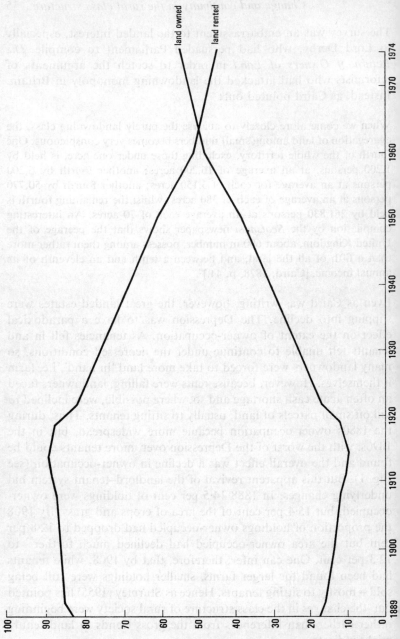

Figure 1 *Proportion of farm land rented and owned in England and Wales, 1887–1974 (Source: HMSO*, Century of agricultural statistics; *MAFF*, Land tenure figures.)

following the First World War, therefore began much earlier. Nevertheless a deluge of land sales began in 1919, on a scale unprecedented since the dissolution of the monasteries in the sixteenth century. Within three years, it has been estimated, one-quarter of the land surface of the United Kingdom changed hands. However, as Hobsbawm (1969, p. 202) has remarked, one of the most noteworthy aspects of this forced aristocratic abdication was that it took place almost unnoticed at the time, outside the restricted coterie of landowners, farmers and estate agents who were directly involved in the transactions. This, Hobsbawm adduces, indicated just how far the agricultural interest and the landowning aristocracy had become removed from the centres of economic and political power by the early decades of the twentieth century.

By 1927 one-third of the land used by farmers was owned by them. During the 1930s continued depression slowed down the advance of owner-occupation, although it is interesting to note that during this period a few farmers, by being in a position to purchase while the majority were selling, were able to compile some extremely large holdings at rock-bottom prices (e.g. Gavin, 1967). Many were new entrants to the industry; others, like the many Scotsmen who moved to East Anglia, were the products of hitherto frustrated ambition. They succeeded where others failed largely on account of their entrepreneurial acumen, their thrift and their willingness to work extremely hard for few immediate tangible rewards. As will become apparent later in this book, they have remained to take their places in the forefront of agricultural and managerial innovation in farming today.

Since the Second World War there has been a consistent rise in the amount of owner-occupation – much more, as will again become clear later, than the official statistics allow. Large estates have continued to be broken up, occasionally as a result of death duties, more often because of the effects of successive Agriculture Acts which, until 1958, gave almost complete security to tenants. Owners have been inclined to take more land in hand whenever it has become available and amalgamate it with their own existing holdings, thereby achieving economies of scale and ensuring a complete control over the farming practices on the land which they own (Sturmey, 1955; Clive, 1966). Thus, as estate-owners have gradually divested themselves of their tenants and as former tenants have continued to buy up the leases on their land, so, particularly in the lowland arable areas of England, a two-class structure of owner-occupying farmers and landless farm workers has begun to predominate. Although the traditional landed upper class is by no means universally absent, and of course the precise structure is far more complicated than these generalizations indicate, nevertheless in many areas it is the case that the social, economic and political leadership of rural society has passed decisively into the hands of farmers (who may also of course now own the land they farm) rather than the traditional landed aristocracy. How farmers exercise this leadership will be one of the most important themes of this book.

This change in the class structure of English rural society represents one immediate reason why the continuing influence of farmers and landowners in society as a whole cannot be viewed simply as an historical lag. Not only has the power of the landed aristocracy declined but the actual class composition of the rural ruling élite has changed appreciably. In other words, the role of farmers in the contemporary British class structure is not one that is based purely on tradition, for what we have is not continuity but a radical disjunction in rural class relationships. Only in a symbolic sense does the landed aristocracy remain at the apex of British society, buttressed by institutions like the monarchy and the House of Lords whose constitutional position is also more symbolic than real. In any case, most farmers would not claim to be members of a traditional upper class, but see themselves as having at least as much in common with the small, or in some cases large, businessman in industry. However the symbolic importance of owning agricultural land does involve certain social consequences. Urbanization, for example, has strengthened rather than dissipated the prestige of rural life; a move to the countryside is still a move up the status ladder in Britain, especially for the urban middle class.

Despite the small numbers actively engaged in agriculture approximately 80 per cent of the United Kingdom's land usage is classified as agricultural – compared with only 10 per cent urban development. These proportions, as Table 1 shows, are not changing rapidly. Notwithstanding lurid allegations that an area the size of Berkshire is sinking beneath concrete every decade, the expert consensus seems to be that 'urbanization is taking place at a decennial rate of about one per cent' (Cullingworth, 1973, p. 88). Losses of agricultural land have been more than made good by increases in agricultural productivity (Gasson, 1966a) and agriculture remains protected by what are – by western standards – draconian planning controls. These controls have often enhanced the market value of agricultural land, most spectacularly on the urban fringe where prospects of development zoning have been high. This serves as a reminder that even in a highly urbanized (though small and densely populated) island like Britain, the ownership of land is a considerable resource, which stretches beyond its mere use-value. Land is also *capital*, a highly secure, long-term investment and a sound collateral, which can be a source of enormous wealth to those who should wish to realize their assets. While there is no accurate information on the distribution of landownership in contemporary Britain, there seems little doubt that land remains one of the major sources of private and institutional wealth and that it is distributed among a tiny percentage of the population (see Atkinson, 1974).

Table 1 *Major land uses, England and Wales, 1900–60*

Year	Agriculture %	Woodland %	Urban development %	Unaccounted for %
1900	83·6	5·1	5·4	5·9
1925	82·9	5·1	6·2	5·8
1939	81·3	6·2	8·6	3·9
1950	80·6	6·4	9·7	3·3
1960	79·3	6·8	10·8	3·1

Source: Best and Coppock (1962), p. 229.

In addition to the economic importance of land, agriculture, as should be clear from the broad comparisons cited at the beginning of this chapter, is not without economic significance in its own right. During this century, the huge urban majority of the British population has received two salutary reminders of the strategic importance of the British farming industry to an island nation. More recently an awareness of its importance has been renewed by emphasizing the vital import-saving role of an expanding indigenous agriculture in a stagnating economy racked by recurrent balance of payments crises (Economic Development Committee for the Agriculture Industry, 1968; MAFF, 1975). The production of food remains the most essential and fundamental form of productive activity, and therefore farming retains an almost unique intrinsic importance which cannot be disregarded. Arguments like these have prompted the British government, in common with governments all over the world, to step in and interfere with the operation of the market in order to protect its sources of food. Agriculture in this country has, indeed, long been in the vanguard of state interference and control of the free market. As Attwood has pointed out, 'The approach to agricultural affairs is a very good indicator of the national economic philosophy at any given time, since it reflects relatively quickly the changes in that philosophy. Far from being the last, farming is among the first in the queue for government action' (Attwood, 1963, p. 148).

It would be ingenuous to believe that this promptness owed nothing to the skill with which these arguments have been marshalled by a superbly organized farming lobby, which has sought to impress upon successive governments the importance of sustaining a healthy British agriculture. In other words, agriculture has in no small way maintained its influence in national affairs by the remarkable adaptability of farmers to changed political circumstances. The agricultural industry has subtly adapted itself to a situation whereby it is one interest among many, whereas earlier it also was *the* ruling interest in society. Its most influential representative organizations – the National Farmers' Union (NFU) and the Country Landowners Association (CLA) – have become almost model political lobbies (see Chapter 3 below), while agriculture still retains its own Ministry to look after its affairs, the head of which invariably has a seat in the Cabinet (see Self and Storing, 1962). The political muscle of the agricultural interest is also aided by the over-representation of farmers among MPs (Roth, 1973). The Conservative Party still retains a significant number of landowning members, and in the constituencies the rural vote continues to be assiduously cultivated. In terms of sheer voting strength, the agricultural vote is not especially significant, as those political scientists who have analysed it unanimously agree (Benyon and Harrison, 1962; Self and Storing, 1962; Pennock, 1959; Howarth, 1969). However, farmers are particularly active in both local politics (Moss and Parker, 1967) and as officers in local constituency associations in the Conservative and Liberal Parties (see below, Chapter 6). Their political strength is therefore considerable and extends beyond the size of their vote to 'less tangible influences' (Howarth, 1969, p. 469).

The massive state intervention in the agriculture industry makes the politics of farming at times seem inseparable from the economics of farming. This politicization of agriculture also makes us aware of the need to regard farmers as social and political agents capable, collectively if not individually, of influencing the economic parameters within which they operate. We shall not, therefore, be regarding farmers as mere ciphers of more abstract social and economic structures. While all farmers are constrained to some degree by the necessity to make a profit, we shall argue that sufficient 'slack' in the system remains for farmers to *choose* how to act within these constraints. This is not to say that agriculture is a totally voluntaristic activity. As we shall see in the following chapter, farmers have become increasingly constrained in their choice of methods in order to remain profitable. Moreover the degree of choice available clearly varies according to size of the enterprise and the liabilities the farmer has incurred. Nevertheless by no means all farmers believe that they must pursue the maximum possible profitability without taking account of their own preferences in respect of their life-styles and other non-economic rewards. There is no doubt that agriculture is becoming increasingly rationalized according to the exigencies of modern market conditions, but many of these conditions are themselves amenable to change through political action and we must be aware of the fact that many farmers remain resistant to using a narrowly defined notion of economic rationality as the only guide to their entrepreneurial activity.

2 Of farming and farmers

There is little doubt that since the Second World War farming as a business has increasingly gained the upper hand over farming as a dignified and Arcadian way of life. (For some excellent descriptions of this process, see Donaldson and Donaldson, 1972; Edwards and Rogers, 1974; Beresford, 1975.) We shall examine in much greater detail the intricacies of this change later in this book, but it is worth while to present at the outset a broad descriptive background which will enable the scope of the change to be appreciated. Even this is no easy matter, for one of the characteristic features of British agriculture is its complexity so that the impact of such changes as have taken place since the war has varied considerably, even from farm to farm.

The most obvious, but also the most revolutionary, transformation has occurred in agricultural technology and husbandry management. The extent of mechanization, particularly the introduction of the tractor (which has totally replaced the horse only since the Second World War) and combine harvester, must by now be apparent to even the most urbanized townie, if only because, in the south and east of England, larger and more sophisticated machines have necessitated the removal of hedgerows and thus produced startling changes in the landscape to the passer-by. Other technological changes have been more subtle, but none the less far-reaching. Fertility has been increasingly sustained by artificial fertilizers, allowing animals (except sheep) to be moved indoors to be bred and reared in artificially controlled environments. 'Factory farming', which a generation ago would have been regarded as a contradiction in terms, has therefore become commonplace. Here disease is controlled by vaccination and selective breeding; outdoors, diseases and weeds are controlled by insecticides, fungicides, herbicides, and so on. Rather than reflecting the eternal rhythms of an immemorial way of life, agriculture has become more of a business based upon the application of scientific principles, however much farmers may regret it. Within a lifetime any sense of continuity has been shattered, for as Beresford points out, tradition has been thrown overboard:

What father did, what grandfather did before him, were pointers of vital consequence. Experience was your capital; and the pace of change was so gradual that the passing of time did not devalue it. Rotations were the moral principles of husbandry. You departed from them at your peril. Traditions like these were rooted in the past; and so long as the experience of the past remained the surest guide to practice in the present, these traditions were invaluable and respected. Science uprooted them; analysed, tested, refuted and rejected them. Ancestral lore ceased to count; father-figures and grandfather-figures became slightly ridiculous. Farmers were children of the Enlightenment after all. [Beresford, 1975, p. 14.]

Thus, over the last thirty years agricultural production has been profoundly transformed, increasing by leaps and bounds. Despite a 20 per cent increase in the population between 1938 and 1974, the rate of self-sufficiency of British agriculture has increased from 30 per cent to 55 per cent (nearly 70 per cent of temperate products), so that in all the net output of the 'national farm' is, at constant prices, double the pre-war level. All this was achieved during a period in which the farm labour force – farmers and farm workers – has been halved, so productivity per man has increased fourfold since before the war. Through mechanization and other labour-saving devices agriculture has been able consistently to shed labour to other sectors of the economy to the extent that Britain now has the smallest proportion of its population engaged in agriculture of any country in the world. Whether this is a consequence of mechanization or a response to the cost and availability of labour is a matter of continuing dispute. Within the constraints set by climate and topography British agriculture is now undoubtedly one of the most efficient in the world. And, whatever the vagaries of weather or politics, it has also become one of the most prosperous.

How many farmers are there in Britain today? In spite of an annual Ministry of Agriculture census every 4 June this is not as easy a question to answer as it might seem. To begin with, the term 'farmer', as anyone who has tried to explain it to European acquaintances will recognize, is by no means unambiguous. The Agricultural Census does not count farmers but 'occupiers' of each 'agricultural holding'. An agricultural holding consists of any piece of land used for agricultural purposes. Many of these do not correspond with a commonsense notion of a 'farm' – for example, a golf course which allows sheep to graze occasionally might qualify; so might a very large private garden. The Ministry is constantly engaged in weeding out the small agriculturally insignificant holdings – gardens, pony paddocks, etc. – from its census and excludes *all* holdings (except glasshouses) below one-quarter of an acre. Nevertheless the overall distribution remains highly skewed towards the lower size-groups as Table 2 shows. The clustering of holdings in the small size-groups

Table 2   *Number and size distribution of holdings in England and Wales, 1974*

Crops and grass acreage	'000 holdings			Million acres (crops and grass)		
	No.	%	%	No.	%	%
¼–19¾	56·8	27·3	⎫	0·49	2·1	⎫
20–49¾	39·9	19·1	⎪ 91·6	1·32	5·6	⎪ 57·9
50–99¾	41·7	20·0	⎬	3·01	12·7	⎬
100–299¾	52·5	25·2	⎭	8·90	37·5	⎭
300–499¾	10·7	5·1	⎫	4·03	17·0	⎫
500–999¾	5·5	2·7	⎬ 8·5	3·70	15·6	⎬ 42·1
1000 and over	1·5	0·7	⎭	2·24	9·5	⎭
Total	208·5 (211·4)*	100	100	23·68	100	100

* 2901 holdings have no crops and grass, i.e. consist wholly of rough grazings, woodland, etc.

Source: MAFF, *Annual Agricultural Statistics*.

Table 3   *Agricultural holdings in England and Wales, 1974*

	Holdings		Area (crops and grass) million acres		Average size acres
	No.	%	No.	%	
Full-time holdings	124151	59·7	21·34	90·1	171·9
Part-time and spare-time holdings	87284	41·3	2·34	8·9	26·8
All holdings	211435	100	23·68	100	112·0

Sources: MAFF, *Annual Agricultural Statistics*; MAFF, *Farm Classification Tables*.

considerably affects the average size of holding, which in 1974 was 112 acres, but this figure includes the thousands of holdings which are not 'farms' in the everyday sense. (Even so, it is nearly three times the EEC average size.) A much better measurement of a 'farm' is a 'full-time holding'; that is, a holding having sufficient crops and livestock to provide full-time employment for one man, on the basis of an average labour requirement – known as a 'standard-man-day' – on farms in general. In 1974 there were 124 151 full-time holdings in England and Wales, with a total area of 21·3 million acres (see Table 3). This gives an average size of 172 acres, a better indicator of the average size of 'farm'. Moreover, this figure is increasing: over the past twenty-five years the number of holdings below 300 acres has declined while the number in excess of this figure has increased. Thus the overall trend is towards farm amalgamation with a small proportion of very large holdings producing the lion's share of the country's agricultural output. Indeed the top 10 per cent of farms, measured by standard-man-days, produce half the total output.

In 1974 there were thus 124 151 full-time holdings, but by no means all the 'occupiers' were 'farmers'. Many were managers employed by an absentee owner; others occupied the holding but their main employment or source of income may have been elsewhere. A further complication is the problem of multiple holdings, that is, separate holdings of land farmed by the same farming business or 'farmer'. Again the Ministry has made great efforts to weed out many of these (see Ashton and Cracknell, 1961) but many remain, as we shall see later in this book, to confuse the statistics. However, multiple holdings account for the fact that some holdings have no 'occupiers' although they do, of course, have 'farmers'. Harrison (1965, 1972, 1975) has argued forcibly and persuasively that the chaos of these statistics could be avoided by taking the farming enterprise as a basis of classification rather than the holding of land. In the meantime, however, it is necessary to recognize that the number of holdings and the number of occupiers do not always coincide, while the term 'farmer', whether part-time or full-time, is an omnibus category which does not precisely correspond to any found in the official statistics. The most reasonable estimate would be to assume one for every full-time holding, that is 124 000 in 1974, but this must be regarded as only a rough estimate.

With the amalgamation of holdings, the number of farmers has been falling steadily since the war, though not as quickly as the fall in the number of agricultural workers. Each farmer has therefore become less significant as an employer of labour, so that by 1974 an average of 1·2 regular, full-time, hired workers was employed on each full-time holding. Again, however, the distribution is skewed with many small farms being operated solely by the farmer and his wife, with perhaps some casual or part-time help at certain peak periods, while the largest 10 per cent of holdings account for over 60 per cent of full-time hired labour. Moreover as the hired labour force has declined, so its composition has changed, for in the search for cheap labour agricultural employers have been inclined to substitute females for males and casual and/or part-time labour for full-time employees (see Gasson, 1974; Newby, 1977). Thus farmers have become a much more significant section of the total agricultural labour force. Some of the relevant statistics are set out in Table 4.

Table 4   *Composition of farm labour force in England and Wales, 1974*

	No.	%
Farmers/partners/directors	166981	39·1
Regular family workers	42652	10·0
Regular hired workers	150289	35·1
Regular part-time workers	67549	15·8
Total occupied* on farms	427471	100

* Excludes casual and seasonal workers.

Source: MAFF, *Annual Agricultural Statistics*.

Agriculture is not one industry, but several – at least six, but there is a variety of farming systems that is almost infinite (see Coppock, 1964, 1971). The Ministry of Agriculture uses a thirteenfold classification (Napolitan and Brown, 1963) and the distribution of holdings according to these types is shown in Table 5. There is a distinct association between the type of farm and its size in terms of standard-man-days (i.e. size of enterprise, not size in terms of sheer geographical area). In general the smaller farms tend to be livestock farms, especially dairying and cattle and sheep rearing. On the other hand, over half of the farms in the largest size groups are cropping specialists, either arable farms[1] or large-scale horticultural holdings (see Britton, 1974, pp. 32–3). Since climate, soil and topography continue to exert an influence over the nature of agricultural activity, geographical location is associated not only with the type of farming

Table 5 *Distribution of full-time holdings by type of farming, England and Wales, 1974*

Type of farming	No. of holdings	% of holdings
Specialist dairy	29707	23·9
Mainly dairy	15869	12·8
Livestock: cattle	9374	7·6
Livestock: sheep	2948	2·4
Livestock: cattle and sheep	13753	11·1
Poultry	2620	2·1
Pigs and poultry	7118	5·7
Cropping: cereals	8114	6·5
General cropping	12498	10·1
Vegetables	1211	1·0
Fruit	1631	1·3
Horticulture	10110	8·1
Mixed	9198	7·4
Total	124151	100

Source: MAFF, *Farm Classification Tables.*

but the size of the enterprise. Hence despite important local variations distinct regional patterns of agriculture in Britain can be discerned (Rogers, 1974). The famous distinction noted by Caird (1851) between the arable east and the pastoral west remains important. In the west farms are generally smaller and concerned primarily with dairying (in the lowlands) and sheep and cattle rearing (in the upland areas), whereas in the east large-scale arable agriculture predominates, with localized areas of intensive horticultural production. Moreover, in recent years, with speedier and more reliable access to markets, the degree of specialization, both within each agricultural enterprise and within particular geographical areas, has increased (Gasson, 1966*b*), an agricultural division of labour encouraged by successive government policies since the war.

In general, therefore, farms have become larger and more specialized, but these trends have been far from uniform from one type of farm and one area to another. Arable agriculture has benefited most from mechanization, whereas other sectors – for example, certain types of horticulture and the poultry industry – have been extensively automated. Indeed the poultry industry – both egg production and broilers – has been the area of British agriculture most profoundly transformed since the war, with not only a virtually complete change-over to factory-farming methods but a rapid concentration of production in a few, enormous enterprises. In all sectors of British agriculture, however, the necessity to invest in ever-larger amounts of capital in order to increase production and lower unit-costs has brought continual pressure upon the economically marginal farms. Indeed the size of farm that constitutes the marginal farm has risen continually, creating a new class of marginal farmers every decade or so. It is this process, again encouraged by the intervention policies of successive governments, which has done so much to promote a more business-like ambience in the agricultural industry. It has prompted farmers to concentrate their minds more on the rationality of their economic behaviour, than to allow more traditional attitudes to remain unquestioned. We will be very concerned in this book with the tensions and contradictions that this has caused.

The structure of East Anglian agriculture

Most of these structural changes in British agriculture have been reflected in East Anglian practice. Indeed, because East Anglian farming is dominated by a type of agricultural production – cereal growing – which has been well served by the scientist and the technologist, the region has customarily been in the vanguard of such changes. Certainly East Anglia today presents an entirely contrasting picture to the conditions which predominated in the 1920s and 1930s when thousands of acres of good, productive arable land lay un-farmed and degenerated into wasteland, when fences were pulled down to be used as firewood and when large numbers of farm workers were unemployed and those who had work found wage levels falling. Wartime conditions and sustained state intervention thereafter have, however, transformed this situation so that huge areas of land have been brought back into production and the efficiency of farms (and farmers) has been dramatically improved.

Today arable farming dominates the agriculture of the region. This can be demonstrated by referring to the annual *Agricultural Statistics for England and Wales* and, for convenience, we have taken three years – 1945, 1960 and 1974 – in order to indicate the extent of arable farming in the four East Anglian counties with which we are primarily concerned – Essex, Suffolk, Norfolk and Cambridgeshire. Figure 2 shows the relative pattern of these four counties compared with the national situation.

The overwhelming importance of arable farming could hardly be better demonstrated. Given the fact that almost 90 per cent of all the crops and grass acreage in these counties is used for cropping it is

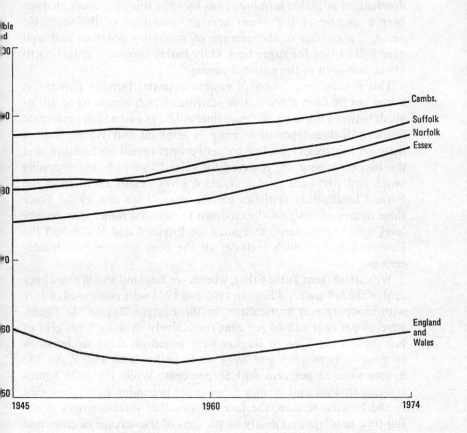

Figure 2 *Proportion of crops and grass acreage taken by arable farming in England and Wales and four eastern counties, 1945–74*

hardly surprising that the contribution made to national arable production is significant. Again taking the period 1945–74 we can examine official figures for acreages of particular crops. They show, *inter alia*, that in 1945 17·3 per cent of the national wheat acreage, 29 per cent of that for barley, 14·8 per cent of the maincrop potatoes,

50·3 per cent of the sugar beet and 22·8 per cent of vegetables were grown in the four counties. The increasing specialization of agriculture since the war together with various technological improvements have, however, combined to produce an even more emphatic domination of arable farming. Thus by 1974 this area accounted for over a quarter of the wheat acreage, one-third of the vegetable acreage, a quarter of the acreage of maincrop potatoes and well over half of that for sugar beet. Only barley showed a reduction to about one-sixth of the national acreage.

This general description of eastern counties farming patterns is borne out by farm classification statistics which enable us to distinguish between full-time and part-time holdings and which enumerate fourteen distinct types of farming in England and Wales. Half of these are livestock types, five concern cropping and horticulture, and the two remaining are reserved for mixed livestock and cropping farms and part-time farms.[2] Table 6 gives details taken from the Farm Classification statistics for the years 1965 and 1974.[3] Since these figures are only produced down to regional rather than county level we compare here the figures for England and Wales and the Eastern Region, which includes all the four counties which concern us.

We can see from Table 6 that, whereas in England and Wales 27 per cent of the full-time holdings in 1965 and 1974 were concerned mainly with cropping and horticulture, in the Eastern Region the figures were 69 per cent and 64 per cent respectively. A mere 8 per cent of holdings in the Eastern Region were based on dairy or livestock farming in both 1965 and 1974 while in England and Wales the figures were 55 per cent and 58 per cent. While the 1974 figures indicate that pig and poultry farming are becoming more significant in the Eastern Region, the fact remains that three-quarters of the full-time holdings and nearly 90 per cent of the acreage of crops and grass is given over to cropping – a remarkable example of regional specialization. Of course, conditions are particularly favourable in East Anglia for crop production. As Rogers (1974, p. 190) points out, ' . . . although most fodder and cash crops can be grown throughout the United Kingdom, it is the large arable farms of the Eastern counties, with their good soils and landscapes which are well suited to mechanised farming, which are at a distinct advantage in crop production'.

The concentration of crop production in the eastern counties is the main factor accounting for the larger overall size of holdings

Table 6 *Distribution of full-time holdings by type of farming, England and Wales and the Eastern Region, 1965 and 1974*

	Number of holdings ('000)							
	1965				1974			
Type of farming	England and Wales	%	Eastern Region	%	England and Wales	%	Eastern Region	%
Dairy	60·8	39	1·6	7	45·6	37	1·1	6
Livestock	24·7	16	0·3	1	26·1	21	0·4	2
Pigs and poultry	9·6	6	1·9	9	9·7	8	2·2	14
Cropping	26·6	17	11·1	51	20·6	17	8·1	48
Horticulture	15·0	10	5·1	23	13·0	10	4·0	24
Mixed	19·5	12	1·8	8	9·2	7	1·1	6
Total	156·2	100	21·7	100	124·2	100	16·9	100

Source: MAFF, *Farm Classification Tables.*

(measured by crops and grass acreage), and farm businesses (measured by standard-man-days). There is an association between type of farming and size of farm business as Table 7 indicates. If we take the national figures we can see that dairying and livestock are dominant in the smaller standard-man-day size-groups but far fewer of the largest farms (2400 + smd) are devoted to these enterprises. Nationally, cropping predominates only on the larger farms, but in the Eastern Region such is the predominance of arable farming that cropping is the most important type for all business sizes. Nevertheless there are proportionately fewer holdings with a labour requirement of less than 1200 smds in the Eastern Region (62 per cent as against 73 per cent for England and Wales) and more holdings with a requirement of 1200 + smds (38 per cent against 27 per cent). So arable farming predominates irrespective of the size of enterprise and larger farms are more common throughout the region than in England and Wales as a whole. Similarly the pattern of crop production in East Anglia has important consequences for the size of holdings measured by crops and grass acreage. We can illustrate this by reference both to the distribution of holdings by crops and grass acreage size-groups, and the average size of holdings for the years 1945–74 (see Tables 8 and 9).

Table 7 Types of farming by standard-man-day size-groups: percentage distribution of full-time holdings, England and Wales and the Eastern Region, 1974

| | Standard-man-day size-groups | | | | | | | | Total | |
| | 275–599 | | 600–1199 | | 1200–2399 | | 2400+ | | | |
	England and Wales	Eastern Region	England and Wales	Eastern Region	England and Wales	Eastern Region	England and Wales	Eastern Region	England and Wales	Eastern Region
Dairy	35	4	42	8	38	9	20	5	37	6
Livestock	29	4	21	3	13	2	5	*	21	2
Pigs and poultry	6	12	7	14	10	14	14	12	8	14
Cropping	14	51	15	46	20	48	29	45	17	48
Horticulture	11	24	9	24	9	21	18	26	10	24
Mixed	5	5	7	5	9	6	14	12	7	6
Total	100	100	100	100	100	100	100	100	100	100
Percentage of all holdings 275+ smds	37	32	36	30	19	19	9	17		

* Less than 0·5 per cent.

Source: MAFF, *Farm Classification Tables*.

Table 8 *Percentage distribution of holdings by crops and grass acreage size-groups, four eastern counties and England and Wales, 1945–74*

	Size-groups	1945 %	1955 %	1965 %	1974‡ %	Percentage change 1945–74 in number of holdings
Cambs*	¼–49¾	73	76	73	58	−58
	50–99¾	10	9	10	16	−15
	100–299¾	12	11	11	16	−29
	300+	5	5	6	10	+13
	Total	100	100	100	100	−47
Essex	¼–49¾	61	66	67	53	−55
	50–99¾	12	10	9	11	−54
	100–299¾	20	18	15	20	−48
	300+	7	6	9	16	+18
	Total	100	100	100	100	−48
Norfolk	¼–49¾	65	68	67	52	−56
	50–99¾	13	12	11	16	−35
	100–299¾	15	14	14	18	−35
	300+	6	6	8	14	+21
	Total	100	100	100	100	−45
Suffolk	¼–49¾	52	57	55	41	−58
	50–99¾	17	15	14	16	−49
	100–299¾	24	22	21	26	−40
	300+	6	7	10	17	+43
	Total	100	100	100	100	−46
England and Wales	¼–49¾	62	63	60	46	−57
	50–99¾	17	16	17	20	−31
	100–299¾	18	17	19	25	−20
	300+	3	4	5	8	+43
	Total	100	100	100	100	−42·5

* Includes Isle of Ely. For 1974 Cambridgeshire (March).

† East and West Suffolk combined where necessary.

‡ In June 1968 47 000 insignificant holdings were excluded from the census.

Source: MAFF, *Annual Agricultural Statistics*.

If we examine Table 8 we can see that the last thirty years have seen a large reduction in the overall number of holdings and that this reduction has been concentrated among holdings of less than 300 acres. In other words there is a clear overall trend to fewer, larger holdings, with the very largest accounting for a high proportion of all agricultural production. This trend, as Table 8 shows, is more pronounced in the eastern counties: whereas 8 per cent of all holdings in England and Wales exceed 300 acres of crops and grass, the figures for Cambridgeshire, Essex, Norfolk and Suffolk are respectively 10 per cent, 16 per cent, 14 per cent and 17 per cent. This greater proportion of large holdings in the east is no new phenomenon, as the table demonstrates.

Thus while the smaller holdings of less than 50 acres may predominate *numerically*, in terms of their significance for employment and production East Anglia is an area of large, arable farms. The figures presented in Table 9, which concern the average size of holdings,

Table 9 *Average size of agricultural holdings in England and Wales and four eastern counties, 1945–74*

	Average size of holding (acres)			
	1945	1955	1965	1974
England and Wales	67	66	76	112
Cambs	62	60	70	111
Essex	84	76	88	145
Norfolk	81	77	88	145
Suffolk	93	90	109	168

thus need to be interpreted with caution. These are necessarily crude averages, being a simple division of the total number of holdings into the total crops and grass acreage. However, as we have already indicated when describing the national situation, such averages mask the pronounced skew towards the smaller holdings.[4] A rather more useful indicator of the average 'farm' size is instead given by data on full-time holdings and in 1974 this was 172 acres in England and Wales, but 190 acres in Cambridgeshire, 234 acres in Essex, 244 acres in Norfolk and 250 acres in Suffolk. However, statistics which differentiate full-time from part-time holdings have only recently become available so that it is not possible to compile a time series for them. Nevertheless what both sets of figures indicate is the generally larger size of holding in the arable east.[5]

We can further illustrate the fact that the part-time holdings and the smaller full-time holdings are of much less importance than their comparatively large numbers might lead us to believe by examining the actual amounts of land farmed within the different acreage size-groups. For example in 1974 in England and Wales 8 per cent of all holdings exceeded 300 acres of crops and grass and yet accounted for (Fig. 2) 42 per cent of all land farmed. In the four counties the comparable figures are: Cambridgeshire 10 per cent and 57 per cent; Essex 16 per cent and 65 per cent; Norfolk 14 per cent and 64 per cent; and Suffolk 17 per cent and 62 per cent. Moreover if we isolate those holdings over 1000 acres in the four counties, from which we selected one of our samples (see below), the differences are even more pronounced. In Cambridgeshire 1·3 per cent of holdings are in excess of 1000 acres but they account for 18·2 per cent of all land farmed; in Essex the corresponding figures are 1·3 per cent and 15·3 per cent; in Norfolk 2·2 per cent and 23·5 per cent; and in Suffolk 2·0 per cent and 18·5 per cent. In England and Wales the figures are 0·7 per cent and 9·5 per cent (all figures for 1974).

When we relate some of these points to production the measure of the importance of the larger holdings becomes clearer still: 'The large (cropping) holdings by themselves account for just over 30 per cent of the total barley acreage, 41 per cent of the total wheat acreage and 48 per cent of the total acreage of maincrop potatoes in England and Wales, a significant example of specialisation' (MAFF, 1970, pp. 19–20). And East Anglia with its larger holdings naturally takes the lion's share of this production, for in 1974 wheat was grown on 65 per cent of holdings in Cambridgeshire, 41 per cent in Essex, 48 per cent in Norfolk and 56 per cent in Suffolk, compared with 22 per cent in England and Wales as a whole. The case of sugar beet is even more stark: Norfolk alone accounts for 25 per cent of total national sugar beet production and this is concentrated further on the largest holdings in the county. It thus becomes obvious that the large, arable farms of East Anglia have a significance in the production of crops in Britain that is out of all proportion to their numbers.

Crop acreage statistics repeat this pattern of not only the concentration of arable production in East Anglia but of the concentration on the region's largest holdings. If we take the example of wheat, then in 1974 nearly three million acres of wheat were grown in England and

Wales, of which almost 70 per cent was grown on only 7 per cent of
the holdings – all of them in excess of 300 acres. No less than 20 per
cent was grown on holdings in excess of 1000 acres, while at the other
end of the scale holdings of less than 50 acres accounted, despite their
large numbers, for less than 2 per cent of the acreage. The four
eastern counties with which we are concerned, however, accounted
for 750000 acres, or 26 per cent, of which 68 per cent was produced
by the 13 per cent of holdings of 300 acres or more. Even yields per
acre tend to be significantly higher in the east, indicating not simply
better physical and climatic conditions for the cultivation of arable
crops, but also the fruits of higher investment in machinery and
agricultural technology as well as the general advantages of scale
which accrue to larger holdings.

So we can see the overall importance of agriculture in eastern
England: large arable farms, capital intensive, and supplying a significant proportion of national arable production. Associated with this
pattern is a higher than average use of farm labour.

We saw earlier that in 1970 12 per cent of all holdings in England
and Wales were classified as large according to standard labour
requirements. By 1974 this figure had increased to 16·7 per cent but
for the four counties the average was around 23 per cent, and in
Essex and Suffolk was over 25 per cent. This gives a general indication of the larger size of farm business and greater use of farm labour
in the east, but we can be more specific. For example in England and
Wales there is an average of 1·2 whole-time hired male workers per
full-time holding; in the four counties the figures are: Cambridgeshire, 1·7; Essex, 2·1; Norfolk, 2·4; Suffolk, 2·2. But this is, of course,
a crude average and we have already seen the effect on other averages
of the large number of small holdings. The fact is that 78 per cent of
holdings in England and Wales employ no full-time hired male
workers, the figure for the four eastern counties being 69 per cent.
It is thus the large holdings which account for most of the farm
labour. In England and Wales holdings of over 500 acres (although
only accounting for 3 per cent of all holdings) together employ 35 per
cent of all full-time male workers. In the four eastern counties the
equivalent figures are 8 per cent and 48 per cent. Whereas farmers,
partners and directors now outnumber regular hired workers in
England and Wales this is not the case in East Anglia. In England
and Wales in 1974 the ratio of whole-time hired male workers to
whole-time farmers was 0·8:1; in the four eastern counties it was
1·6:1. This greater reliance in the east of England on hired labour

is shown in Table 10. Altogether almost one-fifth of the regular whole-time hired male workers in England and Wales are to be found in the four eastern counties. Nevertheless, in common with elsewhere in Britain, the numbers of workers employed in the region's farms has declined and will continue to do so. Since 1960, in fact, there has been a decrease of 62 per cent (compared with 64 per cent nationally).

Table 10 *Average number of regular whole-time hired male workers on holdings employing such workers by crops and grass acreage size-groups, England and Wales and four eastern counties, 1974*

Size-group (acres)	Average number regular whole-time hired male workers				
	Cambs	Essex	Norfolk	Suffolk	England and Wales
¼–49¾	2·6	2·5	2·9	3·0	2·6
50–99¾	2·1	1·8	1·8	1·9	1·6
100–299¾	2·8	2·1	2·5	2·2	1·8
300–499¾	4·2	3·5	4·5	3·7	3·1
500–999¾	7·5	5·4	7·8	6·9	5·7
1000+	16·0	17·6	17·0	16·1	13·9
Overall average	4·5	3·6	4·8	4·0	2·9

Source: MAFF, *Farm Labour Tables.*

Finally, what of the farmers themselves? Given all that we have said so far about the pattern of farming in East Anglia it should be clear that a comparatively small number of farmers – most of them, as we shall see later, owner-occupiers – employ most of the East Anglian farm labour force and are responsible for a not insignificant amount of national agricultural production. These few men are, therefore, not at all typical of most farmers in this country, since most farmers employ little in the way of assets or labour (see, for example, Harrison, 1975). Altogether in 1974, as we saw in Table 4, there were 167 000 full-time farmers in England and Wales and 124 000 full-time holdings. In the four eastern counties the corresponding figures were as follows: Cambridgeshire 3063 and 2276; Essex 3685 and 2710; Norfolk 5076 and 4082; and Suffolk 3655 and 2771. But if we think again of the overwhelming importance in terms of production of the very largest farms and recall that, for example, 48 per cent of the hired male labour force is employed on holdings of over 500 acres, we could express the same fact by saying that 11 per cent of the farmers in the four counties employ 48 per cent of the hired male workers; or that roughly the same proportion of farmers are responsible for over half of the wheat production in the four counties, and therefore a considerable proportion of national production.

It is these farmers, those employing relatively large amounts of labour and capital and producing between them a significant amount of all agricultural output, with whom we are primarily concerned. Of course, the largest holdings may be atypical: there are small farms in East Anglia, some of which were included in our survey, but in terms of their overall importance to the 'national farm', and, not least, because of the sociological problems which we set out to investigate, it is these larger farms which provide one of our main objects of interest. How we set out to investigate them is a matter to which we can now turn.

Methodology

We have already discussed in Chapter 1 why it was we chose to locate our study of farmers in East Anglia and given some idea of the sociological problems we wished to investigate. It is important to understand at this stage that in terms of both location and methodology the research was largely predetermined by its own historical evolution. The idea of conducting research on East Anglian farmers emerged, as was indicated in Chapter 1, from previous work begun in 1970 by Howard Newby on the social situation of agricultural workers (see Newby, 1977). Newby had collected his data by interviewing 233 farm workers on seventy-one farms in an area of forty-four parishes in central East Suffolk, around the market town of Framlingham, between March and August 1972. During the same period he was also involved in extensive participant observation, living in a tied cottage in the fieldwork area with a farm worker and his family.[6] By virtue of this, these forty-four parishes became, then, a focal point of our interest. Moreover, in order to obtain some comparative data to that already obtained from agricultural workers, it seemed sensible to adopt similar research techniques. Thus, our major data-collection instrument was a survey, not least for the very good additional reason that no basic sociographic data on entrepreneurial farmers existed and we had to create our own.

Given, then, the fact that we intended to locate at least one part of our study in the forty-four parishes and also that we intended to interview farmers using a questionnaire, the first problem was to find an adequate sampling frame in order to obtain respondents. It was intended, for comparative purposes, to re-interview all those farmers (N = 71) whose employees Newby had interviewed during his previous research and also to use the forty-four parishes as the location for our study of the role of farmers in local affairs, including local politics (see below, Chapter 6). But we also wished to obtain a sample of the very largest business farmers in East Anglia: clearly, given the broader aims of our research, we could not for ever confine ourselves to one small area of Suffolk. It was quickly apparent, therefore, that we would need two separate samples of farmers to meet the different aims of the research, *viz.*, one sample from the forty-four parishes of farmers regardless of size of holding – this would allow an extension of Newby's work, facilitate our study of the local influence of farmers and also, by virtue of their representativeness, act as a 'control' sample, and a second sample of the largest farms throughout East Anglia in order to investigate those problems directly associated with large-scale farming discussed in Chapter 1. (A description of how we obtained our samples is given in Appendix 1.) Since Newby's original sample was not a random one we decided to obtain a random sample from the forty-four parishes and in addition re-interview those of Newby's original sample not included in the new random sample. So we had in effect three samples: (1) a random sample known as the 'forty-four parishes' sample; (2) Newby's original sample, the 'HN' sample to be used solely for comparative purposes with the research on farm workers; and (3) a random sample of all holdings in Cambridgeshire, Essex, Norfolk and Suffolk of over 1000 acres of crops and grass, the '1000 + acres' sample.[7]

Finally, we should say a word about the respondents themselves. For the most part we managed to interview the farmer, or one of the principals in the case of partnerships and companies. However, nineteen of our respondents were not farmers but farm managers: this could not be avoided for on these farms it was the farm manager who ran the enterprise; the actual owner may have been an absentee, a trust, or employed in an entirely different capacity elsewhere, the farm being a business on the side left to the farm manager to run. We have not excluded data obtained in interviews with farm managers, however; it is true they did not own the land, but in most senses they were 'the farmer' and made all the crucial decisions.

The sociography of East Anglian farmers

In this final section of this chapter we shall present some basic sociographic data on our respondents. We can begin this task by looking at how the farmers that we interviewed came to be involved in farming in the first place. As Table 11 indicates, family inheritance is often decisive in this process and thus the family remains crucial to most farming enterprises. Moreover it is, by and large, families who own farms whether by means of partnerships, trusts or in the form of limited companies. Harrison has aptly summarized the positions based on his research into farm business structure in England and Wales: 'The overall weight of evidence served only to emphasise the narrowing of opportunities for entering farming unless strong and tangible links with the industry already existed. Usually these were family links; families ran farms, and though not true to the same degree, farms were run for families.' (Harrison, 1975, p. 21.)

This position is reflected when we consider the reasons our respondents gave for entering agriculture in the first place. No less than 70 per cent of those in the 1000 + acres sample and 56 per cent in the forty-four parishes sample inherited their farms or had become partners with their fathers and would eventually inherit. A further 11 per cent and 21 per cent respectively had had relatives able to give them a start in agriculture, so that in each sample approximately four out of every five respondents had relied upon their families for a start in agriculture. When we consider that the remainder include tenants (many of whom succeeded to their father's tenancy) and managers (of whom a number came from non-farming backgrounds and so had no realistic hope of farming for themselves) we are left with few who made their way into farming independently by climbing the 'farming ladder'. Only 10 per cent of those in the 1000 + acres sample had begun their farming careers as farm workers or farm managers, while in the forty-four parishes sample this was the case for 17·5 per cent of our respondents.

Consequently, when we examine the source of capital which enabled our respondents to become farmers in their own right, the family looms large whether in terms of the inheritance of land or cash to buy land, or in the form of interest-free family loans or straight cash gifts to set up a farm. It is very much a minority who either first made money outside farming and used this as their source of capital or genuinely climbed the farming ladder by thrift, business acumen and the aid of bank loans or loans from the Agricultural

Mortgage Corporation. Most of those who had made their own way declared that it could no longer be done today at current land prices and interest rates. The position with regard to source of capital for both samples is set out in Table 11. Of course even those who managed to obtain bank loans – especially large bank loans – needed some form of security to offer as collateral and it was generally a family member who provided this.

Table 11 *Respondents' source of initial capital (non-owners excluded)*

Source of capital	1000+ acres		44 parishes	
	No.	%	No.	%
Inherited land	66	69·5	29	60·4
Inherited money	9	9·5	5	10·4
Made money outside farming	8	8·4	2	4·2
Thrift/bank loans	12	12·6	12	25·0
Total	95	100	48	100

Now, given this general situation it is hardly surprising that our samples show relatively low rates of mobility, be it occupational, geographical or social. To begin with, it will already be evident that most respondents' fathers were themselves farmers, for we have seen this is almost a *sine qua non* for entering farming – certainly if one wants a large acreage to farm. Indeed almost 80 per cent of those in the 1000+ acres sample and 72 per cent of those in the forty-four parishes had fathers who were farmers themselves; only 2 per cent of the fathers of those in the 1000+ acres sample were manual workers, compared with 9 per cent of those in the forty-four parishes. It is true, however, that not all our respondents had entered farming immediately as a career. Some made money outside agriculture before purchasing their farms, others inherited land in mid-career, but only 20 per cent of those in the 1000+ acres sample and 12 per cent of those in the forty-four parishes had had more than half of their total jobs outside farming. In virtually all cases these exceptions had spent part of their career in industrial management, commerce or as self-employed businessmen and consequently a change to farming meant using the same skills but in a different environment and, possibly, for the first time as a self-employed person. The fact remains that only one-quarter of each sample had any non-farming experience, the most likely source of which was in the armed services.

When we take into account, therefore, the extreme likelihood of our respondents having (1) a father who was a farmer; (2) inherited the family farm; and (3) no non-farming experience, we would expect geographical mobility to be low in such cases and, therefore, low for the sample overall. And, indeed, this is generally the case, for almost half of those in the 1000+ acres sample and one-third of those in the forty-four parishes were actually brought up on their present farms. Very few of our respondents were born in urban areas and most of those who do not have a lifetime's association with their present farm were, at the very least, born in East Anglia. The relevant statistics can be seen in Table 12.

Table 12   *Location of respondents' upbringing*

Place	1000+ acres		44 parishes	
	No.	%	No.	%
Present farm	48	47·5	19	33·3
Same parish	1	1·0	6	10·5
Neighbouring parish	3	3·0	4	7·0
Within 10 miles	10	9·9	10	17·5
10–49 miles	16	15·8	4	7·0
50+ miles	23	22·8	14	24·6
Total	101	100	57	100

Thus overall mobility rates are low for farmers precisely because entry into farming at the top level is so highly circumscribed, depending largely, as we noted earlier, on family background. All these factors concerning mobility which we have discussed are, however, more markedly true in the case of the 1000+ acres sample. Consequently more of the respondents in that sample had inherited their farms; more had fathers who were farmers; more were born and/or brought up on their present farms; and far more had experience on only one farm – their own and their father's before them. Stability rather than mobility is the most obvious facet of the lives of the larger farmers and this is something which, as we noted in Chapter 1, contrasts with the other occupational groups upon which most studies of the middle class have concentrated. But, of course, just as the modified extended family aids the middle-class nuclear family in its upward spiralist progress (see Bell, 1968) so it is the family which amongst our sample of farmers maintains stability. It is hardly surprising, then, that the most 'stable' of our two samples is the 1000+ acres one, for it is highly unlikely, as many of our respondents admitted, that in modern circumstances a man on his own, unaided by his family, could build up a farm of over 1000 acres. As one of our sample said: 'The means of production are so expensive nowadays that a man who wants to establish a business is forced into the service sector.'

Related to the foregoing analysis is the obvious fact that many of our respondents have never had to enter the labour market as *sellers* of labour and previous research shows that, probably for this reason, the overall educational qualifications of farmers have generally been found to be lower than those of people in occupations of similar standing. Obviously, since the majority of farmers are born into farming they tend to receive most of their occupational training on the family farm (see, for example, Economic Development Committee for the Agricultural Industry, 1972). However previous findings in this area were not altogether borne out by our research, especially in the case of the 1000+ acres sample. We found a much higher attainment in both general educational qualifications and specific agricultural education amongst our samples than national research has shown. This is first reflected in Table 13 which deals with the schools attended by respondents and specifically demonstrated in Table 14, dealing with further education, and Table 15 which concerns formal agricultural qualifications.

Table 13 demonstrates that very nearly two-thirds of those in the 1000+ acres sample and almost half of those in the forty-four parishes went to fee-paying schools. However, there is a striking difference between the two samples in respect of elementary/secondary modern schools and grammar schools. This, as we shall see, is also reflected in terms of school qualifications and further education. But quite obviously any group in which 65 per cent of its membership went to fee-paying schools must be considered unusual, and it is generally true to say that with the 1000+ acres sample we were dealing with an economic and social élite, several of whom were titled and others of whom had either married into or were younger sons of the aristocracy. Traditionally, of course, landowning families have sent their children to public schools but it was noticeable that schools like Eton and Rugby were better represented amongst the

1000+ acres sample, while the parents of those in the forty-four parishes sample had favoured local East Anglian schools like Framlingham and Culford. Divergence in the educational experience

Table 13   *Schools attended by respondents*

Type of school	1000+ acres		44 parishes	
	No.	%	No.	%
Elementary/secondary modern	8	7·9	24	42·1
Grammar	26	25·5	6	10·5
Fee-paying	66	64·7	26	45·6
Other	2	2·0	1	1·8
Total	102	100	57	100

Table 14   *Respondents' further education*

Type of further education	1000+ acres		44 parishes	
	No.	%	No.	%
Oxbridge	19	18·4	2	3·6
Other university	7	6·8	1	1·8
Agricultural college	32	31·0	9	16·1
Other further education	3	2·9	1	1·8
No further education	42	40·8	42	76·8
Total	103	100	55	100

Table 15   *Respondents' formal agricultural qualifications*

Qualification	1000+ acres		44 parishes	
	No.	%	No.	%
Degree	17	16·7	2	3·5
College diploma	29	28·4	7	12·3
Other	6	5·9	4	7·0
None	51	50·0	44	77·2
Total	102	100	57	100

of the two samples, as a consequence of the experience reflected in Table 13, becomes more marked when we consider further education which is shown in Table 14.

We can see from the data in Table 14 that well over three-quarters of those in the forty-four parishes had no further education. Indeed a higher proportion of those in the 1000+ acres sample had been to university than had had any form of further education in the forty-four parishes sample and, as can be seen from Table 15, seventeen of these graduates possessed degrees in agriculture. Perhaps it is also worthy of comment that the agricultural colleges attended by respondents in the two samples also differed in status so that it was more likely that those who attended the Royal Agricultural College, Cirencester, would be from the 1000+ acres sample while local colleges were more likely to have been attended by those in the forty-four parishes. Not surprisingly, there were also marked differences between the two samples in terms of examinations passed at school. Whereas 80 per cent of those in the 1000+ acres sample had passed school certificate or GCE A and/or O levels, this was the case for only 41 per cent in the forty-four parishes.[8]

In reflecting more generally upon the disparities in educational experience between the two samples, however, the matter of family background and resources again looms large. Those in the 1000+ acres sample had, by and large, parents both able and willing to devote large sums of money to ensuring that their sons had the best possible education. However, on many of the smaller farms it is not unlikely that sons would be expected to leave school early because they were needed to help on the family farm and could learn all they needed to know from doing the job, a situation that obviously by no means applies to the larger farmers with a relatively numerous hired labour force. Nevertheless there is probably more to the differences than this. As we shall see in Chapter 3 the farmers in the 1000+ acres sample are far more 'oriented to the market', more businesslike and rational in their approach to agriculture. This may lead them to place a high value on a good education and formal agricultural qualifications. Indeed it was not unusual to find respondents who had not only been to college and/or university but who had also gained experience on other than their family farm, or had even been farming abroad for a short period. Thus, although a recent national survey (EDC for the Agricultural Industry, 1972) showed that the average school-leaving age for farmers was fifteen years and that 90 per cent of farmers had no formal agricultural qualifications, in our 1000+

acres sample the average school-leaving age was seventeen and, as we have seen, 50 per cent possessed formal agricultural qualifications. For the forty-four parishes sample the average school-leaving age was sixteen and a half and 28 per cent possessed agricultural qualifications. Consequently, despite the wide discrepancies between our samples both contain more well-educated and agriculturally qualified individuals than might have been expected on the basis of the national survey. This in turn may indicate the prominence and sophistication of arable farming in East Anglia.

To some extent, of course, educational achievements may depend on age and the age structure of our samples is set out in Table 16.

Table 16 *Age structure of the samples*

Age groups	1000+ acres		44 parishes	
	No.	*%*	*No.*	*%*
Under 30	4	3·9	4	7·0
30–39	27	26·5	13	22·8
40–49	29	28·4	11	19·3
50–59	22	21·6	16	28·1
60–64	12	11·8	6	10·5
65+	8	7·8	7	12·3
Total	102	100	57	100

Whereas for both samples around 30 per cent of respondents were under forty years of age, a rather higher proportion in the 1000+ acres sample were between forty and forty-nine, the reverse being true for those between fifty and fifty-nine and roughly equal proportions were over sixty. Only those under forty years of age among our respondents were capable of benefiting from the provisions of the 1944 Education Act, and thus we found that among those over forty the differences in educational achievement between the two samples was even greater than Tables 14 and 15 indicate.

Age not only affects the educational attainment of our respondents, but also has far-reaching consequences via the stage which they have reached in their family life-cycle. We have already noted the importance of the family in terms of succession to farm businesses, source of capital and so on. Clearly, the precise influence of the family, extended and nuclear, will vary according to the stage in the life-

cycle, but such a processual phenomenon cannot be accurately represented in the necessarily static portrayal which survey-generated
data, based on the situation at a particular point in time, will give.
Nevertheless our data are capable of throwing some light on this
process, as the remainder of this chapter will try to demonstrate. To
begin with, 93 per cent of those in the 1000 + acres sample and 89
per cent of those in the forty-four parishes were married. In fact the
majority in each sample, as Table 17 indicates, were at the second
stage of the family life-cycle, i.e. married with all their children at
home. (For both samples there was an average of 2·5 children per
family.) Given the fact that most of these children were below school-
leaving age, it is not surprising that only 29 per cent of the respondents in the 1000 + acres samples and 27 per cent of those in the
forty-four parishes had their children working on the farm with
them full-time. However, 79 per cent of families in the 1000 + acres
sample and 80 per cent of those in the forty-four parishes had at least
one family member who was directly involved in the work of the
farm.

Table 17 *Family life-cycle stage of respondents*

Life-cycle stage	1000 + acres		44 parishes	
	No.	*%*	*No.*	*%*
Married – no children	4	4·3	3	5·9
Married – all children home	54	57·4	28	54·9
Married – some children home	27	28·7	8	15·7
Married – all children away	9	9·6	12	23·5
Total	95	100	51	100

We asked all respondents about the type of activities members of
their family undertook on the farm according to the following
classification: (a) answering the phone, dealing with callers, running
farm errands; (b) doing office paperwork; (c) giving orders to
workers; (d) working on the land; (e) making farm policies. Since
these data were, of course, derived from interviewing the farmer
rather than the other members of his family directly they need to be
treated with some caution, but they probably correspond reasonably
accurately to the general situation on the farms on which we interviewed. Only a minority of farmers' wives were (allegedly) not

involved at all in the running of the farm business and there was little variation in this between the samples – 23·7 per cent in the 1000 + acres sample and 27·3 per cent in the forty-four parishes. For a broadly similar proportion (23·7 per cent and 20·5 per cent respectively) the wives' involvement was fairly minimal, limited to answering the phone, dealing with callers and running the occasional farm errand. A further 16 per cent in each sample also carried out office paperwork – usually typing letters and compiling accounts. Only 9·0 per cent in the forty-four parishes and 3·2 per cent on the 1000 + acres farms carried out all the functions listed above. Thus, while approximately three-quarters of the wives in both samples were involved in the running of the farm in some way, this mostly concerned ancillary, non-manual tasks rather than work on the land itself – although here there were significant differences between the samples with 17·6 per cent of wives in the forty-four parishes being involved in this, but only 8·6 per cent in the 1000 + acres sample. Perhaps an even more startling illustration of the conception of 'women's work' in agriculture is the fact that over 90 per cent of daughters in both samples had no involvement with the farm whatsoever. Not surprisingly, as the size of the farm increases there is a tendency for the wife to withdraw more and more from any direct involvement in the farm business and assume a purely domestic role – where, it needs to be added, her contribution need be no less significant, economically or psychologically, to her husband's well-being.[9]

The most marked differences between our two samples in the use of family labour concerns the role of sons. In the forty-four parishes sample, 62·5 per cent of our respondents' sons were not involved in the running of the farm at all; but in the 1000 + acres sample this proportion dropped to only 6·3 per cent. The discrepancy was equally apparent at the other extreme: 16·7 per cent of the sons in the forty-four parishes sample carried out all the functions listed above, while 62·5 per cent of those in the 1000 + acres sample were likewise extensively involved. Given that a large proportion of farms in the forty-four parishes sample correspond to 'family' farms – i.e. they employ no hired labour – these results seem to present a paradox. However, many of the small farms in the forty-four parishes find it impossible to 'carry' the farmer's son since there is neither sufficient work nor sufficiently high profits to support him. Sons on these farms are therefore forced to look elsewhere for employment whilst awaiting their inheritance (cf. Williams, 1964). On the larger farms in the 1000 + acres sample, however, there are often ample opportunities for employment, especially in the managerial and supervisory roles which the more bureaucratic nature of these farms has created (see below, Chapter 4). Farmers' sons on these farms will see a potentially lucrative managerial and entrepreneurial career stretching before them, often more intrinsically attractive and rewarding than the drudgery to which their counterparts on the small farms might see themselves consigned.

Farmers are notoriously clannish and the stereotype, at least, is of a highly self-contained and self-perpetuating group, bound together by intermarriage and residential stability. How far is this stereotype confirmed by our data on the farmer's immediate kin? We can begin an examination of this question by looking at the background of our respondents' wives. Our analysis of their employment before marriage is presented in Table 18, the analysis being based on the Registrar General's 1966 *Classification of Occupations*, with jobs being assigned to socio-economic groups. Several points are worth noting. To begin with eighteen of the wives of respondents in the 1000 + acres sample and seven of those in the forty-four parishes had never entered the labour market; in all but three of these cases their fathers were farmers or employers. Equally it can be seen that the socio-economic status of the wife's job before marriage is somewhat higher in the 1000 + acres sample: whereas 72 per cent of wives in the 1000 + acres group are covered by the two groups 'intermediate' and 'junior non-manual', 67 per cent of those in the forty-four parishes are covered by the groups 'junior non-manual' and 'personal service workers'. This point is further reinforced if we look at the backgrounds of their fathers. Amongst the 1000 + acres sample, 27·3 per cent of our respondents' fathers-in-law were farmers, a further 25 per cent were employers or own-account workers; 17 per cent were self-employed professional workers; and 12 per cent professional employees; only 5·7 per cent were manual workers (and they were all skilled) and 9·1 per cent were routine non-manual workers. More than one-third of the fathers-in-law of the 1000 + acres sample who were farmers had themselves run farms of over 1000 acres. When we turn to the forty-four parishes sample we find farmers even better represented amongst fathers-in-law (39 per cent). A further 20 per cent were employers or own-account workers, but only 6 per cent and 8 per cent respectively were self-employed professionals and professional employees; 10 per cent were manual workers, 4 per cent members of the armed forces and 10 per cent

were routine non-manual workers. Thus the general pattern is for
our respondents to be the sons of farmers, but while there is a tendency for them to marry farmers' daughters this tendency is much
weaker than their own inter-generational continuity. Overwhelmingly, however, farmers tend to marry women who are themselves
from a non-manual background.

Finally, in our consideration of our respondents' families we can
look at the occupations of brothers, sisters and brothers-in-law of our
samples. Altogether we obtained details from those in the 1000 +
acres sample for ninety-seven brothers and ninety-seven sisters/
brothers-in-law (since we took details of brothers-in-laws' occupations where sisters were married). Details are given below in Table 19.
We can see that, as with farmers' fathers-in-law, farmers, employers
and the self-employed also predominate. The largest group represented is farmers and, indeed, 55 per cent of brothers and 25 per cent
of sisters/brothers-in-law who were farmers also had holdings of over
1000 acres. Some of these were partners with the respondent, but
most were not. Corresponding details for the forty-four parishes
sample are tabulated in Table 20. The results here are quite similar
to those for the 1000 + acres sample, especially in terms of siblings
who are farming. Manual occupations, however, are more highly
represented and employing and professional occupations are less
common. Nevertheless we can see from these figures that farming is
not simply the occupation of our respondents and the vast majority

Table 18   *Socio-economic groups of respondents' wives prior to marriage*

Socio-economic group	1000 + acres		44 parishes	
	No.	%	*No.*	%
Employers – small establishments	4	5·3	—	—
Professional employees	3	4·0	1	2·8
Intermediate non-manual	28	37·3	6	16·7
Junior non-manual	26	34·6	13	36·1
Personal service workers	4	5·3	11	30·6
Own-account workers	2	2·7	—	—
Farmers – employers	1	1·3	—	—
Agricultural workers	5	6·7	2	5·6
Armed forces	—	—	2	5·6
Inadequate description	2	2·7	1	2·8
Total	75	100	36	100

Table 19 *Socio-economic groups of respondents' siblings*
(1000 + acres sample)

Socio-economic group	Brothers		Sisters/brothers-in-law	
	No.	%	No.	%
Employers – large establishments	5	5·2	9	9·3
Employers – small establishments	13	13·4	11	11·3
Professionals – self-employed	4	4·1	6	6·2
Professionals – employees	11	11·3	7	7·2
Intermediate – non-manual	2	2·1	10	10·3
Manual	5	5·2	4	4·1
Own account	2	2·1	1	1·0
Farmers	53	54·6	28	28·9
Others	2	2·1	21	21·6
Total	97	100	97	100

Table 20 *Socio-economic groups of respondents' siblings*
(44 parishes sample)

Socio-economic group	Brothers		Sisters/brothers-in-law	
	No.	%	No.	%
Employers – large establishments	2	3·8	3	5·9
Employers – small establishments	4	7·5	2	3·9
Professionals – self-employed	3	5·7	1	2·0
Professionals – employees	2	3·8	8	15·7
Intermediate – non-manual	7	13·2	11	21·6
Manual	5	9·4	9	17·6
Own account	1	1·9	1	2·0
Farmers	29	54·7	14	27·4
Others	—	—	2	3·9
Total	53	100	51	100

of their fathers, but that of many of their brothers, brothers-in-law
and fathers-in-law, too.

The stereotype of the farmer belonging to the somewhat enclosed
and self-contained world of the farming fraternity therefore has some
basis in reality. This raises the question of the extent to which
farmers form, in a loose social sense, a 'class'. Certainly, as we have
seen, entry into farming is almost entirely on the basis of birth, either

by direct succession to the farming business or by inheriting the capital whereby one may be purchased. Even those who had acquired their current holding by virtue of self-generated thrift and hard work ruefully admitted that it would no longer be possible at the ruling price of land today. The cheap price of land and tenancies, of which they had taken advantage during the Depression, were unlikely to return; indeed the provision of capital which would enable one of their sons to purchase another farm was considered by many to be beyond their means. The ascriptive nature of this social grouping is made even more apparent when one compares the background of farmers with that of farm workers (see Newby, 1977, p. 356). Agricultural workers are also overwhelmingly the sons of agricultural workers, with a high proportion of immediate kin also working on the land. The amount of social mobility between the two groups, even by intermarriage, is minuscule. All this suggests that class divisions in rural East Anglia are clear-cut and easily distinguishable. A full consideration of rural class relationships involves much more than this, however. For the classical definition of class involves the ownership of the means of production, and it is to this that we can now turn.

3 Market situations

The overall economic position of farmers is by no means a unitary phenomenon, but has to be divided into several analytically separate components. For the farmer is not a participant in a single market, but in several, sometimes as seller, but also as buyer, his position being an amalgamation of varying situations, in various markets. Consequently this chapter considers a number of closely related aspects which together comprise an overall market situation.

To begin with the farmer clearly depends a great deal upon his position as a *seller* of unprocessed farm produce in the open market. This is obviously crucial, since it is his activities here which can largely determine his income. However, the open market is notoriously unpredictable, with often wildly fluctuating prices being determined more by supply and demand than necessary production costs. Farming, as anything more than subsistence activity, would quickly go under if it were left to the vagaries of the market, and hence the state has increasingly intervened with price support (subsidies, guaranteed prices, intervention prices, etc.). Hence no consideration of the market situation of farmers can ignore the relationship between the state and the farmer, and this means, in effect, the relationship between the Ministry of Agriculture (MAFF) on the one hand, and the National Farmers' Union (NFU) and the Country Landowners' Association (CLA) on the other. Of course, recent developments have moved an important element in agricultural price structures and decision-making away from London to Brussels and the EEC. However, even with the given structure of state intervention in the market, and the large part played in the farmer's market situation by the success or otherwise of the lobbying activities and negotiating abilities of the NFU, his ultimate profits and income can be very much affected by his own marketing and investment decisions. Farmers are by no means without choice as to how they market their produce and continually seek to extend their control in the market by means other than a reliance on pressure-group politics or a simple resignation to what the open market might seem to dictate to them in terms of prices.

This particularly applies to the kind of capitalist-organized business farming with which we are concerned. Here a number of alternative options are used. First, the farmer need not sell his produce on the open market at all. He can choose to sell directly to food processors by means of a contract which gives him a guaranteed price even before he has sown the seed. This has obvious advantages and disadvantages depending on which way prices are fluctuating at the time he is ready to sell his produce. In terms of the financial management of his business, a contract means that the farmer knows before he grows his crop what profit he is likely to make; that is, it gives him some certainty in what might otherwise be an uncertain situation. Moreover, he may obtain a better contracted price than the prevailing market price, but – and here is the great disadvantage – prices might be much higher in the open market than the guaranteed contract price. In that case, while with luck still making a profit, he may lose out on a potential bonanza. Those who are dependent upon contracts have decided that certainty is important to them, and that a huge profit lost in one year when prices are high on the open market is generally offset in another year by not making an equally large loss when the market is unfavourable. Some crops, it should be noted, especially sugar beet and milk, have to be sold on contract through the British Sugar Corporation and the Milk Marketing Board, but virtually everything else, from seed to livestock, can be sold either on contract or in the open market.

The farmer's choice does not end here, however. By coming together into a producer group farmers can try to obtain some of the advantages of both an open market and a contract. Since several farmers together can sell in greater volume and afford to buy the expertise of someone with knowledge of the market, they can hope to obtain better prices. Alternatively a single farmer, or a group of farmers, can cut out the middle man and sell directly to retailers by investing in the plant necessary not merely to harvest their crops, but to process, grade and pack it, and perhaps even deliver it. Of course, limitations are set here by the type of crop concerned, vegetables being the most feasible for this purpose. Equally the farmer can sell at least some of his produce direct to the consumer – so called 'farm gate' sales of eggs, fruit, vegetables, and produce for the ever-expanding freezer market, which includes meat for the deep freeze ('farm-fresh meat at wholesale prices'), and 'pick-your-own' fruit.

The latter also has the distinct advantage of reducing to nil labour costs involved in harvesting the crop. We thus have a number of basic ways in which farmers can strengthen their market situation by their own efforts.[1]

In addition to being a seller of farm produce, a second element in the farmer's market situation is that of buyer from industry of a whole range of necessary farm inputs – machinery, fertilizer and feedstuffs in particular. One of the major consequences of the recent changes in agricultural technology has been to make farmers increasingly dependent upon inputs to their businesses which originate off the farm. Here, too, the farmer would seem to be in a relatively weak position in the open market. Even the very largest farmer can hardly be expected to drive a very hard bargain with the many multi-national companies – Shell, ICI, Ford, etc. – which dominate the agro-chemical and agricultural engineering industries. Once again, however, group buying and farmer cooperatives can be a means of obtaining a more favourable price. Finally farmers are also buyers of two other important factors of production: land, whose market is one in which agricultural considerations do not always reign supreme, and labour. In a predominantly rural area like East Anglia, farmers are extremely influential in the labour market (Newby, 1977; Rose *et al.*, 1976; Saunders *et al.*, 1978).

The final income of a farmer, of course, is largely dictated by his ability to operate successfully in these markets; for where a business-man has relatively little control, as is the case with farmers, over either the prices he receives for his products or those he pays others for theirs, marketing ability is of paramount importance. This leads us to a further consideration to which we have already alluded. Farming is both a traditional activity – a 'way of life' – and a rational one – a business. In our early deliberations we felt that a tension between the traditional and the rational should be quite apparent in the marketing policies of those in our samples, and this is to a large extent the implicit theme of this chapter. Moreover farming has always been an individual, or at best a family, activity. But increasingly group action in the market may be necessary to maintain and enhance profitability. Hence we have another and related potential source of conflict for farmers. Should they continue to act as individuals or should they join with others, and how do they perceive the relative advantages and disadvantages of such a choice?

The land market

We can begin our analysis with the factor of production which is
most essential to agriculture: land. The control of land is not only a
crucial economic resource, however, for it also has very apparent
social implications. Not only is it true that 'property and lack of
property are . . . the basic categories of all class situations' (Weber
in Gerth and Mills, 1948, p. 182), but property-owners themselves
are frequently not unaware of this fact. Certainly, as we shall seek to
demonstrate below, landowners are not slow to react to any perceived threat to their position, whether this threat comes from the
state or from within the private economic institutions of society.
Moreover, as Stinchcombe (1962, p. 165) has observed, 'agriculture
everywhere is much more organised around the institutions of
property than around those of occupation'. It is especially important,
therefore, that we attempt to understand the meaning and significance of landownership to the owners themselves. In what follows
in the first half of this chapter we shall begin to do this by concen-
trating on two broad themes. First, we shall examine the various
contemporary threats to landownership (and by extension the current
social structure of rural society) brought about by a combination of
recent developments in the land market and in changing fiscal and
agricultural legislation. Secondly, we shall discuss tenurial status in
the light of data we received from the farmers in our samples. This
should provide an empirical basis for the understanding of the more
theoretical arguments presented in the later part of this book concerning the nature of contemporary property rights and property
ownership.

As we indicated in Chapter 1, within the context of modern
British agriculture land is first and foremost *capital*. It is currently
estimated that about £20 000 million pounds is invested in British
agriculture, roughly in the proportion four-fifths landlord's capital,
i.e. land and buildings, and one-fifth tenant's capital, 'the money
involved in the running of the farm, providing for livestock,
machinery, movable plant and equipment, growing and harvested
produce plus working capital' (Clery, 1975, p. 59). Farmers themselves own the overwhelming proportion of these assets as Table 21
demonstrates. Land and buildings constitute the largest single element amongst farmers' assets, the land alone being the more significant of the two in terms of farmers' wealth. Given the comparatively
recent trends towards owner-occupation (see Fig. 1) and the small

scale of farm businesses, this is hardly surprising. But for precisely these reasons farmers are extremely sensitive to any changes in the land market which they deem to be against their interests, and this is the case regardless of whether they are owner-occupiers or tenants. Furthermore, because of the typical structure of farm businesses – individually or family owned (see Harrison, 1975, pp. 18 ff.) – any increase in land prices inflates the owner-occupier's wealth and consequently increases his tax liability. Similarly, any fundamental changes in the tax structure affecting capital gains, capital transfers or wealth have potentially far-reaching repercussions for all farmers and landowners; even tenants are affected because of the situation of landlords (see below).

Table 21 *Estimated balance sheet of UK agriculture, June 1975*

Liabilities	£m	Assets	£m
Banks	1 100	Land, buildings	15 480
AMC, etc.	295	Machinery, plant	1 050
Insurance companies	40	Livestock	1 700
Private loans	300	Crops and produce	1 200
HP and credit	380	Debtors, bank balances	800
Capital owned	18 115		
Total	20 230	Total	20 230

Source: Clery, 1975, p. 28.

From our immediate viewpoint this is of great significance, for in the course of the last five years the land market has entered a volatile period and a Labour government has been elected pledged to a series of new taxes and other measures, some of which are aimed specifically at agriculture but all of which could have fundamental consequences for the existing structure of landownership. Farmers and their organizations perceive this as a threat to their position and have mobilized against it. In agriculture these fiscal threats are particularly important, for the economic structure of agriculture is very different to that in, say, manufacturing. While generally in industry there has developed a divorce between ownership and control and a concomitant rise of managerialism, in agriculture the situation has reversed. As we noted in Chapter 1, at the turn of the present century 90 per cent of agricultural land was owned by others than those who farmed it and one could discern a *landownership* interest separate from, and often opposed to, a *farming* interest. But the break-up of the great estates and the decline of the agricultural landlord resulted in the creation of a new, and now dominant, class of farmer – the owner-occupier. Although a very recent historical development, the idea of farmers owning the land they farm is now so rooted that any distinction between owning and farming land is generally overlooked. A threat to landownership as it is presently structured is interpreted by farmers, the NFU, the CLA and even at times by the Ministry of Agriculture as a threat to farming. It is only when we realize how entrenched in the minds of farmers is the idea of owning the land that is farmed, of how much even tenant farmers aspire to own land, that we can appreciate the vehemence with which farmers attack taxation changes and changes in the land market.

The structure of landownership

Owner-occupiers are certainly the most numerous group of agricultural landowners. Exactly how many there are is impossible to say since official statistics on landownership are not collected,[2] but over one-half of all farmland is now owner-occupied. Nevertheless, despite their decline this century, the traditional private landowners, the agricultural landlords, are still of great importance. In a sense they are even more threatened than the owner-occupiers, for their income from letting land is regarded as unearned and they receive no relief, as working farmers do, under Capital Transfer Tax. Moreover a wealth tax would be a considerable burden to them and the recent extension of security of tenure to agricultural tenants in England and Wales under the Agriculture (Miscellaneous Provisions) Act, 1976, will effectively prevent them from gaining vacant possession of their own land. Between these two groups is divided almost 90 per cent of the agricultural land of England and Wales, but the land market itself is beyond their control and the price of land bears no necessary relationship to its agricultural use-value. This has become a great embarrassment to private landowners in recent years.

Apart from private owners of agricultural land there are the institutional landowners. A recent survey of institutional landownership by Gibbs and Harrison (1974) has pointed out that while 'the acreage of rented farmland has declined markedly this century, the area owned by public and semi-public bodies has increased and is still increasing' (p. 1). In fact figures from their study show that about

10 per cent of the agricultural land of England and Wales is owned by institutions, and its distribution is shown in Table 22.

Table 22 *Institutional ownership of farm land, England and Wales, 1971*

Institution	Acreage owned
Monarchy	325055
Forestry Commission	80555
Ministry of Agriculture	28112
Other government departments	121663
Nationalized industries	359233
Local authorities	929559
Universities	180385
Conservation bodies	201452
Agricultural Research Council	6622
Church land	157814
City institutions[3]	170000
Total	2560450

Source: Gibbs and Harrison, 1974, p. 5.

There are, then, broadly three types of institutional landowner, viz.:

1. *Traditional institutional landowners* – institutions with a long history of landowning and who generally observe the normative prescriptions of landlord–tenant relationships, e.g. the Church, the monarchy, Oxbridge colleges.
2. *Public landowners* – bodies responsible directly or indirectly to Parliament or whose membership is open to members of the public, e.g. nationalized industries, departments of state, the National Trust.
3. *Financial institutions* – the City element in farm landownership consisting of public companies, especially insurance companies and property groups, some public farming companies whose boards of directors are not related to one another, and pension funds of public and nationalized industries.

This enables us to produce a simple taxonomy of agricultural land-ownership as follows:

80   *Market situations*

I   PRIVATE   II INSTITUTIONAL
A. Traditional landlord   A. Traditional
B. Owner-occupied   B. Public
C. Private trusts/charities   C. Financial

Figure 3   *A taxonomy of landownership*

A very rough calculation, based largely on Ministry of Agriculture
tenure figures, would indicate that about 56 per cent of farm land is
owned by the owner-occupiers, approximately 33 per cent by traditional private landlords and trusts, 6 per cent by public institutions,
3 per cent by traditional institutions and 1·5 per cent by financial
institutions.

Land and inflation

The background, therefore, against which we must set our discussion
of the land market is one where perhaps two-thirds of all farm land is
farmed directly by the owners of the land.[4] The vast majority of these
owners have a direct interest in seeing a stable land market in which
prices rise only slowly and which ensures that a continuation of
private landownership is possible. To put our discussion of land
prices in a historical perspective, Figure 4 shows the trend of prices
over the last 200 years.[5] We can see from this that the trend since
1945 has been for land prices to rise quite steadily – from £45 an
acre in 1945, to £76 in 1949, £101 in 1959 and £299 in 1969. (These
are Oxford Institute figures for land with vacant possession.) However, the sudden and very rapid rise in land prices which took place in
1972/3 followed by an almost equally dramatic fall in 1974/5 and
yet another boom in 1976/7 has put the land market in turmoil and
led to a great deal of acrimonious comment in farming circles.

The precise causes of these market events are difficult to analyse
but the reaction of farmers is of great interest. Figure 5 gives a
graphic picture of recent market trends, although the kind of average
prices on which it is based hide some of the starker realities faced by
farmers in certain areas. In parts of East Anglia, for example, land
prices rose from £300 per acre to as much as £1400 per acre in the
space of twelve months in 1972/3 and many farmers were somewhat
embarrassed to find they were suddenly millionaires. This was a
mixed blessing since, while it made borrowing easier, it made for a
heavy capital tax liability in the future and the possibility of tech-

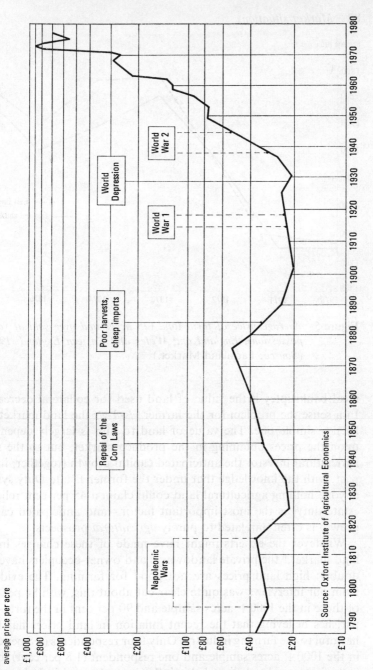

Figure 4 *The cost of farmland, 1790–1976 (Reproduced with permission from the* Sunday Telegraph, *19 August 1973.)*

average price per acre

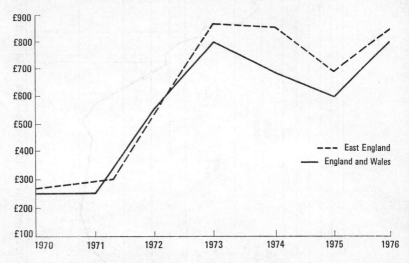

Figure 5   *Average price of farm land (25 acres and over sold at vacant possession), England and Wales and Eastern England, 1970–6 (Source:* Farmland Market.)

nical bankruptcy if the value of land used for collateral decreased. In a sense the problem for the farmer *vis-à-vis* the land market has been a simple one. The value of land to him is largely dependent upon the prices obtaining in the produce market, but to the non-agricultural investor the anticipated capital growth (together, in the past, with the knowledge that under the former Estate Duty system anyone holding agricultural land could claim a 45 per cent relief of estate duty) is the most important factor – and anticipated capital growth is often unrelated to purely *agricultural* prospects.

Whatever the experts might have made of these changes in the land market,[6] the private landowners and owner-occupiers have few doubts: high land prices are not good for farming. The evidence from our interviews was quite clear-cut about this, with 84 per cent of those in the 1000 + acres sample and 90 per cent in the forty-four parishes believing that the recent inflation in land prices has been harmful to the farming industry. Only four respondents (3·8 per cent) in the 1000 + acres sample and one respondent (1·8 per cent) in the forty-four parishes believed this inflation to be positively beneficial (the remainder had mixed reactions). A variety of reasons were given for regarding this inflation as harmful and they are set out in Table 23. We can see that these reasons vary little between the two samples, although those on the generally smaller farms in the forty-four parishes see succession as less of a problem. Certainly most of our respondents became both animated and voluble when asked about land prices and few of them would disagree with any of the seven major reasons noted in the table as to why inflation in the price of land was injurious to them. We must also assume that those who did not mention taxation problems explicitly implied them when they cited succession problems and/or a threat to private landownership. A more detailed examination of these replies revealed that taxation problems were mentioned by only 11 per cent of those in the 1000 + acres sample who owned less than 50 per cent of their land, but by 42 per cent who owned more than 50 per cent. In the forty-four parishes sample the equivalent rates were 31 per cent and 50 per cent. Similarly farmers who mentioned succession problems were more likely to be found among those who owned most land. There was thus a relationship between proportion of land owned and reasons given for inflated land prices being harmful. Below are a selection of comments by farmers on land prices:

Of course it's harmful because it puts landownership at risk. It has produced a situation where the medium-sized farmer with 1000 acres [*sic*] is in
the millionaire bracket when he shouldn't be. Landownership is important
but, in this situation [of high prices], is becoming socially unacceptable
with people thinking 'bloody millionaires'. And it leads to the break-up of
units at the death of owners. [Suffolk farmer, 1200 acres, all owned.]

It's terribly harmful because you can't afford to die. Death duties will be
so heavy that I doubt if my son will be able to take over from me. Taxes
can make a business disappear, and if estates have to be split up there is
less land for tenants. Land is for farming. I don't want to be this 'wealthy'
– if I did I would sell my land and live off the income doing nothing.
[Norfolk farmer, 1300 acres, 55 per cent owned.]

But there were owners who believed high land prices were not entirely bad news:

I can't say it's been harmful to me when I have paid £200000 for land now
worth £1500000. . . . I have never made much from day-to-day farming
but increased my assets from capital gains. [Norfolk farmer, 2300 acres,
all owned.]

Similarly some tenants saw advantages in high land prices:

It's not necessarily bad for us. It brings in new finance. [Norfolk farmer, 1050 acres, all rented.]

However, most tenants recognized that in so far as high land prices caused problems for landlords, then those who rent land are in a vulnerable position. The general point to note, however, is that it is not *farming* which is necessarily put at risk by high land prices, but landownership and the family business which owner-occupiers equate with farming. As one tenant put it (a man who made a rigid distinction between *farming* and *owning* land):

It's harmful to owners but not to tenants. It affected the demand for tenancies but not the rents. It is the family business which really suffers. [Norfolk farmer, 1800 acres, 60 per cent rented.]

Many tenants, however, aspire to ownership and deplore high prices because they make that aspiration less likely to be realized:

It makes it difficult to climb the farming ladder. You can't farm land at these prices and that is why the institutions have bought it. If you are sitting on the land you are all right; but for tenants high prices mean high rents. [Norfolk farmer, 1720 acres, 90 per cent rented.]

You can't make a profit as a farmer . . . and the traditional landowners are being replaced by financial institutions – and that may not be good for farming. [Cambridgeshire farmer, 1100 acres, 60 per cent rented.]

So all farmers perceive inflation as a threat to their position as land-owners now or at some future date. Many were not slow to point an accusing finger at those financial institutions who had begun to invest in land and who were believed to be responsible for land price inflation. In addition the government was equally held to blame for taxation changes (either actual or imminent), especially Capital Transfer Tax, Wealth Tax and Capital Gains Tax with its roll-over relief provisions for agriculture.[7] We can examine each of these in turn.

The City institutions

No recent development in agricultural landownership has created more controversy within farming circles than the activities of the City institutions – insurance companies, unit trusts, pension funds, etc. – in purchasing land to add to their investment portfolios. These City interests, many farmers maintain, have no real concern for agriculture, but merely seek safe havens for their money. The City,

Table 23 *Reasons why inflated land prices are harmful to farmers*

Reasons harmful	1000 + acres (N=95) %	44 parishes (N=54) %
Creates tax problems	36·8	50·0
Restricts recruitment of young farmers	30·5	25·9
Creates succession problems	23·2	7·4
Farming becomes uneconomic	31·6	42·6
Prevents expansion	28·4	27·8
Threatens private landownership	21·1	20·4
Distorts farmers' wealth	8·4	3·7
Other reasons	10·5	5·6

Note: Percentages do not equal 100 as most respondents gave more than one answer.

it is believed, has no sensitivity to the 'needs of the rural community' in their relentless pursuit of Mammon. For example:

For centuries the countryside has been populated by people who contributed more to life than they extracted, be they landowners, owner-occupiers, tenant farmers, tradesmen, craftsmen, or the rector.

The rural population . . . rely on each other and help each other. . . . Most voluntary organisations in the countryside are manned by people who would never think of taking a salary for their services. Rural people are always on the look-out for those less fortunate than themselves, from the grave-digger to the squire they see their occupation as a respectable and worthy one contributing to the betterment of the community in which they live.

They need reimbursement, but this is not the main yardstick of their success as in urban society, for once profit becomes the sole aim and people become labour units, then the quality of life disappears almost overnight. . . .

The participating landlord-tenant who earns his living from his estate should be encouraged by tax law, and so should the owner-occupiers. The rest, who look upon land as similar to gold or a Canaletto purchased solely for its growth potential for personal gain, will I hope, be completely discouraged by taxes. . . . [Hew Watt, Essex owner-occupier with 800 acres, in an article, 'Stop Exploiting the Land', *Farmland Market*, No. 3, January 1975, pp. 12–13.][8]

Since the institutional involvement in the land market was so clearly identified by nearly all farmers as the factor which caused the chaos in land prices after 1972 it is hardly surprising that a certain amount of acrimony crept in. Some of this was due to the persistent tendency among farmers to stigmatize any 'outsiders' connected with the wider urban-industrial world (see below, Chapters 5 and 7). However, much of this antipathy was directed at institutions which clearly did not intend to take the passive role that had hitherto been associated with traditional institutional landowners. Thus the debates about the new 'farming institutions' were, in fact, largely concerned with the style of ownership and control of farmland. It was the economic rationality of the City institutions which was so objected to.

If it did nothing else, the rise in land prices in 1972–3 showed that a very great deal of any farm's equity is tied up in land. The CLA, the NFU and the Ministry of Agriculture all made this a central issue in their submissions to the Select Committee on the Wealth Tax,[9] the implication being that if farming did not receive special case status under any wealth tax then private landownership was doomed. What was not asked was whether it is necessary or desirable to own the land that is farmed since it is assumed in farming circles that owning land is practically a *sine qua non* of farming. Yet this is, in a sense, the question which is posed by high land prices, and this is also where the actions of some of the City institutions have considerable relevance. For example, the managing director of one City-backed farming company has challenged the conventional wisdom as follows:

Many owner-occupiers decry any rise in land values because of increasing their personal tax problems, totally forgetting – or conveniently ignoring – that reasonable increases in land values are essential if they are to remain economically sound in terms of collateral for their borrowings. . . . 'I am not interested in capital appreciation; all I want is for my heirs to farm this land.' . . . Let the rare owner-occupier who believes this form a limited company, let his farm to the company then sell the land to an investor. . . . He then has capital to spare, his heirs have the tenancy in perpetuity, and everyone is happy. [Rosen, 1975, p. 9.]

What Rosen is here attacking is the hypocrisy of the owner-occupier, but it is precisely ownership which they will not relinquish even though, in the opinion of Rosen, the land is not farmed as efficiently as it might otherwise be as a result. Even the representatives of landowners and farmers, it should be added, do recognize that owner-occupancy can hinder agricultural efficiency, but they fall back on non-economic arguments to justify their position:

Few proprietors of family businesses of any sort, are motivated by profit *alone* and considerations other than maximisation of profits affect farming and landowning to a varying degree, either consciously or subconsciously.

Maintenance of the countryside and village life, the provision of sport, improving amenity, providing continuity of employment, minimisation of taxation and many other considerations provide reasons for doing or not doing something which would improve profitability. These motives are perfectly acceptable on personal social and environmental grounds. . . . [CLA, 1974, p. 3.][10]

Indeed to be a *real* landowner means precisely not to be as efficient as possible, while farmers, in their judgements and evaluations of one another, by no means place profitability at the head of their list of attributes (see below, Chapter 5). For example, the CLA's recent discussion paper on landownership stated that:

Other activities of landownership reflect a sense of stewardship which may well be so strong as to dictate courses of action which are totally illogical in terms of maximising the commercial benefits accruing to an owner. The stewardship concept encourages landowners to think and act in the long-term interests of the land and the community it supports. . . . The land-owner's vision and his belief in improving his heritage for his heirs encouraged him to subsidise the local community in many practical ways and to improve and maintain the countryside. Despite the economic absurdity of this type of activity many, albeit a steadily reducing number, still carry on. [CLA, 1976, p. 5.]

And an agricultural correspondent, himself a farmer, has recently stated a similar view more baldly:

To state that owner-occupied land produces more than tenanted land is patently not true. . . . [Wormell, *East Anglian Daily Times*, 31 July 1976.]

It is not surprising, then, that most farmers react defensively to the activities of the City institutions and generally view their activities as no less threatening to their long-term interests than fiscal measures aimed at a more egalitarian distribution of wealth. For this reason the institutions themselves have been quite keen to publicize their activities in order to demonstrate that their attitude to land is not the rapacious one which many farmers believe it to be.[11] However when, as has happened, City investors predict the imminent restructuring of agricultural land tenure and the separation of ownership and control, all the fears of the private owner are exacerbated. For example, Peter Hutley of Property Growth Assurance has argued the case as follows:

It seems to me that the industry has gone full circle and the high price of land will in the next decade bring about the restructuring of farming. The land owner or long term investor, because of his desire for security and capital growth, will accept a low yield on his capital and will probably increase his holdings. The farmer, who actively seeks a high return on his working capital and who is capable of earning 15 per cent + on this, will transfer the ownership and increase his farming acreage by tenanting land. [*Essex County Standard*, 27 April 1975.]

How do farmers react to these threats to their market situation? Among our respondents we found slightly less of a unanimity of view than on the question of inflation. Their attitudes seemed to depend partly on whether the City institutions were blamed for high land prices, partly on a knowledge of City landlords and partly on the amount of land owned by the respondents. The greatest hostility was registered by those in the forty-four parishes where only 3·7 per cent saw the involvement of the City in landownership as beneficial while 74·5 per cent saw it as inimical to agricultural interests and 21·8 per cent thought it something of a mixed blessing. The equivalent figures for the 1000+ acres sample were 29·0 per cent, 55·1 per cent and 15·9 per cent.

We can obtain a better idea of the views of respondents from Table 24. Clearly we received more responses which were hostile than favourable towards City institutions. There are three basic reasons for this: the impersonal nature of such landownership; the fact that such owners have other than agricultural interests at heart; and economic factors – high prices, unfair competition for land, and succession problems. A few quotations from our respondents can illustrate these points:

It's all too impersonal. In the past, when land in the village was owned by a local person, the local landlord was the benefactor. He knew everyone in the village by more than nodding acquaintance. Institutions are impersonal and the village suffers and splits up. [Norfolk farmer and landowner, 3000 acres, all owned.]

The most efficient and human way to conduct a business is by personal contact. If these insurance companies and so on keep coming in we'll finish up like the rest of British industry, especially in labour relations. You can't make agriculture work on an industrial footing. That does *not* mean we can afford to be yokel about farming – but you do have to *care* about farming. Those who own *must* have a personal interest. [Suffolk farmer, 2700 acres, 60 per cent owned.]

But other owner-occupiers were less adamant in their views:

I don't think it's so bad provided the institutions will take a real long-term interest in their investment. But in today and out tomorrow is frightful. However, if they use the land properly, it can be a good thing because it brings in outside capital. Such companies also have greater investment resources. A hundred years ago most land was tenanted from the great estates, and these institutions are the modern equivalent of the feudal estates. But they must go the whole hog and employ decent managers and so on who know what they are doing. Where you have a landlord who is not prepared in any way to see for himself what is going on around his estate but is only interested in figures on paper, this can't be good. The practical farmer's view is to be completely committed to farming, to making a success, and that means a close landlord–tenant relationship. [Cambridgeshire farmer, 2500 acres, 60 per cent owned.]

Some owners see nothing but good from the system because they are enabled to expand through the institutions:

It allows people like us in. We buy at £750 an acre and then sell on lease back for £600 to an institution. This costs us £150 an acre 'key money'. That's what we are doing at present and it's financed from roll-over money. [Essex farmer, 1000 acres, 50 per cent owned.]

It's done no harm; it's the *reasons* for the investment I don't like. But if we need City money and the City will buy at viable agricultural values, it's all right. . . . I am resigned to institutions owning more of the land by 2000 and that is fair enough because it will continue the landlord–tenant relationship after the private landlord has been taxed out of existence. Owner-occupation will decline, too. [Norfolk estate manager, 6600 acres, all owned.]

Of course, many such comments are grudging acceptances of a hard truth: if the private landlord is becoming an anachronism because of heavy taxes, then someone must take his place – and since City institutions do not die they have a lesser tax burden. We view it as extremely significant that one-third of the rented land on farms in the 1000+ acres sample now belongs to such institutions. Many of the tenants in this sample, therefore, had first-hand knowledge of the City landlord. Moreover those renting land from such institutions tended to be favourably disposed towards them. Below are a selection of comments of those favouring the City landlord:

They weren't responsible for the high prices – that was roll-over relief. If we had bought land the amount of money we'd have needed for a farm this size would have been fantastic. As it is we got the lease-back, which I can see nothing wrong with and the insurance company is happy with its 4 per cent return. [Suffolk farmer, 1050 acres, 65 per cent rented.]

It's good: it creates more tenancies and you can only become really large scale as a tenant. Separation of owning from farming is a good thing and that's what these companies offer. They are investing in agriculture and they are landlords like any other. [Norfolk farmer, 1800 acres, 60 per cent rented.]

All of these farmers were tenants of City landlords. Other tenants, however, viewing the relationship from outside, were much less sanguine and expressed similar attitudes to the financial institutions as the majority of owner-occupiers. For example:

No. You reach a stage where you have large, corporate landowners and the relationship between landlord and tenant becomes as far removed as it can be. Those who live on the farm begin to lose interest and the owner never sees the land. [Suffolk farmer, 2500 acres, 55 per cent rented.]

They might have the money but it means an impersonal landlord–tenant relationship and I prefer a more personal one. [Norfolk farmer, 1150 acres, all rented.]

Table 24   *Farmers' views on City investment in farm land*

	1000+ acres (N=93) %	44 parishes (N=55) %
Brings in outside capital	30·1	16·4
Institutions are good landlords	12·9	7·3
Other positive views	6·5	3·6
Institutions remote from farming	26·9	34·5
Caused land price inflation	33·3	38·2
Stops real farmers expanding	18·3	40·0
Institutions are bad landlords	4·3	7·3
Other negative views	8·6	3·6

Note: Percentages do not equal 100 as most respondents gave more than one reply.

Respondents in the forty-four parishes were, as Table 24 reveals, much more condemnatory of the City institutions. In particular they were concerned that they would be prevented from expanding their businesses and younger people would be prevented from ever entering farming because of high land prices consequent upon institutional interference in the land market. Equally, farmers in the forty-four parishes were more shocked at the thought that the institutions should be allowed to purchase land when they had no real love for it. Again, a few quotations from respondents typify this outlook:

I think it's shockingly bad. Basically these people are not trading in land for agriculture, but to safeguard money. They buy large blocks of land farmed by *companies*. Any country that loses its yeoman farmer has lost something. [250 acres, all owned.]

Institutions aren't good farmers. They aren't close to the soil. [5 acres, all owned.]

But interestingly the larger, more go-ahead farmers in the forty-four parishes often took a different view. For example:

The Arabs can buy it for all I care. You can't stand in the way of evolution. . . . The public can take a stake in land through the City and we'll get greater public – not state – ownership. . . . God gave land to the people, not the State. [750 acres, 75 per cent owned.]

In summary, when considering how farmers tend to view the entry of the City into land purchase, it would seem that those who have direct experience of their activities are in favour of recent trends. After all they have generally achieved the very security of tenure which is seen as a principal advantage of *owning* land. Those who are more suspicious of the financial institutions either cannot expand or are already guaranteed tenure of their land for at least one more generation. Equally, tenants used to the traditional landlord–tenant system, which guaranteed to them the succession of the next generation, have already experienced an almost *de facto* security of ownership and are wary of innovations in the system. However, as we have argued, innovation in the landlord–tenant system is becoming more likely as government policies threaten to disrupt the traditional system. We seem to be arriving at a point where, as a result of the likely demise of the traditional private landlord, only institutions will be able to offer security of tenure to tenants for succeeding generations. This need not mean fewer tenancies available in the long term (although it may well do so in the immediate future), but it will almost certainly lead to less close relationships between farmers and their landlords. This could have quite profound effects on the rural social structure, especially in a county like Norfolk where the traditional landlord–tenant relationship has tended to survive longer.

In the meantime, there are those who feel that the financial institutions can be socialized into farming norms:

It is commonly supposed that the new faceless City Moguls will adopt a ruthless policy or rent revisions of capital starvation to their tenants. . . . Fortunately, there is a buffer of long-standing tradition in the old-established estate agents who act on behalf of the new investors and can

surely acquaint them with the more gentlemanly aspects of country living.
[Wormell, 1974.]

Recently, indeed, the President of the CLA has appealed to the
values of a property-owning democracy:

It is when things look blackest that sensible men remember that the
pendulum always swings back, that political wind does not blow for ever
in the same direction. . . . We must not lose heart too easily. Private
property is not unacceptable to the mass of our fellow countrymen. It is
not something of which to be ashamed. [Barker, 1976, p. 47.]

In other words, the fight is on. Recent legislation, to which we now
turn, has, however, made the fight harder to win.

The taxation threat

It is, of course, precisely to try to ensure a property-owning democracy that successive Liberal and Labour governments have introduced fiscal measures which threaten the continuation of private
landownership. Thus the agricultural landlord has for a number of
years now had his rental income assessed as unearned and therefore
subject to the top rate of 98 per cent. This has encouraged many
landowners to take possession of tenanted land as it became available
in order to farm it themselves ('taking the land in hand') and thus
qualifying for earned income relief. To some extent this has been
undertaken reluctantly since estate practice has been to allow son to
succeed father into a tenancy, but economic sense dictates having a
large earned income with a top rate of tax of 75 per cent. But at least
the landowner was in an advantageous position when it came to
Estate Duty. He could claim the 45 per cent abatement relief on
farm land, designed to allow his heirs to succeed to his estate, and
even, by taking advantage of the seven-year rule, could avoid Estate
Duty altogether.[12]

However, he now finds a very different situation under the new
Capital Transfer Tax, exacerbated by some of the clauses in the
Agriculture (Miscellaneous Provisions) Act of 1976. For a private
landowner whose income comes entirely or mainly in rents there is
no relief under CTT. The only relief goes to 'working farmers'.
Moreover, there is no way of escaping CTT since it applies to any
major transfers, whether *inter vivos* or at death, except between
spouses. Hence the tax can, by skilful juggling, be minimized, but
not avoided. Nor can the landowner simply take land in hand and

become a 'working farmer', since to qualify for working farmer relief 75 per cent of income in five of the previous seven years must have come from farming. Neither can the landowner claim business property relief as working farmers can. Moreover, the Agriculture (Miscellaneous Provisions) Act extends tenant security to allow close relatives to succeed, almost automatically, as tenants when the existing tenant dies or retires. So taking land in hand will become more difficult. Consequently the position of the private agricultural landlord has been made more tenuous by recent legislation. However, the institutional landlord is, as we have already indicated, entirely unaffected, so the conclusion must be, *ceteris paribus*, that private agricultural landlordism will decline and institutional landlordism increase. The proposed Wealth Tax can only serve, if implemented, to hasten this process. Of course, an alternative scenario is a creeping process of land nationalization, if land and not cash is used to pay off tax demands; for the fact is that any landowner's assets are illiquid. Many will find it difficult to raise the cash to meet their tax bills and will therefore have to sell land to raise money or offer land in lieu of cash to the Inland Revenue.

The position of the owner-occupier is different but still very much threatened by the tax changes. Below 1000 acres or £250 000 assets there is a 50 per cent relief across the board and even a 30 per cent business relief above those levels. However, as with the agricultural landlord, the tax cannot be avoided and rising land prices, given that land is the most valuable asset the owner has, cause him to have to pay higher taxes. Once again, of course, few owner-occupiers will have the cash available to pay the necessary taxes without neglecting future investment and/or mortgaging or selling land – a process which obviously has finite limits. To obtain any of these exemptions from CTT an owner-occupier must again qualify as a 'working farmer', although some of those in our 1000+ acres sample would not have qualified since they received less than 75 per cent of their income from farming. If a wealth tax were implemented, owner-occupiers would find the burden hard to carry. The CLA estimates that 30 per cent of *all* those who will be subject to wealth tax in the UK will be owner-occupying farmers. It is thus hardly surprising, considering the foregoing, that farmers would like to see their assets treated in a far different way under CTT and any wealth tax. As things stand, however (and here we can refer back to Table 21), 'agriculture is bearing a capital burden [land] which it cannot afford' (MacGregor, 1973, p. 46).[13] Meanwhile, the institutions continue to buy land, the price rises and owner-occupiers face bigger-than-ever future tax bills. Farmers were especially bitter about capital taxation which they see as a threat to their continued existence:

> There are no advantages to ownership today because of existing and proposed taxes which threaten to kill agriculture as we have known it. . . . You know, I have had a tough life. I worked myself stupid for ten years to build up this farm and I have succeeded and I'm doing well. But these ten years will have been wasted in vain if taxes take what I have achieved away from my children. I did it for them. If I lose it, I shall regret the loss of my youth. . . . It will be the end if personal gain and initiative for your children are taken away. Why should the hard-working half of the country be made to help the scrounging half? [Suffolk farmer, 2700 acres, 60 per cent owned.]

What preliminary conclusions may we draw, therefore, from this consideration of the various threats to landownership? Without doubt the long-term market situation of farmers as property owners is threatened, but their resilience and that of their organizations is quite remarkable (see below). For this reason alone our conclusions have to be tentative. To begin with, it is clear that, as a result of land-price inflation, owner-occupiers and landlords have experienced a massive increase in wealth in recent years. Yet they are not rejoicing. On the contrary it is an embarrassment, for in so far as land becomes expensive it becomes a tax liability. This not only threatens the very ownership which this wealth signifies but fails to guarantee succession for future generations. Consequently *farming*, as we shall see again in the next section, is seen as inseparable from *owning* land. Unlike City institutions, however, owner-occupiers are not immortal and so Capital Transfer Tax and Capital Gains Tax eventually have to be paid; but paid out of what? The real wealth of most farmers *is* their land, but land is an illiquid asset. Heavy tax liabilities might well mean selling some land. If land is sold to pay, say, Capital Transfer Tax, then the most likely purchasers are financial institutions, at any rate where relatively large blocks of land are concerned. Other private landowners will be too busy protecting their own future to afford the luxury of purchasing more land. The tenant farmers will also be affected via the squeeze on private landlords.

What does this imply in terms of medium- and long-term change as a direct result of recent movements in the land market? There are those who see a return to a tripartite landed social structure of institutional landowners, tenant farmers and landless workers. However, we are by no means convinced that this must happen, since so much depends upon the future political climate surrounding land-ownership – and not least because we are aware of the tremendous influence of the NFU and CLA upon governments of both parties and their ability to defend farming and ownership interests. There can be no doubt that the farming organizations know what their interests are, and can recognize a threat when they see one. We shall see below how they mobilize their membership against these threats in order to secure favourable changes. The bulk of farmers will not easily yield their status as owners and entrepreneurs for those of employees and managers. In order to appreciate this we need only look to their current perceptions of tenurial status.

Tenurial status

As elsewhere in England and Wales, there have been great changes in landownership in East Anglia in the last hundred years. On the basis of figures from Bateman's (1883) analysis of the 'New Domesday' survey undertaken in the 1870s, we calculate that a century ago land-ownership was very exclusive indeed in the eastern counties. For example, 5 per cent of Norfolk landowners together owned 87 per cent of the land, and less than 1 per cent owned 62 per cent of it; in Suffolk 6·5 per cent owned 88 per cent and 0·6 per cent owned 55 per cent; and in Cambridgeshire 6 per cent owned 81 per cent and 0·4 per cent owned 40 per cent. Altogether about 350 individuals owned between them 55 per cent of the agricultural land of these three counties, to say nothing of what they owned elsewhere. However, from this point onwards we only have land occupation rather than landownership statistics to guide us and these were collected at infrequent intervals until the 1960s, and these, again until the 1960s, are not regarded by authorities as very reliable with the exception of the National Farm Survey of 1941 from which we have published data for East Anglia (University of Cambridge, 1947).[14]

The 1941 study showed, *inter alia*, that 39 per cent of the total land area was held in estates exceeding 1000 acres, representing a decline of about one-third from the 'New Domesday' survey of 1873, but of this only 23 per cent was owner-occupied. The overall rate of owner-occupation was 43 per cent, compared with about 20 per cent for the period 1887–1922 (see pp. 35 ff.). Taking only the four counties with which we are mainly concerned overall owner-occupation rates were as follows: Cambridgeshire, 34 per cent; Essex, 53 per cent; Norfolk, 38 per cent; and Suffolk, 50 per cent.[15] The lower figures

Table 25 Distribution of holdings by form of tenure and total area size-groups, 1973

County	Tenure	0–99 No.	0–99 %	100–499 No.	100–499 %	500–699 No.	500–699 %	700–999 No.	700–999 %	1000+ No.	1000+ %	Total No.	Total %
Cambs	Wholly owned	1001	32.2	220	25.3	23	26.7	6	10.0	11	20.0	1261	30.3
	Wholly rented	1044	33.7	204	23.4	23	26.7	18	30.0	15	27.3	1304	31.3
	50%+ owned	518	16.7	283	32.5	21	24.4	16	26.7	18	32.7	856	20.5
	50%+ rented	535	17.3	163	18.7	19	22.0	20	33.3	11	20.0	748	17.9
	Total	3098	100	870	100	86	100	60	100	55	100	4169	100
Essex	Wholly owned	1783	63.4	512	40.9	53	27.0	31	28.7	17	26.6	2396	54.0
	Wholly rented	557	19.8	328	26.2	49	25.0	29	26.9	14	21.9	977	22.0
	50%+ owned	303	10.8	301	24.0	60	30.6	31	28.7	24	37.5	719	16.2
	50%+ rented	171	6.0	111	8.9	34	17.4	17	15.7	9	14.0	342	7.8
	Total	2814	100	1252	100	196	100	108	100	64	100	4434	100
Norfolk	Wholly owned	1972	42.6	557	33.7	65	27.7	31	20.7	35	22.2	2660	39.0
	Wholly rented	1434	31.0	452	27.4	86	36.6	63	42.0	63	39.9	2098	30.8
	50%+ owned	725	15.7	426	25.8	50	21.3	33	22.0	33	20.9	1267	18.6
	50%+ rented	500	10.8	217	13.1	34	14.5	23	15.3	27	17.1	801	11.7
	Total	4631	100	1652	100	235	100	150	100	158	100	6826	100
Suffolk	Wholly owned	1414	57.5	682	45.1	49	31.4	28	26.4	25	23.8	2198	50.8
	Wholly rented	513	20.9	327	21.6	29	18.6	20	18.9	31	29.5	910	21.0
	50%+ owned	347	14.1	374	24.7	53	34.0	32	30.2	35	33.3	842	19.4
	50%+ rented	184	7.5	129	8.5	25	16.0	26	24.5	14	13.3	378	8.7
	Total	2458	100	1512	100	156	100	106	100	105	100	4327	100
Eng/Wales	Wholly owned	68824	50.9	25594	37.4	1199	28.2	614	24.8	591	26.5	96822	45.5
	Wholly rented	37160	27.5	21433	31.3	1280	30.1	768	31.1	700	31.4	61341	28.8
	50%+ owned	17800	13.2	13545	19.8	977	23.0	580	23.5	502	22.5	33404	15.7
	50%+ rented	11542	8.5	7902	11.6	801	18.8	511	20.7	438	19.6	21194	10.0
	Total	135326	100	68474	100	4257	100	2473	100	2231	100	212761	100

Table 26 *Distribution of (1) owned and (2) rented land by total area size-groups*

Size-groups		0–99 Acres	%	100–499 Acres	%	500–699 Acres	%	700–999 Acres	%	1000+ Acres	%	Total Acres	%
Cambs	(1)	35019	43·7	110566	56·6	26977	53·7	19591	38·9	42381	50·7	234543	51·0
	(2)	45419	56·3	84935	44·4	23254	46·3	30811	61·1	41254	49·3	225403	49·0
Essex	(1)	41617	67·0	185253	61·6	64346	57·0	49757	56·5	69639	63·6	410612	61·0
	(2)	20542	33·0	115685	38·4	48616	43·0	38236	43·5	39842	36·4	262921	39·0
Norfolk	(1)	63488	49·3	221465	57·3	67964	48·9	53485	43·1	112465	43·8	518867	50·2
	(2)	65059	50·7	164899	42·7	70995	51·1	70611	56·9	144093	56·2	515657	49·8
Suffolk	(1)	49640	65·5	237778	68·3	57625	63·5	49435	56·8	99992	63·2	488470	65·1
	(2)	26146	34·5	110541	31·7	33143	36·5	37536	43·2	54734	36·8	262100	34·9
Eng/Wales	(1)	2778286	59·2	7837200	54·8	1261417	50·9	983430	48·3	1734691	47·9	14595024	53·8
	(2)	1918063	40·8	6469224	40·8	1216096	45·2	1052462	49·1	1886199	52·1	12542044	46·2

Source: MAFF, *Land Tenure Tables*.

for Cambridgeshire and Norfolk reflect the high proportion in those counties of the total land area still held in 1941 by large estates which let their land to tenants. Consequently when we consider owner-occupation on holdings in excess of 1000 acres we find the following rates: Cambridgeshire, 16 per cent; Essex, 32 per cent; Norfolk, 22 per cent; and Suffolk, 31 per cent.

When we come to the present situation the continued trend to owner-occupation is very marked. In 1973 the rate of owner-occupation in the four eastern counties varied between 50 and 65 per cent overall and 43 and 64 per cent on holdings of over 1000 acres. As can be seen from Tables 25 and 26 the previous pattern of higher-than-average owner-occupation rates in Essex and Suffolk, compared with Cambridgeshire, Norfolk and England and Wales as a whole, has continued. However, on the basis of our own research, we have good reason to doubt the accuracy of the land occupation statistics with regard to holdings of over 1000 acres in area because they fail to take account of the sometimes exceedingly complex nature of landownership at the level of the individual farm business.[16]

Much of the problem stems from the fact that, as Harrison has observed, '. . . the use of a seemingly firm descriptive term – the landlord/tenant relationship – covers up a complexity of relationships – legal, social, commercial and other – and has probably lulled us into thinking we understand something we do not' (Harrison, 1965, p. 333). Simply asking a farmer how much of his land he 'owns' and how much he 'rents', for example, is just not adequate. Moreover, the section on land tenure in the 4 June Return is by no means unambiguous, as our discussion with farmers confirmed (see Rose *et al*, 1977), so that farmers were found to have entered land held under similar tenurial arrangements in an inconsistent manner. This is because it is quite common, mainly for fiscal reasons, for farmers to create partnerships, trusts and companies because of the disadvantages of sole ownership of land. This is especially the case among the larger farms where the incentive in tax avoidance terms is significantly greater. Harrison has commented upon this in the light of his recent research into farm business structure:

The number of partnerships has increased in recent years and now represents 27% of the total number of farms (28 per cent of the total area and 38 per cent of total assets) but most have been formed with narrow income tax advantages in mind. Only 5 per cent of farm businesses are companies and are, almost without exception, virtually indistinguishable in terms of capital and business structure, finance and general management from family partnerships; they occupy, however 9 per cent of the total area of the national farm and employ 15 per cent of the total assets. [Harrison, 1973, p. 356.]

In addition Harrison found that sole proprietorship is four times as common as partnerships or companies for businesses employing less than £200000 in assets including land, with an exact reversal of that situation for businesses employing assets over £200000. Of course these remain private farming concerns, companies being formed to reduce taxation not to raise capital. Indeed, we discovered that in East Anglia there is a quite marked relationship between size of holding and business status (see Rose *et al.*, 1977, p. 71). The effects of the creation of companies, partnerships and trusts on tenurial arrangements can be quite significant. Land may become the *de jure* property of a family trust or family members and be *let* to the farming company as tenant. In our experience it is then usually returned in the annual census as *rented* land because legally that is what it is – a rent changes hands even though it may be the same individual who passes the money with his tenant's right hand to his landlord's left hand. The fact that the trust and the company are the same people wearing different hats has no bearing on the official statistics yet, *de facto*, ownership remains in the hands of the farmer concerned – he has the majority shareholding or effective control of the trust or whatever. In other words his property rights in respect of the land are basically unchanged. To call his land tenanted is strictly correct, formally and legally the case and that is what the tenure statistics show. But the effect of this in terms of those statistics is obvious: the *real* extent of owner-occupation is underestimated in favour of *apparent* tenancy, the distortion being greatest among the largest farms. The conclusion that is drawn is that the larger the farm becomes the greater will be the likelihood of a significant element of rented land. Our research shows that, in *de facto* terms, the largest farms in our sample have a much higher incidence of owner-occupied land than official statistics would indicate.

In our terms, then, these farms – owned by family trusts and rented to family companies – are owner-occupied or, to use the term in the official statistics, 'wholly owned'. The following tables illustrate our point by comparing official land tenure statistics for farms of over 1000 acres in the counties of Cambridgeshire, Norfolk and Suffolk with statistics we have collected from our sample of farms over 1000 acres in the same counties.[17]

As part of the comparison we have evaluated our own figures on the Ministry's *de jure* basis and on a *de facto* basis, which we consider to be a more accurate reflection of the actual pattern of landownership. In the case of Table 27 we can see that the consistent pattern between rows 2 and 3 for each county is an increase in the wholly-owned category in row 3, accompanied by a reduction in the wholly-rented category. Similarly, the 50 per cent plus owned category tends to increase in row 3. Table 28 confirms the pattern: instead of between 32 per cent and 48 per cent of land being owned, as the *de jure* figures would indicate, the *de facto* figures show between 65 per cent and 76 per cent of the land wholly owned.[18] Our conclusion here, therefore, must be that, in terms of conception of land tenure, official statistics are not sufficiently flexible to cope with the almost baroque tenurial arrangements often encountered on large holdings.[19]

Table 27 *MAFF statistics on distribution of holdings of total area 1000+ acres by form of tenure in 1973* (1)
compared with sample statistics evaluated on (*MAFF*) de jure *basis* (2)
and de facto *basis* (3)
for Cambridgeshire, Norfolk and Suffolk

County		Wholly owned No.	%	Wholly rented No.	%	50%+ owned No.	%	50%+ rented No.	%	Total No.	%
Cambs	(1)	11	20·0	15	27·3	18	32·7	11	20·0	55	100
	(2)	1	5·6	6	33·3	6	33·3	5	27·8	18	100
	(3)	4	22·2	0	0	11	61·1	3	16·7	18	100
Norfolk	(1)	35	22·2	63	39·9	33	20·9	27	17·1	158	100
	(2)	7	14·9	19	40·4	8	17·0	13	27·7	47	100
	(3)	20	42·6	4	8·5	11	23·4	12	25·5	47	100
Suffolk	(1)	25	26·3	21	22·1	35	36·8	14	14·7	95	100
	(2)	8	30·8	5	19·2	7	26·9	6	23·1	26	100
	(3)	9	34·6	2	7·7	9	34·6	6	23·1	26	100

Source for (1): MAFF, *Land Tenure Statistics*.

Bearing this in mind, we can now examine in more detail the pattern of ownership and related matters in our samples. Table 29 details the proportion of land farmed by our respondents which is also owned by them. While in both samples approximately 75 per cent of all respondents owned 50 per cent or more of the land they farmed, we can see that 100 per cent ownership is, as we might expect, much higher in the forty-four parishes sample where holdings are smaller.[20]

For those renting some or all of their land we found a large number and variety of landlords. Of the sixty-four respondents in the 1000+ acres sample who were renting some land, 45 per cent had only one landlord, 25 per cent had two and a further 16 per cent had three. But we also found a few cases where there were between six

Table 28 *MAFF statistics on distribution of owned and rented land on holdings of total area 1000+ acres (1)*
compared with sample statistics on owned and rented land evaluated on (MAFF) de jure basis (2)
and owned and rented land on de facto basis (3)
for Cambridgeshire, Norfolk and Suffolk

County		Owned		Rented		Total	
		Acres	%	Acres	%	Acres	%
Cambs	(1)	42 381	50·7	41 254	49·3	83 635	100
	(2)	14 289	31·9	30 570	68·1	44 859	100
	(3)	34 126	76·1	10 733	23·9	44 859	100
Norfolk	(1)	112 465	43·8	144 093	56·2	256 558	100
	(2)	38 031	40·4	56 174	59·6	94 205	100
	(3)	61 691	65·5	32 514	34·5	94 205	100
Suffolk	(1)	93 992	63·2	54 734	36·8	148 726	100
	(2)	21 657	48·0	23 461	52·0	45 118	100
	(3)	32 870	72·9	12 248	28·1	45 118	100

Source for (1): MAFF, *Land Tenure Statistics.*

Table 29 *Proportion of land farmed by respondents in de facto ownership*

Percentage owned	1000+ acres (N=104) %	44 parishes (N=57) %
0	6·7	14·0
Less than 25	8·6	7·0
25–49	10·6	3·5
50·74	15·4	3·5
75–99	20·2	10·5
100	38·5	61·4
	100	100

and eight landlords involved, although the mean number of land-lords per respondent with rented land was just over two. Among the forty-four parishes sample 86 per cent of those renting land had only one landlord and the remainder had two. Although private landlords accounted for the majority in both samples institutions figured more prominently among the 1000+ acres sample at 43 per cent of land-lords compared with 22 per cent for the forty-four parishes. This, again, is not surprising since institutions have always held fairly large units of land. In fact the City institutions, while only accounting for 14 per cent of all landlords among the 1000+ acres sample, nevertheless accounted, as we have already indicated, for over one-third of all the rented land. The next largest group of landlords, with just under 30 per cent of all rented land, was the traditional private landowners, and a further 20 per cent was accounted for by non-farming individuals and owners. In the forty-four parishes, on the other hand, other farmers were by far the most important group of landlords both numerically and in terms of the amount of land rented. This tenurial complexity is further accentuated by the fact that 30 per cent of those in the 1000+ acres sample, the vast majority of them traditional landowners with their own farms, were landlords of other farmers. In fact of the 40000 acres of land let by those in the 1000+ acres sample to other farmers, 90 per cent was accounted for by the traditional private landowners. Obviously this group remains an extremely important and influential one in East Anglian agri-culture; eleven of this group in our sample were each letting in excess of 1000 acres to other farmers.

To summarize the complex tenurial situation found among the 1000+ acres sample, we have categorized landownership according to the taxonomy set out earlier in this chapter (see above, p. 80) in Table 30 and show the relative amounts of land owned, rented and let by each category. (This exercise is not necessary for the forty-four parishes sample where there was a simple division between tenants and owner-occupiers.) Several of the points already noted are reinforced by Table 30, but in addition we can note that, when considering this table alongside Tables 27 and 28, it is possible to infer that the higher levels of owner-occupation in Suffolk and Essex, compared with Norfolk and Cambridgeshire, are largely due to the fact that there is a greater amount of landownership by category IA in the latter two counties. In other words the larger, private estates were more numerous in Cambridgeshire and Norfolk in the past and have survived for longer than in Essex and Suffolk.

Table 30 *Categories of landownership by counties, area of owned, rented and let land, and number of holdings, 1000+ acres sample*

Category		County	Owned	%	Rented	%	Let	%	Holdings	%
IA	Traditional private	Cambs	9946				12500*		2	
		Norfolk	23943		630		17200*		8	
		Suffolk	5200				6000		2	
IA	Total		39089	(25·5)	630	(1·2)	35700	(89·1)	12	(12·2)
IB	Owner-occupied	Cambs	26480		11058*		540		16	
		Essex	15849		520		890		13	
		Norfolk	37208		25956*		506		34	
		Suffolk	32870		12248		1210		22	
IB	Total		112407	(73·3)	49782	(97·9)	3146	(7·9)	85	(86·7)
IIC	Financial institutions	Norfolk	1940		451		1182		1	
IIC	Total		1940	(1·2)	451	(0·9)	1182	(3·0)	1	(1·0)
	Total		153436	(100)	50863	(100)	40028	(100)	98	(100)

* Includes a 'double count' of 1850 acres owned by farmers in our sample and let to others in the sample.

Finally in regard to Table 30, it is obvious that all farmers who own some land, even though they may rent the larger part, are categorized as owner-occupiers. Only *de facto* tenants are excluded (N = 7).

As we have already suggested, the complexity with regard to land tenure is matched by complex business structures among the 1000 + acres sample. Indeed, the situation was actually a little more complex than we have indicated, for although half of the 1000 + acres respondents operated their businesses as companies, a further 10 per cent had both partnerships and companies involved. In all cases except one, however, the partners or boards of directors were entirely drawn from the family, the exception being the public farming company in Norfolk which is represented as the sole farming financial institution in Table 30. In the forty-four parishes sample there were three companies and two company/partnerships but again entirely composed of family members. Nor did 'company' necessarily mean only one company. Ten of our respondents had two or more companies operating and a further five had more than one partnership. Often the second company or partnership was responsible for farm machinery which it hired to the farming company. Further complexities were introduced by the presence of trusts in 30 per cent of the 1000 + acres sample and 15 per cent in the forty-four parishes. It was clear in most cases where partnerships, companies or trusts were involved that the basic reason for their existence was to reduce liability to taxation and make it easier to hand land on within the family. For example, we encountered one farm where there were seven different companies, trusts and partnerships involved in owning the land, all of which was rented to a farming company, and where the respondent had made provision to turn partnerships into companies overnight, if necessary. As the farmer concerned said:

All our businesses pay a commercial rent to the family trust; the whole thing is income regulating in the sense that we decide what profit each part will make and work to that goal. Part of the business is a limited company and part is not. The farm company owns all the machinery and has the highest turnover but we own the land as a family *not* as farmers.

This was, admittedly, the extreme of sophistication as far as tax avoidance and income regulation was concerned, but many respondents went some of the way towards these kind of provisions. The results of these tax avoidance measures can be quite startling, as the respondent quoted above explained to us:

Last year, before depreciation, we made a profit of £180000 on a turnover of £500000. After valuation we took £40000 from the profits, in other words we carried it forward to next year. Then we took off depreciation and capital improvements worth £130000 and so we paid virtually no tax. One of our companies, which is responsible for 450 acres, was begun two years ago on £1000 capital. It owns nothing except seed, fertilizer and two men. It hires all the machinery from another company and it made £31000 last year after paying rent and contracting charges. But you can jumble the figures any way you want and charge for office expenses, rents, machinery servicing and so on.

It will now be apparent why our data on farmer's incomes (see below) must be treated with *extreme* caution. Other farmers had established trusts for female relatives and grandchildren and combined these with partnerships or trading companies. More commonly, companies were formed to own the land and partnerships to farm it.

Once we had elicited basic information concerning the tenurial situation on each farm we proceeded to ask more general questions about ownership or tenancy. Outright owners and tenants were asked whether they thought owning or renting land led to any distinctive outlook. Those who both owned and rented land were first invited to rate themselves as either primarily owner-occupiers or tenants and then asked the appropriate question. In addition we asked what respondents felt were the advantages and disadvantages of ownership or tenancy and whether as owners they would rather be tenants and vice versa. Finally we asked tenants about their relationships with their landlords.

We found that most farmers did think there were important differences between owning and renting and these differences were recognized equally by owners and tenants. Tables 31 and 32 summarize answers to the relevant questions. It can be seen that we had broadly similar answers from owners in both samples with about one-quarter in each who did not perceive any real difference in outlook between owners and tenants, about one-third who stressed the long-term aspects of ownership and a further third mentioning more than one of the positive aspects of landownership. In broad terms the kind of issues stressed mainly by the owner-occupiers reflected ownership ideologies concerned with stewardship, independence, and farming in the long rather than the short term. (We alluded to such ideologies in Chapter 1 and shall return to them in Chapter 8.) We have chosen a few comments from respondents to illustrate this theme:

Table 31   *Owners' 'outlooks on life'*

Outlook	1000+ acres (N=75) %	44 parishes (N=44) %
All farmers the same	26·7	25·0
Land gives status	2·7	4·5
Continuity/long-term view	32·0	34·1
Independence	5·3	9·0
Combined reasons	33·3	27·3
Total	100	100

Table 32   *Tenants' 'outlooks on life'*

Outlook	1000+ acres (N=24) %	44 parishes (N=10) %
All farmers the same	50·0	20·0
Owners have status	4·2	—
Short-term view/no security	33·3	50·0
No independence	—	—
Combined reasons	12·5	30·0
Total	100	100

Owners are more identified with the land and are more concerned with their position in local society than tenant farmers. They also care more about conservation and this is materially different from tenant farmers and especially true on estates like this which have been in one family for generations. Owners feel a greater responsibility to the locality than other farmers. [Norfolk estate manager, 6500 acres, all owned.]

This estate was begun from peasant farming roots. The family made money out of wool and became landed gentry by buying this estate from the Duke of Norfolk in the time of Henry VIII. But since the 1914 war a lot of land has been lost through the female line of the family and the estate has shrunk. But I love it – and not for the money. I only drive a Mini-van. Money doesn't interest me. When land increased in price I was a millionaire but that's just a nuisance. I am very fortunate but there's a lot of hard work and worry and responsibility. Yet when I go for a stroll I think, 'how many others have their own 60-acre wood to walk in with no one else around?' [Suffolk farmer, 650 acres, all owned.]

Even some of those who claimed there was no difference in outlook were primarily thinking in terms of status. For example:

There's no difference except that you have a greater incentive to work hard and keep the place clean and tidy. But I don't think I am big because I own land. I just wanted my own land so I could farm my way. We are traditional in atmosphere but not in our use of the land. But I'd die for this place. [Suffolk farmer, 3400 acres, all owned.]

When we consider the tenants, where numbers are admittedly small, we can see that those in the 1000+ acres sample are less likely to perceive any significant differences. But eleven of the twelve respondents who said this owned *some* land, while only one of the seven outright tenants perceived no difference. This latter group, it should be noted, had a noticeably instrumental attitude towards the land:

You feel you are in farming more purely to make money and have a short-term attitude. [Norfolk farmer, 3500 acres, all rented.]

For us farming is a business, not a way of life, especially as far as —— Farm is concerned, because we don't even live there. We think entirely in commercial terms not 'pretty' terms. [Suffolk farmer, 1720 acres, 90 per cent rented.]

Owning is completely different from renting. *Owning* is investing against inflation whereas *farming* gives a reasonable cash flow. [Norfolk farmer, 1800 acres, 60 per cent rented.]

Being a tenant is different from being an owner. I pay a rent, a significant sum of money, and it makes you work the land much harder and treat it more as a profitable business. [Suffolk farmer, 2500 acres, 60 per cent rented.]

In some of these statements we have an echo of the ownership and control arguments discussed earlier. But among tenants in the forty-four parishes feelings of inferiority compared with owner-occupiers were more common – not necessarily any social inferiority but a business inferiority:

The owner-occupier is better off simply because he gets the benefit of everything he does. [Suffolk farmer, 125 acres, all rented.]

We do and we don't have a different outlook as tenants. We aren't quite so free to make the improvements we would like to – like drainage – which could improve our position. And when its unlikely that the land will pass to the next generation you have less of a long-term interest in the farm. [Suffolk farmer, 240 acres, all rented.]

It would be tempting to argue that, in some respects, 'farming as a way of life' sums up the attitude of owners and 'farming as a business' that of tenants. While there would be some truth in this, it is by no means the case that all tenants are instrumental and all owners expressive in attitude. Tenants who had once owned land, or who still owned some land, certainly did not have an exploitative attitude. This was especially the case where farmers had either entered into sale and lease-back arrangements or had a guarantee from their landlord that the next generation could keep the farm:

Some tenants may be out for a quick return but I treat all my land as if it were my own. [Norfolk farmer, 1200 acres, 75 per cent rented.]

We work the same way we always did when we owned the land. But then it's worth it because my sons will carry on after me. [Norfolk farmer, 1500 acres, all rented via lease-back arrangement.]

A few tenants recognized status differences between themselves and owners, especially in Suffolk where, as we have seen, owner-occupation rates are very high. For example:

If you own land, you have security and that must mean a different outlook. I think some owners look down on tenants. [Suffolk farmer, 1200 acres, all rented.]

One is regarded differently around here if you are not a landowner. To them I am just a farmer. [Suffolk farmer, 1700 acres, all rented.]

Equally some landowners are quite aware of the status aspects of ownership:

It's a matter of upbringing. Owners have a higher standard of living and can afford to send their children to public schools. [Norfolk farmer, 6500 acres, all owned.]

Some of those who own consider themselves several degrees up in the social strata compared with tenants. Owners have a much more impressive status – they are men of substance. [Cambridgeshire farmer, 3600 acres, 85 per cent owned.]

Not only does the owner think 60 to 100 years ahead while the tenant looks for a return on capital, there's also the question of the 'county' set. That means owning land: the more land you own, the more the doors open. [Norfolk farmer, 2500 acres, all owned.]

Such comments were particularly common in Norfolk – but virtually absent in Essex, a county more influenced by urban criteria of status.

But at the end of the day neither owners nor tenants value land for its status-enhancing qualities alone. Owners are well aware of the economic aspects of landownership and when asked what were the

advantages and disadvantages of landownership they replied largely
in economic and financial terms as Tables 33 and 34 indicate.

Table 33 *Advantages of landownership*

Advantages	1000+ acres (N=77) %	44 parishes (N=46) %
Independence	48·1	45·7
Stewardship/succession	15·6	6·5
Economic	55·8	69·6
Source of status	2·6	2·2
None	9·1	8·7
Other	3·9	4·3

Note: Percentages total more than 100 since most respondents gave more
than one reply.

Table 34 *Disadvantages of landownership*

Disadvantages	1000+ acres (N=70) %	44 parishes (N=46) %
Capital taxation	28·6	28·3
Low returns and high land prices	17·1	10·9
Raising capital	17·1	28·3
Too much capital tied up	27·1	26·1
No disadvantages	34·3	23·9
Other	1·4	8·7

Note: Percentages total more than 100 since some respondents gave more
than one reply.

The prime economic advantage of landownership was the use of
land as collateral for borrowing, and hence the opportunity to take
advantage of capital appreciation. Furthermore 'independence' frequently included an element of business freedom, i.e. freedom of
economic action in terms of investment compared with the tenant
who has to persuade his landlord of the desirability of spending
money on any capital project. Equally neither independence nor
general economic advantages can be divorced from the desire to
ensure succession. Typical of comments made by farmers were the
following:

You can farm as you please with no worries about any landlord to consult or persuade. Our landlord is only interested in his shooting and his political friends who come here to shoot. He runs the estate for the pheasants. As an owner you have no problems provided you have the capital. [Norfolk farmer, 1300 acres, 50 per cent owned.]

Owning land is the best form of security. It lasts a lifetime, it's like owning gold or diamonds. We are here for such a short time, but the land is there for your family after you have gone. [Cambridgeshire farmer, 1300 acres, 50 per cent owned.]

For many of those we interviewed, however, it was precisely the erosion of these advantages which concerned them most. We can see from Table 34 that a large number of our respondents considered landownership to have a number of economic disadvantages, especially in terms of capital taxation, which is a threat to their family succession, and in terms of the amount of capital tied up in their businesses. At the same time inflation makes the cost of capital improvements or of buying more land much greater, especially at a time of high interest rates.[21] Yet the fact remains that 34·3 per cent in the 1000+ acres sample and 23·9 per cent in the forty-four parishes sample saw no disadvantages to landownership. For tenants, however, the whole situation is reversed. Their advantages are the owner's disadvantages. Of the twenty-three farmers in the 1000+ acres sample who were wholly or mainly renting land all but one mentioned the fact that tenants needed less capital – both initial and working – and could therefore farm more land on the same capital than an owner-occupier. In the forty-four parishes sample eleven out of the twelve tenants made this point. But the disadvantages of tenancy were equally recognized, with sixteen (70 per cent) of the 1000+ acres tenants citing the lack of security and independence and five (22 per cent) mentioning the difficulty of raising money and the loss of capital appreciation to tenants. In fact, those who saw no problems in tenancy had entered into lease-back arrangements which guaranteed succession for the next generation. The following are a selection of typical comments:

As a tenant you can farm a larger acreage with a given amount of capital and your rental is lower than an owner would pay in interest for borrowed money. On the other hand I have an unpleasant landlord, I get no capital appreciation on land values, and my son can't succeed. So, if the capital was available, I would buy land and become wealthy and enhance the farm. But I can't afford it. [Suffolk farmer, 1700 acres, all rented.]

[The advantages are] more than ever financial. There's little to be said for owning land now because you can't hand it on – or soon won't be able to. There are no real disadvantages for tenants today and there's no point in owning if you are prevented from handing your heritage to your children. [Norfolk farmer, 1050 acres, all rented on lease-back from insurance company.]

We asked all owners whether they would prefer to be tenants and vice versa. Significantly, while no owner would prefer to rent his land, two-thirds of the tenants in the 1000+ acres sample and three-quarters in the forty-four parishes would prefer to own, if that were possible. Despite the economic problems of landownership the fact that it gives security for future generations (or has in the past) and independence of action consistently proved to be decisive. Perhaps, therefore, the situation for landowners is not quite so precarious as their advocates frequently maintain, merely that the circumstances of landownership are changing.

We have seen that the term 'landlord–tenant relationship' can cover a multitude of different forms. The easy distinction between landlord and tenant made by Caird (1878), who, as we saw in Chapter 1, was able to describe not just what was meant by landlord and tenant but precisely what rights and duties were involved, simply no longer applies. What we have discovered broadly confirms the findings of Harrison in Buckinghamshire:

The landlord–tenant system in this country has long been unique in several respects. Both system of government and public conscience alike permitted its establishment, with little regard for any social costs it involved. . . . It not only set up a pattern which was for some two centuries appropriate to available technology and the role of farming in the economy as a whole but . . . it never attracted any semblance of social stigma to renting. In addition, it granted tenants an exceptional measure of security of tenure. . . . There are signs, nevertheless, that the sort of continuity of tenure which, in the past, lasted from generation to generation is no longer a material part of farm renting. Consequently, the significant part which tenants contribute to fixed and longer term capital formation, is being weighted towards the short and medium term. In the second place, the general tenor of legislation under the Agricultural Holdings Acts, setting out the law governing landlord–tenant relationships, and the general economic pressure to which landlords have been subjected may have been socially acceptable. Nevertheless, so far as landlords are concerned, things may have gone so far as to cause them to alter their traditional role. One of the more significant factors for change which the study revealed was the high proportion of farmer-landlords who were taking land in hand . . . over a half of the farmers who were landowners were pursuing a policy to this end. [Harrison, 1965, pp. 334–5.]

In other words tenants are being pushed into short-term capital investment because of their lack of security, and landlords are being forced to farm land, rather than let it, because of the financial burden upon them. Moreover we have found in addition to the traditional landlord–tenant system, now under pressure, new types of relationship based on lease-back and partnership.

Such developments clearly have the potential to create new forms of landlord–tenant conflict. In the pastoral areas of Britain in particular such conflict has not been uncommon, and the last two decades have seen a spate of tenants' associations being formed, with echoes of the agitation for 'tenant rights' at the end of the nineteenth century (Perkin, 1973). We thus asked all those farmers who rented land whether they had had any particular problems with their landlord and whether they had heard of any particular landlord–tenant problems locally. Those who let out land were asked similar questions about tenants. Six of the seven farmers in the 1000+ acres sample who rented all their land described their relationships with their landlords as good, only one of the tenants viewing his relationship with his landlord unfavourably. The importance of close landlord–tenant relationships was strongly emphasized by the tenants. For example one of our respondents had two traditional landlords, from whom he rented roughly equal amounts of land, whom we shall call Lord A and Lord B. When asked how he regarded his landlords he gave the following reply:

Lord A lives locally and we meet him frequently, but Lord B only visits this estate for a couple of days a year so that he doesn't have to pay UK taxes. He flies in and out and so there is no chance of a close landlord–tenant relationship. He has no interest in his estate at all and wouldn't know me from Adam. But we see Lord A quite often because he and his family join in a lot of the local activities and we play tennis at his house. Of course, all the villages around here are really estate villages and Lord A isn't at all stand-offish. He expects respect, to be called 'My Lord', but he's willing to pay his way although he never seems to have any money on him when he attends local functions. But he commands your respect. [Suffolk farmer, 1200 acres, all rented.]

This emphasis on *personal* relationships was universally regarded as the touchstone of a successful landlord–tenant relationship (just as farmers in turn regard it as a key to successful labour relations – see

Chapter 4). As with many other tenants, the only problem this respondent reported was with regard to game. Tenants do not usually have shooting rights and frequently grumble about the amount of damage done by pheasants and deer to growing crops, regarding game protection as not commensurate with good farming practice. However, we would maintain that there is a far more real problem for the landlord–tenant relationship than game and shooting rights. Many landowners and tenants mentioned it, but not usually when asked about landlord–tenant problems. The problem is the one alluded to earlier – landowners taking land in hand rather than allowing sons to inherit tenancies from fathers as had been the rule in the past. Sometimes concern has been caused when new landowners have taken possession of an estate and have demanded a more businesslike approach; but often economic problems have forced longstanding landowners to review their policies. Nine out of the twelve traditional landowners in our sample have been increasing the amount of land they themselves are farming, at the expense of tenancies, in the last few years. In addition, tenants of landowners not in our sample reported the same situation. This is a great cause of concern to tenants who could normally have expected their sons to take over their tenancy but we found no evidence that tenants blamed the landlords for this. As one tenant said:

You can understand Lord G's position. As he said to me, 'If I rent the land to you I pay tax at 98 per cent. If I farm it for myself I only pay 75 per cent.' [Norfolk farmer, 1600 acres, 75 per cent rented.]

The following comments are representative of the views of landowners on their changed circumstances:

We have taken over 13 tenancies so that's 13 tenants and their families out of farming, their children inheriting nothing and we'll be taking 3 more farms soon. It was a matter of logic. [Norfolk farmer/landowner, 3000 acres, now farming 1600 acres but only began farming in 1964.]

Our farm is rather marginal in size for this area. We could do with another few hundred acres. But I have always allowed a good son to take over a tenancy from his father. Recently a tenant died and I really wanted his land but in the end I let his son stay on. I am an old-fashioned landlord you see, but I am afraid I shall have to take the next farm which becomes available. We are all having to take land in hand. [Norfolk farmer/landowner, 6000 acres.]

Not surprisingly, this kind of policy by landowners makes tenants keenly aware of their lack of security and the problems which will face their sons. This seems to be particularly true where the landowner employs an agent who sees his job entirely in terms of extracting higher rents from the tenants:

I am renting half of my land, principally from [a Cambridge] College. They took me on as a tenant before I was 21 and I always had a good relationship with them. But now they are employing a firm of land agents who are very greedy. Rents have been considerably increased and the relationship is no longer happy. I can't get my son's name on the tenancy because the agents won't play ball. To some extent this is understandable but you would think an older tenant would be better treated. How else will my son be able to succeed? [Cambridgeshire farmer, 1100 acres, 60 per cent rented.]

Lord X never was a farmer but now he has an agent. We can no longer be sure that my son will take over the tenancy. Until recently the estate almost guaranteed it but now it's different because they are farming more. [Norfolk farmer, 1000 acres, 85 per cent rented.]

Recent legislation which has virtually ensured the hereditability of tenancies has, however, tipped the balance of advantage back against the landlord. One result of this is likely to be an increase in landlord–tenant partnerships and lease-back arrangements. One such 'tenant' in a partnership explained the system:

I don't have a normal lease . . . I farm on a partnership basis with my 'landlord'. I don't really favour the arrangement but it works to the 'landlord's' advantage, i.e. the income they receive from the land this way is not deemed unearned. . . . They pay for fertilizers, seeds, sprays and so on and for fixed equipment such as grain dryers, and I am paid so much per acre for the cultivations, harvesting and disposal of crops. At the end of the year all the accounts are worked out and we split the profits on a 50–50 basis. So they can't lose and it works well for me as long as things go well. [Suffolk farmer, 2700 acres, 40 per cent rented.]

Partnership would seem to work mainly to the advantage of the landowner, therefore, and can be less secure than a normal tenancy for the farmer. However, a tenant may prefer a lease-back arrangement, whereby he sells his land and then rents it back from the new owner. By so doing he seeks the advantages of both owning and renting with few of the disadvantages of either. It also enables a farmer to expand his holding. Several of those in our sample had used lease-back in this way.

We rent all but a couple of hundred acres of our land but we have owned around two-thirds of it – not all at the same time. We began to sell land on lease-back in order to get the capital to buy more land, beginning in 1960. It took us thirty years to go from about fifty acres to around 1000 and then 10 years to go from 1000 to 3500. Mind you, the way land prices have gone, I think it was a mistake. It's not that we are at any disadvantage compared with owner-occupiers because they can't get a return on their investment at current land prices. We lost in terms of the increased value of the land. In my generation farmers were always thought better if they owned land, but my financial advisers tell me I would be wrong to own land today. [Suffolk farmer, 3200 acres, 97 per cent rented.]

We financed the purchase of a new farm venture in the west of the country by a lease-back of some of our fenland. We were approached by the insurance company and we asked for quite ridiculous terms for what was poor land. We got our terms! The land is declining and will present real problems in a few years. We have a company tenancy and [the insurance company] doesn't interfere with our farming. However, they want to put up some buildings and spend money which we don't think is necessary. How did we manage the company tenancy? You'll laugh at this. [The insurance company] sent us a normal commercial tenancy – they didn't even know about agricultural tenancies! [Cambridgeshire farmer, 8000 acres, 80 per cent owned.]

But not all farmers use lease-back for expansion. Some have used it to avoid death duties and guarantee succession for their sons, for whether the lease-back is with an insurance company or a private individual it is possible to insert clauses guaranteeing succession or sale back to the original owner. For example:

I used to own all my land, including that now farmed by my sons. I sold to [an insurance company] on lease-back because they wanted a large parcel of land in one unit. They never interfere here and my sons were given the option of keeping the land when my tenancy expires. So I get the best of both worlds – I retained security for my sons while avoiding heavy estate duty. Mind you, I could have made more money if I had sold later, but at least my sons will carry on. I'd rather own but I thought it was the best thing to sell when I did. [Norfolk farmer, 1200 acres, all rented.]

So ownership is still regarded as the preferable situation but harsh economic realities persuade some to sell provided they can guarantee security and succession. It is this need to guarantee the future which is the overriding factor for most farmers and landowners.

Attitudes towards expansion

Our comments on land tenure clearly demonstrate that the way in which land is held can crucially affect the size of the holding and hence the efficiency of the farm business. Of course, this also applies in a more straightforward manner: larger holdings can take advantage of economies of scale, particularly in a highly-mechanized agriculture like that which predominates in East Anglia. Moreover technological innovation is constantly altering the optimum size of holding – usually in an upwards direction. Thus the legal and social framework of institutions which surround landholding can determine – according to how far they help or hinder what is known as 'farm adjustment' (Ashton and Rogers, 1967) – the economic health of British agriculture. Judging the optimum size of holding is not, however, a simple matter, for not only does it vary according to the nature of the land itself (soil, topography, price, etc.), but the cost of other factors of production. Decisions over expansion can therefore be extremely difficult if the farmer believes himself to be at or near the optimum size already. Indeed, such decisions are often regarded as a test of the farmer's entrepreneurial acumen. But what precisely constitutes the optimum size of holding sometimes seems to depend as much upon the whims or prejudices of the farmer as any rational assessment of the situation.

We asked our respondents to tell us whether they would expand the size of their farm, if they had the opportunity, and to give us reasons for their answer. Among the 1000 + acres sample 68 per cent said they would expand, and in the forty-four parishes 65 per cent wished to do so. Table 35 indicates the reasons why they wished to expand, with the need to make more efficient use of resources the largest single reason in both samples. However, we can see that this is overwhelmingly the case among the forty-four parishes sample –

Table 35 *Reasons given by farmers for wanting to increase farm size*

Reason for expansion	1000+ acres (N=70) %	44 parishes (N=36) %
Land needed for sons	14·5	8·3
Need more challenge	14·5	11·1
'Natural' to expand	9·7	2·8
More efficient use of resources	19·4	41·7
Wanted specific but small piece of land	6·5	2·8
Necessary to expand	3·2	13·9
Other reasons	32·3	19·4
Total	100	100

something which is hardly to be wondered at. With the necessary farm inputs all rising so steeply in price, especially fixed equipment and agricultural machinery, it makes sense for farmers to try and achieve economies of scale wherever possible and especially if the farm unit is relatively small as is, of course, the case among most of the forty-four parishes sample. Equally other farmers, especially in the 1000 + acres sample, simply felt that they needed to 'stretch' themselves more. They wanted the extra challenge of running a larger business and were quite willing to expand beyond the point where they would need to employ a manager or other intermediary to help with the extra work load. But, of course, the greatest limitation on the desire to expand often lies in the high price land is currently obtaining. Not all farmers, by any means, are in a position where they could afford to borrow the necessary money. Some will take the risk, others who have inherited land and so have no outstanding debts are much better placed.

With this in mind, we asked our respondents if they thought that in farming 'bigger means better'. While in both samples a majority of respondents acknowledged that size was important, only 16 per cent in the 1000 + acres sample and 19 per cent in the forty-four parishes were unqualified in their enthusiasm. Roughly 25 per cent in each sample felt that bigger farms brought disadvantages as well as advantages, and 25 per cent in the 1000 + acres sample and 17 per cent in the forty-four parishes felt that there were diminishing returns beyond a certain size. However, 33 per cent in the 1000 + acres sample and 39 per cent in the forty-four parishes stated unequivocally that bigger did *not* mean better. The reasons for their answers are set out in Table 36. There was general agreement that while bigger farms could obtain economies of scale, they also tended to become less efficient, remoteness and loss of control being seen as a danger. A balance had to be decided between, say, growing more but lower-yielding crops and obtaining a bigger return while losing close contact with workers and being forced to delegate. Or, to put it in other terms, between continuing a traditional 'way of life' and rationally seeking profit-maximization. The following quotation illustrates the self-imposed limits of some farmers:

I admit size does have advantages in some respects. For example, 500 acres is better than 300 acres in terms of the efficient use of machinery and labour. But you must have a personal interest because that's what farming is all about – a close worker-to-boss relationship. Again a lot depends on individual factors. I am sure I could manage another 500 acres but what if I doubled the size? I would be dependent on having good people to whom I could delegate and I'm no good at that. . . . But as far as the general point is concerned I know my crop yields now are less than when my farm was smaller. For example, I am more dependent now on the weather. If the weather changes while I am harvesting, I could lose half my crop. [Suffolk farmer, 2700 acres.]

Table 36   *Advantages and disadvantages of large farms*

Reasons	1000+ acres (N=97) %	44 parishes (N=57) %
Size irrelevant	1·0	5·2
Economies of scale	59·8	61·4
Greater bargaining power	8·2	8·8
Less efficiency	32·0	28·1
Remoteness/loss of control	49·5	29·8
Worse crops/further from land	21·6	17·5
Threat to small farms	0·0	5·3
Other	7·2	7·0

Note: Percentages total more than 100 since most respondents gave more than one reply.

We can contrast this answer with that of another, farming a similar acreage only a few miles away from the previous respondent:

You can't justify certain expenditure without a large unit. . . . You can sell better. The small farmer doesn't have the feel of the market because he is so insignificant and a weak seller. Size leads to a different approach to marketing because you can get closer to the final market. You can be a better buyer, too. People don't want to lose your custom. So much depends on the farmer himself. Small farmers *can* be good farmers. [Suffolk farmer, 2200 acres.]

Not surprisingly the smaller farmers, even though they may acknowledge the advantages of scale, are more suspicious of size:

Some of these big farms are all wrong. They make one farm out of eight and so that's eight farms gone west. [Suffolk farmer, 70 acres.]

I've seen many a farmer on 500 acres do better than those on 1000 or 2000 acres. It's business sense that counts. [Suffolk farmer, 120 acres.]

We also compared the size of our respondents' farms at the time they first became farmers in their own right with the current size of their farms. Altogether we were able to derive adequate information for seventy-nine of the 1000+ acres sample, of whom 62 per cent had expanded their farms. Just under half of these had been able to expand through purchasing land, 10 per cent by taking land in hand, and 45 per cent by renting land. What is perhaps more interesting is that, whatever the means of expansion, 80 per cent of those who had expanded had more than doubled the acreage they began with. Indeed 26 per cent had achieved a 300–500 per cent expansion and 24 per cent had expanded their holdings by more than a factor of five.

Clearly, however, we need to examine these figures more closely in the light of the length of time in farming and the conditions under which expansion was possible. It would be an exceptional farmer under current conditions who could make such rapid advances and many of those among our sample who achieved this did so at times when land was cheap (such as during the 1930s) and they were willing to take risks which others were not. Others in the sample were given loans or cash gifts by members of their family to aid their expansion, and some made money from other businesses to finance land purchase. Again it would be an exceptional family or an exceptional business which could finance large land purchases today. At the same time renting land in order to expand becomes more difficult as the pressure on landlords increases and the supply of land to rent diminishes. It is likely that any young farmer today who desires considerably to expand the size of his holding by renting will need to look to the City institutions. There is something of an irony in this situation, for it is quite likely that such a young farmer is himself the son or the grandson of a farmer who benefited when the financial pressures on agricultural landlordism broke up the great estates earlier in this century: 'They or their fathers stepped in and bought when others were forced to sell. They did not then worry about the poor rich who were taxed out of their inheritance . . . ' (Cherrington, *British Farmer and Stockbreeder*, 1 February 1975, p. 37).

The produce market

While the wealth of all but tenant farmers lies in the land which they own, the return on land as an investment is comparatively small when compared to the return on tenant's capital. The bulk of the farmer's income derives from, and its size depends upon his success in, the marketing of his produce. However, the market itself, in overall terms, has its basic parameters, set by the state. As we saw in the first chapter, state intervention in the operation of the market is by no means a recent phenomenon in agriculture. The first effective steps were taken during the First World War when guaranteed prices were introduced for cereals and compulsory cropping orders were made. Guaranteed prices were continued for three years after the war but then revoked as world trade recovered and cheaper imports became readily available once more. Home agriculture was allowed to return to the depressed state it had been in prior to the war and it was only after the beginnings of the Great Depression that the state once more intervened. However, as Self and Storing (1962) relate in their admirable, but now rather dated, study *The State and The Farmer*, it is from this period we can date the beginnings of 'the modern period of state intervention, assistance and control' (p. 18).

Agriculture, in common with other basic industries like coal and steel, was treated as a depressed industry and similar measures applied to it, such as taxation relief and trade protection. Equally the reorganization of agriculture was promoted by the Agricultural Marketing Acts of 1931 and 1933, designed to give producers more stable markets and prices for their products. Import quotas and price subsidies were also introduced. These subsidies were of far greater benefit to the arable farmers of eastern England than any other group. As Self and Storing (1962, p. 19) note:

... four-fifths of the £104 millions paid out in the inter-war period related to wheat and sugar beet and was primarily of value to the arable farmers of Eastern England. This concentration of support on arable production protected the remains of the old 'high farming' and inhibited the shift to livestock products which was economically desirable.

Nevertheless the agricultural industry generally remained depressed until the onset of the Second World War, during which the government introduced unprecedentedly sweeping controls while farmers were given the chance to make better profits. The consequence was that by the end of the war farmers were quite firmly wedded to state intervention since it meant guaranteed prices. However, they feared that once again, as after 1918, they would be ignored by governments in the search for cheap food from abroad. Thus the 1947 Agriculture Act, which formed the cornerstone of agricultural policy until entry into the EEC, was at first viewed with suspicion, but a series of favourable price reviews and the concomitant continuing prosperity of agriculture served to restore confidence.

We are concerned here only with those aspects of the 1947 Act which affected marketing. The twin aims of government policy were to provide both stability and efficiency by means of an Annual Price Review for specified farm products which was to be conducted by the Minister of Agriculture in consultation with the farmers' interests groups, principally the NFU. The purpose of the Price Review was to determine the guaranteed price to the farmer of products like wheat, barley, milk, eggs, potatoes, sugar beet, beef, and pig meat for the following year. If market prices fell below guaranteed prices then farmers received the difference in cash – a 'deficiency payment' – from the state, while the consumer was able to take advantage of cheap food prices in the shops. Subsidies for such inputs as fertilizers, and grants for investment were also made to farmers. In consequence both stability and efficiency were expected to ensue.

But why should farmers need any protection from the free market? In simple terms it is basically due to the low price-elasticity of demand for food and the fact that agriculture is an industry with a relatively large number of producers. Self and Storing (1962, pp. 24–5) explain the problem well:

. . . the supply of some products fluctuates sharply while demand for them is relatively inelastic. The yield of crops varies with weather conditions, but consumers do not eat much if any more bread or potatoes when production is high and prices fall. Another reason is the tendency of producers to over-react to market changes, through decisions being taken independently by hundreds of thousands of farmers. There are cases when an increase in price leads to a sharp expansion of output, followed by a collapse of prices and an excessive contraction of output.

The major problem with this policy, as with price guarantees before the war, is that it tends to lead to certain inequities. Donaldson and Donaldson (1972) calculated that up to 1964 almost two-thirds of subsidies had gone to arable farmers, and that between 1955 and 1964 subsidies to arable farmers increased by 200 per cent and those to pastoral farmers *decreased* by 30 per cent. As they conclude (p. 32):

. . . farms of over 300 acres, which produce the bulk of the nation's corn, constitute about 5 per cent of the 270,000 holdings of over five acres. Without going so far as to say that 5 per cent of the farmers have been getting 55 per cent of the subsidies, one can legitimately say they have received the lion's share, while the main body of farmers, for whom the subsidy is primarily intended, have recently been given comparatively little support.

This is a point also commented on by Self and Storing (1962, pp. 34–5) and was brought about largely because Britain is less self-sufficient in cereals than in livestock products. Since most of the cereal crop is used to make animal feed, the arable sector becomes the hub of the farming system, for to expand livestock production requires a prior expansion of the arable sector. As we commented in an earlier paper:

Arable farming is therefore the centre of gravity of British agriculture. The cereal market is a *world* market and therefore cereal growers essentially bargain with the government for support prices. Livestock rearers, however, are less dependent on a world market for prices, but they bargain with arable farmers for feedstuffs. The prices granted to arable farmers, therefore, control not only the profitability of arable farming, but of pastoral farming, too. The argument has been put forward, then, that an expanding British agriculture means, initially at least, an expanding arable production, with all the incentives that this implies. [Bell and Newby, 1974, pp. 90–1.]

Undoubtedly this system of subsidizing agriculture would have continued but for Britain's entry into the EEC in 1973, but, of course, membership of the Community involved switching to the Common Agricultural Policy which, rather than being based on deficiency payments, is based on the protection of agriculture from cheap imported produce and the use of intervention price levels. The Community purchases agricultural produce when the market price falls below the intervention level (hence the production of 'wine lakes' and 'beef and butter mountains') releasing it on the market again when (if) the price rises. Consequently many important decisions concerning agriculture are no longer made in Whitehall but in Brussels. However, the Price Review machinery continues in order to assess the condition of the industry and to set prices for those products not at present covered by the CAP. Nevertheless despite the changeover from a system financed by the taxpayer to one largely paid for by the consumer, the CAP still leaves decisions concerning marketing arrangements to the member states to decide and hence the structure of the market for individual farming products varies from country to country in the EEC.

The farming organizations

Whatever the legalistic interpretation of the situation in terms of 'consultation', the period which surrounds the Annual Price Review is in fact a process of negotiation between, in Britain, the Ministry of Agriculture on the one hand and the NFU, and to a lesser extent the CLA,[22] on the other. (In Brussels a somewhat similar system operates involving the EEC and COPA, the European federation of farming organizations, although this is also complicated by the often divergent interests between the member states.) To a not inconsiderable degree, therefore, the profitability of many, if not most, farmers depends upon the strength of their representative organizations and the latter's success in what amounts almost to the collective bargaining of their members' incomes. The NFU therefore has some of the characteristics of an orthodox trade union (although attempts are often made to understate this, since its membership – as we shall see in Chapter 7 – is on the whole virulently anti-trade unionist), except, of course, that its members are not employed by the state, merely supported by it. Furthermore, in other respects, most notably its negotiations with farm workers' representatives on the Agricultural Wages Board, it acts as an employers' organization. This ambivalence, which is added to by the wide disparity in the membership between, say, Welsh hill farmers and East Anglian cereal growers, means that the NFU prefers to work 'behind the scenes' by classic pressure-group methods and dislikes open confrontation.

The NFU has been recognized by many commentators to be one of the most superbly-organized pressure groups in Britain (see, for example, Self and Storing, 1962; Beresford, 1975; Wilson, 1978). Ostensibly it might appear that the NFU would be in a weak bargaining position *vis-à-vis* the state, but in fact it has a quite remarkable influence within the Ministry of Agriculture. Indeed, the Ministry itself, as Sampson (1971) points out, can be regarded as the greatest monument to its influence. As we discovered in the initial stages of our research the Ministry is most reluctant to take any action which might be considered by the NFU to be detrimental to the interests of farmers and, as Wilson (1978) notes, there is a close and abiding relationship between those in the top echelons of the civil service in the MAFF and the national officers of the NFU. It would probably be true to say that not a single day passes when someone from the Ministry is not in negotiation with someone from the NFU. As Self and Storing comment, when those from the NFU appeal to 'keep farming out of politics' they really mean 'keep the decision making process behind closed doors in Whitehall rather than have it argued about in Westminster between the parties' (1962, p. 47). This close liaison has been neatly summarized by Green (1975, p. 136):

It continues to maintain something very like a Parliamentary Lobby. . . . It keeps a large propaganda and information service at work. It has a department for research into agricultural economics. . . . It makes representations, whenever necessary, to the general public, the food trade, Parliament, the Treasury and any other relevant Whitehall department. Above all, it negotiates closely and almost unceasingly with the Ministry of Agriculture. Indeed, its relations with the Ministry are so close that the Union is always in some small danger of becoming as much an adjunct of it as a pressure group engaged in warfare with it.

And we would add that the Ministry sometimes appears to be in danger of being an adjunct of the NFU. It is small wonder that Wilson concludes in his cross-national study of farmers' organizations in advanced societies that the NFU 'is arguably the best and organisationally strongest of western agricultural interest groups' (1978, p. 31).

Even a cursory glance through the farming press is sufficient to reveal the extent of the NFU's activities. For example, a leading article in the NFU's fortnightly journal, *British Farmer and Stockbreeder*, at the time of Labour's return to power in 1974, had this to say: 'Labour may be fresh in office, but hardly unaware of the industry's problems or the representations it has made over the years to bring about urgent reforms in our tax system. The N.F.U. takes good care to keep opposition leaders well briefed when out of office' (vol. 3, No. 75, 1974, p. 3). And in a recent letter to *Farmers' Weekly* the NFU Deputy President asserted that the NFU leader is as frequently consulted by the Labour government as any trade union leader. In making representations to the government on Capital Transfer Tax and Wealth Tax, for example, the NFU were instrumental in setting up an inter-departmental committee 'to examine the cumulative effects of all these taxes' on agriculture. He went on to say that the relief granted to farmers in relation to CTT in the 1976 Budget were acknowledged by the Chancellor to be based on the findings of that committee to which the NFU gave evidence (but whose report remains unpublished). He concluded: 'Moreover, the fact that [the Chancellor] has made no mention of wealth tax suggests that the Government is hardly likely to bring forward plans for such a tax at an early date. If this is revived he will be obliged to take account of the strong arguments that we have deployed as he has indeed now done in the case of capital transfer tax' (*Farmers' Weekly*, 16 April 1976, p. 43).[23]

For many other pressure groups, such statements could be taken rather as indicative of the bravado of the leadership and a desire to impress the grass roots, but this hardly applies to the NFU. To be sure the NFU has very successfully argued that in pursuing its own sectional interest, it is also pursuing a very genuine national one. Not only have two world wars provided sharp reminders of the strategic importance of an indigenous British agriculture, but expanding home production can save hundreds of millions of pounds on imports and help to alleviate Britain's chronic balance of payments problem. The NFU has utilized these and other arguments with remarkable skill in order to achieve favourable treatment for its members. A careful examination of any NFU annual report reveals the wide-ranging activities of the union in its promotion of members' interests. For example, the NFU Parliamentary Committee employs parliamentary agents to aid in the task of scrutinizing all proposed legislation which might affect farmers. Where it is deemed necessary the union seeks exemption from or special assurances concerning the bill in question. In 1975 the union obtained exemption for farmers under the Wild Creatures and Wild Plants Protection Act which had extended statutory protection to species in danger of extinction. In consultation with the Ministry of Agriculture farmers were excluded from prosecution 'in respect of unavoidable damage caused to these rare species in the course of responsible agricultural operations' (NFU, 1976, p. 20). Similar exemptions or assurances were given with regard to other Acts of Parliament and in the case of private bills NFU headquarters ensured that county branches were made aware of any matter which might affect their interests.

However, the major legislation of concern to the NFU in 1975 was the Community Land Act. The union had made its objections known to certain aspects of the Community Land Scheme when it was first outlined by the then Labour opposition in 1973. By 1975 the Parliamentary Committee was able to report as follows:

Extensive discussions were held with Ministers and civil servants, and throughout the passage of the legislation detailed lobbying of MPs and Peers of all parties took place. NFU inspired amendments and briefs were debated on many occasions – often with all-party support. Whilst the legislation remains suspect and unnecessary in the Union's view, there have been substantial changes made to the original widespread and un-fettered powers of local authority land organisation. Many of these changes are specifically aimed to protect agricultural land and the farming industry. [ibid., p. 21.]

In addition to the activities of the Parliamentary Committee, the Economics and Taxation Committee negotiated with the Ministry of Agriculture and the Treasury for greater relief for farmers under Capital Transfer Tax, with some success (ibid., pp. 38–9). Meanwhile the Publicity Committee, responsible for keeping the media aware of the activities of the NFU, quoted an article from the *Sunday Times* which praised the union for its successful mastery of the EEC political machine in Brussels in the following tones: 'The farmers' lobbying system in Brussels is the best mounted by any British organisation.... Agriculture has achieved major political importance in the UK and a formidable international reputation' (quoted in ibid., p. 99).

During 1975 the NFU issued 162 press notices and held twelve major press conferences: 'all were well attended and produced positive results for the NFU' (ibid., p. 100). In addition the Publicity Committee noted that the amount of coverage given to agriculture on radio and television 'remains the envy of other sectors of the industrial world' with 'about 31 hours of material on farming and allied topics' *each week* (ibid., p. 100). The NFU's monitoring service picked up no less than 1200 references to the union during 1975 on radio and television, and the expansion of local radio was seen as giving 'a very useful platform for speakers from the industry to talk to significant numbers of urban consumers' (p. 100). Not only does the Information Division provide press releases, it also gives editorial material for the agricultural supplements of local papers. After reviewing its activities for the year it is hard to disagree with their boast that 'no other industry has a comparable network of news and publicity outlets' (p. 101). The union's regional information officers serviced over 1000 local papers, sent out 800 press releases, placed 200 special articles, were involved in 100 local radio programmes and reinterpreted national press releases in the light of local interests. All of these activities are, of course, in addition to the publication of the union's own journal, *British Farmer and Stockbreeder*. Given this arsenal of publicity talents it is small wonder that a NFU-commissioned survey of the views of the general public towards farming, conducted in 1973, produced such favourable results from the NFU's viewpoint.

It must, therefore, be all the more galling for the NFU to know that so often their membership is not appreciative of its efforts. Indeed the NFU leadership becomes very indignant when, as often happens, there are calls for a more militant approach – as the following from a *British Farmer and Stockbreeder* lead article indicates:

The calls for a Joe Gormley [as NFU leader] are made by those who falsely equate a disciplined body of paid employees ... with farmers who are self-employed, under no obligation to support their own union or even to belong to it, and a substantial number of whom would decline to do so if they believed the advice mistaken or the consequences financially damaging. Those who want an industry with strike pay had better find other employment. [11 May 1974, p. 3.]

But the real problem for those who disagree with the NFU within the industry is that of being heard. As Wilson observes (1978, p. 39), the MAFF maintains the NFU's monopoly position by effectively refusing to negotiate, or consult, with any splinter group. This, of course, has advantages for both the NFU and the government.

Although the NFU publishes no details of its actual membership, informed estimates (Self and Storing, 1962; Donaldson and Donaldson, 1972) put it at around 75 per cent of its potential membership. This is an amazingly high figure when one considers the diversity of its membership.[24] Among our respondents 90 per cent in the 1000+ acres sample and 70 per cent in the forty-four parishes were members. We asked them why they had initially joined and their replies are categorized in Table 37. No clear and consistent pattern emerges with almost equal numbers of respondents believing that they had an obligation to join, that there were particular benefits (e.g. favourable insurance facilities) in joining, that they had never thought otherwise, or had inherited membership. As with the members of most trade unions few attended branch meetings regularly but 40 per cent in the 1000+ acres sample and 26 per cent in the forty-four parishes did claim to go to some meetings and only six respondents altogether expressed 'no interest' as the reason for not attending meetings. In addition 44 per cent of members in the 1000+ acres sample and 31 per cent in the forty-four parishes were or had been in an elected position within the NFU at either local, county or national level, so for many their membership of the union is meaningful. The few respondents who had either been in the NFU and subsequently left, or who had never been members, nearly all gave instrumental reasons for their action – generally an inability to afford the fees. In both samples over 70 per cent of members were satisfied that the NFU was acting in their interests, although those in the forty-four parishes were less sure that the union represented all farmers equally. This was perhaps reflected in the fact that 43 per cent in the forty-four parishes felt the NFU should be more militant compared with 24 per cent in the 1000+ acres samples. Nevertheless most respondents tried to draw a clear line between the actions of the NFU and that of trade unions, and in so far as they were willing to condone militancy it was only because 'that appears to be the only way you get heard today'. But for most members responsibility and restraint in their dealings was seen as a positive virtue of the NFU.

Table 37   *Reasons for joining the NFU*

Type of reason	1000+ acres (N=80) %	44 parishes (N=42) %
Ideological	22·5	28·6
Instrumental	22·5	23·8
Automatic	23·8	9·5
Company membership	20·0	21·4
Combination	5·0	9·5
Other	6·3	7·1
Total	100	100

The CLA is of lesser importance in terms of the produce market, since it is basically a defensive organization of landowners. But, while a less public organization than the NFU, there is no reason to believe that it is any less effective or insistent in those matters which most concern it. We have already seen how quickly the CLA has mobilized against the perceived threats to landownership implied by recent government policies and by the changed land market. Not unimportant in this regard has been the ability of the CLA, by what can only be regarded as a 'hard-sell' approach, to persuade owner-occupiers, of all sizes of farms, to join the Association – an association which was after all initially formed to defend landlords. Indeed, the increased rates of owner-occupation have made it easier for the NFU and CLA to cooperate since they are no longer identifiably organizations which represent the tenant on the one hand and the landlord on the other.

Undoubtedly, as Green (1975) points out, the CLA has to adopt more defensive postures than the NFU since it is basically concerned with defending property. As one respondent summed up the difference, 'The NFU helps you to make money, the CLA helps you to keep it.' Frequently, then, the CLA in its statements tries to seek common cause with all property-owners. For example: 'There is an enormous range [of landowners] but the closer the owner of the land, whether owner-occupier or resident landlord, is identified with the smaller working farmer, the less the likelihood that he will have to bear the brunt of political attack arising from envy' (CLA, 1975, para. 5, pp. 1–2). These sentiments partly account for the recruitment of smaller landowners into the CLA. The fact remains, however, that while the CLA has gained the right to be consulted on all matters concerning landownership, and is represented on many official committees, it does not have the kind of relationship with the government that characterizes the NFU, although it still maintains many vital unofficial contacts with decision-makers and is well represented in the House of Lords. Moreover, it offers to its members extremely useful advice concerning such matters as taxation and grants which can be used in improving returns to landownership and enhancing income.[25]

Not surprisingly, we found that the CLA's membership was much less comprehensive than that of the NFU with only 37 per cent of those in the forty-four parishes being members, compared with 75 per cent in the 1000 + acres sample. A variety of reasons were given for joining the CLA, the most common being instrumental: they wanted the advice the CLA could give concerning, for example, taxation. Given the more specific functions of the CLA it is far easier for members to see the positive advantages of their organization. This largely explains why almost 90 per cent of CLA members thought the national organization was adequately representing their interests. It was generally felt that leading members of the CLA 'moved in the right circles' and had a lot of behind-the-scenes influence, not least, it was claimed, because Ministers and top civil servants could be invited to go shooting on the estates of CLA officers and consequently observe estate problems at first hand.

The crowning achievement of both the NFU and the CLA has been successfully to adapt the agricultural interest to changing political circumstances, successfully to mobilize their members in an era when the interest of the farmer and landowner has become merely one among many. The NFU has been particularly successful in retaining all the various groups within agriculture – often with mutually conflicting aims according to the commodity with which they are concerned – under the umbrella of one predominant organization (despite the breakaway Farmers' Union of Wales, formed in 1955). In so doing it has immeasurably enhanced both its influence and the interests of farmers in the country as a whole. Along with the Law Society, the British Medical Association and the British Roads Federation it is probably one of the most powerful parliamentary lobbies, to the extent that if it is not, as Self and Storing suggest, 'almost . . . an arm of state' (1962, p. 37), then at times it has seemed that the Ministry of Agriculture has been almost the political arm of the NFU. Nevertheless the NFU clearly cannot please all of the farmers all of the time. For many years it was accused of being in the hands of East Anglian cereals growers (ibid., p. 45), but now the balance has shifted slightly towards the more medium-sized mixed farmer. Certainly some of our respondents on the very largest enterprises felt little need for organizational help. 'I think some of our managers might be in it,' one farmer on 16000 acres remarked vaguely, 'but I don't bother with it. If I want something done I go straight to the Minister.' Nevertheless most of England and Wales's 180 000 farmers must speak with one voice to be heard at all by a population of 56 millions (ibid., p. 55). Its cohesiveness, effectiveness and influence are, by any standards, extraordinary.

Market orientation

While the various farming organizations provide a framework for the prosperity of agriculture through their lobbying activities, they can do no more than offer a series of favourable conditions. The weather, of course, remains a factor beyond their control – and so does the success with which individual farmers market their produce. There is a basic complexity in the market for agricultural output since marketing varies according to the commodity concerned, where it is produced, when it is produced, how perishable it is, how much processing is required and so on.[26] In addition any one crop or product may have a variety of potential uses which affect marketing – for example, wheat may be grown for seed, for animal feed, or for flour; peas may be grown for canning, freezing or for sale on the open market and so on. All this makes it potentially difficult for the individual farmer, concerned as he is with the basic problem of producing his crops or rearing his animals, to be aware of all the marketing possibilities for his produce. Most farmers simply do not have businesses large enough to make any substantial improvement in their market situation (for example, by processing food themselves) and many, characteristically individualists, are suspicious of, if not hostile to, any suggestion that they should combine into groups or cooperatives to improve their position. Such changes in the food market that have occurred in recent years tend to have, moreover, favoured the larger business farmers – for example, contract growing for food processors or supermarkets, who demand fairly large quantities of uniform produce preferably graded, packed and ready for immediate sale. Any farmer who anticipates entering such an arrangement, even as a member of a group, will probably need to make a substantial initial capital outlay and employ extra personnel at all levels. But the advantages of cutting out 'middle men' and selling direct to the consumer are obvious.

For most farmers, however, marketing means selling to a wholesaler and it is up to the farmer to use his acumen and his knowledge and anticipation of the market to obtain the best possible price. In many ways this makes the farmer a professional gambler, although often he may be forced to sell produce at a lower price than he might later obtain (in the case of non-perishable produce) for cash-flow reasons. Cereals are nearly all sold to local agricultural merchants who may process it themselves or sell on to brewers, millers, feed manufacturers and so on. Since merchants are willing to offer credit to farmers, and given the length of time which elapses from planting to harvesting, it is hardly surprising that many farmers find it necessary to sell their cereals immediately they are harvested; by this time they need the cash but, of course, prices may be depressed since so many farmers are similarly committed. Those farmers who can afford it usually have storage facilities for cereals so that they can be more flexible in their marketing, but again this is an activity mostly confined to the larger farmers who grow a sufficient acreage to justify the cost of storage and who suffer less acutely from cash-flow problems. Horticultural products, fruit and vegetables, tend to be sold through the main wholesale markets like Covent Garden, although the contract trade with food processors and retailers is rapidly growing. Livestock tends to be sold either at auction or on contract to wholesalers and manufacturers. But these can only be generalizations and many farmers come to gentlemen's agreements with butchers, local vegetable merchants and so on in an attempt to get better prices.

For some products, however, farmers may sell or may be required to sell through a marketing board. Marketing boards were initially established in the 1930s in order to stabilize farmers' incomes. The boards are essentially producer-controlled cartels. Where farmers do not sell to the boards, they still have to comply with directives that may be laid down by them. Although there were at first marketing boards for only milk, hops and potatoes, the scheme was extended to eggs, bacon pigs, wool, tomatoes and cucumbers. These later boards have now been wound up and the only new organization is the British Sugar Corporation which, though not a marketing board, operates very much like one and sets a quota to the amount of sugar beet grown as well as providing technical services.[27] Milk is almost entirely sold via one of the five Milk Marketing Boards and potatoes are controlled by a marketing board which only buys to protect the market price at a reasonable level, but which sets a limit to the acreage of potatoes a farmer can grow, can control the flow of potatoes on to the market for human consumption and licenses potato merchants.

A further marketing option open to farmers is to form producer groups or cooperatives. This can increase both buying and selling power and can be carried out on a large or small scale. The basic reason for group formation is obviously to perform a function beyond the scope of any individual farmer in either production or marketing, and, as we discovered, it is a particularly popular practice in the production and sale of vegetables, and in the promotion of 'new' crops like oilseed rape. Such schemes are notoriously difficult to organize, however, since they must overcome the widespread individualism of farmers and counteract the prevailing rationality of agricultural production which is a competitive one.

We were particularly interested in the extent to which those farmers in our two samples were sensitive to changes in the market for various farming products – that is, the extent to which, within the limits set by location, physical conditions, soil type, etc., they attempted to maximize their profits. The results are shown in Table 38.[28] The differences between the samples are hardly surpris-

Table 38 *Market sensitivity of farmers*

	1000+ acres (N=104) %		44 parishes (N=55) %	
Very high	28·8	} 61·5	1·8	} 21·8
Quite high	32·7		20·0	
Quite low	24·0	} 38·4	21·8	} 78·2
Very low	14·4		56·4	
Total	100·0		100·0	

Table 39 *Market sensitivity by acreage farmed for the two samples*

Market sensitivity	Acreage farmed Less than 50	50/150	150/399	400/999	1000/1499	1500/1999	2000+
High	0	10·5	15·8	71·4	50·0	57·9	80·0
Low	100	89·5	84·2	28·6	50·0	42·1	20·0
Total	100	100	100	100	100	100	100

ing. Many of the smaller farmers, lacking the flexibility and resources of their larger-scale counterparts, were at a positive disadvantage in the market. Indeed among the larger farmers in the 1000+ acres sample there was a significant relationship between acreage farmed and market sensitivity. In Table 39 we have combined these data for the two samples for ease of presentation. Those farmers who were very highly sensitive to the market typically commented as follows:

Our main crop is fruit and here I am very sensitive to what is going on· I spend the first half-hour of each working day telephoning the markets about prices. If the price doesn't look good I hold back the crop for a while. We have plenty of storage facilities, and we are spending more money on them so that we can get better prices. . . . We have spent a lot of time, money and effort in finding the best market for each different fruit. If you find the right place you make a lot more money. Some things seem to sell better in different parts of the country. I am also in milk, which we produce and deliver to the doorstep via our own milk rounds-men; and cereals, half of which I sell through a producer group and the rest I store and sell when the market looks good. [Cambridgeshire farmer, 2800 acres.]

I follow the grain trade very closely – twice or three times each day I get reports, and I watch the futures market. Pigs I follow on a weekly basis, but sometimes daily. I get reports on the beef market three times a week and all this influences the volume of selling I do. . . . Money is what I am in farming for so I need to know exactly where I am at from day to day and what margins I can expect. Total financial control is an absolute must. We have just had 4000 tons extra grain storage. You can't farm on this scale without proper facilities for cleaning, storing, drying and marketing. [Cambridgeshire farmer, 3500 acres.]

When I took over this farm ten years ago it was a typical Norfolk arable farm. There was no livestock at all, it was all sugar beet and cereals. We don't grow sugar beet now because there's no profit in it; I have cattle so I grow the grain for them but I don't grow any for the market because vegetables are more profitable. I also grow a lot of grass. This is lovely land for grass and I could see there was a potential market for it so I have installed a grass-drier and I sell that through a broker. Apart from the potatoes which we sell on contract to merchants, all our vegetables are sold through our own co-op. We employ a professional salesman there. [Norfolk farmer, 2300 acres.]

Within the limits of good husbandry we try and follow the market, i.e. try and judge what we *think* the market will be like. For example we have reduced our barley acreage and increased the wheat because we feel demand for barley for animal feed will fall because the livestock market is so depressed. We have cut down on our own calf-rearing activities because of the market and have made three men redundant due to the market slump. We have paid for a survey of our farm business and this shows we can make more profit by diversifying so we are going into oilseed rape and more beet. We built a 2000-ton grain store twenty-five years ago because we could see bulk handling would come and we have no fields of less than 40 acres. [Norfolk farmer, 1800 acres.]

The diligence and single-mindedness of these highly market-oriented farmers contrasts starkly with those farmers who take a more easy-going attitude or who recognize, and are unwilling to pay, the costs of such single-mindedness. For example, the following respondent put good relationships on his farm ahead of profitability, in contrast to the last farmer quoted above:

[Despite high prices] I have kept my corn acreage constant. . . . If I had grown more corn this year, I would have had to have dismissed some men. I am reasonably happy as I am, but I shall grow more corn as men retire. [Cambridgeshire farmer, 2000 acres.]

Most typical, however, of the responses of the low market-oriented farmers were comments like the following:

We always keep doing the same thing and hope it works out from year to year. [Suffolk farmer, 1200 acres.]

I just carry on regardless of what is happening. [Suffolk farmer, 1150 acres.]

I don't follow the market. I am more interested in the *land*. [Suffolk farmer, 1600 acres.]

You can't really do anything. Everything is too short-term because of government interference. [Norfolk farmer, 1100 acres.]

Interestingly all of the above were owner-occupiers who had inherited their land and had not expanded the acreage of their holdings significantly. Rather they were content to continue much as their fathers had farmed before them since it gave them a comfortable living. Often the more market-oriented farmers had either expanded their acreage considerably or had completely overhauled their farm business and practices, for example moving out of unprofitable products and into profitable ones, selling all their livestock and so on. It is impossible on the basis of our rather small samples to judge whether such factors are merely coincidental – certainly not all those in our sample who inherited a well-established farm simply sat back on their laurels, but, unfortunately, our own data are not adequate to take the beginnings of this hypothesis concerning market orientation and inheritance any further.

Whereas high market-orientation was the norm among the 1000 + acres sample, it was the exception in the forty-four parishes. Even where farmers are oriented to the market in ways similar to the majority of the larger farmers, they often felt inhibited in what they could achieve. For example:

I have limited storage facilities and so I have to sell nearly all my crop at harvest. I'm very well aware of the market, but I just can't act upon it. . . . I have to take incredible risks in order to get the returns I do. [Suffolk farmer, 415 acres.]

I am highly price conscious. The market is the major factor and so I grow for the best market. But there are limitations in the cost of land, labour and machinery. [Suffolk farmer, 750 acres.]

Other of the larger farmers in the forty-four parishes made similar comments, but the majority, with few acres and little capital to invest, could not be expected to be very market-oriented:

This last year has been my worst ever. I never know the right time to buy and sell because prices are so erratic. [Suffolk farmer, 200 acres.]

I do what I want to do and hope for the best. [Suffolk farmer, 35 acres.]

You have to stick with one thing. If it finishes you, well. . . . I've taken a hammering this year but I'm hoping things will change. [Suffolk farmer, 94 acres.]

The small, lowly market-oriented farmers are somewhat fatalistic in their attitudes. They 'hope for the best' and feel unable to control their fate, while the highly market-oriented farmers, instead of waiting for things to happen, try and make them happen instead. Of course, the strong relationship between farm size and market orientation does indicate that for much of the time in arable farming one can only hope to take advantage of the market if one has the resources necessary to invest in machinery and buildings. Hence it is only the larger farmers who have storage facilities, or who can afford to entertain the idea of not simply producing the crops but grading, packing and selling direct to the retailer as well. Indeed, most marketing options which give the arable farmer a chance of greater profit necessitate a larger operation to make them worthwhile. Hence, as we shall see, the tremendous disparity of incomes between farmers of different business sizes.

Although the marketing options open to farmers are many and varied, in recent years there has been an increase in the number of farmers entering into contracts with food-processing firms. We asked all our respondents whether or not they had any such contracts, or had ever had them, for which products and how they assessed such marketing arrangements. The results of this question are given in Table 40. The effects of size are again apparent. More of those in the 1000+ acres sample have contracts and only one-quarter have failed even to consider them. Obviously the food-processing firms are mainly interested in farmers who can offer them a relatively large supply of produce and who have the resources to meet the various demands concerning, for example, harvesting and delivery of produce.[29] The biggest single reason given by farmers in the forty-four parishes for not considering contracts was that they were not 'big enough' whereas in the 1000+ acres sample the main reason given was a preference for marketing produce by other means.

Most of the contracts held by farmers were with companies like

Table 40   *Contracts with commercial food-processing companies**

	1000+ acres (N=103) %		44 parishes (N=56) %
Has contract(s)	56·3		37·5
No contract	43·7		62·5
Has had contract		6·8	12·5
Considered contract		10·7	16·1
Never considered contract		26·2	33·9
Total	100	43·7	100 62·5

* Excludes marketing organizations, e.g. MMB and BSC, and farmers' cooperatives.

Bird's Eye and Batchelor's for vegetables, and Sainsbury's and Wall's for pigs. A common allegation is that large companies like these put farmers in a very weak bargaining position and that farmers find that the companies interpret the contracts to suit themselves. However, of those farmers who had contracts, 71 per cent in the 1000+ acres sample were quite satisfied with them and 57 per cent in the forty-four parishes. Indeed, many farmers noted the enormous help and technical expertise given free by the companies with whom they had contracts, as well as the advantages of knowing in advance how much profit a particular crop was likely to yield. But contracts do pose a dilemma for the farmer, especially for those who enjoy 'playing the market' to try and obtain the best price. All farmers are aware that prices for their produce can fluctuate wildly, and a contract with a guaranteed price can be useful when prices in the open market fall. The problem can be particularly acute with pigs, a major enterprise on many of the farms we visited. In the short period in which we were interviewing profitability in pig farming went through two booms and one very bad slump. It is in situations such as these that 'traditional' and 'rational' considerations can come into conflict, often, as we discovered, in one family. For example, one of our interviewees complained that his father refused to entertain the idea of contracts for their pigs because he enjoyed selling on the open market:

I would favour more contracting but my father prefers to play the market. He believes you may make more sometimes. But I prefer to know what I shall get. Farmers really are poor at marketing. What other industry is as haphazard at marketing produce as farming? The closer we can get to the consumer market, the better off we and the consumer would be. [Suffolk farmer, 1200 acres.]

There was no doubt that many farmers did find marketing a real problem, especially with the very fluctuating market in cereals which has been a feature in recent years. As one farmer commented:

It's crazy! There are such great variations of price today – £20 a ton in wheat in the last year. . . . I'm not at all happy with the way we sell. And, of course, *we* can't increase prices in response to higher costs. [Norfolk farmer, 1200 acres.]

All these tensions of marketing were neatly summarized by one Cambridgeshire farmer:

It's no use just being a good farmer nowadays. You can produce all the crops you like of top quality but it's knowing when to buy and sell that counts. It's more profitable to the farm for me to stay in my office on the telephone talking to the corn merchant, or finding out other prices, than it is for me to work with the men. That's why I don't do much *proper* farm work – what I call proper farm work. It's not enough now to know when to sow and when to harvest, when to drill and when to spray. You have to know when to *sell* – what prices will do next. I've just bought all my fertiliser for *next* year. It was cheaper to borrow the money to do that than to wait for next year's prices; they are bound to be higher because prices of the constituent products have gone up 100 per cent. And I can see no end to it. If the price of steel goes up, the price of cars goes up. But fertiliser price-rises don't mean I'll get more for my corn. I may get *less*. [Cambridgeshire farmer, 1050 acres.]

In conclusion we may note that, of all the markets in which he is involved, the produce market is the most crucial, yet there is a diversity of approach to marketing by farmers ranging from the fatalism of some to the skilful and intricate arrangements of the most highly market-oriented. But the explanation of varying marketing strategies is more problematic. Size is the most obvious feature, as we saw earlier, in explaining market orientation, but size of scale is as much a consequence as a cause of market sensitivity and attitudes also depend on the extent to which a farmer is committed to a traditional pattern of farming or sees the necessity to intervene more positively in order to move the market his way. We suspect that the explanation of these traits may lie in the area of pre-adult socialization, but our data on this are insufficiently sensitive to make any positive statements and our attempts to correlate market orientation with a variety of 'face-sheet variables' simply produced a depressingly long list of negative findings. In any case if the produce market continues to show the kinds of fluctuations it has evidenced recently, and if costs continue to rise at the recent rate, more and more farmers will become increasingly anxious about their marketing arrangements. As with the land market inflation has given rise to many problems in the produce market but it has also given a boost in recent years to those arable farmers who have been able to take advantage of the higher prices obtained for their products by their vigorous and aggressive marketing strategies. Here, as elsewhere, economic pressures are continually pushing the farmer towards a more rationalized business structure and away from an easygoing 'way of life'.

Farmers as buyers

The significance of farmers to the British economy extends beyond the value of farm sales, for farmers also make important purchases of farm inputs – as the vast amount of research and advertising expenditure by farm machinery and chemicals companies, for example, would indicate. Indeed, farmers spend around £3500 million a year on goods and services (including labour which we discuss in the next chapter) as Figure 6 indicates. Here again the farmer is brought into contact with large-scale industrial enterprises from whom he has to purchase his machinery, animal feed and fertilizer. Where possible some farmers do purchase direct from manufacturers but even in the wholesale trade large firms, like Dalgety, are swallowing up many of the local agricultural merchants. Consequently, farmers are in a relatively weak bargaining position as buyers and we expected that they might be somewhat hostile to business. After all, the large companies with whom the farmer deals are not slow to pass on to him their increased costs, but the farmer often cannot do the same. In the forty-four parishes 65 per cent said they felt that 'big business' was too powerful, but only 44 per cent answered similarly in the 1000 + acres sample. The following are some typical responses:

They are virtual monopolies. . . . This is bad for farmers because they become a speck in the ocean. You have to accept their prices. [Norfolk farmer, 1000 acres.]

I ring up some of these merchants now and offer a few tons of wheat but they aren't interested in dealing in such small amounts. [Suffolk farmer, 180 acres.]

It used to be a buyer's market but these big firms have made it a seller's. [Suffolk farmer, 400 acres.]

You used to know who you were dealing with. Now it all goes through the sausage machine. [Norfolk farmer, 3500 acres.]

But although many of our respondents regretted these changes, were often harsh in their criticism of large organizations and heavy in their praise of the individually-operated businesses, most accepted the changes as a fact of life at best, and at worst a sign of the general ills of society. They did not, however, appear to resent their weak bargaining position until personal experience brought it home to them – for example, waiting several weeks for a supply of fertilizers and then finding the price had risen since they ordered. One farmer, on investigating such a case, learned that the chemicals company concerned had been stockpiling while awaiting a price increase. For most of the time, though, a fairly sanguine view is held of the relationship to big business.

Purchases	£m	Sales	£m
Feed	1234	Crops	987
Seed	106	Livestock	1573
Fertilizer	305	Fruit and vegetables	512
Livestock	107	Eggs, milk and wool	1219
Machinery	326	Grants	242
Other	488	Valuation increase	388
Total direct costs	2566	Total	4921
Labour	683		
Interest	102		
Other, including depreciation	438		
Net income	1133		
Total	4921		

Figure 6 *Estimated trading account of UK agriculture, 1974–5 (Adapted from Clery, 1975.)*

How long this will remain is not altogether clear. The degree of vertical integration in British food manufacture is remarkably low by the standards of other advanced industrial societies. Whatever the reasons for this (and this area has hardly been touched upon by academic research) the British farmer has instead become more dependent upon big, often multi-national, corporations for both inputs and outputs. This absorption into an agro-industrial food-producing complex has seen the farmer's share of the retail price of food falling steadily since the war. The high capital cost of land may continue to deter food processors and the major retail chains from developing links backwards into agriculture, although even here they may feel tempted by recent threats to the continuation of private landownership, with a view of ensuring the continuity of their supplies. But all this is essentially speculative. The current pattern is likely to persist for some considerable time to come, with farmers largely oblivious to, or indifferent towards, their weakening bargaining power which these trends suggest.

Farmers' incomes

The income of farmers is, of course, an area of great dispute. To begin with most farmers are quite convinced that their incomes are depressed to the benefit of the urban majority and the government which represents it, neither of whom care where the food comes from as long as it is cheap. But there is another sense in which the picture is by no means straightforward. Farm incomes vary according to a variety of factors, many of which we have already touched upon. There is the determination of prices made by the state, the operation of world markets in the case of crops like cereals, the selling and buying ability of the individual farmer, the type of farm, the size of farm, the quality of land, the weather, and so on. The list could become almost endless. With these qualifications in mind we can review the trend of farm incomes in recent years before discussing the particular views of our respondents on their incomes.

Notionally, the farmer's income consists of three elements: a return on capital invested, a return to his entrepreneurship and a payment for his labour. But even the Ministry of Agriculture has found the task of dividing the three elements impossible in any but a completely arbitrary way. Consequently it is fruitless to compare rates of return in agriculture with those for industry as a whole, even if one discounts the cost of land. But we can examine, on the basis of Farm Management Survey data, the trend in net farming income in East Anglia over time, as Figure 7 demonstrates. We can see from this diagram that the period 1971–4 produced a dramatic increase in the incomes of East Anglian farmers, and this was especially the case on cropping farms. Even increased prices of farm inputs and higher fixed costs did not offset this trend. But Figure 7 does not give any real idea of the level of farm income which obviously varies quite considerably from farm to farm. Again using the available Farm Management Survey data published by Cambridge University, the average net income per acre was £17·1 in 1971 and £36·9 in 1974. Since the average size of farms in the sample was 303 acres in 1971 and 317 in 1974, the average net income of farmers rose from £5180 in 1971 to £11700 in 1974 – an increase of 125 per cent. Of course there were great variations according to size and type of farm. Most

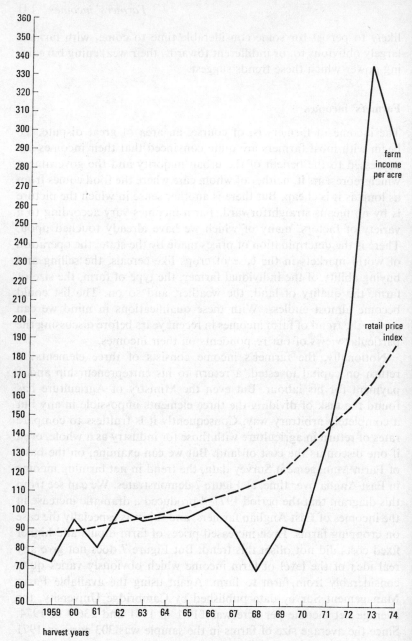

Figure 7 *Index of farm income per acre* v. *retail price index* (1964 = 100) (*Source:* CSO, Monthly Digest of Statistics *and Cambridge FMS.*)

profitable in 1974 were the cropping farms, especially the mainly cereal farms where average management and investment income was £42·0 per acre, reflecting, of course, the rise in the world market price for wheat. Although farm incomes have fallen back in the last two years, the MAFF Farm Incomes Survey for 1974–5 showed that cropping farms of the kind widely found in East Anglia still fared better than average. For example, farms of the type included in our 1000+ acres sample of over 2400 smd business size returned an average income across all types of farm of £19282 but on mainly cereal farms one of £44786. Even on farms of business size 275–599 smd, while average income was £2353, the mainly cereal farms averaged nearly £6000.

Consequently, while we were interviewing in 1974 and 1975, East Anglian farmers, although worried by inflation, were on the whole enjoying higher returns than ever. We asked all our respondents to give us details of their annual turnover and profit margins but we found the quality and reliability of answers too variable to analyse in any systematic way. Some farmers were plainly reluctant to give any answer, while many claimed not to know or simply handed us their accounts and invited us to see if we could make sense of them. It must further be admitted that we were made very much aware of the likely reliability of responses by one of our first respondents who asked whether we wanted to know his income according to the set of accounts prepared for him or for the Inland Revenue. The difference in profit between the two sets of figures amounted to £170000. However, we did ask in addition how satisfied farmers were with their 'present level of income' and, if they were dissatisfied, whom they blamed. The results of this question are given in Tables 41 and 42.

We can see from Table 41 that the larger farmers, not surprisingly, were rather less likely to complain about their level of income, and (Table 42) slightly more likely to blame themselves than the government for their problems. Many of those who were dissatisfied with their income regarded it as insignificant compared with the amount of money they had invested; that is, they regarded the return on capital as being too low when the cost of land, especially, was taken into account. It would appear that many farmers, as we saw earlier, resent their land being regarded as wealth but complain when their incomes represent a poor return on the value of their land. However, on most of the larger farms, and on a number of the smaller ones, the return on tenants' capital appeared to be quite healthy, and it

Table 41   *Income satisfaction*

	1000+ acres (N=101) %	44 parishes (N=57) %
Completely satisfied	7·9	8·8
Quite satisfied	55·4	42·1
A little dissatisfied	24·8	38·6
Very dissatisfied	11·9	10·5
Total	100	100

Table 42   *Factors blamed for dissatisfaction with income*

	1000+ acres (N=35) %	44 parishes (N=28) %
Government policies	48·6	65·5
Individual problems	17·1	3·4
Market factors	11·4	10·3
Others	22·8	20·7
Total	100	100

was only on farms where livestock played an important role that farmers were really worried about their returns. Moreover many farmers, while expressing satisfaction with current income, said their feelings were contingent upon prices keeping pace with increased costs.

However, one obvious point has to be made concerning income of farmers. Since many farmers, certainly most of the more substantial owner-occupiers, have inherited their houses and land, and can obtain many expensive consumer items, such as cars, as business expenses, any true assessment of their income would need to take this into account. There are many perquisites in farming, as in other businesses, for those at the top.

Conclusion

Paradoxically, as we pointed out when discussing the land market, it is precisely the increase in the paper-wealth of farmers which seems to be the major threat to their market situation. If taxation really bites, and if the City continues to purchase farm land, then there could be a move back to a tripartite landed social structure. Consequently farmers who are at present owners and entrepreneurs may (or their sons may) become employees and managers on land owned by financial interests or the state. That some farmers are wealthy no one can doubt. Apart from the evidence we have already given in this chapter it is quite obviously the case that since families tend to control farms and the indebtedness of farmers is low, the capital structure and wealth structure in farming are similar. As Harrison (1975, p. 65) has observed: 'Comparisons with wealth holdings of the rest of the community are notoriously hazardous, but, whereas 16 per cent of the farming community . . . had net farming wealth of over £20000 each, only 1·7 per cent of the community in general had this amount of wealth according to Inland Revenue statistics.' Moreover, as we shall see in the next chapter, some farmers have sources of wealth and income outside farming (see also Harrison, 1975, p. 66). All this makes them potentially vulnerable to capital taxation.

Are we, then, about to encounter the rural nemesis which has haunted the mind of the private landowner since, at least, 1910? Since, as we have shown, this is essentially a political matter, much will depend upon the vagaries of the ballot box. In any case, there will be no sudden cataclysm, only a piecemeal change to one form or another of corporate landownership. As far as food production itself is concerned, however, the rationalization of British agriculture is likely to continue: fewer, larger farms, fewer workers, new technological innovations, increased output. The cost–price squeeze on farmers is likely to intensify, which will in turn lead to this process of rationalization being accelerated, and this in turn will lead to a greater uniformity. As Beresford (1975, p. 215) has summarized these trends: 'The same determinants are driving us towards the same solutions. . . . Farming will be no less efficient; no less resilient; but different. In the lowlands, stockless arable systems and landless livestock systems will develop side by side.' Farming as a rational business activity will consummate its victory over farming as a traditional way of life. How successfully this can be accompanied by the maintenance of traditional relationships at the workplace and in the community is the concern of the rest of our argument.

4 The work situation

During the heyday of mid-Victorian high farming, a succession of foreign visitors, attracted to East Anglia by its justifiable reputation for technological advance, gazed in wonderment at what was for them a unique spectacle. East Anglian farmers, they observed, *did not work* (Hobsbawm and Rudé, 1971, p. 33). Accustomed to the largely peasant-based agriculture of continental Europe and elsewhere they equated work with manual labour and were slow to recognize that the work of the East Anglian farmer involved not so much his labour power but his entrepreneurial skill. Economically, his importance was as a provider of capital. Such considerations illustrate the care with which the concept of work situation (Lockwood, 1958, p. 15; 1975, pp. 240–1) must be handled when applied to an occupational group which is not only very diverse in its composition but whose economic activity does not fit readily into the categorizations derived from the study of manual workers in industry. As an outside onlooker it is easy to fall prey to the popular prejudice against the 'feather-bedded' farmer; farmers themselves, on the other hand, will stoutly maintain that they work 'all hours that God sends'. For each 'gentleman-farmer' who cannot be said to work in any popular meaningful sense of the word, there is the small farmer who will spend fifty to sixty hours a week in manual work, with administrative and accounting duties in addition.

Much of the problem stems from what is defined as work. The vast majority of farmers live at their place of work: they are continually on the job. The cliché that farming is a 'way of life' recognizes the fact that there is no separation between home and workplace, and that the division between work and leisure is purely a matter of subjective interpretation. When a farmer walks his dog around the fields on a summer's evening inspecting the state of the crops; when he spends a day shooting pigeons or rabbits; when he spends one morning a week at the local market – is this business or pleasure? When completing census forms (or answering questions from inquiring sociologists) the farmer will count any agriculturally-associated activity as 'work', and his working week will therefore constitute virtually his entire waking hours. This needs to be borne in mind when considering the data presented below. In absolute terms the figures for the working week need to be regarded with some scepticism: they almost certainly exaggerate what the farmer himself would subjectively define as work while engaged in that activity. Nevertheless a more satisfactory approach might be to attack the very distinction between work and non-work when applied to farmers, since, for the majority, their economic role is an all-embracing one which they can never completely escape except on the rare occasions when they go away on holiday.

It makes more sense, therefore, to break down the farmer's time into a number of discrete activities and to assess the significance of each. The farmer – as agricultural economists have long recognized – encompasses a number of important roles in the productive process. He may perform manual labour of a kind indistinguishable from that of hired workers (the only kind of work which counted as such to nineteenth-century visitors); he is also engaged in strictly entrepreneurial activity – buying, selling, planning, etc. – which is most often performed in an office rather than out in the fields; and he is engaged in various kinds of managerial (in a sociological rather than an economic sense) activity, supervising and directing the activity of workers out and about on the farm. The proportion of time taken up by each of these activities will vary according to the time of the year. In East Anglia, in particular, the rhythm of work is a peculiarly fluctuating one, given the predominance of arable agriculture in the region. While recent technological innovations have slightly evened out the distribution of work across the farming year, it is still dominated by periods of quite frenetic activity – seed-time and harvest – interspersed with periods of relative calm. If one adds on to this the fluctuations caused by changes in the weather, then the daily and weekly work of the farmer carries no set pattern. A rain-affected harvest, for example, can mean several days of virtual inactivity (beyond impatiently shuffling papers around the office desk) followed by up to eighteen hours a day of manual labour.

In this chapter, therefore, the data on the nature of the farmer's working week need to be regarded with some care. Most of our respondents had great difficulty in arriving at estimates of the amount of time they typically spent on various activities, and some did so only after considerable protest. Nevertheless some interesting differences *within* our sample do emerge and it is likely that these comparative indications contain a much greater validity than the absolute figures. Bearing this in mind, and also that the previous chapter has dealt with much of the farmers' entrepreneurial activity, this chapter will concentrate upon the role of the farmer as employer and examine the modes of control which farmers extend over their labour force in the work situation (cf. Newby, 1977, Chapter V). While, clearly, other aspects of the work situation are not irrelevant, such an emphasis enables some of the theoretical issues outlined in Chapter 1 to be pursued, as well as providing comparative data with material previously collected on the work situation of agricultural workers (ibid.).

Work and work satisfaction

The average length of the working week, as estimated by our respondents, was 49·8 hours for all the farmers that were interviewed. There were, however, considerable variations within our samples, as Table 43 shows. In the forty-four parishes, where a cross-section of farmers was interviewed the average number of hours per week worked on the farm dropped to 45·2, whereas on the larger farms in the 1000+ acres sample the average was considerably higher at 55·7 hours. Much of this difference is accounted for by the greater significance of other employment activity among the farmers in the forty-four parishes, where a small but significant proportion were part-time farmers, particularly the smaller, marginal farmers who had

Table 43   *Distribution of total number of hours per week worked on the farm*

Total hours worked on farm per week	1000+ acres (N=82) %	44 parishes (N=53) %
Less than 40	14·6	28·3
40–49	15·9	17·0
50–59	21·9	15·1
60–69	33·0	18·8
70–79	8·6	18·9
80+	1·2	1·9
D.K./N.A.	6·9	—
Total	100	100

perforce to supplement their meagre agricultural earnings with income from employment elsewhere. Thus in the forty-four parishes, 21·1 per cent of those interviewed were engaged in other employment for twenty hours or more per week, compared with only 3·8 per cent in the 1000 + acres sample.

Not surprisingly there were also variations in how the working week on the farm was divided between performing manual labour alongside hired workers and supervisory and administrative duties. These data are shown in Table 44. Again there are significant differences between the samples which are related to the size of the enterprises concerned. Among the respondents interviewed in the forty-four parishes 66 per cent spent less than one-tenth of their time on office work – routine paperwork, telephone calls, personal callers, accounts, planning and so on – and a similar proportion spent more than three-quarters of their time actually working alongside their workers. On the 1000 + acres farms, however, there was considerable contrast: 72·1 per cent spent less than one-tenth of their time working alongside their workers and 34·4 per cent spent more than half of their time in the office. Similarly, 22·2 per cent of the 1000 + acres sample spent more than half their time supervising the workers, compared with only 8·6 per cent in the forty-four parishes. The statistics in Table 44 clearly demonstrate the effects of bureaucratization on the large-scale farmer. The majority are not so much *farmers* as full-time administrators and managers, who might as easily be working in an office or factory in a large city. Subjectively, of course, nearly all these farmers would regard themselves as being very different from industrial managers; nevertheless, as far as their work situation is concerned, many of these larger farmers do not farm in the generally accepted sense, i.e. they do not themselves drive tractors or milk cows. Indeed the figures slightly understate their degree of separation from the land, for most of the 25·6 per cent who worked alongside their workers less than 10 per cent of their time would only do so during periods of peak labour activity, such as harvest or autumn drilling. Apart from these few weeks they would routinely be performing no manual labour on the farm at all.

On the small farms this situation is almost completely reversed. Here the farmer himself constitutes a high proportion of the total labour force and on those farms employing only two or three workers a considerable proportion of his time will be spent actually working on the land. This brings the farmer into much more frequent and pervasive face-to-face contact with his employees (to be considered

Table 44 *Proportion of time spent on certain activities on the farm*

Proportion of working week	Office work 1000+ acres (N=90) %	Office work 44 parishes (N=53) %	Supervision of workers 1000+ acres (N=81) %	Supervision of workers 44 parishes (N=35) %	Work alongside workers 1000+ acres (N=56) %	Work alongside workers 44 parishes (N=52) %
Nil	4·4	7·5	16·0	37·1	46·5	13·5
1%–9%	7·8	58·5	25·9	25·7	25·6	1·9
10%–19%	11·1	7·5	14·8	5·7	5·8	—
20%–29%	17·8	3·8	9·9	5·7	1·2	7·7
30%–49%	24·4	7·5	11·1	17·1	8·1	5·8
50%–74%	23·3	13·2	11·1	5·7	5·8	5·8
75%–100%	11·1	1·9	11·1	2·9	7·0	65·4
Total	100	100	100	100	100	100

Note: All farmers not employing hired workers, together with 'don't knows', have been excluded.

in detail below). Consequently the farm is run in a much less formal and impersonal manner and this in turn has consequences for the 'industrial relations' of agriculture. In addition, the small farms tend to be much more an extension of family identity, and this applies equally in the work situation where the other members of the family are much more likely to be involved if they are of a suitable age: for example, 25·3 per cent of the wives of the 1000+ acres farmers had 'no interest' in the farm, compared with only 8·3 per cent of farmers' wives in the forty-four parishes; similarly, 27·8 per cent of the latter were involved to the extent of working on the land, compared with only 8·0 per cent on the 1000+ acre farms. Although no farmer can completely divide 'home' from 'work', therefore, the intertwining of the two is particularly complete on the smaller enterprises. (But see data on involvement of wives in Chapter 5.)

As noted above, a substantial minority of farmers possessed other business interests than those represented in their own farm. The number, type and significance of these interests could vary considerably, however, and these variations are somewhat concealed in the information contained in Table 45. Among the 1000+ acres farmers, for example, their farming *persona* could be something of a sideline to their major activity as, say, director of a multi-national industrial company, chairman of a merchant bank, head of a City stockbroking firm, or whatever. Moreover, even those farmers for whom agriculture was their most significant economic activity could have quite important interests elsewhere, particularly in agriculturally-related companies such as merchants, marketing organizations, etc. In each case, 'other business interests' would be an accurate descriptive term. However, when this phrase is applied to the non-farming activities of the smaller farmer then it can be misleading in that it implies something rather more grandiose than what is often simply a part-time (or even a full-time) job. One respondent, for example, had 'other business interests' which emerged on further inquiry to be a newspaper round for a local newsagent. This sits somewhat uneasily in a table which also includes Lloyd's underwriters and merchant bankers. It is a distinction which is also conveyed in the finding that while these activities were significant, either financially or emotionally or both, for 16·2 per cent of the 1000+ acres farmers, they were significant for 28·0 per cent of the farmers in the forty-four parishes. As a broad generalization (to which there were exceptions in both samples) the larger farmers tended to be somewhat passive recipients of non-agricultural incomes from directorships, etc., while the smaller farmers were actively engaged for a substantial proportion of their working week in other forms of employment. In both cases, however, a majority had no other interests outside their farms.

It is already apparent, therefore, that what constitutes the 'work' of the farmer is by no means straightforward. It may consist of employment both off and on the farm. It involves a varying amount of administrative office work, supervision of employees out and about on the farm, and carrying out manual labour alongside the workers themselves. The work of the farmer is therefore extremely varied, especially so when one considers the variety introduced into working on a farm by the widespread lack of any extensive division of labour, the influence of the weather, inbuilt seasonal changes in the pattern of work activity, and so on (see Newby, 1977, Chapter V).

Table 45   *Other business interests*

Nature of business	1000+ acres (N=101) %	44 parishes (N=57) %
Director of agriculturally-related company	41·6	19·3
Agricultural contractor	2·0	7·0
Haulage contractor, garage owner	4·9	5·3
Builder	1·0	—
Lloyd's underwriter	4·9	—
Other directorship	10·9	14·0
Other paid employment	12·9	10·5
None	53·5	64·9

Note: Percentages total more than 100 since some respondents possessed more than one other business interest. Of the 1000+ acres farmers, 47 individuals held 79 other interests; and of the farmers in the 44 parishes, 20 individuals held 32 other interests.

Moreover, the farmer has the enviable autonomy of being his own boss and often the necessary resources to move around a good deal outside the farm on albeit localized trips to markets, agricultural shows, dealers and so forth. In addition the farmer has available to him what many would view as the intrinsic satisfaction of watching plants and animals grow. It would not be too difficult to present an idyllic view of the farmer's work situation, but set beside this must be the long hours; the poor working conditions, especially in bad weather; the responsibility for the livelihood of the employees; and the worry stemming from the unpredictability of weather, disease, market conditions, etc. While the close relationship between home and work carries its own peculiar advantages it also makes the job impossible to escape from whenever this might be desirable.

In order to provide some comparative information with the data collected on farm workers, all the farmers interviewed were asked a number of questions concerning work satisfaction. In Table 46 there are listed those aspects of farming which our respondents said they most valued. Among the 1000 + acres farmers the most frequently cited aspect was the autonomy or independence which being a farmer conferred. For example:

You're your own boss and you can please yourself. You have responsibilities to undertake.

Being independent and able to take a day off when I want. You are your own boss.

Independence. I enjoy running the business and planning the work. You get a sense of achievement.

Table 46 *Most valued aspects of the farming occupation*

'Can you tell me what aspects of the farming occupation you most value?'

Most valued aspect	1000 + acres (N=105) %	44 parishes (N=57) %
None	1·0	—
Variety	10·5	10·5
Husbandry	21·9	38·6
Outdoor life	11·4	8·8
Stewardship/ownership of a 'piece of England'	3·8	—
Living in the country	7·6	12·3
Other expressive	9·5	3·5
Money	1·0	1·8
Risk/entrepreneurship	11·4	5·3
Autonomy/independence	26·7	24·5
Other instrumental	1·9	—
Way of life/total involvement	9·5	12·3
Sense of achievement	19·0	5·3
D.K./N.A.	5·7	3·5

Note: Percentages total more than 100 since most respondents gave more than one reply.

However, among the farmers in the forty-four parishes the most frequently cited factor concerned husbandry – the intrinsic satisfaction to be gained from watching crops and animals grow. This probably reflected these farmers' greater contact with working the land, as well as their relative lack of independence compared with the large-scale farmers on more than 1000 acres. Some examples of this intrinsic satisfaction are given below:

It's the satisfaction of seeing good crops grow and your cows yielding well. I can't think of anything else which could give the same satisfaction or pleasure.

The closeness to nature – I'm attuned to nature. The sanctity of life it entails. The unexpectedness of it.

Living in the country and producing something where you can see the results of your work. Producing food without which people can't operate.

It's the satisfaction of doing a job well. My MLC records came out at 22 pigs per sow sold. There's not many people can equal that. I get over 3 tons per acre of wheat which means I've joined the 3-ton club. You get a tie.

Overall there was a slight tendency of the 1000+ acres farmers to give more instrumental reasons, 41 per cent of all replies compared with 31·6 per cent in the forty-four parishes; similarly they were less expressive in their replies (64·0 per cent, compared with 73·7 per cent).

We also asked our respondents what they liked least about farming. Their replies are shown in Table 47, and they illustrate once again the greater separation of the large-scale farmers from mundane agricultural labour (they are less likely to cite specific tasks such as mucking out, hedging and ditching, etc.), their greater degree of immunity to economic pressures, but also their greater awareness of, and irritation with, government 'interference' in the agricultural industry. Despite working on average fewer hours per week, the farmers in the forty-four parishes were none the less more prone to cite long and/or awkward working hours. In addition the much greater proportion of 1000+ acres farmers citing office work, despite spending such a large proportion of their time in the office, indicates the degree to which they are frustrated from working out on the land and thus pursuing their occupational identities as farmers. Nevertheless, these data should not be allowed to convey a gloomy view. A substantial number of respondents could find nothing which they particularly disliked about farming and the proportion who had ever seriously thought of leaving farming (still less had actually done anything about it) was 28·1 per cent in the forty-four parishes, and 18·1 per cent of the 1000+ acres farmers. Moreover, when asked whether, if they could go back and start life all over again, they would choose a different occupation, only a very small proportion stated that they would do so (16·2 per cent of the 1000+ acres farmers; 5·3 per cent in the forty-four parishes).

Table 47 *Least valued aspects of the farming occupation*

'. . . And what do you like least?'

Least valued aspects	1000+ acres (N=105) %	44 parishes (N=57) %
Specific farming tasks	3·8	14·0
Long/awkward hours	4·7	19·3
Worry	11·4	10·5
Office work	10·5	1·8
Bad weather	21·9	21·1
Economic pressures/low returns	13·3	21·1
Politics/government interference	19·0	8·8
Other	5·7	3·5
None/no dislikes	17·1	15·8
D.K./N.A.	5·7	5·3

Note: Percentages total more than 100 since most respondents gave more than one reply.

These data can usefully be compared with those collected from farm workers in the forty-four parishes by Newby (1977, Chapter V). The workers were much more inclined to give specific tasks as either their most or least favoured aspect of the job – for example, 'working with machinery' was the most highly valued (20·6 per cent), while specific tasks were mentioned by 28·4 per cent of the workers as being the most disliked aspects of the job. In a very limited way this confirms previous observations on the more limited and pragmatic aspects of working-class culture (Converse, 1965; Mann, 1970). However, it is also clearly related to the subordinate nature of the farm worker's work situation compared with that of the farmer; 'autonomy' as a valued aspect of the job was cited by only 7·7 per cent of the workers. More telling differences emerge when one considers the propensity to leave agriculture. Among the farm workers,

38·2 per cent had seriously thought of leaving (compared with 24·7 per cent of the farmers) and 55 per cent stated that they would not choose to work on the land again if given the chance to do so (compared with 12·1 per cent of farmers).[1] Clearly, therefore, what determines the 'job satisfaction' of the farmers cannot be regarded simply as a function of the job itself but is equally related to their role as property-owners and entrepreneurs (see Chapter 8). For this reason, this chapter will be concerned less with this aspect of the work situation than with the role of the farmer as employer.

Employment practices

So capital-intensive is contemporary arable agriculture that East Anglian farmers are not, by industrial standards, large-scale employers of labour. The average number of full-time, non-family workers in the forty-four parishes was 3·5, rising to 20·3 on the 1000+ acres farms. By agricultural standards, however, those figures are very high (the national average is 1·2), so that, as noted in Chapter 2, East Anglia represents one of the highest regional concentrations of agricultural labour. The distribution of the labour force among the various samples is shown in Tables 48–50. (Since some direct comparisons with data collected from farm workers by Newby will be made later in this chapter information from the HN sample is shown in Table 50.)

The structure of the agricultural labour market was dealt with in some detail by Newby (1977, Chapter III) so that only its main features need to be reiterated here. The geographical extent of the labour market was found by Newby to be highly localized, with over 60 per cent of farm workers in employment located in either the same or a neighbouring parish to that in which they were born. However, the predominantly local nature of the labour market did not mean that agricultural workers were completely sedentary; the pattern was, rather, that of considerable geographical mobility but usually over very short distances indeed, certainly over a range within which the choice of occupation and of employer was extremely limited. Such localization, taken with the sparse spatial distribution of employers in rural areas resulted in a highly particularistic market situation, where employers and employees knew one another – and one another's reputation – on a personal basis before the question of seeking and granting employment arose. As Newby discovered, and as our present research confirmed, agriculture is an occupation in

Table 48 *Type and distribution of farm workers, 1000+ acres sample (N=105)*

Size-groups	Hired full-time workers		Total full-time workers		Hired part-time workers		Total part-time workers	
	% of farms	% of workers	% of farms	% of workers	% of farms	% of workers	% of farms	% of workers
0	—	—	—	—	38·0	—	34·0	—
1	1·0	0·05	—	—	14·6	3·8	16·5	4·2
2–7	18·1	5·2	12·4	3·5	36·9	31·7	36·9	32·6
8–19	50·0	32·6	52·4	28·8	7·7	28·2	7·7	27·7
20–29	14·5	15·9	18·1	21·5	20·0	11·3	2·0	11·1
30+	16·3	46·3	17·1	46·2	2·0	24·9	2·0	24·4
Total	100	100	100	100	100	100	100	100

Table 49 *Type and distribution of farm workers, forty-four parishes sample (N=57)*

Size-groups	Hired full-time workers		Total full-time workers		Hired part-time workers		Total part-time workers	
	% of farms	% of workers	% of farms	% of workers	% of farms	% of workers	% of farms	% of workers
0	34·5	—	32·1	—	71·4	—	66·1	—
1	25·5	7·3	19·6	5·2	17·9	34·5	21·4	40·0
2–7	25·5	25·0	33·9	31·3	10·7	65·5	12·5	60·0
8–19	12·7	54·2	10·7	40·8	—	—	—	—
20–29	1·8	13·6	3·6	22·7	—	—	—	—
30+	—	—	—	—	—	—	—	—
Total	100	100	100	100	100	100	100	100

Table 50 *Type and distribution of farm workers, HN sample (N = 54)*

Size-groups	Hired full-time workers		Total full-time workers		Hired part-time workers		Total part-time workers	
	% of farms	% of workers	% of farms	% of workers	% of farms	% of workers	% of farms	% of workers
0	9·8	—	7·4	—	78·0	—	74·0	—
1	25·5	5·5	22·2	4·4	8·0	19·0	12·0	34·6
2–7	43·1	32·6	42·8	32·7	14·0	81·0	14·0	65·4
8–19	19·6	48·3	18·7	43·0	—	—	—	—
20–29	2·0	13·6	3·8	15·8	—	—	—	—
30+	—	—	—	—	—	—	—	—
Total	100	100	100	100	100	100	100	100

which the personal relationship between employer and employee so predominates that farmers sometimes go to what – by urban standards – seem extraordinary lengths to investigate the 'character' (i.e. private life) of prospective employees who are not familiar to them. This is not necessarily a surreptitious matter (and where a worker can afford to be choosy the process is sometimes reversed), but farmers generally will prefer workers they have known intimately from childhood and remain, as we shall see, somewhat suspicious of formal qualifications and impersonal methods of hiring.

This particularism emerged from information given to Newby concerning the farmers' hiring practices (i.e. by the sample we have termed the 'HN sample' in this study). Informal contact by the farmer accounted for 30·2 per cent of all hirings, with personal application by the worker accounting for a further 35·4 per cent. However, a small minority (15 per cent) of highly trained and specialized workers (e.g. herd managers) were recruited by more universalistic and impersonal methods (30 per cent from press advertising) and greater attention was paid to their formal qualifications. This group, indeed, formed an exception to the overall characterization of the farm worker's market situation – they were highly trained, highly mobile (including many 'spiralists'), highly paid and often participating in a national, or at least regional, labour market. Nevertheless this group is exceptional; in general, as Newby put it, 'The overall typification of the agricultural worker's market situation which emerges from this analysis is one of considerable powerlessness compared with urban, industrial workers' (Newby, 1977, p. 165).

Except on the urban fringe, therefore, farmers remain in a dominant position in the rural labour market. Despite the increasing penetration of many rural areas by urban labour markets, and despite the increasing reluctance of many rural school-leavers to accept the social stigma of working on the land, the continuous mechanization of agriculture, along with other labour-saving devices, has ensured that the demand for labour has accompanied the supply in an ever-decreasing spiral. Moreover, the tied cottage has restricted the outward mobility of labour, particularly among the older age-groups – and over one-half of the agricultural workers in East Anglia are now over the age of forty-five. These factors help to explain why the earnings of agricultural workers are among the lowest in Britain and why, since the Second World War, the average hourly earnings of agricultural workers have deteriorated markedly *vis-à-vis* those of industrial workers. In addition, in East Anglia where there is little industrial competition for labour agricultural workers' earnings are lower than those which prevail in agriculture generally.

Farmers themselves, however, rarely acknowledge that they are in such a dominant position. During our interviews the commonest view, even away from urban areas, was that there was a shortage of labour and that what was available was extremely expensive. This apparent inconsistency can partly be accounted for by the somewhat outdated views which farmers held of what constituted a high wage, perhaps indicating their unfamiliarity with current conditions in the urban industrial situation. We would frequently be told, with some pride and a touch of incredulity, that tractor drivers were now (i.e. in 1974) earning £2500 or even £3000 per year (which included overtime, but excluded the notional value of a tied house), as though this were an astronomic figure. In fact it was below the industrial average. The belief in labour shortages, despite often high local rates of unemployment, probably owed itself to the farmers' desire for quality as opposed to quantity, particularly now that the mechanization of agriculture has resulted in a requirement for a much more skilled labour force than in the past and now that the amount of capital tied up in a piece of farm machinery (such as a combine harvester) is so great that the farmer is less inclined to take a risk in allowing any worker who happens to come along to operate it.[2] This emphasis on quality, it should be added, is regarded mostly as a function of the particular personality qualities of the worker rather than his universalistic qualifications for the job. Thus farmers often possess a particular image of an ideal worker and then seek to find one; their protestations of labour shortages therefore indicate not so much a literal assessment of the state of the labour market as their high (some might say unrealistically high, given the wages they are prepared to pay) ideals (cf. Black, 1968).

Certainly, farmers are in general very suspicious of formal qualifications, except for those involved with highly skilled animal husbandry, and prefer to make their own personal assessment of the worthiness of their prospective employees. We asked our respondents to list the qualities they looked for in applicants for jobs on their farms and followed this with a question as to whether they thought that the possession of formal qualifications made a man a better farm worker. Their replies are summarized in Table 51. Rather surprisingly, given the often highly bureaucratized nature of the 1000 + acres farms, there is little distinction between the two samples. In the majority of cases in both samples hiring practices appear to be highly particularistic and concentrated upon the personal character of the worker. Further probing revealed a familiar catalogue of qualities which would be produced by most employers – honesty, conscientiousness, adaptability, reliability, etc. – as well as their background, experience and ability. The typical way in which farmers operate in the labour market can be better illustrated by selecting some of their own accounts which may be regarded as representative of the general pattern. The following are some examples:

First, you judge the man as a character. Is he a likeable fellow or not? Is the man likely to be dissatisfied or a trouble-maker? Once you've satisfied yourself of that you want a man with initiative, responsibility, especially for livestock men. If a man is to work with machinery he must be familiar with all types of machinery. Stockmen and tractor-drivers must be willing to work weekends and overtime. [Suffolk farmer, 1100 acres.]

Honesty. I always contact the previous employer. This is very important. You can make a lazy man work, but dishonesty causes problems. We also want docile men, because you can rely on them to do as they're told. [Norfolk farmer, 5000 acres.]

Inevitably one goes on impressions of respectability. But I do go to his house to see what his standards are and I'm also interested in the motives he has – why does he want to work for me. I don't want men who are out for money or perks. I'm always interested in men with craft certificates and I never employ a man at a lower level than his capabilities. This causes discontent. [Norfolk agent, 7000 acres.]

I look for a nice family. You have to look at the man as a whole. You must have a happy man and you must look at the wife and children especially when they're going to live in your house. I want a man who'll want to earn money and work overtime; a man who's done well in the army makes a good worker, so do anglers and paper-boys. [Suffolk farmer, 2000 acres.]

Well, *certainly* not bits of paper! Practical working ability is important. We leave the employing of men to the foremen and they usually know who they set on. They get local men. There's a good local grapevine. [Norfolk farmer, 1500 acres.]

I want a man of good appearance with a good work record. Someone with very long hair I would regard as *very* unlikely. References are useless. I'm more interested in what the man says and whether he looks honest. But it is very difficult to judge. [Norfolk farmer, 3000 acres.]

We tend to work on a common-sense basis. We thought of going to professionals to get us a manager, but we couldn't define what we were looking for. Yet we do know who we want when we see him. We want good, steady sloggers and in management straightforward men of intelligence and balance. Sometimes you sense these things. We take it very seriously because it is important. We house them because we want people who are the right people. Certainly a trade certificate of some kind is very important, especially in animal husbandry, but I've got nothing against the man with experience and you can have some people who are over-trained. [Cambridgeshire farmer, 1200 acres.]

Table 51   *Desired characteristics of employees*

'When you have an applicant for a job on your farm, what qualities in him do you look for?'
'Do you think the possession of formal qualifications makes a man a better farm worker?'

Desired qualities	1000+ acres (N=80) %	44 parishes (N=39) %
Character	47·5	48·7
Skill	12·5	10·3
Both character and skill equally	40·0	41·0
Total	100	100

Desirability of formal qualifications	(N=92) %	(N=38) %
Very important or useful	26·1	26·3
Marginally important or useful	16·3	21·1
Irrelevant	38·0	26·3
Important for management only	4·3	2·6
Both qualifications *and* experience important	5·4	10·5
Harmful	9·8	13·2
Total	100	100

Note: All farmers not employing hired workers, together with 'don't knows', have been excluded.

Most farmers, then, operate informally in the labour market and pay attention to formal qualifications only when recruiting highly specialized or managerial employees. The emphasis on the character of the workers is understandable in terms of the strong belief in farming as a practical activity, as something which 'you can't learn from books', but also, as many of these quotations indicate, the degree of personal intimacy between farmer and worker while at work places a premium upon personal compatibility which hardly arises in most industrial settings. In addition, however, it is also apparent that farmers take considerable care to select out any prospective workers who might give them 'trouble' – however this may be defined – so that the workers who are eventually employed are more likely to be conducive to the normative prescriptions which the farmer tries to promote. This forms an important basis for the smooth running of the work situation and the modes of control which the farmer operates within it which will be considered later in this chapter.

The careful selection of a worker who will not cause 'trouble' is regarded by most farmers as being doubly important, for not only does a troublesome worker jeopardize the smooth running of often complex and arduous farming operations, but he is often an inhabitant of an important and costly piece of farm property – a tied cottage. No farmer wishes to see his housing stock vandalized, but since this is a somewhat unlikely possibility as far as most farm workers are concerned, the farmer's caution is directed towards the risk of less obvious sources of trouble. Since many tied cottages are situated on the farm itself (rather than in the local villages) the farmer and his employees live in close proximity to one another and a familiarity with his employees' private lives is often an inevitable consequence of such propinquity. Farmers are therefore able to observe at first hand the close interplay between the condition of the worker's domestic life and his performance at work. A troubled marriage or family life can be seen to affect considerably a worker's efficiency as well as increasing the likelihood that the farmer will be drawn willy-nilly into an involvement with his employee's private affairs. On both counts, therefore, farmers try whenever possible to vet not only the worker's character, but that of his wife, too. A settled marriage and an attentive wife is viewed as both a useful asset of a reliable worker and a guarantee that the farmer is less likely to have to intervene in an unseemly domestic dispute. Hence farmers regard as entirely normal an extensive investigation into the character of prospective employees which would be regarded as remarkable – and slightly offensive – in an urban industrial setting.

The tied cottage is also a key institution in the operation of the labour market, regarded as such by both farmers and farm workers alike. At the time of interviewing, the tied cottage, always a vexed issue, had become highly contentious once more due to the return of a Labour government in 1974 and the later publication of its discussion document on tied cottage abolition (DOE/MAFF, 1975). The arguments for and against changes in the tied cottage system (see Newby, 1977, Chapter III for a summary) were therefore part of a public debate and each week the farming press contained correspondence or a feature article on the relevant issues. It was a debate in which the vast majority of our respondents had a personal interest: only one farmer in the 1000+ acres sample did not possess any tied housing, and only 38·5 per cent in the forty-four parishes, many of whom did not employ any labour in any case. The crux of the case put forward by the abolitionists – principally the NUAAW – was that the tied cottage increased the social and economic dependence of the farm worker on his employer, reducing his social status to that of a serf, whilst economically tying him to agriculture by posing the insurmountable barrier of finding a new house as well as a new job should he wish to move off the land. This produced a 'captive' labour force which led in turn to depressed wages. The NUAAW also gave considerable prominence to the feelings of insecurity which the tied cottage system engendered: while eviction remained possible it was bound to produce an atmosphere of fear, particularly among the old, the sick and the injured, irrespective of the (very low) number of actual evictions which occur each year.

Newby (1977, p. 186) argued that the issue of the tied cottage represented in microcosm the wider issue of class relationships in agriculture. Because the customary divisive issue of wage negotiations had been banished beyond the farm gate in most cases (to the national negotiating body, the Agricultural Wages Board), only the tied cottage remained as a potentially irreconcilable conflict of interest which threatened the generally close and harmonious relationships which employers wished to foster.

The response of agricultural workers to the tied cottage [Newby observed] may therefore follow a similar pattern to varying patterns of class consciousness in general, ranging from outright opposition, through varying degrees of ambiguity, to outright endorsement of the existing system. Nor is this merely a matter of analogy: because the tied cottage involves rights over property, the purchase and disposability of labour and the level of monetary and non-monetary rewards, then class relationships are, because of the peculiar circumstances of agricultural employment, *reducible to* the tied cottage in most cases. In striking a particular attitude towards the tied cottage system, the agricultural worker is therefore saying something, albeit in a modest, restricted and situationally-defined way, about class ideology *tout court*. [ibid.]

Newby discovered that only 49·8 per cent of his sample of farm workers wished to see any changes in the tied cottage system and only 29·6 per cent wanted complete abolition.

If one regards attitudes towards the tied cottage as an indicator of perception of class interests, then it is interesting to compare this situation with the views of the farmers in our samples. There was a total unanimity to retain the tied cottage system, although many of our respondents saw that some changes were necessary in order to attune the system more closely to the exigencies of the modern world. In practice, this meant a system whereby retired farm workers would be guaranteed a council house, while the tied cottage as an institution continued exactly as before. Farmers were committed to the continuation of the tied cottage system because they saw it as an essential part of their ability to function properly as a business. Without being able to offer accommodation, they argued, it would be impossible to attract any labour at all into agriculture. Moreover, the unpredictable and fluctuating nature of farming activity made it imperative that employees, especially stockmen, should live in the immediate vicinity of farm buildings. The tied cottage is therefore viewed as being not only essential but inevitable, particularly given the chronic shortage of council houses in rural areas. For these reasons, whatever the minor defects of the system, there is simply no realistic alternative – if it were abolished it would render incalculable harm to British agriculture and leave the farm worker worse off than before. Agitation for abolition is merely the ignorant meddling of politically motivated agitators, often from outside the industry. The following examples are fairly typical:

A lot depends on the farmer and farm workers concerned. Frankly I don't see what's all that wrong with the system. It saves us a lot of income tax in that farm wages would have to go up if tied cottages didn't exist – the state loses there. But food prices stay down. It's not a bad economic proposition for anyone because it helps keep prices down. The crunch comes at the end of a man's service. No one minds a rent-free house, but what happens when a man retires? And here the importance of the individual farmer comes in. Do you look after him or try and get him out? We try and help people get a council house. We have houses for all our employees, including the mechanics and the builders and the blacksmiths, so we're finding it difficult to get accommodation for all of them, but the country planners don't like us to build more houses because they seem to think I shall sell them at a later date. Nor do they see the need to provide housing for everyone, but I do. I've written long letters about this to the council but to no avail. So we've bought on the open market and that can't be good for anybody. I did once have to resort to legal action. I didn't want to, but I had a herdsman who was still in the house one and a half years after leaving the farm, and herdsmen, of course, need to be close at hand so we wanted the house. We went to the courts. The man concerned wasn't awkward – he just couldn't find anywhere else to live. The council moved when we moved and he got a house. But we aren't beastly about it. If we were, it would get around. [Cambridgeshire farmer, 1200 acres.]

I've only once had to tell a man that if he didn't like his job, he'd have to leave the house. Since that day he's never upset me. But I don't like to use it as a means of persuasion. Employees don't realize the cost of rented housing on the open market. [Suffolk farmer, 1300 acres.]

Agriculture is too political and Labour politicians are too hypocritical. There are other industries which have tied cottages. I don't believe good farm workers have any problems. A good farm worker can choose from any of thousands of jobs. Just look at the vacancies in the farming press: it's the bad ones who face problems when they're sacked. Some men only take farm work to get the house. I think in many ways the tied cottage is essential. For example, when we're combining and we decide to work until dark instead of finishing at six, it's easy to contact the wives and let them know. The whole system depends on the attitude between boss and men. Personal contact's the thing. [Norfolk farmer, 1200 acres.]

The most disinterested opinion which any farmer would express was that in an ideal world, there should be no tied cottages, but that under present circumstances there was no doubt that it was a necessity. One or two farmers even complained about the amount of capital that was tied up in their housing stock. Nevertheless all were adamant that it must be retained. The following answer – which, it must be emphasized, is a minority view – is typical of this attitude:

If I could run my farm successfully without them, the sooner I could get rid of them the better. They're a liability. All that capital tied up! They're worth at least £7000 each and we'd love to sell them. All my workers wouldn't come if I had no tied cottages. I've built houses specifically for them. I'd prefer to lend them money to buy their own, but they prefer the tied cottage. Yet here there's no sort of feeling to being tied to the job. [Suffolk farmer, 2500 acres.]

There is little doubt that the majority of farmers operate the tied cottage system as humanely as circumstances will allow. Many are fully aware of their responsibilities to their workers, particularly elderly or retired workers, and do not use the tied cottage as a weapon with which to keep their workers in line. Rather it is a carrot which they dangle in front of them in order to persuade them to take a lower-paid job than elsewhere. Unfortunately, no matter how humane the individual farmer may be, circumstances often demand that he threaten the tied cottage tenant with eviction, especially on the smaller farms where the housing stock is usually insufficiently large to carry retired workers and where the house is essential to attract a replacement. The threat of eviction is therefore by no means as idle as many farmers would like to believe: among the 1000 + acres sample, for example, 42·3 per cent had at some time used legal action to remove tenants (12·5 per cent of which were 'colluded' cases where a mock 'eviction' was arranged to force the local council's hand). Although, it should be emphasized, such legal action was much less drastic than actual eviction – usually the conveyance of a solicitor's letter and/or a possession order – we would nevertheless estimate that over one in three of farms employing labour engage in such action (cf. Irving and Hilgendorf, 1975, p. 48) so that the insecurity which the tied cottage generates among farm workers cannot be dismissed lightly.

Such is the dependence of the individual farm worker on the farmer for both employment and housing, therefore, that he is usually powerless to bring about an improvement in his plight through his own efforts (Newby, 1977, Chapter III). Moreover such is the scattered nature of farm employment that it is extremely difficult for farm workers to combine to force an improvement in their pay and conditions collectively. The trade union, the NUAAW, has found it no easier to escape these constraints than the individual farm worker (see Newby, 1977, Chapter IV). It has found it impossible to bring about the kind of drastic improvement in farm workers' conditions of employment that would place them on a par with industrial workers and has been disinclined to engage in militant action in the pursuit of its claims. The NUAAW hardly represents a threat to the farmer, therefore. Among our respondents, only 12·4 per cent of the 1000 + acres farmers were hostile to the NUAAW and 44·3 per cent were positively favourable towards it; in the forty-four parishes, the respective proportions were 19·3 per cent and 45·6 per cent. Nor could this be accounted for by a sympathy with trade unions generally; indeed most farmers were extremely hostile to trade unions – 71·7 per cent among the 1000 + acres farmers and 82·0 per cent in the forty-four parishes (see Chapter 7 below). One cannot help but conclude that the reason why most farmers are not hostile to the NUAAW is that it is so ineffective (for whatever reason) in fighting for its members' interests. Again, some of our respondents' comments bring this out most clearly:

They're trying to do the best for their membership that they can, but they're such a small battalion, like the NFU. It's the day of mob rule. You can see that at your university. Farmers and farm workers are in such a small minority they can't shout loud enough. [Suffolk farmer, 100 acres.]

I'm all in favour of it! I've got the local branch secretary on my farm and he's the most reasonable man I've got. It's a fine union. Doesn't do the farm workers much good. [Essex farmer, 1200 acres.]

Anyone working for us can join the union. We have the local branch secretary working for us and we give him time off with pay to attend union conferences and so on. We like to try and work in with the union rather than against it. [Suffolk farmer, 8000 acres.]

All our men are members of the union, but the union seems to be an irrelevance. The farm workers work in intimate involvement with the farmers and this militates against unionization. [Norfolk farm manager, 5000 acres.]

Until just very recently I thought it was very responsible and had the utmost respect. But now it's got into the hands of militants, especially Joan Maynard. Now Collison was quite a statesman, but from the workers' point of view very ineffective. [Essex farm manager, 14000 acres.]

For the most part, therefore, this relationship between the farmer and his employees is undisturbed by the decisive intervention of the NUAAW. The corollary of this is that the powerlessness of the farm worker is entirely unmitigated by any intervention in the labour market: it is the market which determines, one way or another, what the farm worker's level of rewards shall be (see Cowling *et al.*, 1970, p. 85). That farm workers are among the lowest paid workers in British society (see Newby, 1972*a*; 1977, Chapter III) is indicative of their continuing dependence. The low pay of the farm worker is, indeed, something of an embarrassment to many farmers. Their economic instincts teach them to pay no more than the market demands, yet their social responsibilities for their employees equally demand that they look after their workers as best they can. The implications of this will be explored later in this chapter, but here we may merely note that the apparent contradiction between these two aspects of their role as employers makes farmers extremely defensive when discussing wages in agriculture. They are acutely aware of a gap between their principles and their actions and nothing seems to excite such a collective guilty conscience among farmers as their relationships with their workers, particularly the issue of pay. Thus 71·4 per cent of the 1000 + acres farmers and 77·8 per cent of the sample in the forty-four parishes agreed that farm workers' wages were unjustly low. However, the blame for this was primarily attached to the cheap food policy of successive governments since the war, which held down returns to farmers and farm workers alike. While this argument must be treated with some scepticism – farmers in East Anglia are among the most prosperous in the country while farm workers' wages are among the lowest and it is the lack of alternative employment rather than an inability to pay which keeps wages down (Newby, 1972*a*) – it performs a useful social function in both providing a plausible explanation to the workers which absolves the farmer of responsibility, and expiating the farmers' collective guilt by invoking a scapegoat which is far removed from the farm and is in no position to answer back (see also Chapter 7).

In many respects, of course, the most interesting aspect of the farmers' attitudes towards their employees' pay is the fact that they are unwilling to explain the level of wages by reference to their entrepreneurial role and the operation of market factors. Farmers are not charity organizations and the fact that the state of the rural labour market, the tied cottage and weak unionization conspire to depress wages need not be hidden beneath intricate and complex explanations about how they wished they could pay more but for a variety of reasons are unable to do so. Farmers are so powerful in the labour market that in one sense they have no need to resort to such explanations. But in another sense, of course, they are essential. All farmers are instinctively aware of the fact that they need to cultivate the identification of their employees rather than rely entirely upon their dependence. A pleasant and harmonious working relationship, particularly in an occupation like agriculture where workers are granted such workplace autonomy, is not only desirable but essential: a labour force which grudgingly works under the threat of sanctions is of no use to any farmer. Thus the low wages of the farm worker need to be 'explained away' in a manner which will leave this identification intact. This serves to show that while the dependence of the farm worker forms a basis for this identification it *is* only a basis. The conditions which promote such dependence do not in themselves create the necessary identification. In addition the farmer must constantly try to cultivate the desired relationship with the employees and interpret their situation to them in a way which is commensurate with the smooth running of the farm. The mechanisms by which this is achieved can now be explored in some detail.

Maintaining the deferential dialectic

How is the identification of farm workers to be retained, given the hierarchical authority structure of the farm and the highly inegalitarian distribution of rewards between employer and employees? This is the key problem which underlies the daily dealings of a farmer with his workers. On the one hand it would be possible for the farmer to rely purely upon a contractual bargain, reduce the relationship with his workers to purely that of cash nexus and rely upon the size of the pay packet to obtain their identification. As one farmer put it:

The involvement largely ends at the farm gate. I don't have a friendship relationship with anyone here. Personal relationships and business relationships don't mix. After all, I don't expect my doctor to be a personal friend.

Such contractual relationships can be contrasted with a much more common pattern: the employer who extends his involvement beyond the work situation through a complex web of paternalistic authority. For example:

You have to have the right relationship with your men. All my men are really interested in the work. We give them a day's outing once a year, give them a pound each, give them port and sherry at Christmas, a gold watch at thirty years and a party. I'm a great believer in looking after the men. . . . We gave our foreman a Mini car when he retired. . . . I visit their homes and make sure everything is O.K. The men know when management cares.

One aspect of the farmer's relationship with his workers is therefore the *content* of the normative prescriptions which he offers, by which the relationship is to be interpreted and regulated. However, equally important is the *structure* of the work situation which will largely determine the efficacy with which these prescriptions may be communicated to the workers and the extent to which they have access to, and are capable of supporting, other interpretations of their situation than those offered by their employer. We shall examine each of these in turn.

As we noted in Chapter 1, the conditions most favourable to the growth of stable paternalist rule are those exemplified by Coser's notion of a 'greedy institution' (Coser, 1974; Newby, 1976). The personal aspects of traditionalism imply that it is most effective on the basis of face-to-face contact, a condition to which most farms obviously correspond. Moreover an element of totality is of considerable importance, for it will ensure that access to other sources of legitimacy than those offered by the paternalist employer will be difficult to obtain. Once again the social situation of many farm workers, particularly those living in tied housing, remains a total one. Such a total social situation immediately confers upon farmers a considerable advantage when it comes to trying to cultivate the identification of their workers, and of encouraging a 'team' or 'family' atmosphere among their workforce. Where workers live on the farm, the pervasive contact between employer and employee provides ample opportunities for such personal identification to proceed; but even where workers live off the farm farmers may try to extend personal ties beyond the work situation and into the local community. We shall examine the role of the farmer in the local community in more detail in the following chapter, but here we may merely note that the involvement of the farmer in the life of his workers outside the work situation may be regarded as a key indicator of attempts to gain the identification of workers by traditional, paternalist means.

While it is possible to argue that traditional authority is the most stable form of the legitimation of power (Weber, 1964; Newby, 1975, 1976), it is clear that by no means all farmers wish to pursue such traditionalism, or indeed are able to do so. For farmers, while remaining somewhat culturally isolated from the mainstream of British society, have increasingly divested themselves of the cult of the gentlemanly amateur and adopted instead an air of professional expertise – a change dictated by both wider cultural changes in British society and by the exigencies of the modern, scientifically-based business of agriculture. Against this, however, is the fact that the diminution of the labour force and the growing proportion living in tied housing have enabled a much greater degree of personal contact to ensue between farmers and workers and thus provided the conditions for such traditionalism to prosper. This indicates that farmers to some extent have a considerable choice over how they wish to maintain their authority over their workforce. Many continue successfully to do so by engaging in traditional forms of authority outside the work situation.

In general, a majority of farmers stated that they were involved in the life of their workers, but there are also significant differences between the samples. The so-called 'size-effect' (Ingham, 1970) does not operate in a straightforward manner since among both farmers and their wives there is less involvement on the smaller farms in the forty-four parishes than on the larger farms in the 1000+ acres sample. This is partly due to the smaller farmers ceasing to possess the wherewithal to exercise paternalism – for example, a large tied housing stock, the ability to offer various perquisites, the time and resources to engage in home visits, charity, etc. Moreover, not all such examples of involvement are prompted by the farmer: where a worker perceives his employer to be sufficiently influential he may approach him over a whole variety of personal matters, ranging from help with his children's education, arranging hire purchase for consumer durables, completion of tax forms and a myriad of other examples of personal aid which will obviously be weighted towards the larger, more recognizably educated – and locally powerful – farmers. However, there may be a structural explanation of such differences which we shall elaborate later in this chapter.

One manner in which farmers, particularly in the 1000+ acres sample, attempt to obtain the identification of their employees is thus to enter into a web of paternalistic relationships outside the work situation itself. We shall consider this in more detail in Chapter 5. Within the work situation, however, farmers also attempt to manage their workers not only in an organizational sense, but ideologically through providing definitions of the situation and transmitting a series of values and beliefs which are conducive to social harmony on the farm.[3] With this in mind we asked our respondents what, in their view, was the best way to handle workers on the farm. The replies often contained a whole variety of recipes, many of them highly idiosyncratic and applicable only to a particular farm or even a particular worker. Such particularism is hardly surprising, and, indeed, given the prevalence of traditionalism indicated above, very predictable. However, it makes the data unamenable to quantification, so that instead of presenting them in a tabular form we shall draw upon the major themes of the farmers' comments and illustrate these themes liberally with their own words. We were not only interested in a static picture of labour relations in agriculture, however, for we also asked our respondents how (if at all) relationships between farmers and farm workers had changed since they began farming.[4]

Overwhelmingly the recipe for good labour relations advocated by the farmers that we interviewed could be summed up in two words: good communications. They emphasized the need to provide a constant interpretation of the work situation in a way that would reinforce harmony and identification. So that the workers could 'properly understand' the situation there was also an emphasis on personal contact.

My father taught me to discuss everyday problems with the men. They are not unintelligent: they know their jobs and have a lot to offer. I can always talk to the men and they can always come to me. Mutual discussion is the key. [Cambridgeshire farmer, 1200 acres.]

How to handle the workers? Make sure they're fully in possession of the facts and what you're trying to achieve. For example, I've just bought two new combine harvesters. Both of them are in the barn. I'd just heard that they'd gone up in price, so I told my men, 'If you found there's two new Rolls-Royces and they're yours, what would you do? Well – there's two new combines out there which cost as much as Rolls-Royces and you're being given them to drive.' You've got to put it in terms they'll understand. [Norfolk farmer, 1200 acres.]

The pursuit of good communications frequently extends to consultation over everyday working matters. Indeed for those farmers who could remember conditions before the war, the growth of informal consultation, replacing the old authoritarian regime, was regarded as the most fundamental change.

Father can remember when there were many men out of work. It was quite feudal in those days, but now the boot is turned. We don't have industry's problems, we have more respect for the men now. My father's generation just sacked men. We have to be more careful and get a good relationship with the men, which is what I have. But it goes deeper than that, we have more respect for each other. It's a two-sided relationship. [Suffolk farmer, 1100 acres.]

Yes, things have changed. You have to handle men more carefully because a good man can get a job anywhere. Before the war men were regularly sacked and so they jumped to it. But now you have to be careful and it makes things difficult. [Norfolk farm manager, 8000 acres.]

The reasons for these changes are manifold. One, as is indicated by the last comment given above, is the change in the labour market situation today, compared with the Depression. 'It's all a question of supply and demand', as one farmer put it. Additionally, however, farmers have been forced to move with the times and the growth of citizenship among farm workers and of a more democratic ethos in society generally has necessitated some kind of adaptation among employers.

Relationships have changed, especially on the owner-occupied farms· There's much less paternalism now. Workers are more independent· Farmers have stopped trying to change the workers, stopped trying to make them conform to a set life-style. It does still happen around here, but even my boss allows the workers to put Labour posters in their windows now. Farmers realise now that the men aren't fools and the men won't put up with interference outside working hours. The farmers have learned while the men have asserted. [Norfolk farm manager, 2000 acres.]

These two factors are, of course, interrelated: the farm workers' market situation has often determined the speed of their acquisition of citizenship and other rights. Within the work situation, however, the massive change in farm technology has itself brought about far-reaching changes in the relationship between farmers and farm workers. It has conferred upon farm workers far more workplace autonomy, while also giving him control over an expensive farm investment (Newby, 1972*b*; 1977, Chapter V). In these circumstances no farmer wants a disgruntled worker driving out of the farmyard to begin his day's work: farmers are thus prepared to accept some 'give and take' over the organization of everyday farming activities. The farmer will, of course, expect – and usually be allowed – the 'last word' but equally the worker will expect to be consulted. Thus, in a variety of ways, many of our respondents echoed the farmer cited above who compared his combine harvesters with Rolls-Royces.

It may just be local but we have gone away from an orders situation to a talk-back situation, which is very healthy. I'm all in favour of craftsmen and there's no doubt that those who do the job know more of the detail than the managers. You *tell* the men *when* to do jobs, but you *ask* the men how to do them. [Cambridgeshire farmer, 1200 acres.]

There's a much closer relationship between farmers and farm workers because both sides know what's at stake – a great deal of money. We have four or five farm meetings a year which are supposed to be two-sided, although it's usually me talking a great deal to them about what goes on. I impress upon them the prices of goods and products. . . . I show trust in them. [Suffolk farmer, 1700 acres.]

Employer–employee relationships are not so autocratic now. We see the men every Christmas for a meal and a drink and we talk the year over. . . . They know what we have to pay for the machinery they use. [Norfolk farmer, 1000 acres.]

Such consultation makes it even more imperative that farm workers possess a set of beliefs and values which will not lead them to be uncooperative. (Indeed, contained within the consultative process there is often the transmission of such values by the farmer.) Our respondents referred to this bundle of values and beliefs which they wished to promote by a number of metaphors, most commonly involving the creation in the work situation of a 'team', 'family', 'community' or, less emotively, 'partnership'. By this they meant a strong sense of identification with the aims and methods of the farming enterpise and, at the personal level, a sense of stable harmony, cooperation, shared pleasure in the work and *Gemeinschaft*. The following are examples:

Farm workers are very much more equals now. Independence is very important to us all. None of us want to be one of 20000 at Ford's. It's the same for me as it is for one of my tractor drivers and so we establish a sense of partnership. You use Christian names and make them feel part of the business. [Norfolk farmer, 5000 acres.]

Managers are responsible for making sure the men are well looked after and have time to themselves. We have good personal relationships and pay the men while they are sick, lend them money and so on. We want to create a community, a secure and happy framework for their lives. That's the job of a farm. We even have our own football team and so on, we have parties. This all helps the social situation of the farm. The best way to handle workers is to give a sense of pride in the job. . . . We encourage them to take pride in what they do. We also encourage team spirit and working together. [Suffolk farmer, 3700 acres.]

Once the correct team spirit is inculcated, of course, then the whole system will run reasonably smoothly. Farmers will be pleased to consult their workers for they will usually be given the advice they want to hear. Moreover the workers will themselves suggest improvements in the running of the farm of which the farmer, who is perhaps removed from the daily experience of actual working conditions, may be unaware. As a farm manager pointed out:

I never talk to them as a group, but always as individuals. Talking to them is important for me. I can't work any other way. I often ask for their opinions and they usually agree with what I would have said but feel it is their idea. Some men like to be involved in decision-making.

One candid farmer also disclosed his secret of good labour relations as follows:

Farm workers are a funny lot. They like to feel they're part of the place, but you've also got to be boss. So what you do is make sure you can have a quiet word with them, then you can sow a few seeds in their minds. You say one day you're thinking of doing something in such-and-such a way and then you don't talk about it again. Then a few weeks later you say to them that you're thinking of doing such-and-such and you ask them how they think it should be done. Then they'll tell you the way you told them a few weeks before, but now they think it's *their* idea. So you take them up on it and they feel involved and that they've contributed to the farm. That way they're happy and they probably wouldn't have done it if I'd ordered them straight out. It sounds bad, I know, but that's how it works.

Most farmers implicitly recognize, however, that the extension of such a complete ideological hegemony in the work situation is a difficult, and even an impossible, matter. The farm worker, even when living on the farm, is never completely isolated from disruptive influences outside. Indeed, the 'greedy institution', which many employers would like to create of their farm and locality has been successively undermined as the twentieth century has proceeded. This has created added difficulties which a number of farmers acknowledged. One farmer on 200 acres in Suffolk for example, attributed a deterioration in labour relations to:

Unionisation caused by low pay and television. This television is a hell of a thing. Ninety-nine per cent of those who watch TV are influenced. Men get disturbed. They can't help themselves when they see Scargill, Foot and company. . . . I'm becoming less and less involved with my men. They come in in the mornings with long faces. I feel like saying, 'Don't you enjoy coming in to work in the mornings?'

Against the encroachment of such alien influences, farmers feel relatively powerless for those which are most frequently cited – the mass media, the workings of the 1944 Education Act, the weakening of the work ethic wrought by the welfare state – are often a product of centralized government legislation. However, a more surmountable, if not entirely tractable, barrier to 'good communications' often lies in the organizational structure of the farm itself – and this is something which farmers can, and do, go about combating.

Almost all farmers subscribe to Lord Percy's dictum, cited in Chapter 1, that they can 'manage men with whom they can talk'. They therefore place a premium on being able to enter into personal and pervasive interaction with them, partly because an awareness of them as individuals enables farmers to cope with their foibles:

You have to treat men as individuals. You have to know your men and their moods and their ways. Establish a good personal relationship and listen to them and their ideas. There's no one way – you have to know each man and his strengths and weaknesses. They're all individuals and you treat them therefore as they need to be treated. One likes abuse, another likes persuasion. [Cambridgeshire farmer, 3500 acres.]

Problems of contact occur, however, where the scale of the farming business requires a number of intermediaries, such as foremen and/or managers, between the farmer and his workers. Here face-to-face interaction becomes highly attenuated and there is a consequent risk that workers may lose their identification with the farm and subscribe to more oppositional values. This particularly applies to the most pervasive and continuous form of contact – through working along-side each other around the farm. Table 52 shows how the frequency of this decreases as the levels of hierarchy in the farm organization proliferate. The absence of the employer from the work situation,

Table 52 *Frequency of working alongside employees against levels of hierarchy in organization of farm*[5]

Frequency of working alongside employees	Levels of hierarchy			
	Two (N=73) %	Three (N=59) %	More than three (N=39) %	All farms (N=171) %
Regularly	65·8	11·9	15·4	35·7
Occasionally	24·7	27·1	23·1	25·1
Rarely	2·7	33·9	41·0	22·2
Never	6·8	27·1	20·5	17·0
Total	100	100	100	100

together with the larger number of workers on the more bureaucrati-cally organized farms, is thus regarded as a hindrance to the kind of attitudes among the workforce which the farmer may wish to engender. As one Suffolk farmer observed,

I find the most dangerous times are when the men are working together. Mucking out and doing sugar beet, they get talking together and start grumbling.

It is in this respect that recent changes in the work situation have come to the aid of so many farmers. Mechanization has both reduced the number of workers on farms, allowing many of them to de-bureaucratize, and it has reduced the opportunities for those workers who have remained to work alongside each other under conditions that allow easy communication (Newby, 1977, Chapter V). This has enabled farmers to become much closer to their workers in the work situation.

When I was a boy my father had over twenty men on 700 acres. I've got six men on 1200. That's the difference. I've got very close to them. . . . [Essex farmer, 1200 acres.]

On those farms which are still sufficiently large to support a bureau-cratic structure, however, problems of non-contact remain. Never-theless many of these employers are not only very aware of the risks inherent in this situation, but take considerable care to do what they can to avoid them.

Relationships are polarising now. It's more an us-and-them attitude. But then factory conditions create factory problems. It's amazing how quickly trouble can brew up. The best way to handle workers, then, depends on farm size. With two or three workers, that's fairly easy to cope with, you can be personal, but the more employees you have, the more you have to take a harder line, otherwise people tend to take advantage. You have to make more rules and more conditions. [Norfolk farm manager, 10000 acres.]

The larger you get, the more labour problems you get. You need good labour relations if you are to progress. The bigger you get the more difficult it is to motivate people and keep them involved. But this is the only real problem of size – farming will become more like industry in this respect. [Norfolk farm manager, 7000 acres.]

On the large farms such is the awareness of this problem that many employers take considerable steps to try to mitigate the consequences, and this would seem to account for the *higher* degree of involvement in the lives of workers outside the course of work. One farmer, who had recently been removed from frequent contact with his workers owing to the increased scale of the business following an amalgama-tion with neighbouring properties, exemplified this approach:

I now have a manager, whereas I was my own manager before. Therefore I no longer see every man every day and I now don't see them for four to five days. This is where farming, if it's not careful, will meet the same problems as industry. I have a roster to see people every so often. My secretary makes sure I stick to it. I hope it's not obvious, but it is necessary to keep in touch.

On the small farms, however, contact in the work situation is often so continuous that there is no need, or even desire, to continue it outside. As one Suffolk farmer put it,

Their private lives are theirs, and I must keep away or else it will restrict them. Of course they live in my houses but I try not to interfere unless they do unsavoury things. We see enough of each other at work.

This last comment indicates how delicate a matter maintaining the desirable state of labour relations may be. While farmers take considerable trouble to cultivate the identification of their employees, they also recognize that they must not overdo it. For on occasions over-identification may create as many problems as opposition. The farmer, after all, must remain in charge of the farm. He expects and demands the last word, and ultimately the structure of the relationship with his workers, however matey its content, is an extremely hierarchical one. The farmer cannot therefore allow this identification to go too far: he has his authority to maintain. Rather he must convey the correct mixture of social intimacy and social distance which will enable the exercise of his authority to proceed smoothly (Newby, 1975). Much of this involves the ostensibly petty nuances of behaviour – demeanour rather than articulated speech (Goffman, 1973). However, some of our respondents voiced the necessity of 'drawing the line' between authority and mateship in transacting their labour relations.

Some farmers still think men must do exactly as they are told, but we believe in giving men responsibility. Farm workers are the most adaptable and flexible men in industry and our men get at least £2000 a year and a free house. Mind you, I'm not saying you don't have to be autocratic now and again. I remember one case involving a foreman who lived in one of the farm houses. We were introducing a manager and we wanted him to have the house. It was absolutely necessary for him to be there at the centre of things. Now it was no use my being namby-pamby about the change. I told the foreman that we'd build him a new bungalow but that he'd have to move into temporary accommodation until it was completed. He wasn't happy, but I know it was best for him in the long run. Sometimes you have to think of them as children – they don't always know what's best, so you have to be autocratic about things. We had a lot of trouble, but he's happy now in his bungalow. He did have a nervous breakdown, in fact, but he's fine now and really enjoys working for the manager. [Cambridgeshire farmer, 1100 acres.]

At one level I'm not involved at all. I tell them, 'It may be my house, but it's your home', and I only go in at their invitation. I'd never talk politics other than with their consent. I try to keep out of their lives. Privacy is important. At another level I'm very involved because I know that if a man has family troubles – if he's unhappy – then he won't work well. Fifty-two humans depend on this business. That's what it's about – a happy life for fifty-two people. Therefore I am concerned, but I don't interfere. [Suffolk farmer, 750 acres.]

[You should treat workers] as human beings, as equals, diplomatically. You get the best by knowing their strengths. You must never embarrass them and never give orders, always *ask*. Never ask them to do something you can't do, but you make sure they work hard and know you're the boss. I try and discuss jobs with them and let them do things their way as far as possible. But sometimes they're a bit too conscientious. The other day one of my men wanted to change the oil on the combine harvester half-way through harvest. I said, 'Bugger the combine harvester! You get on with the harvesting.' [Suffolk farmer, 2500 acres.]

It is thus apparent that maintaining the tension between identification and differentiation in employer–employee relationships on the farm often requires some skill in being able to strike the correct balance. Hence a pervasive personal relationship is required for such management to be effective rather than its mediation through impersonal abstractions or rules. It is in this sense that the 'size-effect' must be understood, for bureaucratization involves a decreasing efficacy of traditional authority as the opportunities for personal contact are reduced. However, as the above examples illustrate only too clearly, the exigencies of producing for a market are always likely to break through such niceties when the situation demands it. This factor should not be overlooked, for while the foregoing has been concerned with the sources of stability in agricultural labour relations these relationships remain underpinned by economic factors. But the point is that few farmers are willing to rely upon market relationships alone. The Essex farmer who said of his workers, 'We pay them to work and that's all' was very much in a minority. Much more common were those who would prefer not to be quite so involved with their workers, but who wearily resigned themselves to the inevitability of it in the cause of good labour relations. As one Suffolk farmer put it,

It's one of the drawbacks of farming. You're too involved with the men's families because they live with you on the farm. I don't like it, but on the other hand it does mean you never get strikes.

A typology of farmers

In conclusion to this chapter it is possible to develop a typology of farmers based upon key aspects of their market and work situations. In Chapter 3 we noted that while all farmers produce for the market, by no means all farmers behave in what we termed a 'market-oriented' manner. For many, farming continues to be as much an expressive and affective form of activity – a 'way of life' – as an instrumental one of making money. Market sensitivity therefore varies between those whose primary interest in farming is a certain life-style, in which agriculture itself may be of only minor significance, and those who could be considered first and foremost as business entrepreneurs who happen to be in the business of growing crops and rearing animals. We have also noted that farm size *per se* is only imperfectly related to market sensitivity: though market conditions may be such that bigger generally means better in terms of rates of return on capital investment by no means all large farms were more market-oriented, nor did farmers generally believe that increasing size in itself connoted a more market-oriented approach. However, as the size of enterprise increases farmers are forced to bureaucratize in the sense of introducing intermediary levels of authority in the farm organization between employer and employee, thus removing the farmer from pervasive and personal contact with his workers. We have demonstrated in this chapter how many such farmers, aware of the dangers which such tendencies represent to the fostering of harmonious labour relations, have taken steps to counteract this by making a conscious effort to extend a system of paternalistic authority both within the work situation and outside. However, this itself suggests that farmers have an ability to choose the legitimating strategies which they wish to operate. Some highly market-oriented farmers, for example, may be unwilling to expend resources on what they would regard as an outmoded paternalism – although it should be emphasized that there is in principle no necessary conflict between market orientation and paternalism since the latter may turn out to be a cheap form of labour control, cheaper, for instance, than paying high wages; rather it is likely that the values that produce high market orientation also tend to coincide with a disdain for paternalism.

Taking the degree of direct involvement in husbandry and the degree of market orientation together, it is therefore possible to derive a typology of farmers which helps to explain some of the observed differences in attitudes and behaviour among our various samples. This typology is shown in Figure 8.

		Market orientation	
		Low	High
Degree of direct involvement in husbandry	Low	1. Gentleman farmer	2. Agri-businessman
	High	3. Family farmer	4. Active managerial farmer

Figure 8   *Typology of East Anglian farmers*

Cell 1 consists of farmers whose orientation to the market is low and who take little direct part in the actual farming operations of their enterprise. Indeed even the managerial functions may be delegated to a hired manager or agent. In our sample such farmers consist mostly of traditional landowners, primarily concerned with maintaining a distinctive life-style involving many of the traditional gentlemanly pursuits of hunting, shooting, civic involvement, charitable activity and so on. We have followed a familiar colloquialism by dubbing such farmers 'gentleman farmers'.[6]

Cell 2 consists of farmers whom we have called, slightly corrupting an American expression, 'agri-businessmen'. By this term we do not just mean the narrower American usage which describes the penetration of agriculture by food processing and other industrial corporations in a process of vertical integration, although in East Anglia such enterprises are included in the category. Rather we mean farmers, whether individuals or companies, who regard agriculture as primarily a means of making money and regard the farmer's expertise as lying in administration and financial accounting rather than in husbandry. This category includes some of the largest farming companies in Britain and collectively their proportion of national agricultural output far exceeds their numerical significance (for examples, see Beresford, 1975).

Cell 3 consists of the farmer who spends most of his time working on the land himself, working alongside his employees where hired workers are engaged or quite frequently relying solely upon the labour of himself and his family. The major concern of such family farmers is to maintain an equitable degree of profitability (and, by

extension, standard of living), rather than go for profit maximization
with the attendant extra work, increased risk, extended borrowing
and greater capitalization that this would often involve. 'Keeping the
name on the land' (Arensberg and Kimball, 1968) is therefore as
much a goal as obtaining a maximum rate of return on capital
invested. Such 'family' farmers have been well documented in the
sociological literature (e.g. Rees, 1950; Williams, 1956, 1964;
Nalson, 1968; Jenkins, 1971). They dominate the farming economy
of the pastoral areas of Britain, but even in East Anglia, while they
do not typify the agriculture of the region, they commonly exist in
the interstices between the larger farming enterprises.

Cell 4 consists of a group of farmers whom we have termed 'active
managerials'. They form a group which is highly instrumental and
market-oriented in its approach to agriculture but they continue to
be closely involved in the husbandry of their farms. They are not
simply desk-bound administrators but have a high degree of technical and agricultural expertise and often an innovatory approach to
agricultural technology. They spend a great deal of their time out and
about on the land, personally supervising and being involved in the
day-to-day farming operations and dealing with cropping and livestock problems as they arise. They may indeed, take a pride in being
able to 'turn their hand' to any job on the farm and will be scornful
of those 'armchair' farmers who cannot.[7]

The distribution of these four types of farmers within our samples
is shown in Table 53. This is shown in order to provide a context for
the analysis which follows. It should be emphasized that we are *not*
making any claims about the representativeness of our samples in

Table 53 *Distribution of types of farmers among 1000+ acres,
forty-four parishes and HN sample*

Type of farmer	Sample 1000+ acres (N=105) %	44 parishes (N=57) %	HN (N=54) %
Gentleman	30·5	14·0	27·8
Agri-businessman	54·3	12·3	14·8
Family	—	56·1	40·7
Active managerial	15·2	17·5	16·7
Total	100	100	100

terms of the four ideal-types and that these proportions can therefore be extended beyond our samples. Such claims would clearly be ridiculous in view of the highly distinctive nature of East Anglian agriculture, the selectivity of one of our samples (1000+ acres) and the non-random nature of another (HN). Rather what we are looking for is not the absolute level of representation of these types among our respondents, but the systematic variation between them that can be attributed to their location in the typology. We shall proceed by considering those variables which have been dealt with in this and the previous two chapters.[8] How far location in this typology affects the nature of the farmer's relationships with other members of the local social system outside the farm will be considered in succeeding chapters.

There were some significant differences between the four types of farmers in terms of their general social backgrounds. Our data confirmed common observation in that both gentleman farmers and family farmers tended to be more local in their backgrounds (though how far this is matched by a 'local' orientation will be taken up in Chapter 5). For example, both types of farmers tended to be born in the immediate locality (in the same or neighbouring parish). By far the most geographically mobile were agri-businessmen although this was *not* accompanied by any pattern of occupational mobility. This suggests a link between geographical mobility and economic instrumentality which reflects findings among manual workers, most notably in *The Affluent Worker* study (Goldthorpe *et al.*, 1969). However, since agri-businessmen exhibited no disproportionate tendencies towards either inter- or intra-generational occupational mobility, nor are they over-represented at any particular stage in the family life-cycle, we feel justified in accounting for their mobility in terms of a purely *agricultural* spiralism (Watson, 1964; Nalson, 1968) linked to the expansion of the farming business.

Such spiralism is partly related to educational background. Only 30 per cent of the agri-businessmen had not undergone some form of further education, compared with 42·5 per cent of the gentleman farmers, 60 per cent of the active managerials and 79·2 per cent of the family farmers. Agri-businessmen were also more highly educated in terms of their length of education – 61·7 per cent were educated beyond the age of eighteen, compared with 39 per cent of the gentleman farmers, 16·7 per cent of the family farmers and none of the active managerials at all. Moreover only 38·7 per cent of the agri-businessmen had no formal qualifications in agriculture, compared with 50 per cent of the gentleman farmers, 66·7 per cent of the active managerials and 83·3 per cent of the family farmers. The possession of such educational qualifications is undoubtedly an aid to mobility, but one may also infer that not only has it provided agri-businessmen with the technical know-how to indulge their expansion plans but it has resulted in the inculcation of a more universalistic set of values which has enabled them to break with the ties of localism. While many of the gentleman farmers have also been highly educated, one suspects that this was always, as far as they and their parents were concerned, purely a form of training as a means of obtaining a particular range of skills and expertise in farm management. Our data, however, do not allow us to go beyond such surmise.

There seems little doubt that the spiralism of the agri-businessmen is linked to expansion. Only 21·3 per cent of them were still farming the same acreage as when they began in agriculture, compared with 46·2 per cent of the active managerials, 48·6 per cent of the gentleman farmers and 68·6 per cent of the family farmers. Moreover, the proportional increases were much greater. Thus 67·6 per cent of the agri-businessmen had more than doubled their acreage since they began farming, compared with 22·8 per cent of the gentleman farmers, 38·5 per cent of the family farmers and 16 per cent of the active managerials. Initial farm size obviously plays a part in this by providing greater collateral for expansion; nevertheless these differences remain between agri-businessmen and the other three groups even allowing for farm size. Similar differences also emerge in their attitudes towards further expansion. For example, 22 per cent of agri-businessmen could see no ultimate limit to the size of their farms compared with 14·6 per cent of gentleman farmers, 9·3 per cent of family farmers and 6·7 per cent of active managerials. Indeed 22 per cent of the gentleman farmers desired no further expansion at all, indicating their stronger attachment to the farming life-style, and this was much higher than either family farmers (11·1 per cent) or active managerials (6·7 per cent) both of whom could see an economic rationale for expansion on their generally smaller holdings. Again, these differences remained even allowing for farm size.

The type of farmer was linked with the size of the holding, though by no means in a straightforward manner. We encountered no family farms over 750 acres, for example, while 85 per cent of the agri-businessmen were farming more than 1000 acres, compared with 63·3 per cent of the gentleman farmers and 56·7 per cent of the active managerials. However, all types were represented in the lower size-groups: farmers could, it seems, be 'gentlemen' on quite small acreages, often supported by income from other business interests. The presence of agri-businessmen on small acreages, however, probably owes itself to the inappropriate use of acreage to determine size of farm business in certain types of agriculture – for example intensive livestock rearing and horticulture. Obviously, on the smaller acreages family farms tended to predominate: 72·3 per cent of the farmers that we interviewed on less than 400 acres were family farmers. It is the active managerials who are most evenly distributed among the farm size-groups. Like the agri-businessmen, active managerials are highly market-oriented and thus their outlook on general agricultural matters closely resembles the former's. Often, however, active managerials have made a deliberate decision not to expand to a level which would remove them from an active role in the husbandry of the farm; hence, they are less inclined to expand further. However, this group also includes some frustrated agri-businessmen thwarted by the non-availability of land or capital for expansion as well as embryonic agri-businessmen that the survey method has frozen at a particular stage in their development.

Agri-businessmen were not only much more inclined to expand the acreages of their holdings, but they were prepared to engage in a very catholic series of arrangements in order to do so. Agri-businessmen alone had entered into the full range of expansionist schemes that we coded – purchase, agricultural tenancy, other rental arrangements and lease-back. The most popular form of expansion was through renting land under an agricultural tenancy (29·8 per cent) which was in marked contrast to the other three types of farmers each of whom preferred to expand by purchase. Indeed, all the active managerials that we interviewed who had expanded the size of their farms had done so through purchase. As a corollary of this we found that only 28·3 per cent of the agri-businessmen farmed land which they owned entirely, compared with 56·1 per cent of the gentleman farmers, 55·6 per cent of the family farmers and 66·7 per cent of the active managerials.

These differences raise some intricate chicken-and-egg questions. How far, for example, can the higher tendency of agri-businessmen to rent land be accounted for by their prior expansionist outlook and hence their greater willingness to engage in arrangements of whatever kind in order to achieve this? Or, how far do the incentives offered by tenancy (as opposed to owner-occupation) to maximize profits (rather than derive an equitable standard of living) push farmers into a high degree of market orientation? One of our key informants, for example, himself a successful and highly market-oriented managing director of an expanding tenanted-farming company, put it to us very strongly that our typology could be replaced by a simpler scheme based upon tenurial status. Owner-occupiers, he suggested, were the least market-oriented group of farmers, content to allow their businesses to idle away, so long as they produced sufficient income to keep them in the life-style to which they, and their wives, had become accustomed. Tenant farmers, however, were forced to be more market-oriented by virtue of their need to produce a surplus over and above their rent and the fact that (except where tenancies became totally hereditable) they had no guarantee of family succession. The most market-oriented of all, though, were farm managers who could be dismissed if they did not produce results. While this argument has some appeal, our data suggest it is somewhat over-simplified. It does not account, for example, for the active managerials who are both owner-occupiers *and* highly market-oriented (nor for the managers of the estates of landed gentlemen, whose main concern is as much to provide a good shoot as to improve barley yields). We would therefore tend to account for the greater significance of tenancy among agri-businessmen in terms of their prior value orientation – in this case their desire for expansion. They may usefully be compared with the active managerials who equally are imbued with a strong market orientation but unlike their agri-business counterparts place a greater emphasis upon personal independence and thrift, making them less inclined to become either tenants or large-scale debtors. Either way expansion is inhibited.

Location in the typology also affects the various 'managerial styles' which farmers adopt in their relationships with their employees. Thus the farmers who felt most involved in the life of their workers were the gentleman farmers and agri-businessmen. However gentleman farmers tended to pursue their interests outside the work situation by partaking in a range of activities in the local community and in this sense they corresponded to the traditional role of the country squire (see below, Chapter 6). Agri-businessmen, however, were more disdainful of local involvement and tended to restrict their activities more to the farm itself. Whereas the gentleman farmer almost instinctively accepted the obligations of traditional authority, it was apparent that a number of agri-businessmen adopted a policy of 'caring' for their workers as a deliberate and conscious policy of labour management. Hence their reluctance to enter into local leadership roles outside the farm (and even, as some of the quotations cited in the previous section illustrate, to adopt a paternalist role inside the farm gate). Agri-businessmen are, on the whole, much more conscious of the risks of employer–employee separation on the larger enterprises and take steps to counteract them; gentleman farmers tend instead to operate with a set of taken-for-granted assumptions about how to handle their men.

Only half as many family and active managerial farmers felt as involved in the lives of their workers as the gentleman farmers and agri-businessmen. Both family farmers and active managerials, however, maintain continuous contact with their workers in the work situation and it is likely that they neither see the necessity nor have any desire to extend this still further. However, there are also important differences between the two groups in their attitudes towards farm workers which suggest that the active managerials are the most economically instrumental of all employers. For example, active managerials were the group most likely to consider farm workers adequately paid and they exhibited a considerably greater hostility to the NUAAW – 26·7 per cent were very hostile, compared with 18·6 per cent of the family farmers, 12·3 per cent of the agri-businessmen and 10 per cent of the gentleman farmers. This instrumentality ties in with the active managerials' basis of authority on the farm. They place considerable emphasis in their dealings with their workers on their own expertise and their ability to keep 'one step ahead' of their workers. The authority of the active managerial is therefore more role-specific – it is limited to his role as farmer, and his performance in the work situation (especially his knowledge of farming techniques and his ability to apply them) becomes crucial. Hence, perhaps, the more active nature of his managerialism.

Conclusions

The very impersonality of the organizational structure on the more bureaucratic farms is bound to conflict to some extent with the general desire of farmers to cultivate the identification of their labour force. The propensity of increasing size to bring about functional specialization often necessitates the use of a more formal, impersonal administration of the farm and renders the employer a more remote, authoritarian figure. It also restricts the opportunities open to the employer to socialize his workers into the required norms and values of the enterprise and to obtain their personal commitment. As the labour force has diminished due to mechanization, these opportunities have without doubt increased. Only on those very large units that have resulted from farm amalgamation has this trend been reversed and the tendency for farms in general to de-bureaucratize been halted. However, even on the very large enterprises which are quite common in East Anglia, many employers are, as we have seen, aware that 'factory conditions create factory problems'. Hence most farmers are quite prepared to construct an intricate web of paternalistic labour relations in order to obtain the identification of their workers; on the smaller farms this will occur spontaneously out of the much closer involvement of employers and employees in the work situation, whereas on the larger farms it is often a matter of conscious or unconscious policy.

However, a complete identification of the workforce can only be ensured when some degree of totality is present in the situation – that is, where access to alternative definitions of the situation are in some way restricted. For many farm workers working in intimate involvement with their employers, often living in a tied cottage situated on the farm, such a totality remains virtually guaranteed. But by no means all workers are in this situation (Bell and Newby, 1973). This chapter has concentrated on associated aspects of scale in the work situation, particularly the mode of control which is exerted there and its implications for the kind of workplace interaction and worker identification which ensues. However, in order to assess the extent to which farmers attempt to extend the boundaries of their 'greedy institution' beyond the farm gate and thereby encompass those workers whose work situation does not constitute their total social situation, it is necessary to examine the role of farmers in the social structure of the village community.

5 Status situation and the local community

During the nineteenth century farmers and landowners were often assiduous in their attempts to create a greedy institution out of the local village. Ideally they wished to create an harmonious and self-contained 'organic community' within which the identification of the 'lower orders' could be ensured. The rural village was to become, as Best has put it (1971, p. 85), 'a beautiful and profitable contrivance, fashioned and kept in smooth working order by that happily un-doubting class to whom the way of life it made possible seemed the best the world could offer'. How many villages actually corresponded to this vision must remain in doubt; certainly their 'Beau Ideal' (Davidoff *et al.*, 1976) was regarded as a fragile and delicate creation easily subverted by the agents of the apparently troublesome world beyond the village boundaries where there was no guarantee that subordinates would 'know their place' (see Newby, 1977, Chapter I, for an extended discussion). However, it was towards this vision of an 'organic community' that local landowners and farmers worked, towards an ideal village with its protective squire, prosperous farmers and contented labourers marked by deference and service from below and kindly, benevolent patronage from above.

Such a smoothly running edifice often depended upon an isolation from alternative, contaminating definitions of the situation. It also depended markedly on the pattern of landholding – and hence the nature of the local class structure. This, for example, underpinned the familiar distinction between 'open' and 'closed' villages that is made by historians of nineteenth-century rural areas. Hobsbawm and Rudé (1971, pp. 152–7) have a perceptive discussion of this point. They cautiously and correctly indicate how only a few villages corresponded to these ideal types. Concerning 'closed' villages, for example,

. . . we may occasionally encounter (a) genuine monopoly villages owned entirely by one landlord, or villages, so dominated by one or two land-lords as to make the description 'closed' quite realistic. It is also true that in practice this may not be a very different situation from type (b) which may be described as *oligarchy*, *i.e.* a parish dominated by a group of gentry and noble familes none of which owns an overwhelming proportion of it. Such oligarchies were common in some parts of East Anglia (possibly the result of the familiar medieval multi-manor villages in that region). [Hobsbawm and Rudé, 1971, p. 152.]

Hobsbawm and Rudé note that in the Hartismere Hundred of Suffolk – an area which includes part of the forty-four parishes – seventeen out of thirty-four parishes in the 1830s were dominated by 'some combination of Henniker, Wilson, Kerrison, Frere, Adair, Tomline, Cobbold, etc.' – but only five could be described as 'closed' in the narrow sense. Hobsbawm and Rudé also create type (c) 'in which a strongly established landlord or occupier co-exists with a fair number of small owner-occupiers'. They again illustrate this from Hartismere Hundred, where there were six parishes in which more than 30 per cent of the land-taxed properties were owner-occupied, while between 60 and 90 per cent of the tax was paid by one mono-polistic landlord or by an oligarchy. Mixed parishes, however, may have been much more common than either 'open' or 'closed'. The genuinely 'open' parish, mainly in the hands of small owners, was, they feel, very rare. Much more frequent was the case of a *'village within a parish whose building land was owned by small men – publicans, shopkeepers, artisans and the like, while the bulk of the farming land was monopolized or owned by an oligarchy'*. Ixworth and Earl Soham (the latter being one of the forty-four parishes) are good examples in Suffolk.

What is so significant about these different types of village is that during the Swing disturbances 'open' villages were much more riotous, while the degree of control and domination in the 'closed' and 'mixed' parishes was frequently sufficient to prevent riots from occurring. Not, Hobsbawm and Rudé (1971, p. 154) suggest, that the pattern of landownership *per se* was crucial: ' . . . it is doubtful whether the ownership of land mattered very much to the labourers themselves, who certainly owned none and demanded none. From their point of view the presence or absence of the local squire or gentry might have been more relevant.' Hobsbawm and Rudé are, however, tantalizingly brief on what might be the precise mechanisms of social control and domination in the locality and what might lead it to break down, for they recognize that the particularistic nature of these relationships renders it extremely difficult to derive any generalizations (Hobsbawm and Rudé, 1971, pp. 154–5; see also

Newby, 1975). The character of such relationships was 'obscure', they conclude. On the other hand, relationships between farmers and workers are much clearer: there is a very marked correlation between a propensity to riot and a high concentration of employment. Thus it would appear that even in the 1830s, during a most important challenge to the rural authority structure, the closer the farmer was to the worker (as indicated by the ratio of farmers to workers) both at work and in the community, the less disaffected the worker would be. Taken together these factors could be decisive – as Hobsbawm and Rudé (1971, p. 156) indicate: 'As against size of village and pattern of landownership and employment, poverty alone gives us no reliable clue to riotousness.'

In the village, as well as on the farm, farmers encouraged an identification with their interests as opposed to those of others, especially working-class-based interests. Through such mechanisms as charity, sponsorship and patronage, the village inhabitants were encouraged to see their individual interests as similar, if not identical, to those of local landowners and farmers. These values were supported from the pulpit (in many villages the incumbency was in the gift of the local landowner) and in the schools. The content of the school curriculum and the pace of the educational year was made harmonious with the cycle of agricultural production. The only escape from this all-encompassing institution was to leave. And many did go – to local towns, to London and to industrial towns in the midlands and the north. Many also emigrated to Canada and Australia. Perhaps the most striking illustration of both the exploitative and stifling nature of social relationships in these communities is provided by Blythe in his description of how gladly East Anglian agricultural workers enlisted in 1914 to be slaughtered in the fields of Flanders (Blythe, 1969, Chapter 1). And yet the rhythm and the routine of village life, the comforting pace of the agricultural year – immutable, irreversible and solid – were also socially safe and supportive. *Gemeinschaftlich* social relationships within and between status groups were enduring and even encouraged by the locally dominant. Place, land and kinship were the basis of the local community. Many lived out their lives in the same village – it was familiar and comfortable. When times were hard and when one had personal troubles it was to the community – to the squire or to one's family – that one turned for charity and a little largesse.

Outside the agricultural community was a frequently only dimly perceived urban and industrial world where social relationships were thought to be very different. Kinship, it was believed, must be less important as you obviously left your family behind when you migrated to the towns. In factories you were a mere extension of the machine. There an employer would not know his workers and they would not know him. What is more, outside the countryside workers 'combined' into trade unions, there was a Labour Party and an increasing disinclination to accept things as they were, to accept the *status quo*. Everywhere, especially in the years just before the First World War, there seemed to be challenges to the established and traditional order. Rural areas were not untouched by these great changes in British society, but there was a stubborn rearguard battle fought against the social forces mobilized by urbanization and industrialization. In the end agriculture and the social relationships based on it has largely come to terms with these changes, but any sociological account of East Anglian agriculture must take these changes into account. For one of the most significant consequences wrought by urbanization and industrialization was the disruption and reconstitution of the local community.

During the nineteenth century virtually all East Anglian villages, however 'open' or 'closed', were organized around a particular kind of work. Agriculture dominated the lives of their inhabitants and those who were not directly employed on the land were usually engaged in various service and ancillary occupations. The village therefore formed an 'occupational community', not dissimilar to urban counterparts associated with industries like mining, ship-building, and so on. Such occupational communities could even support (how widely or continuously is not clear) a working-class sub-culture based upon 'oppositional' values (see Bell and Newby, 1973; Newby, 1977, Chapters I and VI). During the twentieth century the decline of rural employment opportunities, the 'drift from the land' and the influx of urban commuters, weekend cottagers and holiday home dwellers to many rural areas has undermined both the village as an occupational community and the rural working-class sub-culture which it formerly contained. Two analytically separable local social systems have been emerging. They are what we wish to call the 'encapsulated community' and the 'farm-centred com-munity'. Both can be seen as a response to the urbanization and industrialization of the countryside, processes which have threatened the continued ability of the farmers and landowners to dominate the local community.

Nowadays there are many people living in the countryside who are not dependent for their employment on local farmers. This is a very dramatic change from the time of the Swing riots and has obviously undermined the ability of farmers and landowners to dominate whole communities. These newcomers/outsiders/aliens – all common terms among our respondents – have had the effect of bringing elements of the national housing market into East Anglian villages, which had hitherto been insulated, by distance as much as anything else, from such direct urbanization. This influx has led to the creation of one of, or in some cases, both of the local social systems that have emerged as alternatives to the traditional occupational community. The 'encapsulated' community, for example, consists of the rump of the former occupational community who now become a self-contained and tightly-knit group of locals, often physically encapsulated from the rest of the village in a council house estate. We would emphasize, though, that this physical separation is by no means absolutely necessary – it is the extent of social separation which leads to a 'community within a community' being formed. There is, as we shall illustrate later, a tremendous feeling within many East Anglian villages of having been *overrun* by an invasion of outsiders. It is no wonder, then, that there has been a social retreat into encapsulated communities, consisting of 'true country people', who 'really understand agriculture' *and* 'respect local farmers and landowners'. A second reaction to the urbanization and industrialization of the countryside is the creation of the 'farm-centred community'. As we have described elsewhere (Bell and Newby, 1973) an increasing proportion of farm workers now live on the farm, usually in tied cottages, a reaction to changes in the local housing market as much as to changes in the local labour market. The potential that this gives for farmers to dominate *their* labour force is, of course, enormous (this has been discussed at length in the previous chapter), so that in many cases there is no longer any need for the farmer to behave like a squire *in the village* because he can control his labour force at the point of production.

Thus in both types of community situation workers and farmers have come closer together. As farms have de-bureaucratized (see the previous chapter) and villages have become urbanized, workers and farmers have sought a common identity as 'locals' (yet, of course, remain vitally differentiated in income, life-style and authority). Farmers – and, as we shall see below, their wives – now feel themselves to be more than ordinarily closely involved in the lives of their workers, *on the farm* as well as in the village. The class divisions and status distinction between farmer and worker can, for the farmer, be conveniently forgotten in the conflict with the outsiders. Though farmers do, of course, have social relationships with the newcomers (while feeling very hostile towards them) they no longer need to dominate the local community in order to protect their economic position. As they need less and less labour and as more and more workers live on their farms (rather than in the village) farmers no longer have to play authority roles in the village. Indeed, as we shall see, many farmers, especially the more market-oriented ones directly involved in the day-to-day running of the farm, viewed these local authority roles as both anachronistic and a waste of their time. They are more concerned on the one hand to continue to maintain their control of their workers on the farm and on the other to protect what they see as the wider political interests of farmers at the district and county council levels. Increasingly, though, the control of the local village is irrelevant to the farmer.

Nevertheless the village retains an important *symbolic* significance. Recent changes in the social composition of the rural village allow, for example, both farmers and farm workers to continue to feel misunderstood and to be threatened by outside forces, both urban and industrial, so creating a 'community of feeling' (or 'communion' as we now prefer to call it – see Bell and Newby, 1976) as locals. It helps what is actually a very diverse group with conflicting interests to unite and speak with one voice. 'Localism' has, we feel, largely replaced 'community' (though the latter always subsumed the former) as an ideology to which both farmers and farm workers can subscribe. In the face of television and the motor car it is no longer possible for farmers to provide the only definitions of reality in the countryside, yet their continuing economic domination means that *their* notions of community have continued to be important and significant. Localism lines up farmers and workers *on the same side*. Moreover, in the conflicts with newcomers that occur in villages over farming practice and access to and use of the land, the workers' interests frequently *are* those of the farmer.

Local social status

Farmers in East Anglia – especially if they are also landowners – have never been merely farmers. They have also been at the pinnacle of the local status system – and some, of course, have simultaneously been at the pinnacle of the national status system. Status relies for its efficacy upon a consensus of prestige allocation. This was clearly more feasible in a social structure at once more coherent and uni-dimensional (in 'closed' villages, for instance). Each member of the system knew his place and the system as a whole was regarded as natural. The urbanization of the British countryside has, however, disrupted this system by introducing new criteria of status and dissolved the former, albeit imposed, consensus. The contemporary status situation is thus far more complex.

Parallelling the 'metropolitanization' of Britain under the impact of such innovations as the mass media and the growth of the Welfare State, with its associated notion of *citizenship* (which is surely most antipathetical to notions of local interactional status), are the *local* consequences of the urbanization of the countryside. As we have already indicated, there are now living in virtually every village in East Anglia people who owe nothing to farmers. They are often middle-class, well educated and have *chosen* to live in the countryside. They are not trapped there in a mesh of economic and social ties. They are *competitors* for the local social roles that had hitherto been the monopoly of landowners and farmers (Pahl, 1965; Ambrose, 1974; Connell, 1974). Furthermore, they are in opposition to farmers over a number of issues – especially concerning the use of the countryside. This is one important way in which at the ideological level, the traditional community is breaking down. In short, local/newcomer distinctions are now very important in the status systems of East Anglian villages (Newby, 1977, Chapter VI).

Much of the coherence of the former local status system has dissolved under the impact of these changes. The village squire, for example, is no longer always the universally acknowledged head of the village's status hierarchy that he was once supposed to be. His declining influence is associated with the 'eclipse' of the village from its former role as an occupational community, but this in itself has been a patchy and somewhat haphazard process, since there are still isolated areas of East Anglia, cut off by poor roads from urban centres, where many villages remain essentially occupational communities. In parts of the region, therefore, the squirearchy continues to fulfil its time-honoured role as provider of largesse, custodian of moral values, and leader of the local community. Thus 56 per cent of the farmers interviewed in the survey believed that some of their colleagues still behaved like squires. They pointed to the sense of obligation towards the local community felt by many larger farmers and landowners, and to the self-assertive belief held by some of them in their right and duty to lead:

Sir P. is squire of the village. He employs a lot of people, I wouldn't say because he needs them, but almost from tradition. He feels they need him. They have to be supported. [Suffolk farmer, 300 acres.]

We've got a squire called the Major. He's regarded in a squire-like way. He's the major employer. He owns a quarter of the village. His family's been here since 1550 – it's a continuity of interest. [Suffolk farmer, 75 acres.]

I can name several. . . . They are JPs, pillars of society and the church, school governors. They're feudal. Their approach to labour is that labour should be grateful to have a job for which they should grovel in return. They think they have a divine right to rule. [Norfolk farmer, 3000 acres.]

Indeed, some farmers whom we interviewed complained that they were obliged to fill such positions in the village as a result of a generalized social expectation, often despite their own reluctance to do so:

Farmers are forced to behave like squires because people still expect it. In a village like this, people expect you to lead. . . . You try to look after people at Christmas. Basically, there's four farms of any size in this parish, and they are expected to give assistance when required. [Suffolk farmer, 2000 acres.]

I support the different village organizations financially, and I make facilities available – for example, they have the parish bonfire night on my land, my mother arranges coffee evenings here, we were closely involved in a recent turkey trot – I supplied the tarpaulins and the labour. The family is considerably involved, but I don't want to get too personally involved because it would tie me here more than I want. The trouble is that being one of the larger landowners, one is looked to for help in these sort of things. [Suffolk farmer, 1300 acres.]

When I came here, a lady said to me, 'Oh, I'm so glad you've come, now we have a squire.' I told her I'd have nothing to do with it. But where does being a squire begin, and being concerned for your workers end? [Suffolk farmer, 110 acres.]

If, however, some farmers are 'attached' while not wholly 'committed' to their socially-defined roles as squires (see Goffman, 1969), it is equally the case that others are both attached and committed. In other words, although there may be moral pressures on the larger landowners to perform with at least some grace the customary functions associated with ownership of a local estate and tenure of the 'big house', many appear to accept them willingly. For them, a sense of 'responsibility' and a conviction in their own destiny to lead are unshakeable. They distribute charity and dominate the community just as their ancestors have done for centuries, and they expect (and generally receive) due gratitude and respect:

When I was a small boy, old ladies in the village used to curtsey to me at the age of seven. . . . I still run a charity which I use to give Old Age Pensioners half a ton of coal. I have another charity which was originally used to dress the kids at the local school – which I maintain – but now I use it to make Christmas presents to them of coats – Marks and Spencer gave us wonderful terms. [Suffolk farmer, 1000 acres.]

The local V I P – if you want to call me the local V I P – the local peer should be chairman of the Parish Council, and I've put my views into practice. . . . But the day of the local V I P being chairman of this and chairman of that is over. It's much better if the village run their own show. I don't mind being President of things. . . . I've spent a lot of time finding good chaps to take over from me. . . . I guaranteed a debt to the bank for the village hall. I lend them my land for the annual fair. I lend them access to my land for the children's playground. They help each other – there's a first-class community spirit and I take great pride in it. [Suffolk farmer, 2000 acres.]

Such men, however, are in the minority among farmers and landowners today. Thus, it is worth noting that although over half of our informants claimed that some farmers were still like squires, only 9 per cent admitted that they themselves were, and many pointed out that the squirearchy was a declining breed.[1] Some argued that the significance of the squire had decreased in proportion to his declining economic stranglehold on local communities, and especially on labour market opportunities:

Some farmers are like squires, but it's only with the consent of the squired because they can leave or tell him to piss off. Our neighbour owns a whole parish and he's a major influence. But his workers could go elsewhere if they wanted to. [Suffolk farmer, 750 acres.]

People don't need that squire business now. We aren't relied on for work any more. Try and be a squire today and you'd be in for it – you'd get all the kicks. [Essex farmer, 1200 acres.]

Clearly, the power of the squirearchy has diminished considerably. Indeed, a number of our informants recognized, implicitly or explicitly, that the role of squire today has little to do with economic or political power. The country squire, that is, may still exist in some occupational communities, but even there his position is more a source of interactional status (or, indeed, a reflection of that status) than of economic might or political domination:

There's no squire round here – not in the sense of a squire riding through the village, seeing a bit of paper, and telling someone to pick it up, or of thinking that people are privileged to work for him. Nobody today thinks working for Lord H is a privilege – they enjoy working for him. He knows the majority of people in the village. [Suffolk farmer, 200 acres.]

It's all past. There's no lords of the manor now. There may be in title, but not in wealth or position. [Suffolk farmer, 500 acres.]

The urbanization of the rural village has, however, also threatened to undermine the status of the squire, even where he may retain his control of the surrounding land and local employment opportunities, for so few village inhabitants now work locally. As one self-confessed squire wistfully informed us:

There were good and bad squires. Someone like myself – I own all the land around [the village] – I attempt to behave like a good squire. A lot of people today have a lot of power and no responsibility. My position is the reverse – responsibility without power.

The position of the individual village squire today may indeed be one of 'responsibility without power', but this need not imply farmers and landowners in general are no longer the dominant political group in rural society (see Chapter 6). Some (though not all) farmers do continue to maintain a very close and direct interest in the local village, including a number of positions of authority in local clubs, societies and voluntary associations. For instance, even in the 1000+ acres sample 94 per cent were interested to some extent in their village and 60 per cent belonged to some local clubs and associations. Yet 64 per cent had *no* official positions in these formal associations, indicating both their displacement by newcomers and the difference in orientation of some farmers. An examination of Table 54 shows that the degree of interest in the village in the 1000+ acres sample was stronger than in the forty-four parishes. This variation between the samples is consistent with those data we have on membership of local clubs and societies – 39 per cent of the 1000+ acres sample did not belong to any, but the proportion rose to 56 per cent in the forty-four parishes. Agri-businessmen among the 1000+ acres sample were, again consistent with our data, much more likely *not* to belong to local organizations.

Perhaps the clearest difference between the farmers of the 1000+

acres sample and those in the forty-four parishes can be illustrated by the number of positions of local responsibility that our respondents held. Many of the farmers that we interviewed occupied prominent positions of responsibility in local affairs – positions such as school govenors, trustees of local charities, chairmanships of village hall committees and Parochial Church Councils, and even membership of the local bench. Only 36 per cent of the 1000+ acres sample did *not* hold such a position while another 36 per cent held two or more; in the forty-four parishes sample 65 per cent did *not*

Table 54 *Degree of interest in local village*

'How interested are you in what goes on in . . . ?'

Degree of interest	1000+ acres (N=100) %	44 parishes (N=55) %
Very interested	41·0	26·3
Fairly interested	37·0	38·6
A little interested	16·0	28·1
Not at all interested	6·0	7·0
Total	100	100

Table 55 *Positions of responsibility locally held*

	None %	One %	Two or more %	Total %
1000+ acres (N=102)				
Gentleman	9·8	5·9	13·7	29·4
Agri-businessman	18·6	14·7	14·7	48·0
Family	—	—	—	—
Active managerial	5·9	9·8	6·9	22·6
Total	34·3	30·4	35·3	100
44 parishes (N=55)				
Gentleman	3·6	5·5	5·5	14·6
Agri-businessman	3·6	3·6	5·5	12·7
Family	42·9	3·6	9·1	55·6
Active managerial	14·5	1·8	1·8	17·1
Total	64·6	13·5	21·9	100

hold such a position while only 21 per cent held two or more. This is a very good indication of local authority off the point of production and its full political significance is elaborated in the next chapter. What this means is that farmers, whether they feel like squires or not, *are* still behaving like them in some localities. There are, however, some interesting variations by the type of farmer, as Table 55 shows. For instance, notwithstanding that the agri-businessmen among the 1000+ acres sample were not so interested in the village nor belonged to so many local clubs and societies, they were much more likely to hold one or more positions of authority. Those least likely to do so were family farmers in the forty-four parishes. Indeed outside the forty-four parishes almost two-thirds of the farmers that we interviewed held positions of authority in the locality. Thus, while farmers have certainly been displaced from some local authority positions, and may feel their status to be threatened by newcomers, it is clear that farmers continue to fill a remarkably high proportion of them – and that this is especially true of the larger farmers. We shall return to this issue in Chapter 6.

The disruption of 'community'

Whatever the reality of the situation, a paramount feeling among most of the farmers that we interviewed was that an harmonious and well-ordered village community had recently been disrupted, or was threatened with disruption, by the arrival of urbanite newcomers. Around 77 per cent in both samples felt that there had been a 'loss of community' in the rural village. However, it was in their more extended remarks on the nature and meaning of community that our respondents really reflect the ongoing changes in the local social system.

First of all, what did the farmers mean by 'community' anyway? Several of them provided us with short and pertinent definitions:

Group of people living in an area who see each other frequently and who don't want to get away from each other . . . but the weekenders break this up, so do cars, second homes. [Suffolk farmer, 1000 acres.]

Community was also felt to mean continuity and was created over time:

People who know one another. At X we knew everybody, you made your friends at school, you had relations all around you. Even the village policeman we knew, but now they only drive past in a van. [Suffolk farmer, 90 acres.]

202 Status situation and the local community

Community for East Anglian farmers (as for many sociologists) gains in perspective when the rural is specifically contrasted with the urban. For example, in answer to a question that we asked about the *meaning* of community we were told that they were:

Natural villages – anything that serves the purpose of the village. Towns aren't communities. It's like cattle, the herd identity. It's the same with humans. You can only identify with a group up to a certain size. [Suffolk farmer, 760 acres.]

Earlier in this chapter we noted that one of the central social changes that has been occurring in East Anglian agriculture is the recreation of 'community' on the farm itself. So it is significant in this respect to quote this 1600-acre farmer from Norfolk:

Men regard the farm as an essential part of their life and are attached to it – it's the same with the village. It's a matter of allegiance and loyalty.

It is interesting to indicate what these ideas of community might do to support the farmers' authority roles. For instance, a farmer who *denied* any loss of community said:

We still have the WI in the village and an old people's party every year. Bingo is quite strong and we have football and cricket teams. There's no big industries or towns round here, that's why. *That's why we have no labour problems.* [Norfolk farmer, 1200 acres; italics added.]

Farmers were very clear what was destroying the local community – it was the urbanization of the countryside. One cause of the loss of community was the motor car.

I should think that 75 per cent of men go out of the village to work – it's due to the motor car. Pre-war there were half a dozen cars in the village, but today every man has a car, therefore he's mobile. Whereas country courting couples used to walk up lovers' lane and sit on the stile, now they drive up there in their cars and throw out the Kleenex when they have finished. [Suffolk farmer, 2600 acres.]

Another was the effects of television, so that no one, not even the locals, are interested in entering such symbols of a vigorous community as the best-kept village competition. But easily the single most destructive social change was the influx of newcomers. One respondent, who farmed 1700 acres in Norfolk, was in no doubt as to the consequences that would result from this penetration of the 'organic community' by outsiders:

We're getting a lot of strangers in the area now. They have a different life-style which the long-term residents long for. It causes real problems and it's a bad thing. *People in the country should be left docile and happy and not be made to want things* ... but it's changing and it's a pity. [Italics added.]

Demographic occupational changes were also clearly understood to lead to changes in social relationships:

The old country people are dying out, the young ones are going to work elsewhere and the weekenders and retired people are coming in. Week-enders might as well fill the empty houses but they don't understand the countryside, you've got to keep an eye on them. [Suffolk farmer, 90 acres.]

For those villages nearer large towns, especially around Ipswich, there have been much more dramatic changes than those wrought by the motor car, television and the odd weekender. For instance, we were told that:

There's been a splitting between the ex-urban dwellers and the local villagers – that's why we formed a parish council at X with the express intention of welcoming and absorbing Ipswich people moving in. But it was totally impossible – they set up an alternative tenants' association to the parish council, it was a fiasco. Now the parish council is overrun by urban dwellers and the locals have retired behind walls and given up. Here we have had a spate of totally immoral speculative building and commuters from Ipswich. They take no part in parish affairs whatsoever. [Suffolk farmer, 235 acres.]

And certainly feelings often ran high; there was talk of 'invasion', of 'aliens' and of 'natives'. Sometimes though both sides were blamed for the loss of community:

... the natives aren't sufficiently involved to accept the invaders, but the invaders aren't sufficiently sensitive to integrate, they bring aggression with them into the community and produce resentment. The natives feel insecure. Like at X – a rapid influx of aliens have taken over the council and now they want to tell the natives they can't park on the green in front of the pub when they have been doing it for years. [Suffolk farmer, 760 acres.]

And,

We're full up with newcomers to the village. New housing estates are full of Ipswich commuters. We've just lost everything – it's changed from a community to a community centre. I just wish they wouldn't take it over, otherwise they'd be welcome. In the old days the church, the village hall, and perhaps even the cricket, WI, and that sort of thing, but it has all gone by the board nowadays. We don't talk to people in the pub like we used to. [Suffolk farmer, 72 acres.]

The feeling of being taken over was expressed deeply and many times. As one respondent put it:

.. they get on to committees and run them and try to override people who have been here all their lives. There's too many do-gooders who don't understand the country way of life. They try to run the whole show instead of the locals who know all of the ways of the countryside. [Suffolk farmer, 560 acres.]

Occasionally, however, the newcomers' enthusiasm for running things seems to actually create a community that did not previously exist:

... people who come here and try and make more of the community thing than there really is. It happened at X – the newcomers decided, 'Ah! we're in a community! Where is it?' Then they half made it in the process. The older residents just laugh at it a bit. The farmers and the new people: never the twain shall meet – they just don't understand farming. [Suffolk farmer, 10 acres.]

So in their reasons for believing that there has been a loss of community newcomers are blamed by farmers most frequently. Either they come in and try to run everything or they are 'stand-offish' and set up their own organizations which is equally frowned upon:

I don't like newcomers . . . they aren't of anywhere. They don't want to be involved too much. They won't identify too much. They're like someone in a nudist camp who wants to keep his trousers on. [Suffolk farmer, 100 acres.]

It is difficult sometimes to see how the newcomers can win – they certainly seem to provide a convenient scapegoat for any recent undesirable changes. Table 56 shows just how hostile farmers were to the newcomers who have moved into 'their' villages and so disrupting 'community', unsettling 'their' workers and competing for authority positions. Such sentiments will come as no surprise to anyone who is familiar with the public statements of farmers on this issue, both in the farming press and elsewhere. It would not be too much of an exaggeration to suggest that farmers exhibit almost a collective paranoia towards the outside world. We discovered, for example, that there were marked differences between how they believed farmers were viewed in general in contemporary Britain and the local view 'here in the village', as we put it to them. Table 57 vividly illustrates this point – only 6 or 7 per cent of those interviewed thought that people in general were friendly towards farmers. One wonders whether any other occupational group believes that they are so unpopular with the country as a whole. Locally, however, farmers feel much more secure. No wonder they regret the passing of community.

Table 56 *Attitudes to newcomers*

	1000+ acres (N=100) %	44 parishes (N=50) %
Hostile	55	40
Neutral	21	32
Friendly	16	22
Indifferent	3	2
Mixed	5	4
Total	100	100

Table 57 *Farmers' views of how others regard them*

'*What sort of view do you think people in general have of farmers?*'
'*What about here in the village?*'

	1000+ acres (N=102)		44 parishes (N=55)	
	Generally %	Locally %	Generally %	Locally %
Hostile	74·4	12·9	81·1	13·8
Neutral	3·9	2·0	—	9·8
Friendly	6·9	64·8	5·2	61·9
Indifferent	3·9	1·0	8·5	2·0
Mixed	10·9	18·3	5·2	12·5
Total	100	100	100	100

We can illustrate these feelings vividly with quotations, for the farmers that we interviewed were prepared to talk about this at very great length. It was perhaps summed up most crisply when we were told (by a 760-acre farmer in Suffolk) that farmers were seen by the rest of the population as 'idle, too well off, exploiters of their employees, careless of the countryside and of people's health'. Many farmers felt that the rest of the world was in some ways jealous of them. For instance:

I hate townspeople and they hate us. They think that we're oversubsidized and I think they are jealous . . . let me give you an example. Take the case of a bookmaker with two thousand pounds invested and a Rolls-Royce. He'd be regarded as a clever bloke. But a farmer with a Rolls-Royce and two million pounds invested is seen as a lazy sod who's made his money from taxpayers' subsidies. Yet who is doing a service and who doing a disservice? I could buy five Rolls but I'm still poorly paid for my investment. [Suffolk farmer, 1600 acres.]

Farmers thus believe themselves to be unpopular and misunderstood:

It's because we don't like people with dogs chasing cattle and leaving french letters on the fences and old television sets chucked in the fields. They only see us when the sun is shining. They don't see us in the winter, up to our arses in mud. They think we're wealthy – it's due to the press; except the *Daily Express*. Farmers aren't loved. [Suffolk farmer, 2600 acres.]

And 'they' think that 'we':

. . . put seed in the field, shut the gate and harvest a lot of money in the autumn. I mix with a lot of people in the City and they think that farmers are uneducated with straw sticking out of their ears. [Suffolk farmer, 400 acres.]

Yet locally they feel a lot more secure. Farmers would stress that:

The locals are O.K. – they hold us in awe. They still think we're the squires because we live in a big house. [Norfolk farmer, 1000 acres.]

Country people realize what farmers do and what they are up against. [Suffolk farmer, 90 acres.]

Thus an important aspect of the perceived loss of community was the disruption of the older and more unified view of local status wrought by the arrival of the newcomers to the village. This was frequently commented upon. As one respondent put it:

Older people have been led to believe that they rely on farming. They were brought up to think, 'Farmers, that's where the money is, that's where the work is' – rightly or wrongly. The newer people don't understand this feeling and they resent like hell the prestige that farmers get. [Suffolk farmer, 10 acres.]

Despite all these changes, there is still a feeling among some farmers that local interactional status is the key determinant of their personal social position. This is still accompanied by a willingness to be 'placed' by the village. Recent changes have, however, made it more uncertain as to what this 'place' is, or how widely it is shared among the inhabitants. Occasionally, it seemed that while the farmer himself was prepared to retain an adherence to the old certainties, the next generation might be rather more confused by the confused complexities of the local status system:

My children say to me, What are we? I say we are what the village say we are. The village will decide who is gentry and who is not and who is in between. The village has a rating system of farms – where it is good to work and where it is bloody awful. All houses are rated according to the wife: if she's a lady, does she interfere, is she bad tempered. For example, I've given all my men a tot of whisky for the new year. This is the sort of thing that counts. [Suffolk farmer, 100 acres.]

This quotation also serves to illustrate how this particular farmer felt that his behaviour towards his workers was significant in 'placing himself locally. In this way it may be said that authority roles on the' farm tend to 'spill over' into the village. Because of the elision between work relationships and the local rural community, farmers are much more likely to be involved in the lives of their employees outside working hours. This is, as we noted in the previous chapter, often a key factor in attempts by farmers to gain the identification of their workers by constructing a web of traditional, paternalistic relationships outside the work situation. Table 58 shows how far farmers

Table 58 *Involvement of farmers and their wives in the lives of their employees outside the course of work*

Degree of involvement	Farmers		Wives	
	1000+ acres (N=102) %	44 parishes (N=37) %	1000+ acres (N=82) %	44 parishes (N=30) %
Very involved	31·4	2·7	25·6	16·7
Quite involved	39·2	56·8	29·2	6·7
Not much involved	21·6	21·6	14·6	33·3
Not at all involved	7·8	18·9	30·5	43·3
Total	100	100	100	100

believed themselves and their wives to be involved in the lives of their employees.[2] The scale of this involvement, though it might be found in some other small entrepreneurial concerns, indicates its perceived importance in agriculture. It should be remembered, though, that in many cases the workers actually live on the farm so that 'popping in and out' is very easy.

In order to take account of this we also asked our respondents whether they actually met their workers off the farm. In fact there was less actual interaction off the farm than the farmers, by their answers to the previous question, had led us to expect (see Table 59). This indicated to us how far the local social system based on agriculture has moved out of the village and on to the farm. The village may remain an important arena for the symbolic or 'attributional' status (see Plowman *et al.*, 1962) for, as one farmer, speaking for many who were very conscious of this, put it:

They expect you to set standards around here and behave in a certain way and they don't like it if you don't. My men don't like to see me drive a small car. [Norfolk farmer, 1000 acres.]

However, although these villages thus remain, for the agriculturally-based population at least, potentially or latently interactional status systems, not all that much interaction between farmers and farm workers appears to be occurring off the farm. When we recall the extent to which many villages have been denuded of their agricultural population, this is not perhaps surprising; moreover, this situation becomes even more understandable when we examine the composition of our respondents' friendship networks.

Table 59 *Employer–employee contact off the farm*

'Do you ever see your workers off the farm?'
'Whereabouts?'

Location	1000+ acres (N=102) %	44 parishes (N=37) %
At home	3·9	2·7
Pub	11·7	18·9
Sports/clubs/societies	7·8	13·5
Other	3·9	—
No social contact	72·7	64·9
Total	100	100

The farmer's social network

In order to gauge to what extent farmers formed a distinct group living in an insulated social world consisting only of other farmers, we asked our respondents to nominate up to four friends, and we then collected some information (occupation, place of residence, etc.) on each.[3] Table 60 shows the composition of their friends, broken down by the Registrar General's social class categories. It is quite clear that farmers' friends are resolutely middle-class (some of the consequences of this are developed in Chapter 7 on class imagery and ideology). Moreover, they live out their social lives in middle-class and *farming* circles. A very high proportion of their friends were also farmers – so they are largely insulated from countervailing values and influences at the interpersonal level. None of this is perhaps very surprising – but it should be borne in mind that it exaggerates and magnifies the influence of their familial background, and that of their spouses, which, as we saw in Chapter 2, is also overwhelmingly agricultural and middle-class.

Table 60 *'Social class' of farmers' friends*

Class*		1000+ acres No.	%	44 parishes No.	%	HN No.	%
'Middle class'	I	52	14·8	35	15·4	37	17·1
	II	89	21·2	33	14·5	39	18·1
	'Farmer'	188	42·8	132	57·9	104	48·1
'Working class'	III	12	2·9	15	6·6	23	10·6
	IV	—	—	6	2·6	9	4·2
	V	—	—	1	0·4	—	—
Unclassifiable		7	3·0	2	0·9	—	—
N.A.		66	15·7	4	1·8	4	1·9
Total		420	100	228	100	216	100

* Defined by the Registrar General.

Those friends who were not farmers were to a large extent 'self-employed' and again we would want to argue that their values would be to a very great extent consistent with those of the farmers, particularly as many of these individuals owned businesses which were closely connected to agriculture, such as agricultural contracting, wholesale merchandising, etc. Altogether 67·4 per cent of the 1000+

210   *Status situation and the local community*

acres sample's friends were either farmers or self-employed and 71·5 per cent of the forty-four parishes sample's friends. These farmers live out their non-working lives, then, mainly in the company of other farmers and in that of the entrepreneurial self-employed middle class. Furthermore, the farmer's social world is extraordinarily *local*, though not as confined to the immediate parishes as that of their workers (see Newby, 1977, pp. 154–8). Table 61 presents our information on this. The farmers in the forty-four parishes and HN samples were much more 'local' in their friendship nominations than were those in the 1000+ acres sample – 68·2 per cent in the forty-four parishes and 62 per cent in the HN sample lived within ten miles of our respondents as opposed to 39·7 per cent of the 1000+ acres sample's friends. The propinquity of farmers' friends and the fact that frequently they are other farmers strengthen their feelings about the locality, for the setting for their social world – markets, shoots, agricultural societies and shows, cocktail parties and so on – is predominantly local. In general, they simply do not have non-rural, non-local friends – and, of course, virtually none from the working class. Largely insulated from urban, industrial and working-class influences they rarely meet socially people from outside the countryside or even from outside of agriculture or agriculturally-related industries. Moreover this social exclusivity worked even *within* the farming friendships, where large-scale farmers tended to be friendly with other large-scale farmers. Thus 31·1 per cent of the 1000+ acres sample's friends were farmers who worked 400 or more acres, whereas this proportion fell to 18·9 per cent in the forty-four parishes sample. The 1000+ acres farmers only nominated two (or 0·5 per

Table 61 *Location of farmers' friends*

| | 1000+ acres | | 44 parishes | | HN | |
	No.	%	No.	%	No.	%
Same parish	35	8·3	52	22·8	42	19·4
Neighbouring parish	13	3·1	29	12·7	22	10·2
Within 10 miles	119	28·3	74	32·7	70	32·4
10–50 miles	107	25·5	38	16·7	40	18·5
50+ miles	63	15·6	29	12·7	33	15·3
Abroad	6	1·4	1	0·4	1	0·5
N.A.	77	18·3	5	2·2	8	3·7
Total	420	100	228	100	216	100

cent) friends who farmed less than 150 acres compared with thirty-one (13·6 per cent) in the forty-four parishes.

It is, of course, only with considerable difficulty that we can move from these data to making statements about the interactional status system of farmers. Yet in their friendship patterns – indicated both by the overwhelmingly middle-class composition of the friends and the matching size of farm run by their farming friends – farmers' interaction patterns *are* clearly stratified. The picture that emerges from this analysis is one of farmers having a local middle-class and farming social network that generally reflects the farmer's own social position – small farmers interact with other small farmers, large with large, and so on. We were also interested in the extent to which the friends that farmers nominated knew each other – this we are using as an indicator, admittedly not a very powerful one, of the structure of the social network in which the farmers lived. Our data show that the larger farmers (in the 1000+ acres sample) *do* tend to live in 'tighter', more socially exclusive networks of friends – 60·2 per cent of their friends knew each other, compared with 53·6 per cent in the forty-four parishes. However, the more heterogeneous nature of the forty-four parishes sample masks important internal differences. Breaking down the samples by size of holding, we find that the most socially exclusive groups are the very large and the very small farmers, each of whom seem to form tightly-knit friendship networks consisting of farmers of comparable scale. This pattern is also reflected when the data are analysed by types of farmer, with agri-businessmen on the one hand and family farmers on the other form-ing the most exclusive networks. We had thought, before we began our research, that the larger farmers would be altogether more cosmopolitan than the smaller farmers – but this was not so.

The generally exclusive nature of the farmers' networks of friends and kin obviously affects the judgements and values which underlie their allocation of prestige. Farming, as we have pointed out earlier, is a highly visible activity – visible, that is, to other local inhabitants and for that matter to anyone who passes through the countryside. Farming activity in all its complexity is particularly visible to other farmers. The tightly-knit nature of most farmers' friendship networks would suggest a high degree of consensus over prestige allocation as well as facilitating normative control over what constitutes 'good' farming practice. We asked our respondents for their ideas on what made a good farmer. Their replies are shown in Table 62. Not all their answers proved very useful and not all of them answered these questions fully, but some gave several replies. These are, of course, normative statements – their actual personal practice is discussed elsewhere. About one-third of their replies focused instantly on the very traditional *farming* criteria of growing good crops, having clean land (by which they mostly mean the absence of wild oats) and 'knowing' the land. Their answers also reflect the business pressures that they are under in that the second most popular reply concerned good marketing, efficiency and productivity. Only 11·9 per cent in the 1000+ acres sample and 4 per cent in the forty-four parishes cited profitability. It is, however, in their fuller replies, from which we quote below, that we get the flavour of their views on what makes a good farmer.

Table 62   *Farmers' ideas of what makes a good farmer*

	1000+ acres No. of replies	%	44 parishes No. of replies	%
Knowing when to do things	11	7·2	7	9·3
Profitability	18	11·9	3	4·0
Good marketing/efficiency/productivity	26	17·2	18	24·0
Progressive/innovatory	5	3·3	2	2·6
Good relationships with employees	14	9·2	3	4·0
Personal commitment/involvement	15	9·9	9	12·0
Grows good crops/clean land/knows land	52	34·6	23	30·6
Stewardship/looks after land	7	4·6	7	9·3
Other	3	1·9	3	4·0
Total	151	100	75	100

The actual practice of farming is extraordinarily varied, and the farmers that we interviewed represented almost the full variation – from 2-acre pig units to 15 000-acre 'prairie' farmers, from traditional landowners who seemed more concerned with pheasant shooting than yields per acre to very hardheaded hedge-destroyers and stubble-burners. Elsewhere in this chapter we shall be concerned with the effects that some of these practices had on farmers' local standing, but here our concern is with the farmers' views of themselves and of other farmers. Most of our respondents were very willing to make normative statements about what, in their view, makes a good farmer. They usually had very clear and definite opinions. The tensions between the two key aspects of their answers – between what could be called their expressive feeling for their land and their instrumental attitude to the farm as a business – was frequently expressed. For example:

Interest makes a good farmer, interest in the farm and the land, although today it's not good enough to be a good farmer, you've got to be a good businessman as well. That's where a lot of farmers feel the pinch, they are not good enough businessmen to make as much as they could. [Suffolk farmer, 120 acres.]

In their notions of good farming practice many respondents also expressed deeply-felt values and attitudes about property that we shall elaborate in Chapter 8. Many farmers, for example, felt strongly that they were not just farming for the present generation:

A good farmer produces as much as possible from the soil but keeps it in very good nick. He leaves it better than he found it. He keeps wild oats out and keeps the farm clean. [Suffolk farmer, 500 acres.]

A good farmer will farm as if he is going to farm for ever, a bad farmer as if he is going to die tomorrow. [Suffolk farmer, 217 acres.]

The smaller farmers in the forty-four parishes did tend to stress the virtues of being a working farmer with the proverbial muck on their boots, having feeling for the land and a clean farm, understanding nature and sheer hard work. One farmer also told us that a good farmer was one who looks after his men as well as he looks after his cattle and machinery. Though he meant well, we wondered whether his workers would have preferred him to put it the other way round. However, the larger farmers, while they were just as capable of waxing lyrical about nature and the land, and while they too tended to stress tidiness and cleanliness, exhibited a different edge to these kinds of comments. For instance:

A good farmer is enthusiastic and efficient and on the ball and one jump ahead. Those who will have an early go at a new idea are good farmers. I also think a good farmer is a tidy farmer. Above all you have to be dedicated. [Norfolk farmer, 1000 acres.]

This was also reflected in comments concerning financial matters. Larger farmers tended not only to give profitability more importance but to regard it as a purely rational matter:

A good farmer: financial success first and foremost. If he's achieving that, the other things follow naturally. He'll look after his land because it is in his financial interest to do so. [Cambridgeshire farmer, 4500 acres.]

The smaller farmers who referred to this, however, did so with a slightly bemused air, as though profitable farmers were simply uncannily prescient, with a genius for doing the right thing at the right time:

... they are all good round here, but there are certain people – it's not good luck, they'll cut hay, bale it, cart it and soon as the last lot goes through the gate into the barn, the rain will start pouring down. It's not luck, 'cause the same chap can do it time after time. [Suffolk farmer, 100 acres.]

Perhaps a good concluding remark is one that shows the kind of pressures that farmers now feel themselves to be under to alter their farming practice, despite their traditional notions of good husbandry:

Good farmers aren't necessarily the cleanest any more. You have to be a financial success. There aren't really any bad farmers today because you can't afford to be. [Norfolk farmer, 1300 acres.]

This comment was in many ways typical – a somewhat regretful recognition that farming has moved from a 'way of life' to a 'business' and that old standards of 'good farming' are either outdated or impractical under modern conditions.

In general, however, what emerges most strongly from our replies is the *uniformity* and *homogeneity* of normative response across and between our samples; nor was there any striking variation between types of farmers. There are, indeed, strong pressures on farmers to conform to the standards of husbandry and general farming practice of their peers. Those who try to step beyond the permitted boundaries of behaviour can meet with considerable disdain (for an example involving employment practices, see Newby, 1977, pp. 304–7). We know of at least one group of farmers in East Anglia who pride themselves on their ability to be profit-conscious and to subsume all other considerations beneath that of profit maximization. Their unashamed instrumentalism is so frowned upon that they have formed themselves into a club – only a dozen or so strong – in order to seek some sanctuary in each other's company. They feel – and indeed are – a beleaguered minority.

Farming practice and the environment

One of the themes of this chapter has been the disruption caused to established patterns of interaction and status by the arrival in most rural villages of ex-urban newcomers. We have already adduced a number of reasons for the apparent antipathy which exists between these recent immigrants into rural areas and farmers. The new-comers appear to many farmers to have undermined the previously accepted social order of the village and have challenged farmers for positions of community leadership which had hitherto been almost entirely within the farmers' domain. The tendency to stereotype or even scapegoat the village newcomers becomes even more under-standable when we realize just how little social contact they actually have with farmers. All this social friction comes to a head when farmers and newcomers clash over issues connected with both the use of and access to agricultural land, issues which lie under the broad heading of environmental conservation.

The newcomers' expectations of rural life are dominated by what Pahl (1968) has called their 'village in the mind'; that is, by an aesthetic notion of the countryside which stresses its visual aspects and which largely ignores those economic functions of the country-side concerned with the production of food. For many ex-urbanites the countryside is, indeed, an idyllic retreat from the world of work and hence there is a tendency for them to oppose any changes which will affect the visual aspects of either the village itself or its surround-ing rural landscape. Modern farming practice, however, necessitates often widespread and thoroughgoing changes in the landscape, especially in intensively farmed lowland areas like East Anglia. Uprooted hedgerows, diverted footpaths, the construction of tower silos and asbestos barns, the burning of straw and stubble: these are the accoutrements of modern farming methods. And none of them has a place in the newcomers' 'village in the mind'. Usually well educated and articulate, the new adventitious population is often not slow in making its feelings known to those farmers whom they are prepared to brand as arch-destroyers of the nation's heritage. Farmers in turn have a tendency to regard them as interfering busy-bodies who have no knowledge or understanding of agriculture. Once the stereotypes have been established there is a tendency for this cleavage to become perpetuated through elements of self-fulfilling prophecy in the behaviour of one side towards the other. And so there is potentially a great deal of *local* conflict over the use of land. Farmers become very irritated by newcomers who, as one respondent put it, 'say these are my rights to walk a line of a map through your disease-free animals'. Many farmers echoed this point; the countryside could not be treated as the equivalent of an urban municipal park:

Farming is a business and one can't afford to have people running loose over the farm – same as BMC wouldn't like people wandering over their factory. It's the same thing – farming is big business. [Suffolk farmer, 1000 acres.]

There's a classic crassness in the Londoner who comes out here and complains about pig smells and mud on the road. In a way it's my stupidity that I didn't go and explain to him what we're doing but it is crass on his part to have an idyll far from reality. [Suffolk farmer, 760 acres.]

Real locals have a fair regard but commuters . . . we find [here] that they expect an awful lot. We have a lot of footpaths through our land and they expect to do what they like. But real Suffolk folk have a terrific respect for the countryside. The weekenders expect too much freedom on our land. [Suffolk farmer, 2000 acres.]

Access is not the only problem, however, for it is in their actua-farming practice that farmers also come into conflict with the newl comers:

Last winter I was cutting down a hedge and two or three local worthies, suburbanites, stood and swore at me and told me I was a murderer – yet the county council had told me to cut it down in the first place! Nature has to be managed like anything else. Yet they just don't understand. [Suffolk farmer, 110 acres.]

This antagonism leads some farmers to be deliberately provocative – such as one farmer who said, 'I'm a great burning man – I spend hours with my box of matches . . . ' In this context footpaths seemed to be a particular bone of contention. We were told over and over again that local amenity associations, and the Ramblers' Association in particular, were just too inflexible in their attitudes. Footpaths, it was often emphasized to us, were originally designated so that local villagers could walk to and from work, the church, etc. As far as farmers are concerned it was therefore the ultimate absurdity to maintain footpaths when they had long outlasted their function and to put up footpath signs when the locals had always known where they were. And anyway:

It's not the locals who want the footpaths but the outsiders. We know what the interests of the countryside are and so do the real country people. [Cambridgeshire farmer, 1100 acres.]

Again farmers are quite capable of being deliberately provocative:

I've ploughed up two footpaths. I don't stop people walking them. Trouble is now nobody knows where they go! When they stray off them I threaten them with prosecution for trespass. [Suffolk farmer, 1600 acres.]

Such behaviour is both a cause and a consequence of the stereo-types that have arisen between farmers and newcomers over their respective attitudes towards the countryside and environmental conservation. Yet many farmers feel that they must make changes in the rural landscape, restrict access and indulge in environmentally questionable farming practices in order to stay in business. Many uproot hedgerows, say, with genuine regret, but feel compelled to do so by the economic exigencies of modern farming. Hence the com-ments presented above need to be placed in the context of the generality of farmers' attitudes towards environmental conservation, as shown in Table 63.

Table 63 presents data from a deliberately general question which we asked about how our respondents viewed the effects of recent changes in agriculture on 'traditional' features of the rural landscape. Their replies show a number of separate dimensions, occasionally cited in isolation, but more often used in combination. One dimen-sion is a straightforward pro- or anti-conservationism; another is approval or disapproval of the activities of environmentalists; and a third is an acknowledgement of a conservation problem, but dis-agreement over whether a solution did or did not lie within the hands of the farmers themselves. Thus 87·3 per cent of the 1000+ acres farmers and 72·3 per cent of those in the forty-four parishes expressed what might be termed a 'sympathetic' view to the problem of environ-mental conservation, but 60 per cent and 39·5 per cent respectively were hostile to conservationists. Only a minority of farmers – 27·7 per cent in the 1000+ acres sample and 22·9 per cent in the forty-four parishes – believed either that there was no environmental problem or that if there was one then farmers had no part in it. Similarly only a minority – 5·7 per cent in the 1000+ acres sample and 21·1 per cent in the forty-four parishes – were willing to accept that farmers had gone too far in changing the environment, although a higher proportion – 20 per cent and 36·8 per cent respectively – were prepared to acknowledge that there was *some* justification for criticisms of farmers in this regard. The most common response was an acknowledgement of an environmental problem, but to see this as having been created by impersonal factors – economic and techno-logical – with which the farmer had little choice but to comply.

Observation of Table 63 also reveals significant differences between the two samples. In general those farmers in the 1000+ acres sample were more hostile to conservation; for example, they were more than twice as likely as farmers in the forty-four parishes to regard concern

218 Status situation and the local community

Table 63 *Farmers' views on environmental conservation*

Views on conservation	1000+ acres		44 parishes	
	% of respondents citing reply (N=105)	% of replies (N=200)	% of respondents citing reply (N=57)	% of replies (N=102)
In favour of conservation but regard environmentalists as ignorant/misguided	31·4	16·5	17·5	9·8
Continually creating new environment by replanting, etc.	15·2	8·0	12·3	6·9
Hedge-removal, etc., technologically unavoidable	42·9	22·5	43·9	24·5
Hedge-removal, etc., unavoidable due to cheap food policy	16·2	8·5	8·8	4·9
Problem manufactured by environmentalists	28·6	15·0	14·0	7·8
Farmers have gone too far in changing environment	5·7	3·0	21·1	11·7
Some justifications in criticisms of farmers	20·0	10·5	36·8	20·6
Not a problem of farmers' making	14·3	7·5	12·3	6·9
No problem/nothing wrong with modern methods of farming	13·4	7·0	10·6	5·9
Other	1·0	0·5	—	—
D.K./N.A.	1·9	1·0	1·8	1·0
Total		100		100

for the environment as a problem manufactured by environmentalists and only 5·7 per cent of them believed that farmers had gone too far in altering the environment, compared with 21·1 per cent who expressed this view in the forty-four parishes. Similarly there were differences between the different types of farmers with those most hostile to conservation being the agri-businessmen, whereas the group most sympathetic were the family farmers, 22·2 per cent of whom believed that farmers had already gone too far in altering the environment, compared with only 2·9 per cent of the agri-businessmen. Moreover 53·4 per cent of the agri-businessmen denied that there was a problem, compared with 22·2 per cent of the family farmers. However, hostility towards environmentalists remained constant over all types of farmers in both samples.

We asked our respondents a specific question about whether they were troubled by preservation or amenity societies. In each sample only a minority expressed concern, though the size of the minority was substantial – 39 per cent in the 1000 + acres sample and 30 per cent in the forty-four parishes. When we questioned the farmers further about what precise 'trouble' they had had locally with either amenity societies or with locals it was clear that *access* to their land, specifically footpaths, was the most important cause of friction, followed equally, but both only about one-third as frequently mentioned, by stubble-burning and hedge removal. That is to say, modern farming practice was not as frequently an irritant to other non-farming residents as access to the land itself. This kind of felt resentment is not purely a reflection of the farmers' activities but also depends upon the degree of vigour with which local amenity societies are prepared to pursue their aims. It should also be remembered – and it is illustrated in the quotations cited above – that the amenity societies are seen by farmers as being run by and for newcomers to the countryside – by outsiders to the local social system who have different attitudes and values and see the countryside as *amenity* not as a factor of production. Little wonder, then, that there is friction between newcomer and farmer.

The attitudes of our respondents towards environmental conservation is, nevertheless, considerably more complicated than the stereotype held of them by newcomers would suggest. By no means all farmers are as antipathetic to the conservationist case as is sometimes assumed. However disputes over access and landscape changes are generally the channels through which friction derived from other factors may run. Undoubtedly farmers are disturbed by the presence of competitors for local status positions who, for once, do not seem to 'know their place' in the local community and over whom farmers do not have the power which stems from being their employers. Disputes over broadly environmental issues can be merely outlets for the frustrations which inevitably arise out of such changes, providing farmers with the occasional excuse to try to reassert their former unquestioned authority. Notwithstanding the trials and tribulations over the arrival of the newcomers, however, we should not lose sight of the fact that the general agreement among farmers over a range of issues – the loss of 'community', the hostility of the outside world towards them, their ideas about what makes a good farmer – suggest that they are highly integrated into a local, rural and agricultural social network. Given both their interactional patterns and the uniformity of their normative replies, there seems clear evidence here of a very high degree of moral integration among farmers. That this is locally based is also an important conclusion – as we shall see in the following chapter.

6 The rural power structure

During the nineteenth and early twentieth centuries, the question of who held power in rural England was hardly problematic. Whatever their internal differences of opinion, landowners and farmers formed, from the point of view of rural workers, a coherent and easily identifiable rural ruling class which retained a firm grip upon all the important institutions of rural society – the land, employment, housing, education and the law. At the apex of this ruling class stood the traditional English landowning aristocracy which, together with the landed gentry and titled families of county society, dominated the social and political activities of rural areas. For generations their power and benevolence enveloped all aspects of rural life, aided and abetted by a respectful tenantry. As Bernard Cracroft complained in 1867:

So vast is their traditional power, so broadly does it sit over the land, so deep and ancient are its roots, so multiplied and ramified everywhere are its tendrils and creepers and feelers that the danger is never lest they should have too little, but always that they should have too much power, and so, even involuntarily, choke down the possibilities of new life from below. [Cited in Guttsman, 1969, p. 151.]

Such power was often personified by the imposing figure of the local squire, who until the First World War was a seemingly permanent and enduring fixture on the rural scene. Over the last hundred years, however, squirearchical rule has come under severe attack, first, as Thompson (1963) has documented, from a farming tenantry increasingly impatient with their economic and political omnipotence, while more recently, as the previous chapter has indicated, both farmers and the remnants of the traditional squirearchy have seen their hegemony threatened by the arrival of middle-class ex-urbanites.

Taken together, these two changes suggest that the class domination of rural England, which was so manifest during the nineteenth century, has become less coherent and less personalized. At the very least such changes suggest that the nature and mechanisms of political power in rural areas are a matter for serious empirical investigation rather than *a priori* assumption. Of considerable significance here has been the growing bureaucratization of local government and the democratization of local politics since 1888, for both have resulted in the development of an increasingly formal and impersonal structure of local administration in which 'public persons' have largely replaced traditional 'social leaders' in positions of local power (Lee, 1963). That is to say that the spread of citizenship (Marshall, 1965) into even the most remote rural areas of East Anglia has ensured that the economic power and status traditionally associated with the landed upper class is no longer an *automatic* passport to political dominance. In part this has been due to the continuing rationalization and professionalization of local administrative functions, something often imposed by central government and associated with the 'eclipse' of community (Stein, 1964) in advanced capitalist societies, but it has also been due to the necessity of modern political leaders to cultivate electoral support.

Yet, despite the undoubted erosion of the personal power of the local resident squire, it is also the case that this power has by no means disappeared. While the break-up of the landed estates shortly after the First World War undoubtedly rendered local village squires increasingly rare and anachronistic figures, anyone with any familiarity with East Anglia will realize that they are far from being an extinct species. Any analysis of the current situation must therefore begin with an assessment of the extent to which squirearchical rule in the area has declined.

The gradual decline of the squirearchy

Prior to 1888 there was no unified system of local government administration in rural areas. Since the Poor Relief Act of 1601, villages had been governed by parish vestries. These were meetings of local householders held under the guidance of the clergy which enjoyed the power to levy a poor rate for charitable use. As Smellie (1968) notes, the vestry was for many years the only popular assembly outside Parliament with the right to impose compulsory taxation, but by the nineteenth century its powers were in decline, and a number of other more formal bodies began to be established for the purposes of local government. In 1834, for example, the Poor Law Amendment Act consolidated the hitherto haphazard growth of Poor Law unions. Each union extended over several parishes (in East Anglia they corresponded to the traditional 'Hundreds') and was controlled by an annually elected board of guardians. Then in 1848, local boards of health were introduced, while later still, burial boards, highways boards, sewerage and drainage boards, and, in 1871, school boards, were added to a growing list of local authority bodies, resulting in a system of rural local government which was hopelessly fragmented and confused:

So far as any principle can be detected beneath this multiplication of local authorities, it was 'for each function, its own authority'. . . . Confusion and fragmentation were probably at their worst in the English countryside where, as the greatest public health expert of the day said, there was one authority (the Vestry) for every privy, and another (the Guardians) for every pigsty. [Best, 1971, p. 37.]

To the extent that there was any unity in this administrative chaos, it derived from the power of the Justices of the Peace, whose functions included not only the dispensation of justice, but also a part in the administration of the Poor Law, highways and bridges, paving, lighting, street cleansing, licensing, property valuation and, from 1856, the police. Local Justices often exerted considerable influence over vestry meetings, and were also accorded membership *ex officio* of the various administrative boards which were running affairs in their area, with the result that they could 'attend meetings when they wished to influence policy, and otherwise allow the elected representatives to carry on the day to day administration' (Lee, 1963, p. 47). Despite their powers, however, they were never subject to popular election, but were rather appointed to their office by the Lords Lieutenant of the county in which they resided. Lords Lieutenant, who were themselves appointed for life by the prime minister of the day from among the peers of the realm, not surprisingly selected local Justices from a highly restricted range of eligibles; indeed, the prohibitive property qualification for magistrates, introduced in 1744, virtually ensured this. The landed gentry and aristocracy which dominated the Quarter-Sessions throughout these years have justly been described by Lee as 'perhaps the purest example of oligarchy to be seen in England' (1963, p. 4). Similarly, Whitfield, in his historical survey of local government in Suffolk, describes the Justices in that county as 'an almost exclusive oligarchy of landowners', and points to the customary restriction of the office of Lord Lieutenant to 'the heads of a very few noble families with extensive estates in the county' (1970, p. 21). It was not until 1909 that Lords Lieutenant ceased to be solely responsible for this particularly significant form of local patronage, but even today they still chair the small and secretive selection committees on whose recommendations magistrates continue to be appointed. Today, however, the power of the Justices is more confined to strictly judicial matters.

It was largely as a result of the confusion of authorities and multiplication and duplication of local government functions through the nineteenth century that Parliament established a system of county councils in 1888, and rural district and parish councils six years later. The two Local Government Acts which introduced these reforms can be understood as attempts not only to rationalize but to democratize rural local government, for the new authorities were to be elected on a universal suffrage. For the radicals, these reforms represented the means by which power would be transferred in the country areas from the hands of the privileged to the hands of the masses – the introduction of the parish councils in particular was widely hailed as a peasants' charter. For the conservatives, on the other hand, these changes were seen as a direct attack on the rural upper classes, and were strongly resented and opposed. The powers of the upper-class Justices, for example, were stripped away and placed in the hands of the new county councils, while the traditional 'social leaders' of the countryside were for the first time to be exposed to the vagaries and vulgarities of public elections. Furthermore, the influence of the church and the squirearchy in parish affairs was seemingly smashed by the replacement of vestry meetings by parish councils. As Arnold-Baker (1958, p. 5) has noted:

In 1894 the squire, the parson, and sometimes the schoolmaster were the leaders of the village. Their influence depended upon their traditional prestige, their superior education, and their relative wealth and, in a hierarchical society, upon their social standing. The vestries had followed their lead, taken their advice, or bowed to their power. The Parish Councils were regarded as an intrusion.

In many areas, this resentment resulted in a sharp conflict between the new parish councils and the old ruling class (cf. Ambrose, 1974). A bloodless revolution, it seemed, was occurring in the countryside, and the days of the squirearchy were numbered.

In retrospect, however, the significance of the 1888–94 reforms was minimal as regards any transfer of power from one class to another.

The new parish councils, for example, never fulfilled the hopes and aspirations which the radicals had had for them. Their functions were limited, and their potential highly restricted through lack of finance. They were, in any case, dominated still by the wealthy and educated minorities of rural society, and in many instances their memberships appeared little different from the traditional social and political leaderships of country parishes for centuries before: 'Despite being hailed as the Peasants' Charter, the Act of 1894 introducing Parish Councils did very little to alter the basic form of local government at parish level; it merely provided the squire and parson with a more useful means of carrying on as before' (Mitchell, 1951, p. 394). Nor did the social composition of the new county councils appear to present any challenge to the traditional hegemony of landed interests. Lee (1963), for example, shows that in Cheshire, no fewer than forty-seven of the seventy-six members of the new county authority were Justices of the Peace. In the country as a whole, twenty-six of the forty-eight new counties selected the chairman of the Quarter-Sessions as their first chairman. Both of the new Suffolk county councils[1] selected magistrates as their first chairman, while their aldermanic benches contained virtually all the leading figures from the Quarter-Sessions, including some names (e.g. Hervey, Rous, Tollemache, Rowley) which remain familiar in local government circles in Suffolk to this day. As Whitfield (1970) notes, the families which had dominated the magistracy from the seventeenth century onwards in Suffolk came to dominate the new county authorities in 1888, and their influence was thereby perpetuated into the present century. Thus, of the eleven chairmen of the East Suffolk County Council between its inception in 1889 and its termination (due to the reorganization of local government) in 1974, no less than eight were titled members of the nobility. In Suffolk as elsewhere, therefore, the reforms of the late nineteenth century did little to overturn or even weaken the traditional domination of landed interests in the county.

If the personnel changed little, however, the basis on which the traditional ruling class continued to exercise its power did slowly alter. Throughout the last eighty years, power in rural areas has come less and less to be associated with particular individuals and families *per se*, and more and more to be the property of certain bureaucratically defined positions. Thus, although the same class continued to exercise power well into the twentieth century, they did so only by seeking public office, through which they were increasingly obliged to exercise their traditional political privileges. There has, in other words, been a slow but progressive shift in the mode of their authority from that deriving out of tradition and custom towards that vested in formal office as legally defined (Weber, 1964). The 1974 reorganization of local government in England and Wales is only the latest of a series of changes which have served to weaken particularistic modes of control, and to rationalize the government of rural areas, thereby impelling the traditional ruling class into increasing dependence for its power on the occupancy of formal office.

None of this, however, should be taken to mean that the *personal* influence of the squirearchy died completely with the 1888–94 reforms. Perrott, for example, notes that at least until the Great War 'an approving nod from the man at the Big House was necessary in most areas of local decision' (1968, p. 184), while Thompson suggests that 'Nowhere before 1914 did local communities altogether repudiate their traditional leadership or throw off their traditional respect' (1963, p. 211). Nor, indeed, was the decline of the squirearchy after the First World War quite as dramatic as is sometimes imagined, for even today the benevolence of the 'Big House' in some rural areas (and notably in parts of East Anglia) appears to have withstood the economic and social upheavals of the last fifty years, while the status and personal authority of its occupants remains clearly in evidence. In Norfolk, for example, Johnson (1973) found that the political power of the 'old families' was still marked, and that the large landowners in the area continued to 'inspire considerable awe and occasionally not a little fear' (p. 18). The significance of the squirearchy in East Anglia in particular appears to have been in only gradual decline this century, for, as Whitfield (1970) notes, the area's relative isolation from the Industrial Revolution and its continuing dependence on agriculture prevented the emergence of any competing industrially-based local leaderships, while, as we shall see later, it is only in the last decade or so that an immigrant 'middle class' has begun to challenge for local leadership positions. This need not imply, however, that farmers and landowners are no longer the dominant political group in rural society. Nevertheless the shift towards a more formalized framework of local government institutions has ensured that the continuing political domination of rural society by farmers and landowners has been carried out through an accommodation to these new conditions.

The farming interest in local government today

Consequently, as a first step in analysing the political significance of farmers and landowners in East Anglia we must consider the extent to which they have achieved positions of dominance within the local authorities which now govern the area. We do so in the full knowledge that the parameters of local power are to some extent set by the central institutions of the state over which local political leaders have little control. However, we wish to argue that over two crucial resources – the provision of employment opportunities (through local planning policies) and the provision of housing – the control of local authorities provides a key to a considerable degree of control over the life-chances of rural workers. Our analysis must therefore take us beyond the farm gate, and even the individual village community, to consider the extent of political dominance exerted by farmers and landowners in the administration of the area.

In particular we shall concentrate upon the county of Suffolk, within which the forty-four parishes are located and where we have carried out an extensive case study of the role of the agricultural interest in local government. This involved an examination of local political issues at both the county council and district council levels. More specifically we concentrated upon the former rural district councils of Deben, Blyth, Gipping and Hartismere, which are contiguous with the forty-four parishes. Since 1974 these councils have formed part of the new Mid-Suffolk and Suffolk Coastal district councils, the former remaining almost entirely rural in character while the latter has involved the amalgamation of the former urban districts of Felixstowe, Leiston and Woodbridge with their rural hinterlands. This has enabled a useful comparison to be made concerning the adaptability of farmers and landowners in local government to changed political circumstances. Because of limitations on space we cannot hope to cover the whole range of activities in which these authorities were engaged. Instead, we shall concentrate upon two – planning and housing – which most directly affect the position of local farm workers. (For a discussion of the reasons for taking a decision-making approach to the study of community power, see Saunders *et al.*, 1978. Details of our research techniques are given in Appendix 3.)

First, however, it is necessary to introduce a note of caution. Clearly numerical representation on a local council body of itself means little. It may be politically significant when it comes to winning votes but it should be recognized that a small number of well-organized individuals holding key strategic positions may regularly dominate a relatively disorganized majority. Such, indeed, is the principle of 'cybernetic hierarchy' of which Parsons (1966), Buckley (1967) and others have written. It is thus necessary to consider not only what proportions of council members in East Anglia are farmers or have economic interests connected with agriculture, but also to ascertain the extent to which farmers and landowners occupy positions as 'gatekeepers' (Pettigrew, 1972) within local authorities. This will generally involve analysis of the occupancy of committee chairmanships, and of key policy-making committees. Moreover, it does not necessarily follow that, if farmers (or any other group) occupy key gatekeeper positions, they are therefore powerful. The point here is that power is a potential quality: political positions represent one type of power resource which must nevertheless be used before power can be said to have been exercised (Martin, 1971). This is important if we are to avoid any naïve positional approach to the analysis of community power (see Bell and Newby, 1971). Too many 'élite' studies have taken the positional definition of powerful groups for granted, yet power, as we shall see, cannot adequately be studied from any such static perspective.

Furthermore, even if farmers are seen to occupy and to use key positions within local authorities, it should not be assumed that they are therefore exercising power in their own interests. Again, as we shall see, farmers and landowners themselves often cite altruism, philanthropy, and public service as their motives for becoming involved in local government in their areas – values, incidentally which reflect the 'gentlemanly ethic' (Wilkinson, 1970) traditionally associated with the rural squirearchy. Such articulated motives should not lightly be ignored. As Giddens (1974, p. xii) writes:

We are surely not justified in making direct inferences from the social background, or even the educational experience, of élite groups to the way in which they employ whatever power they possess once they attain positions of eminence. Because a man emanates from a specific type of class background, it does not inevitably follow that he will later adopt policies which are designed to promote class interests corresponding to that background.

It is not enough then, to look simply at *who* is exercising power without also considering the question of who is benefiting as a result. One group may presumably exercise power in the interests of another. As Westergaard (1974, p. 29) correctly observes, 'The final test of power . . . is not *who* decides, but *what* is decided – and not decided.'

We must then, consider the possibility that any given group may presumably enjoy power (in the sense of the achievement of their interests) even though they actually *do* nothing. This raises a host of theoretical and methodological problems which we shall consider later in the chapter. For the moment, we need only note that if individuals or groups may not always be observed in the exercise of their power, and that if the defining character of power is benefit, then we must be in a position to isolate what the 'interests' of different groups are, and thus to assess the extent to which such interests are furthered or hindered by given instances of the exercise of power (Lukes, 1974). In the present case, therefore, we must consider what is objectively in the interests of farmers if we are to assess their political strength through analysis of empirical instances of the exercise of power.

Let us, however, begin by tracing the nominal strength of farmers and landowners in East Anglian local government. We would expect, of course, that in a rural region whose economy is heavily dependent upon agriculture, farmers would figure centrally in the formal positions of power and responsibility. The Maud committee findings of 1967 indicated that farmers did, at the time of that survey, comprise the major occupational group on rural district councils, accounting for 35 per cent of all rural district members in England and Wales (Moss and Parker, 1967). In order to assess whether this was still the case in the East Anglian region, we conducted a questionnaire survey among virtually all East Anglian local authority members in the autumn of 1973, just six months before local government reorganization came into effect.[2] The results were fairly predictable. Twenty-one per cent of our total respondents were farmers, this proportion rising to 31 per cent among rural district councillors. Furthermore, the 'agricultural interest' as a whole in the region's local government was even stronger, for another 4 per cent of our respondents were part-time farmers (e.g. 'gentleman farmers' among members of the armed forces, and company managers and directors who ran farms as a sideline or a hobby), and 5 per cent were directly involved in, or dependent upon, the agricultural industry in the region (e.g. directors of companies involved in the manufacture, processing or distribution of agricultural implements, chemicals, or foodstuffs, agricultural advisers and research staff, land agents, farm managers, and – in just five individual cases – farm workers). In total, well over 300 of our respondents – 30 per cent of the total – had some form of direct agricultural interest. Again, this agricultural interest group was numerically strongest in the rural district councils, where it accounted for 42 per cent of all members, although it also figured prominently in county councils where it represented 29 per cent of the total membership. In Norfolk, where the proportion of farmers and related occupations involved in local government was highest, no less than 50 per cent of rural district councillors were found to have an agricultural interest. Clearly, at least before re-organization, farmers and their associates were well represented at all levels in the region's local government structure.

We noted earlier, however, that occupancy of strategic positions in decision-making bureaucracies was possibly more significant politically than sheer weight of numbers. Here too, though, farmers and landowners were found to be potentially strong. Thus, taking the chairmanships of councils, council committees, and council sub-committees as indicative of key gatekeeper positions in local authorities (see, for example, the findings of the Maud Report, and of various local government case-studies – notably Bealey *et al.*, 1965), farmers were consistently over-represented in key positions relative to their proportionate numbers in council memberships as a whole. Thirty-five per cent of those of our respondents who were farmers reported occupancy of at least one such position. Farmers were over-represented among chairmen in all types of councils. Thus, although they accounted for less than two in ten of all county council members, they held three in ten of all county council chairmanships. Similarly, while accounting for only three in ten of all rural district council members, they held four out of every ten rural district chairmanships. To the extent that chairmen of committees are in positions of significant potential power in local authorities, it is clear that farmers (and, indeed, those in allied occupations) enjoyed a political capacity beyond the level of their representation in East Anglian local government as a whole.[3]

Before considering whether this pattern was changed in any way by the 1974 reorganization, it is worth noting what types of farmers were found on the old local authorities. Seventy-three per cent of them, for example, employed some labour. Indeed, 42 per cent employed at least five workers, indicating an agricultural enterprise of considerable size. Yet in the East Anglian region in 1973, only 32 per cent of farmers employed labour, while only 8 per cent employed five workers or more. It was thus the larger farmers who predominated on local councils. Furthermore, no less than 71 per cent of the farmers on East Anglian local authorities had attended fee-paying (private or public) schools. Yet as we saw in Chapter 2, even among the 1000+ acres farmers whom we interviewed, only 65 per cent had attended such schools. Clearly, those farmers who achieved election to local authorities in the region were generally relatively large farmers from relatively prosperous, upper- or upper-middle-class backgrounds.

Not only were these farmers atypical in terms of size and background, however, but they were also atypical as regards the depth of their involvement in local affairs. Twelve per cent of them, for example, were JPs, 32 per cent held lay positions in the church such as wardens and membership of parochial church councils; 26 per cent sat on local administrative bodies such as water and drainage boards. In all, 87 per cent of them held at least one local position of responsibility other than membership of a local council. Yet as we saw earlier, among our sample of farmers as a whole in the region, only 56 per cent held any positions of responsibility. A similar picture emerges in relation to participation in local voluntary organizations; only 4 per cent of the farmers in the local government survey did not belong to any local clubs or associations, the equivalent figure among our sample of all farmers being 44 per cent. Clearly, the type of farmer who, at least before 1974, came to participate in local government affairs was somewhat atypical, and when we discuss the size and significance of 'the farming interest' in local government, it is important to keep in mind that we are discussing in the main the larger, higher-status, and more community-conscious farmers. In short, we are looking at much the same class of farmers as that which has dominated rural politics for centuries.

But what of the composition of local authority councils today? The local reaction to the new authorities which were introduced in 1974 was qualitatively little different from that which greeted the 1888–94 reforms, for reorganization posed a severe threat to the size and significance of the farming interest in local government throughout the region. At both county and district levels, old authorities were amalgamated into new, larger authorities, and once distinct urban and rural councils were frequently brought together into a single administrative unit. In Suffolk, for example, the Ipswich County Borough was amalgamated with the predominantly rural East and West Suffolk County Councils, while at the district level, rural district councils were brought in with urban districts and boroughs. Not only did these changes provoke considerable antagonism among rural representatives at what they saw was the challenge (and sometimes the virtual eclipse) posed by the numerical strength of urban representatives on many new authorities, but they also led inevitably to a decline in particularism in local politics, and a corresponding rise in the significance of formal political parties in contesting local elections. Before 1974 many rural councillors on the district and county councils had managed to secure election independently of any party political patronage and support, for wards were relatively small, and the more prominent members of the locality (notably, of course, the larger farmers) were sufficiently well known throughout the area for them to run on a 'personal vote'. With the reorganized larger authorities, however, wards increased dramatically in size, and the personal vote was correspondingly dissipated as indicated by the sharp decline in number of candidates elected independently of party sponsorship (see below). This has significantly affected the level of farmers' representation on the new authorities. On the Suffolk County Council, for example, we estimate the proportion of farmers at 16 per cent of the total, while on the two district councils which we have studied the proportions are 35 per cent in Mid-Suffolk and 11 per cent in Suffolk Coastal. The numerical strength of the farming interest thus appears to have declined slightly overall, but notably so where new authorities have been formed out of both rural and urban areas (e.g. in Suffolk Coastal, where only 58 per cent of the members represent old rural district areas, while the remainder represent old urban authorities such as Felixstowe and Woodbridge).

But how significant is this decline in numerical representation? We saw that in the old authorities farmers were over-represented, relative to their numbers, in positions of greatest potential power – i.e. committee chairmanships. We found that the same was still true at the county level in Suffolk following reorganization. Indeed, although farmers and landowners accounted for only 16 per cent of the total county council membership, they enjoyed something approaching a monopoly over key positions. Thus the chairman and vice-chairman of the county council were both farmers. So too was the leader of the majority Conservative group (who was also leader of the council). The chairman of the Planning Committee owned and farmed over a thousand acres in Suffolk as did the Education Committee chairman. The chairmanships of the key finance and policy sub-committees were both held by farmers, while the chairman of the Social Services Committee was a large landowner. There were, in fact, no major committees on the county council which were not chaired by farmers or landowners.

At the district level, the picture was rather more confused. On Mid-Suffolk Council, where farmers still accounted for 35 per cent of all members, the chairman of the council and the chairmen of three of the four committees were farmers or agricultural landowners. On Suffolk Coastal, however, only one of the five committee chairmanships was filled by a farmer, and he was a Labour Party member (see below). Thus again we see that in Suffolk Coastal where reorganization led to the amalgamation of urban and rural authorities, the potential power of the farming interest dipped significantly, while it was maintained at a consistently high level in both the overwhelmingly rural Mid-Suffolk and the new county councils.

Farmers, then, generally continued to occupy potentially key positions at both district and county levels in Suffolk. Indeed, their potential power extended even further. At the parish level, for example, at least in the more rural areas, local farmers continued to dominate, while the continuing presence of farmers and landowners on rural constituency Conservative Party selection committees has ensured that virtually all of Suffolk's representatives at Westminster are in some way connected with agriculture.[4] None of this by itself means a great deal, of course, for as we noted earlier, it is not enough to point to the political potential of farming and landowning interests in the county. The fundamental question remains: to what extent is this potential realized?

Environment, planning and the farming interest

We saw in Chapter 5 that a widely recognized and often publicized source of conflict and acrimony in rural areas relates to the threat posed by new agricultural techniques to the rural environment. The complaints of newly-arrived residents concerning farmers' apparent disregard for the beauty of the countryside are matched in intensity and frequency only by the complaints of farmers concerning the newcomers' apparent ignorance of the facts of modern farming practice. This cleavage along the classic urban/rural, newcomer/local dimensions regularly manifests itself in various conflicts over rights of way, landscaping, and so on, and thus invariably involves the intervention or mediation of local planning authorities – the district councils in the case of development control questions (such as the granting of planning permission for a new worker's cottage), and the county council in the case of broader strategic planning issues (e.g. decisions on zoning and land use). Many farmers recognize the significance of local authority planning policies in relation to their own farming enterprises – no less than 40 per cent of those farmers interviewed in our survey, for example, cited planning as the single most important aspect of local authority decision-making (the next most frequently identified policy area, mentioned by 22 per cent, related to local rate levels).

The relationship between the planning authorities and the farming community in Suffolk is generally one of harmony and cooperation. In the words of one large-scale farmer:

Farmers are a very strong interest group in rural areas. For example, I've never had any problems over planning decisions. They're generally fairly sympathetic – even on factory farming – in rural areas. Generally, they're very helpful and understanding.

Other informants similarly stressed the sympathy with which the planning authorities generally viewed farmers' interests, and the informality of the relationship between the two:

We don't have many problems on planning matters. . . . We don't have sessions of getting together with all the District Councillors who are farmers, or with the County Councillors. It's just an agreed attitude between us. [NFU official.]

The NFU and CLA work very well. . . . But then again, we see them. I see the secretaries of both organisations if they want to come and see me. What helps is knowing all these people and being really friendly with them. [County councillor and landowner.]

Underpinning this close and informal liaison is a fundamental article of faith subscribed to equally by both parties – namely, that Suffolk's principal industry is agriculture, and that anything which benefits the county's farmers must *ipso facto* benefit the county as a whole:

We are all mixed up with the agricultural thing. I mean, when you boil it down, the towns and villages and what-have-you in Suffolk in the main are dependent on agriculture, so that we really have all got the same ends all the time. [Former rural district council chairman.]

All the decisions that I can remember have accepted that Suffolk is fundamentally an agricultural county – agriculture is our principal industry and will remain so. . . . Generally speaking, this is an accepted idea – it's good agricultural land in Suffolk. [County council committee chairman and large landowner.]

We do want to try to maintain as much good agricultural land as possible. ... We want it appreciated – and it is within the County Council – that the prosperity of the county is highly dependent on agriculture. [NFU officer.]

Farmers are the start of a chain. Others earn a living through the farmer – corn merchants, vets, millers, machinery manufacturers, and so on. If the farmer isn't looked after, these people suffer. [1000-acre farmer.]

In this sense, the agricultural interest and the 'public interest' are synonymous, or are at least seen to be so. Indeed, the identification drawn by local and county planners between the two has often resulted in a marked reluctance on the part of local authorities to invoke such powers as they have in order to force farmers to observe regulations which may hinder the profitability of agricultural enterprises. A case in point concerns the voluntary planning agreements reached with the NFU and CLA in relation to development in the Dedham Vale.

The Dedham Vale, which forms the boundary between Suffolk and Essex, is one of East Anglia's most renowned beauty spots. Immortalized in Constable's paintings, the Vale (or, at least, twenty-three square miles of it) has been a designated Area of Outstanding Natural Beauty since the late 1960s, due mainly to the publication of a survey of the area in 1966, and of proposals for the future of the area in 1968, by the three planning authorities with interests in the Vale (Essex, West Suffolk and East Suffolk County Councils). In their 1968 *Dedham Vale Proposals*, the three sets of county planners noted that while industrial and residential development in the Vale could be strictly controlled (indeed, virtually no such development was to be allowed in the future – see later), agricultural development could not, for the only agricultural buildings ordinarily subject to planning control were those of over five thousand square feet in area, or forty feet in height. Most buildings, needless to say, were small enough to be exempt on the basis of such criteria. However, it was possible to bring these smaller farm building developments under the control of the planning authorities by seeking what is known as an 'Article Four Direction' which would make it compulsory for all farmers in the area to apply for formal planning permission for *any* new proposed development. Such a course of action was apparently considered by the planners, but as the report indicates, the spirit of harmony and cooperation soon reasserted itself:

The three counties had considered that effective control over the erection of agricultural buildings could be obtained only by the application of an Article 4 (Class VI) Direction over all new agricultural buildings in the Vale, but following strong representations from the Ministry of Agriculture, National Farmers' Union, and Country Landowners' Association, it has been agreed that a voluntary liaison system will be adopted as an alternative. [*Dedham Vale Proposals*, 1968, p. 27.]

It was agreed that the NFU and CLA should 'request' their members' full cooperation in submitting any plans for future development to the relevant planning authority. Then, as the report put it:

If no objection is raised, the farmer will be informed by letter as soon as possible, but if any alterations or special requirements are thought necessary, the local planning authority will contact the farmer and discuss the matter with him. . . . In cases where agreement on alterations cannot be reached, the local planning authority would notify the farmer of their intention to report the matter to the Liaison Committee [p. 27].

In other words, if a farmer refused to comply with the suggestions of the planning authority, the dispute was to go before a committee consisting of two NFU representatives, one CLA representative, one representative from each of the three county planning departments and a Ministry of Agriculture adviser.

The committee would consider the proposal, and if agreement could be reached, the National Farmers' Union and Country Landowners' Association would try to negotiate for agreement with the farmer. In cases where the Liaison Committee is unsuccessful in finding a solution, the Local planning authority will resort to reporting to their members, possibly with a recommendation to make a specific Article 4 (Class VI) Direction on the area covered by the proposal [p. 27].

Thus, while householders in the Vale are *obliged* to gain planning permission for as much as the erection of a front-door porch, farmers are *asked* by their own organizations to cooperate in a *voluntary* scheme involving *informal* discussions with local planners, and (in the event of disagreement) *arbitration* by a committee on which planners are in a numerical minority. Only in the last resort will one of the county councils involved even *consider* the possibility of imposing an Article Four Direction. This voluntary system remains in operation today, and is indicative of the relationship which exists between farming interests and planners in Suffolk.

Although the development of farm buildings is one very significant area in which the conflict between farming profits and environmental aesthetics becomes manifest, another of equal importance concerns the erection by farmers of new cottages in which to house their workers. As we saw in Chapter 4, the great majority of farmers believe that, in order to attract suitable labour to work for them, they have first to offer accommodation. This creates problems for those (few) farmers who wish to expand their labour force, and for those who wish to replace a retired worker without evicting him from his cottage, as most farms are by definition in the most rural areas of the county where mains services are largely absent, and where, according to long-established county strategic planning policy (in East Suffolk, at any rate), virtually all development is prohibited. There is therefore a continuing tension between the demands of farmers for permission for tied housing development and the restrictions imposed by the county council's planning policies, and this was strongly reflected in our interviews with farmers in the area:

We're trying to put up some new bungalows and they've messed us about. We eventually got outline planning permission, but now they won't agree to the colour of the tiles and the shape of the windows.

We're affected a hell of a lot – especially on houses. We've had tremendous trouble getting permission for a worker's bungalow. They've got their priorities wrong on these councils. In the country they say that villages should be clustered together, but you need workers on the spot when you've got livestock. In a family, you don't put your children in one place and yourself in another, do you?

This problem tends to affect only a particular section of the farming population and these are often the smaller or medium-scale farmers. The larger farmers, are usually well established, and having seen their labour force decline over the years with mechanization, may well enjoy a surplus rather than a shortage of tied housing. It is, for example, no coincidence that although 40 per cent of our respondents expressed concern with council planning policies, and this proportion remained constant for both samples, there were nevertheless significant differences in the nature of their concern. Smaller farmers were overwhelmingly concerned with development control policies – precisely the area concerned with questions such as the construction of a new tied house. Thus, of the smaller farmers who cited planning as an area of concern, nearly three out of every four discussed development control issues. The larger farmers, by contrast, were generally far more concerned with strategic planning issues – whether industrial growth should be permitted in the countryside, or a sharp increase in population be encouraged, and so on. Only one in four of them discussed such relatively parochial planning matters as the difficulty of gaining permission for a new bungalow.

This difference in emphasis between larger and smaller farmers points to a very real conflict of interests between them, for while many smaller farmers want a relaxation of planning controls in the countryside, a large proportion of the larger, and especially the more traditional, farmers and landowners want a continuation, and even a tightening, of restrictions on rural development. A 300-acre farmer expressed this well when he commented:

The local farmer hasn't got such rigid ideas about preservation. He's more in contact with circumstances – more practical than the aristocratic big landowner who just wants his two and three thousand acres and doesn't want it touched.

These larger farmers, indeed, are often to be found taking leading and active parts in local preservation and amenity groups – the very organizations which the smaller or more economically rational farmers often despise and oppose:

Of course, we have farmers in our membership, but not the local tough farmers – they don't like us because we keep an eye on what they are doing. Our type of farmer is basically the larger owner-occupier. I should think about two or three hundred of that type belong to the Society, but very few of these tough working farmers. [Suffolk Preservation Society member.]

This has at times led to quite bitter public disputes between traditional landed interests dominating a local amenity group, and more 'progressive' farming and entrepreneurial interests on parish councils.

Parish councillors are more – I'm not being disparaging – they're usually go-ahead people who want to get things moving. They tend to be developers. But we are warners against development. So you're bound to get controversy between a Parish Council wanting more council houses and industry, and a Society which says that, if you have houses, you completely wreck the view and won't get people looking at it. [Landowner and amenity society chairman.]

The X Society is not an official body – it's the old tie brigade. It's a society formed by property-owners – not farmers – who wanted to preserve their own outlook, and make sure no one comes along and spoils it. It's a selfish outlook. Now while we fully agree that X has many attractions, there's a limit to which it should be restricted to others. We don't agree with opposing all development. There are local people whose offspring want to live here. Why should a self-formed society say no development? [Farmer and parish council chairman.]

Such opposition between parish councils calling for limited growth, and preservation/amenity societies intent on preventing any development, is characteristic of many different villages in Suffolk, and especially of those in recognized Areas of Outstanding Natural Beauty where environmental groups are usually strong, and planning restrictions severe.

This same conflict between conservationist landowners and expansionist farmers has also at times manifested itself in clashes between the county and district levels of government in Suffolk. Before 1974, for example, there was a history of acrimony between the wealthy and often titled landowners on the East Suffolk County Council, and the medium-sized farmers on some of the more northerly (and hence more 'rural') rural district councils. The old Hartismere RDC was a case in point. As one farmer and ex-Hartismere member explained:

I'm an opponent of the planners. We did things in Hartismere a different way. We used to send them on to the County Council. But the county council had a terrible name in this area. They wouldn't let anybody do anything. A lot of these arty types on it – they wouldn't allow building.

Or, as a former planning officer from a nearby authority reminisced:

It wasn't smooth sailing at all in the old Hartismere area. The members in that area didn't accept the County's policy. What they used to say was, 'If there's a sewer, you can build a house.' They didn't care about scattered development. . . . You used to put the flags out if they refused anything.

Clearly, then, we are faced with a rather more complicated picture than was painted at the beginning of this section, for it appears that while *some* farmers find themselves opposed to the policies of environmental protection implemented by the local planning authorities in Suffolk, others fully support them. There is, therefore, no clear division between agricultural and environmental interests. We shall consider the reasons why certain types of farmers and landowners support the environmental cause while others oppose it later in this chapter. First, however, we should note the political consequences of this situation.

The movement for environmental preservation and conservation in Britain is narrowly-based (Cotgrove, 1976). Eversley, for example, sees it as 'élitist', comprising 'the ever present ancient establishment, the landed aristocracy, the products of Oxford and Cambridge, the landowners, the officer class, and, behind them, the hangers-on' (1974, p. 15). Nevertheless, like terms such as 'progress' and 'equality of opportunity', 'environmental conservation' has for many people become an 'obviously' desirable objective. In other words, though grounded in sectional interests and promoted by a small number of relatively privileged people, conservationist sentiment has to a large extent entered the national consciousness (see Lowe, 1975; Law, 1974). As Herfindahl (1965, p. 229) puts it:

The imprecision surrounding use of the word 'conservation' has been associated with widespread attempts to appropriate its persuasive sound for special interests. If a certain proposal is labelled a conservation proposal . . . there is probably a tendency for more favourable reaction than if a less emotive term is used. After all, if a person is asked whether it is better to conserve or not conserve, he no doubt will vote for conservation.

Thus, just as agricultural prosperity seems obviously to be in everybody's interests when the economic base of a given locality is grounded in the agricultural industry, so too environmental conservation seems self-evidently a 'good thing'. After all, does not the state of the environment concern every one of us?

From such an argument, it follows that for landowners (as indeed for farmers) there appears to be a happy coincidence between the pursuit of self-interest and the defence of the 'public interest'. Thus while farmers can pursue profits in the 'knowledge' that others will benefit from their prosperity, so too landowners can maintain their environmental privileges against all threats of development 'knowing' that conservation serves the nation as much as themselves. Indeed (as we shall see in more detail in Chapter 8), landowners frequently claim to be concerned, not only for their less privileged contemporaries, but even for the environmental heritage of those who have yet to be born. Such worthy sentiments are rarely contested by council members in Suffolk who accept the congruence of conservation and the public interest almost uncritically:

We all want the same thing. We want to preserve the countryside for ourselves, for the people who come to visit us, and for our children. . . . Planning in this area is very very strict compared with other areas. You cannot build. . . . Getting houses built here isn't easy. . . . You don't want industrial development spoiling things. It's all right for those of us who already live here – we're fine, we already live in the country – but it's for people who want to come and see it. [District council chairman.]

There is, therefore, an evident consensus between the preservationist/ conservationist lobby and most local authority members and officers. As with the farming organizations, so for environmental groups this consensus results in a close and informal relationship between themselves and local authorities. As the Suffolk Preservation Society newsletter observed, 'It is increasingly possible to feel that the Society is working with the Planning Authorities to preserve Suffolk, rather than against them in defence of it' (winter 1974, No. 8 p. 3). Landowners and planning authorities are thus allied in their concern to protect the environment on behalf of the people of Suffolk in particular, and of Britain in general.

Problems arise, however, when apparent contradictions occur between the interests of landowners, and the interests of those who may wish to come and view – or, worse still, make use of – the environment which has been protected 'on their behalf'. As Emmett (1971) has noted, the values of conservationists such as traditional landowners tend to be first paternalistic (we know what is good for people), and secondly exclusive (let us keep what is ours for ourselves). Needless to say, these two are not necessarily compatible and may often prove contradictory when they come to be applied in particular instances. This is especially likely to be the case where exclusivity is the dominant motive, and paternalism (or altruism) the ideological justification – i.e. where attempts are made to restrict access of 'the public' to a piece of land which has been protected 'on the public's behalf'. This, however, is precisely what many landowners try to achieve. One landowner and amenity society official clearly recognized the tension involved in such an exercise:

I feel very much a life-tenant. It's my job, having come into it as a well-worked beautiful farm, to hand it on in the same condition. One of my arguments is that we must leave something for the next generation to spoil – we can't spoil everything ourselves. Of course, if you're going to keep the farm beautiful, only a few people can enjoy it, because the moment you introduce more people into the area with their cars and their ignorance of the countryside, leaving gates open, going into the middle of corn fields, filling ditches with refrigerators and cookers, you spoil it. I feel very strongly that I'm a trustee. . . . Of course, people may misrepresent your motives. But – for example – I'm very keen on tree planting. I plant three or four hundred oaks a year. I spend a lot of time going round planting. But I know that unless I look after them and prevent others getting near them, I won't get those oaks up. You've got to be selfish about it.

'Selfishness' is thus transformed into a public virtue. Privacy and privileges are strictly guarded, and the public is resolutely denied access, yet all of this is accomplished 'in the public interest', for only landowners can be trusted to care for the land.[5] Lowe (1975, p. 15) aptly summarizes this point: 'We see built into much preservationist thought an ambivalence: preservation for the nation, but not necessarily for the public.'

In Suffolk, this ambivalence is characteristic, not only of the views of traditional landowners and the environmental lobby generally, but also of county policy on conservation and preservation. Nowhere is this better illustrated than in the county council policy on attracting tourism to the various protected beauty spots in the region. Thus, while county councils in England and Wales spend an average of £10·35 per thousand population on promoting tourism, Suffolk spends only £7·37 (*County Planning Statistics*, 1974/5). The council's policy was clearly revealed by one of its leading members, himself a landowner, when he explained: 'I suppose preservation isn't in everybody's interests. But it is terribly sad if places are ruined by bad development. . . . I'm anti-tourist. We don't want more tourists – they spoil places by coming to them. Perhaps one is being selfish . . . but there is very good reason for being selfish about it.' The low priority (or, indeed, negative orientation) accorded to promotion of tourism in Suffolk appears to indicate that greater emphasis is generally placed on the values of 'exclusivity' than on those of paternalistic altruism in the development of a conservation policy in the county.

It would be misleading, however, to suggest that the landowners' appeals to conservationist sentiment necessarily represent conscious and deliberate attempts to disguise their own self-interested motives. Many of them appear genuinely committed to the aim of conserving what they see as a worthwhile and valuable national heritage. However, it is clearly the case that whatever their motives in defending the environment against threats of development, their support of conservation policies brings them a number of political and economic advantages over and above the advantages of living in an unspoilt and beautiful part of the countryside. In other words, we may draw a distinction between what landowners state as their motives for conserving the environment (and of course there is no check on whether these actually *are* their motives), and the objective consequences which follow from this with regard to their own material and political interests. We can, that is, say something about objective effects as well as subjective motives. Arguably, it is the former which are politically most significant.

The analysis of such objective consequences involves the problematic notion of interests. We must, in other words, determine where the interests of landowners (and of other groups affected by these policies) objectively lie. The problem, however, is that what we consider to be in the interests of, say, Suffolk landowners may not be considered as such by themselves. For example, we shall argue that conservationist policies are objectively in the interests of farmers and landowners in so far as they result in a perpetuation of a low-wage rural economy (through the exclusion of industries competing for local labour) and the maintenance of a Conservative majority on the county council (through the exclusion of potential Labour-voting urban immigrants). But how valid are such arguments if landowners themselves disagree with them?

For Dahl (1961), the answer is, 'not at all'. According to his pluralist theory of liberal democracy, the assertion of 'objective' interests independently of, and in contradiction to, the subjects' own interpretation of their interests, is untenable. Thus, what an individual asserts or believes to be his interests (again we should note that the two may not be the same) *are* therefore his interests, 'even though from the point of view of observers, his belief is false or ethically wrong' (Dahl, 1961, p. 52 fn.). We all therefore know what we want, and nobody is a better judge of what constitutes our interests than we are ourselves.

The problem with Dahl's position is that it assumes that we are all in a position to assess what is in our interests (i.e. that we are not ignorant of possible alternatives), and it ignores the problem (particularly pertinent in the present case) that what people believe to be in their interests may not be what they state to be in their interests. For Dahl there is nothing useful to be said about interests beyond what is reported on a questionnaire return. Articulated preferences and interests are seen as synonymous. Against this, however, Lukes (1974) has argued that objective interests may be discerned in a given situation, even against the articulated preferences of those to whom they are applied. Taking Crenson's study of air pollution legislation in American cities (Crenson, 1971), he seeks to show that, *ceteris paribus*, it is in the interests of a population to avoid being poisoned by dirty air 'even where they may not even articulate this preference' (p. 45). Of course, there is ultimately no philosophical justification for this assumption (Gray, 1976), and even if the argument is accepted in the case of the dirty air issue it does not follow that 'objective' interests can be inferred as easily in other situations. Nevertheless, while avoiding any attempt to make statements about 'human nature', we would argue that it is methodologically viable and theoretically justifiable to infer interests *contextually*. In the context of a capitalist economy, for example, we would argue that it is objectively in people's interests to maximize their economic returns and to minimize their costs, other things being equal. This is not to deny the substantive rationality of altruistic behaviour within a market system, but it is to recognize that the function of the ideal type market lies in allocating values, such that the functionally rational goal of actors operating in the market lies in maximization of returns. In this way, the objective interests of two parties to a transaction may be deduced independently of the subjective meanings which they attribute to their actions.

On the basis of this argument, it may be suggested that it is in the interest of, say, employers to sponsor and support such policies as result in the maintenance of cheap labour supplies. This is not to argue that those employers who do in fact support such policies do so for this express purpose. They may have other subjective motives entirely. But irrespective of such aims and motives, it can be argued that the *effect* of their support is to advance their own interests *qua* employers. Similarly, when property-owners combine to prevent any further residential development in a particular area, we may argue that irrespective of their motives their interests are objectively furthered in that the scarcity of housing thus induced serves to inflate the market value of existing dwellings. Or again, it can be argued that it is objectively in the interests of those relatively prosperous sections of a local population to support low public expenditure policies, for this ensures a low rate of property taxation, while such a policy will objectively disadvantage the least prosperous sections who may be expected to benefit most from increased public expenditure on welfare and other similar services. In all three of these examples, we can see that the objective interests of employers, house-owners and rate-payers respectively can be inferred contextually, independently of any professed motives and preferences which these three groups may voice.

When we turn to consider the case of landowners and large farmers, it is apparent that, irrespective of all the claims to altruism, their support for conservation functions to perpetuate a situation in which they continue to reap a number of political and economic

advantages while less privileged groups continue to bear disproportionate costs in terms of alternatives forgone (Tabb, 1972). Perhaps
the most significant of these advantages relates to local wage levels,
for agricultural wage rates in East Anglia are among the lowest in
England, despite the fact that the region's farmers are among the
most prosperous in the country (Newby, 1972*a*). Now, it is beyond
doubt that even limited industrial development, when permitted in
predominantly agriculturally-based rural areas serves to increase
average wage rates. In his study of industrial migration in relation to
small town development schemes in East Anglia, for example, Lemon
(1975, pp. 29–30) concludes:

Many firms had hoped to pay considerably lower wages in East Anglia
than previously, but had instead seen wages pushed up since their arrival
under the pressure of competition from firms subsequently moving into
the area, expansion of those already there, and the multiplier effect of new
industry on the total employment available. . . . Industrial development
might reasonably be expected to bring earned income levels in East Anglia
closer to the U.K. average and this appears to be the case in the small
towns.

Similarly, in the recent report of the East Anglian Regional Strategy
Planning Team (1975, pp. 1–2), considerable emphasis was placed on
the need to attract more industry if the low wage levels were to be
raised:

Away from the major centres, poor job prospects cause considerable local
concern. Opportunities are limited to agricultural employment and
incomes tend to be low. . . . There should be opportunities for individuals
to increase their incomes and widen their interests through a better choice
of jobs and training opportunities.

In Suffolk, however (and particularly in East Suffolk), opportunities for attracting new industry into predominently rural areas have
consistently been rejected by the county council on the grounds of
environmental conservation. In 1960, for example, when the West
Suffolk County Council, acting on the advice of its officers, entered
into 'overspill' agreements with the Greater London Council thereby
stimulating development at Haverhill, Bury St Edmunds, and
Mildenhall, the East Suffolk County Council stoutly refused to
participate, despite pressure from district councils in the centre and
north of the county (e.g. Halesworth UDC and Wainford RDC). As
a result, West Suffolk issued Industrial Development Certificates for
five times the total floor space sanctioned by East Suffolk in the

period 1958–69, 39 per cent of which was located in small towns in mainly rural areas. In East Suffolk, by contrast, such development as was permitted was concentrated mainly at Lowestoft and, to a lesser extent, Felixstowe, and thus away from the parts of the county which were most dependent on agriculture (see Lemon, 1975).[6]

The decision by East Suffolk not to take London's overspill industries and population was only one of a number of similar decisions taken over the last fifteen years or so. Nor has this anti-development policy been significantly altered since the 1974 re-organization. Indeed, at the time of writing, the new Suffolk County Council is busy opposing any suggestion of large-scale future development in any part of the county. On the coast at Orford Ness, for example, the interest expressed by the Central Electricity Generating Board in some redundant Ministry of Defence land for a large-scale nuclear power plant has provoked much hostility and opposition, while a proposal by the East Anglian Regional Strategy Team that a new town should be developed in the north around Eye and Diss has aroused some consternation. In terms of potential sources of employment, of course, a new power station in the east and a new town in the north could prove highly significant as alternative competitors for local (mainly agricultural) labour – the power station alone could employ 2500 men during its construction, and a further 800 employees on a permanent basis, many of whom would be recruited locally. This is not, though, an argument which finds much support among the county councillors, farming and landowning organizations, newspaper editors, and preservation groups who have all so vociferously and unanimously opposed any development at Orford. Although pointing to the safety factor (despite the site being relatively isolated) and to the loss of land (although the land is of low quality) they are mainly concerned with the effect which such a large-scale development would have on the aesthetic qualities of the neighbouring environment:

Power stations have several effects. They lead to large pylon lines which people simply hate. . . . Also, if it went to Orford, it would open up a remote bit of the coast, and would destroy the whole character of the area. . . . You'd produce lots of jobs for a short time – mainly for the Irish – but not many for the indigenous population once the building was finished. . . . You get pylons going slap across country – that would cause more of an outcry than anything else. [County Planning Committee member.]

Some Labour members, predictably, see the issue rather differently and are openly sceptical about the concern for the aesthetic qualities of Orford Ness:

Landowners stand to lose. . . . It's all a question of control. If you've got the *status quo* on your side, you'd be idiotic to do anything to risk losing it. You attract industry, you get workers moving in, and that destroys the political situation and affects wage levels, so they'll oppose it. Who are the environmentalists anyway? The middle class. Who lives in these rural villages? The working class can't afford to live there and travel to work. To hell with pretty little trees! I'm a concrete and brick man. Work comes first. [Labour district councillor.]

Farmers don't welcome industry in rural areas where they're paying low wages. I can assure you that I've been to meetings at County level where this has been patently obvious. It's a policy that's never been said or publicly proclaimed, but it's a sense they've got towards each other. They don't want factories where they'll lose their labour force. . . . I like the countryside, but if it's going to bring jobs, I'm all for it. But I suspect a lot will vote against, not because they're conservationists, but because they don't want alternative jobs in rural areas. [Labour county and district councillor.]

Their scepticism receives some support from an analysis of expenditure by Suffolk County Council on positive preservation policies. It is reasonable to assume that members' overriding concern with the environment would lead them to sponsor a variety of different policies designed actively to preserve and protect it. Yet the *County Planning Statistics* for 1974–5 reveal that, in its first year of operation, Suffolk's estimated expenditure on rural preservation and development together with the conservation and preservation of its many spectacular medieval buildings amounted to £74·85 per thousand population, compared with a national average of £93·93. As recently as December 1975, the Planning and Countryside Sub-Committee rejected a call from one member (himself a leading figure in the Suffolk Preservation Society) for a further £50000 to be budgeted for 'positive planning' such as tree planting schemes and grants for historic buildings. As one of his Conservative colleagues put it, the suggestion was 'irresponsible'.[7] For most county councillors, the environment must be conserved against development, but not necessarily preserved in any positive sense. Thus, the vigorously pursued anti-development policy suggests that it is as much a priority for most landowners and farmers on the county council to exclude competitors for labour as to maintain the nation's heritage. As one unusually frank landowner (not himself a councillor) put it: 'I'm against the industrialization of the area because we don't need industry and industrial workers round here. It makes the farm labour position worse and it spoils the countryside.' Undoubtedly, some Labour members, looking across the floor of the Council Chamber at the cluster of landed interests in control of the majority group, see almost a conspiracy to maintain a low-wage economy (and, at the same time, a Conservative county). We are *not* suggesting this is so. However, whether it is intended or not, such planning policies are redistributive and generally socially regressive in their effects.

Property and political domination

The most recent threat to the political domination of landowners and farmers in Suffolk (and elsewhere in East Anglia) has been brought about by the influx of predominantly middle-class ex-urbanites, pursuing a rural idyll or 'village in the mind' as Pahl (1968) has called it. We have already examined in some detail the conflict with local farmers into which their arcadian view of the countryside has inevitably drawn them. In the light of such conflict it is easy to over-look how both farmers and immigrants share certain interests as substantial owners of property. Indeed as the anti-development out-look of most farmers indicates, the antagonisms which arise from time to time between them may best be understood, not as a rift between conservationists and anti-conservationists, but as disagree-ments on emphasis between ultra-conservationists and conserva-tionists. Quite simply, for whatever reasons, neither group relishes any large-scale development. As one landowner and county coun-cillor put it:

You always find that people who move into a village out of London are active preservationists. They go there for a reason. They're usually more articulate, and more keen on preservation than the people already there. . . . There's not a running battle with farmers, but there's not an identity of interests either, is there? In some cases, though, a farmer and a retired Londoner are at one – for instance, in not wanting a council estate doubling the size of the village.

Notwithstanding the intensity of the conflict which may arise over uprooted hedgerows and diverted footpaths, both farmers and new-comers desire to preserve the countryside as 'truly rural'. In this sense, all property-owners in Suffolk are more or less on the same side of the conservationist fence, with all that that implies for the low-wage economy in rural areas. Furthermore, not only are their interests fundamentally in accord over conservation, but they are similarly in accord over most other aspects of council policy.

Take, for example, budgetary policy. We noted earlier that concern with rate levels ran high among the farmers interviewed in our survey, although farmland itself is not rated. But farmers *qua* householders appear as concerned at maintaining a low rate as do other relatively prosperous householders. Indeed, objectively, their interests as property-owners lie in securing low levels of public spending, for as relatively prosperous ratepayers, they do not benefit substantially from increased local authority expenditure. With few exceptions, therefore, all sections of Suffolk's property-owners share one common interest in relation to local authority budgetary policy – keeping the rate down. With its fiscal policies, the county council in Suffolk has proved itself very responsive to the interests of property-owners over the years. As the finance committee chairman of East Suffolk County Council explained in 1963, 'It has always been the policy of the council to let the ratepayers keep their money in their pockets, and only to ask them for as much in rates as we really need' (quoted in the *Suffolk Mercury*, 8 March 1963). And this same philosophy has remained in evidence at the county and district level ever since:

We have to defend reasonable services and keep the rates low – and I don't mind saying that. We do have to keep the rates low. [Committee chairman.]

I and all my colleagues accept that the rates are low – although the electorate doesn't seem to think so! Whenever we plead poverty to Whitehall, they say we have the remedy in our hands – 'look at your rates', they say. So we come back here and discuss it, but we all agree to keep the rates down. [Committee chairman.]

Just as conservation of the environment is regularly represented as being in the interests of all classes in Suffolk, so too a low-rate policy is commonly defended in terms of a 'public interest'. Indeed, some councillors go so far as to argue that low rates benefit, not so much the large property-owners, as those on low incomes:

We have to be concerned with low rates because we're a low wage-earning community. [District councillor and 1000-acre farmer.]

We have to keep the rates down because we have so many retired middle-class pensioners who vote Tory, and we are a low wage area with no heavy industry . . . no one would make a public stand for more expenditure in Suffolk. [County councillor and landowners.]

There is, of course, an essential paradox in such arguments, for even allowing for a high degree of efficiency low rates invariably involve lower levels of expenditure on the very services from which low wage earners and pensioners may be expected to benefit most. Far from it being 'necessary' to hold rates down for the sake of low wage earners, it can reasonably be argued that their interests could best be served by putting the rates up. Certainly, Suffolk's political leaders have consistently shown their unwillingness to increase the rate levy, even at the expense of services provided:

It is our duty as members of the council to see that the extra burden on the ratepayers through the development of county services is kept to a minimum. [Finance chairman, quoted in the *Suffolk Mercury*, 8 March 1963.]

Our duty is to do all we can to keep the rates down even though incomes rise. The demands on local government services constantly increase. . . . We have to ask ourselves, can we afford improvements in these conditions? [West Suffolk chairman, quoted in the *East Anglian Daily Times*, 19 February 1971.]

. . . many projects have had to be postponed or even abandoned. Examples of cuts or deferments (far from the complete list) are: The programme for Nursery Provision severely reduced; the replacement of old school buildings not proceeding; some new schools deferred; supplies of school materials reduced; libraries at Stowmarket and Ipswich deferred; fewer new roads to be built . . . no extra services for the chronically sick and disabled; deferment of equalisation of standards in provision of home help and meals services; deferment of improvement to residential homes. . . . The county's existing level of expenditure is relatively very low . . . the need to economise and to get value for money will be continually borne in mind. [County council news-sheet on rates, March 1975.]

The catalogue of cuts made each year in social services, education and elsewhere has produced a situation in which, while only six English counties levied a lower rate in 1974–5, only four spent less *per capita* on education, only four less on social services, and none spent less proportionately on their library services (*Return of Rates*, 1974–5). As with its planning policies, so too with its fiscal policies, the county council has long perpetuated a bias to the disadvantage of working-class interests. It is not simply that the propertied stand to gain most from environmental conservation and low rates, but that the working class stands to lose – through depressed wage levels and inadequate welfare and other service provisions respectively.

Nowhere is this bias more marked and more significant than in its effect on housing policies. The combination of a desire to keep spending down, and a rigid anti-rural development planning policy, has resulted in a disproportionate emphasis on private low-density, high-priced housing development in rural areas, and a shortage of low-rent public housing.[8] Table 64 demonstrates that in the eight years prior to reorganization, local authorities in East Suffolk built council houses at half the East Anglian regional rate, while an average of over four private homes were built in the area for every council house completed. (It is interesting to note here that one of the principal objections voiced by the farming and landowning lobby to proposals to abolish or amend the tied cottage system is precisely the lack of available municipal accommodation in rural areas, yet Suffolk's political leaders refuse to countenance any large-scale residential development in these areas.) Clearly, we are in the presence of a self-fulfilling prophecy. For most sections of the Suffolk working class, private housing is too expensive, while public rented accommodation is too scarce. Little wonder, then, that many farm workers can envisage little alternative to a tied cottage (Newby, 1977). The implications of the growing proportion of workers living in tied housing were discussed in Chapter 4. Here we may merely note how such changes have been wrought not only through the activities of farmers as employers, but by the representatives of their interests in the wider political arena beyond the farm gate.

The disregard for working-class housing interests revealed in county and district housing and planning policies over the years is extraordinary, for the demand for cheap rented accommodation in rural areas remains high. Thus, while not allowing for those families who fatalistically never bother to apply for a council house because they recognize the futility of such an exercise, or for those systematically 'pruned' from waiting lists from time to time, the actual waiting list for public housing in Suffolk Coastal District amounted to over 2000 families at the beginning of 1976, while that in Mid-Suffolk stood at 1400. Such high levels of demand, however, are by no means always regarded by Suffolk's policy-makers as adequate grounds for providing more housing.

This was made very clear by the Suffolk and Essex planning authorities in their 1966 *Survey of the Dedham Vale* where it was noted: 'In our view, the traditional peace and tranquillity of the Vale depends on keeping the population scale more or less the same as it is today. Natural increases from within the Vale should not necessarily be housed within its villages' (pp. 11–12). Thus, despite the

Table 64 Permanent dwellings completed in East Suffolk, East Anglia and England and Wales, comparing local authority and private completions, 1966–73

Year	East Suffolk			East Anglia			England and Wales		
	Local authority dwellings built per 1000 population	Private dwellings built per 1000 population	Private dwellings built per local authority dwelling built	Local authority dwellings built per 1000 population	Private dwellings built per 1000 population	Private dwellings built per local authority dwelling built	Local authority dwellings built per 1000 population	Private dwellings built per 1000 population	Private dwellings built per local authority dwelling built
1966	1·8	6·5	3·6	3·9	6·9	1·8	2·9	4·2	1·4
1967	1·4	6·3	4·5	3·6	6·6	1·8	3·2	4·1	1·3
1968	1·9	6·9	3·6	3·0	7·2	2·4	3·3	4·4	1·3
1969	0·8	5·2	6·5	2·6	6·4	2·5	2·8	3·6	1·3
1970	1·1	4·4	4·0	2·2	5·7	2·6	2·6	3·4	1·3
1971	1·1	5·2	4·7	2·4	6·9	2·9	2·2	3·7	1·7
1972	1·3	5·0	3·8	2·1	6·8	3·2	1·8	3·8	2·1
1973	0·9	5·4	6·0	2·1	6·2	3·0	1·5	3·6	2·4
Average	1·3	5·6	4·3	2·7	6·6	2·4	2·5	3·9	1·5

Source: Department of the Environment, Local Housing Statistics, London: HMSO, appropriate years.

fact that less than three new council houses had been built in the
Vale each year since the war, the planners stipulated in their 1968
Proposals that even this modest level of provision should stop.
Future generations of the indigenous working class thus have either
to find existing tied or rented accommodation in their home area, or
emigrate: 'The existing and anticipated future demand for housing
is not accepted as an over-riding justification for further large-scale
land allocations for residential development. . . . No further private
or public estate development will be permitted' (p. 8).

Now even the most casual observer of recent British political
history will know that, along with education, housing has become
something of a sacred cow for all major parties. This is not to say
that successive governments have necessarily acted in accordance
with their proclamations, but it is to recognize that virtually all
politicians since the war have felt obliged to reaffirm their abstract
commitment to large-scale housing development. How, then, is it
that in Suffolk not only have the houses not been built, but very little
attempt seems to have been made by political leaders and administrators to disguise the fact? Why, in other words, have such policies
as that outlined by the Dedham Vale planners (and, indeed, those
followed in most other parts of rural Suffolk) produced so little
opposition from those most disadvantaged by them? Indeed, how
is it that a pervasive bias continues to be perpetuated against non-
propertied interests in most fields of council policy, virtually without
challenge?

For Dahl, as we saw earlier, such questions make little sense.
From his pluralist perspective, interests can only be analysed in relation to consciously-evolved political preferences, and since all members of liberal democracies enjoy equally the rights to vote and
organize to defend or support their 'interests', political passivity and
inaction can only indicate that these preferences have largely been
satisfied. Despite the evidence of the effects of strategic planning
policies on wage levels, of the effects of low-rate policies on service
provisions, and of the effects of these two taken together on housing
availability for less prosperous groups, Dahl's argument would
therefore seem to lead to the conclusion that Suffolk's working class
has nothing to complain about, the 'proof' of this assertion being
that its members complain so little. Such is, of course, a teleological
argument which fails to take account of any 'causes' other than a
sense of satisfaction which could have contributed to a pervasive
working-class passivity. It is an argument, furthermore, which pre-

supposes two essential conditions in a given political system – community (or at least compatibility) of interests on the one hand, and legitimacy of rule on the other. Thus, although people are seen to have differing goals in any given issue, and although power is seen to be exercised by the few over the many, nevertheless there is assumed to be a fundamental congruence of interests between leaders and led which results in the former enjoying the trust (and hence the attributed legitimacy) of the latter. According to this argument, power involves obligations of obedience on the part of the many in exchange for the benefits rendered them by the powerful few – 'A means of effectively mobilising obligations in the interests of collective goals' (Parsons, 1966, p. 85). In this sense, power is genuinely authoritative in that it is voluntarily ceded from below (and therefore legitimate), and is used for the collective good (and is therefore communal in benefit).

The problem with this entire theoretical position is that it ignores the possibility that power may be used to prevent less privileged groups from expressing their interests. Those with power in a given political system may be in a position to mask, repress or prevent the emergence of any potentially threatening opposition, and thereby create an impression of harmony and consensus (Bachrach and Baratz, 1970). Thus, for example, awkward political demands may simply be ignored by those in power – defined away so that for all practical purposes they were never made. Alternatively, it may be that subordinate groups, recognizing the power of their leaders to ignore them, or even to exact retribution upon them, fail to articulate demands which they nevertheless regard as highly important. In rural Suffolk, where as we have seen the same men often dominate the political system as dominate the local employment market (by virtue of their ownership of land), the local housing market (by virtue of their control of tied housing), the local legal system (by virtue of their position on magistrates' benches), and even the sources of local welfare and patronage, there is likely to be a strong disincentive for less powerful and more dependent groups to mount a challenge against them (see, for example, Vidich and Bensman (1958) on the power of Jones in Springdale and, on a more general theoretical level, Lehman (1969) on 'symbolic power'). Or it may be that the power of propertied interests in areas like Suffolk is so great that subordinate groups not only fail to express their interests, but fail even to recognize them. As we saw in Chapters 4 and 5, the work and community situations experienced by many rural workers tend to bring them into fairly regular and particularistic relations with farmers and landowners. The result may be the encouragement of vertical instead of (or in addition to) horizontal ties of identification, and the consequent transmission to or imposition on them of the values, beliefs, and ideologies of the dominant class (see also Chapters 7 and 8).

Now, taking Parsons' twin criteria of legitimacy ('morally binding obligations') and community (power used 'for collective goals'), it is apparent that both are problematic in situations of political inactivity, such as that in rural Suffolk. Not only is it difficult, in the light of the evidence presented above, to maintain that power has been used for the collective good in Suffolk, but it is also far from well established that this power has been used legitimately – i.e. with the voluntaristic consent of those subject to it.[9] Indeed, far from legitimacy being the source of power for dominant political and economic interests, it may presumably be the case that their power has enabled them to engineer a 'false' legitimacy. As Gouldner has observed, the powerful are in a position to 'enforce their moral claims and conventionalise their moral defaults' (1970, p. 297). However, if we are to argue that the relative passivity of the Suffolk working class does not therefore arise out of the satisfaction of their objective interests, but rather from some form of 'non-decision-making' (Bachrach and Baratz, 1970), then we must demonstrate *how* stability has been maintained. Power, that is, involves causality, and it is thus necessary to investigate the causal means by which power has been used by propertied interests to maintain the passivity of those below them. By following Bachrach and Baratz, we may identify three distinct situations in which the powerful have been able to bring about and maintain the apparent or actual silence of objectively disadvantaged groups.

The first is the way in which opposition is 'defined out' of the political process. Public opposition to council policies in Suffolk is rare, to say the least. Indeed, as we shall see later, when opposition does arise, it tends to come from those groups which objectively appear to have least to complain about. The Suffolk working class, that is, appears extraordinarily placid. One reason for this lies in the passivity of its political representatives – i.e. the Labour Party. In other words, the objectively less privileged groups in Suffolk rarely articulate any discontents, partly because their official mouthpiece in the county remains for the most part firmly shut. Why is this?

One reason is the strong belief held by many councillors that local government is not a matter suitable for the pursuit of party politics. In our 1973 survey of councillors in East Anglia, we found that 51 per cent of all respondents claimed to be 'Independents', this figure rising to 68 per cent among the farmers and landowners who sat on local authorities in the region. Independents were most strongly represented in rural district councils, where they accounted for 71 per cent of all members, and most weakly represented in county councils, where they accounted for 27 per cent (although it is interesting to note that on the East Suffolk County Council, this figure was somewhat higher at 35 per cent). The significance of these figures lies in the fact that over half (and in some authorities, over three-quarters) of councillors in the region were both elected without the official endorsement of any political party, and, once elected, claimed to remain detached from any formal party political grouping in the councils to which they were returned. Indeed, they were positively hostile to the activities of organized political parties in local government:

The emphasis is on 'good government', on 'administration', not 'politics', and on 'businesslike' attitudes. The ideal decision-making process is based on 'common agreement', divisions in the community must be glossed over. From the viewpoint of the parties this produces an unfavourable climate, one in which they are seen as either having no role to play, or only an unimportant one. [Bulpitt, 1967, p. 19.]

The values of 'independence' are well established in Suffolk politics, and although the significance of the political parties has inevitably increased since the 1974 reorganization, it nevertheless remains the case that many councillors continue to stress the importance of what they term 'keeping politics out of local government'. Many, indeed, draw a distinction between party political decision-making on the one hand, and 'efficient' or 'reasoned' decision-making on the other, with the implicit or explicit assumption that the two are mutually exclusive:

There were no politics whatsoever on the old authority – in ten years I honestly never heard the word 'politics' mentioned. The old council was *sensible*. We had our various committees, we knew one another, and we'd talk things out sensibly, not formally. ['Independent' district councillor and chairman of local Conservative branch.]

Nor are such values confined to Independent and Conservative members, for paradoxically, many councillors elected under the patronage of the Labour Party express similar opinions:

Mid-Suffolk unfortunately is political. It's a pity it was allowed to creep in in rural areas. Common sense used to prevail, but I'm not sure it does now. [Labour member.]

I would wish to state that it is to the credit of local councillors, irrespective of political persuasion, that there is a large measure of agreement and co-operation on most issues ... common sense rather than hard line political doctrine has prevailed, and long may it be so. [Labour Suffolk Coastal councillor in a letter to the *Suffolk Mercury*, 11 January 1974.][10]

Many Labour councillors thus subscribe to the very ethic of 'political independence' described by Bulpitt, central to which is an entrenched ideology of harmony and consensus.

We have seen in earlier sections of this chapter how consistent attempts are made by Suffolk's political leadership to represent sectional policies as being 'in the public interest'. Clearly the 'independence' ethic contributes to the success of such attempts, for by stressing harmony, agreement, and above all what one respondent termed 'reasonable men talking to each other in a reasonable way', it serves to produce and perpetuate a managed impression of consensus in which conflicts of interest are seen as in some way pathological. It also enables the Labour Party members to achieve the status of being seen to be participating in a decision-making process from which their powerlessness would otherwise exclude them. Policy options therefore become 'obvious', for if everybody is on the same side, the task for councillors of all persuasions becomes merely the search for the most expeditious means of implementing what is self-evidently in the public interest. As Harris has noted, however, the effect of such an ethic is that real objective conflicts of interest are obscured or totally ignored: ' . . . administration of a status quo that is taken for granted is all, and controversy over the nature of the status quo is eliminated. In this context, important questions can be "taken out of politics", that is, no longer seriously debated from different perspectives' (1971, p. 99). Thus, those who are not prepared to maintain an impression of consensus and harmony, and who therefore ignore the informal and tacit 'rules of the game' (Grant, 1971) by raising contentious issues for public debate, are generally dismissed as 'politically motivated', while attempts are often made to socialize them into an appreciation of the independence ethic:

The bulk of the work of the county council is non-political. When you do get party politics, it's very often brought in artificially by people who are keen on party politics – mainly the Ipswich contingent. A lot of them are former members of the Ipswich Borough Council where things were different – they were rather startled when they got to the new County Council and found these hayseeds from East and West Suffolk who apparently hadn't heard of politics, and who were prepared to listen to their curious views. If they were rude, they found it was greeted with a shocked surprise! They got the point after a while and modified their attitudes. [Conservative committee chairman.]

I was talking this morning to a young chap – a fiery left winger. He's young, he's enthusiastic, and he's upset a lot of people. . . . He said to me this morning, 'You know, I can't get used to the idea that we all sit round the table and the Conservatives don't say what I expect them to say! We had all talked about this and that, and there was no political business at all, and he wasn't used to this. . . . I told him, this is something you've got to accept – that it does work this way. [District council chairman.]

The result of all this is that the consensus ideology becomes self-validating. Thus, if it is assumed that there are no conflicts of interests, then party politics are uncalled for, and if there are no party politics, conflicts of interest over particular policies (e.g. in planning or housing) will at best be obscured, and at worst totally ignored. The few recalcitrants who refuse to cooperate in the perpetuation of this self-fulfilling prophecy may then be simply 'defined out' (Mathiesen, 1974; Saunders, 1975) as 'unreasonable', 'irresponsible', 'naïve' or whatever, such labels occasionally being given additional credence by the hostility of members of their own party on the council. Alternatively they may simply be tolerated, for if members feel that the consensus ideology is sufficiently well established, they can afford to permit some licence to a small fringe minority. This 'repressive tolerance' (Marcuse, 1976) was vividly illustrated in the comments of one Conservative county council committee chairman:

The young councillors from Ipswich thought people like myself – they regard me as a rich man – they thought we would actually dislike them. The first thing I did was to find out their Christian names. They looked rather surprised. And at one of our first meetings, at lunchtime when we all sit down together before the council meets, the chairman went and sat down in the middle of the Labour people and began talking to them. They were astounded!

The institutionalization of Labour Party opposition varied in different local authorities. At county level, where virtually all members belonged to a political group, it was probably weakest, although since the group leadership changed late in 1975, opposition became somewhat more conciliatory. On the old East Suffolk County Council, the Labour leader was for some years vice-chairman of the council, and he and the 'Independent' chairman developed a close and relatively informal working relationship. With the 1974 re-organization, however, the Labour group came to be dominated by young relatively radical members from Ipswich, and they elected one of their own colleagues as leader. He made it clear that no offers of council office would be accepted by members of his group, and he spearheaded a radical attack on majority group policies, and particularly on the need to equalize social service provisions among the three old local authority areas by increasing the rate levy. Within eighteen months, however, the right-wing and rural elements of the group had mustered sufficient support to replace him with the former leader of the East Suffolk group, who has again proved himself a willing partner to majority group consensus politics:

Party politics are getting much less now. People don't sit in party heaps in committees now. It was much more uptight when it all began than it is now. [Conservative committee chairman.]

The Labour group do have some influence on the County Council.... There's a split between the older right-wing members from the county, and the younger left Ipswich group. X tends to be more moderate in his views – when he was elected leader, it was a vote for moderation. . . . Maybe the group felt things had gone far enough. [Local newspaper reporter.]

At district level, party groupings were rare before reorganization, at least in the rural areas, due in large part to the small number of Labour members elected. The 1974 reorganization, however, created larger authorities and greater opportunities for Labour groups to assert themselves. On both Mid-Suffolk and Suffolk Coastal councils, for example, ten Labour candidates were returned in the first district elections. In Mid-Suffolk (the more 'rural' of the two), however, the Labour members came almost exclusively from Stowmarket – the only recognizably urban area in the district – where they had previously controlled the old urban district council. Almost automatically, therefore, they formed a party caucus on the new authority, and the old pattern of informality and 'independence' familiar to those councillors from the old rural district was broken:

The whole thing's changed – it's got formal. We didn't used to call each other Coun. this and Coun. that in the old days. Reggie would say this, or Harry that. [Independent member.]

It is doubtful whether the development of formal party politics has resulted in any significantly increased opposition to Conservative policies in Mid-Suffolk. Nevertheless, it has avoided the almost total incorporation of the Labour opposition which characterizes the decision-making process in Suffolk Coastal where the Labour group was, with only one or two exceptions, totally committed to consensus politics:

We don't waste a lot of time finding maximum areas of disagreement. . . . We spend our time on good administration rather than arguing about issues which don't really come up. . . . Labour groups in other areas want to find an issue and divide the council up. But you get further by looking for areas of agreement. [Labour Suffolk Coastal member.]

Some stood as Conservatives, some as official Labour, one or two Liberals most as Independents. But the minute they were elected, no one had a clue who was what. There's no politics on Suffolk Coastal except for one chap who's very politically motivated, but everyone told him to shut up, and he's since fitted in very well. They decide on common-sense grounds. [Suffolk Coastal chief officer.]

In Suffolk Coastal, despite their minority status, Labour members held three of the five committee chairmanships, including that of Policy and Resources (although, interestingly, excluding that of Planning – indeed, no Labour members sit on the Planning Committee) – despite the fact that the Labour Party at national level had stipulated that minority groups should not accept any political office:

It seems to me that politics are out in local government if you're going to get a real sense of dealing with people's problems. . . . Politics never become a crucial issue in the council at all. There's never been a raging political row about anything. . . . The general Labour Party attitude is that we should never accept chairmanships where we're not in power, so I've fallen out with the Labour Party over this. If you have to deny the council the benefit of your ability for political reasons, I'm not in favour of it. If I thought that accepting a chairmanship involved a loss of principle, I'd resign. . . . Some people take the silly nonsensical attitude that there's got to be a political division. Why should there be? God didn't give the Labour Party the ability to think of all the good arguments. [Suffolk Coastal Labour committee chairman.]

Of course, it is somewhat naïve to argue that Labour chairmen have 'sold their souls' for the sake of political office, for they have their scruples, and they will not lightly preside over the pursuit of blatantly right-wing policies. As one earnestly explained in relation to the low level of council house building, 'There doesn't need to be political disagreement. The council ought to build the maximum amount of council houses, and it's the policy we've always pursued. If they [the Conservatives and Independents] said they wouldn't do it, then I and my colleagues would be after them.' But they rarely do say that they will not build houses. Instead they explain that, despite all good intentions, they simply 'cannot' raise the finance (due, of course, to a low-rate policy which goes unquestioned), or simply 'cannot' find a suitable site (due to their unchallenged development control policies).[11] In other words, given the fundamental consensus on basic policies to which most Labour members are a party, attacks on specific decisions which inevitably flow from these policies are inconceivable, and decision-making is therefore preserved as 'non-political'. As one Labour radical summarized the situation, 'There haven't been any major issues, simply because the Labour Party hasn't made an issue out of anything.'

The case of Suffolk Coastal is clearly extreme. However, there is evidence that as the other authorities investigated settled after the trauma of reorganization, a similar pattern was reasserting itself, such that although the Mid-Suffolk and county council Labour groups were by no means as incorporated as they had been before 1974, they were nevertheless becoming less and less 'coercive', and more and more 'conciliatory' in their opposition. The result in all three instances was that opposition to majority group policies was becoming increasingly contained. In their concern about rocking the boat, Suffolk's Labour councillors were thus losing sight of the direction in which the stabilized craft was heading.

Not all opposition is 'defined out' of the political process, of course, for there are other channels available by means of which it may be articulated by a disgruntled working class. What is important, however, is that even when opportunities are available for the mobilization of opposition, they are rarely grasped. In other words, on those occasions when lower-class interests are not 'excluded' (Parkin, 1974) from the local political process through the adoption of a 'non-politics' ethic, they appear to exclude themselves. One possible explanation for this seemingly resolute inactivity on the part of an objectively deprived section of the population lies in the second exemplification of 'non-decision-making' – the notion of anticipated reactions. That is, discontent may be suppressed if the discontented feel that they would be ignored (or perhaps even negatively sanctioned) were they to voice their grievances. The problem with this argument is that there is seemingly no way in which the observer can determine whether inaction is the result of anticipated reactions unless it follows a prior attempt to 'fly a kite' to assess what these reactions are likely to be (Parry and Morriss, 1974). This problem becomes all the greater when we recognize that power relations will to a large extent be taken for granted in everyday life – rarely will we stop to examine what we ordinarily 'can' or 'cannot' do. Thus what Clegg (1975) has termed the 'structure of domination' is generally taken as given, and in consequence we rarely need to 'fly a kite' in order to 'know' what the likely reception to our demands will be. Indeed, instances where a kite is flown are likely to be quite unique. The question, then, is: how can we demonstrate anticipated reactions in situations such as these where patterns of dominance and subordination are routinized and well established?

Most council members in Suffolk are aware of the passivity and apparent political apathy of the rural working class, but invariably choose to explain it with tacit reference to the model of democratic pluralism advanced by Dahl and Parsons:

Suffolk does produce pressure groups when necessary. But it doesn't have a great deal of cause I don't think. . . . There is not much militancy in anything here. There isn't the cause for militancy here. . . . It's not apathy. It's not apathy at all. It's surprising. The Suffolk person is quite a mule – you can't move him if he doesn't want to be moved. But he is absolutely no fool. [Former district council chairman.]

Well, perhaps it's because of the type of people who live in Suffolk – they're people of the land but they're no fools. They're very astute people. But they don't get terribly involved – no, that's not the right way to say it – they feel strongly, and they expect their representatives to know what they're feeling strongly about almost instinctively, without writing it down, or without saying it. . . . I suppose, being facetious, they choose the right people, and the right people do the right things for them. It can't be like that, but it almost looks like that, doesn't it? [District council chairman.]

In other words, the Suffolk 'working man' is seen as an individual who knows what he wants, and whose wants are 'instinctively' recognized by those he elects to govern him.

There are two problems with this sort of explanation. One is that, despite the assurances by many different respondents that 'there isn't the cause for militancy here', 'there's not much that's contentious in this part of the world', and so on, we saw earlier that objectively there is a range of potential causes for militancy and potential issues in Suffolk which never becomes manifest. Secondly, it will be apparent that there are occasions in a pluralist democracy when opposition between competing (if not conflicting) interests is seen to be a positive and healthy attribute. Indeed, on such occasions, inactivity and political passivity are frowned upon as indicating a level of irresponsibility on the part of abstaining citizens, while 'participation' (or at least the impression of it) is strongly encouraged. We would argue that mass inaction on such occasions can only be seen as indicative of the tradition of political fatalism and apathy which is the *direct result* of a situation of long-term political weakness and exclusion from effective political power. Political activity, that is, cannot simply be turned on or off like a tap, and when a given group is routinely excluded from any effective form of political activity for a long period, it is unlikely to respond with any vigour on the odd occasions when powerful interests deem that it should. This point may be illustrated, first, in relation to local elections and, secondly, with regard to recent planning exercises which have involved some element of 'public participation'.

In Britain as a whole, of course, few people bother to vote in local elections, and Suffolk's voting figures appear comparable with the rest of the country. Thus, in the 1973 elections for the new county and district authorities, the national average turnout of 43 per cent in county council elections was mirrored in Suffolk (42 per cent), while turnout in the two districts analysed was slightly higher than the national mean (44 per cent in both compared with 39 per cent nationally). Our problem, however, is not simply that so few people bother to vote in these periodic celebrations of local democracy, but also that, at least until 1974, so many councillors were unopposed at the polls as so few people could be found to stand as candidates against them. Needless to say, unopposed candidates were invariably 'Independents' of right-wing persuasion. With reorganization, although the proportion of county councillors returned unopposed dipped substantially (just two members of the county council elected in 1973 were unopposed), the shortage of 'competitors' at district level has continued. Indeed, according to the Registrar General's *Statistical Review of England and Wales*, 50 per cent of Mid-Suffolk members, and 27 per cent of Suffolk Coastal members, were automatically returned without a contest in 1973, these figures comparing with a national non-metropolitan district council average of just 13 per cent. Such high proportions of unopposed elections tend to create a 'bad image' for local democracy – it is difficult to argue that

264   *The rural power structure*

councillors have a mandate from the people when 'the people' do not have a chance to vote against them. It was for this reason that one ex-councillor to whom we spoke had regularly engaged in manoeuvrings with a distinct *Alice in Wonderland* quality about them: 'What I don't agree with is what has happened in many cases where people get in unopposed. I'm dead against this altogether, and in fact I used to try to get people to oppose me at one time – it sounds silly, but I think it's right.' It is almost as if Suffolk's politicians see the inactivity as too good to be true, and thus paradoxically feel obliged to stimulate some 'opposition'. Certainly, as we shall see in the last section of this chapter, apparent conflict may be tolerated or even encouraged by powerful interests if the illusion of democracy can thereby be maintained.

A second example of working-class apathy in the face of structured opportunities for political action concerns Suffolk's recent experience of public participation in planning. Following the recommendations of the Skeffington report and the prescriptions of the 1968 Town and Country Planning Act, Suffolk County Council has been engaged since its formation on the development of a new county structure plan which at all stages has been made available to the public for comments and criticism. By 'made available', we mean that opportunities have been offered for interested parties to make their views known, although little or no attempt has been made to go in search of these views. The result, predictably, was that the response to the first consultative document (*Suffolk: The Choice Ahead*) was overwhelmingly a response of the politically articulate minority. Just twenty-nine individuals submitted views, while of the forty-two non-statutory voluntary organizations to do so, ten represented business interests, eighteen were preservation or environmental groups, three directly represented farming interests, and five represented residents' or ratepayers' groups. This level and type of response was, for a leading member of the Planning Committee, satisfactory.

I think the public response to our consultative document is satisfactory. Of course, there's an awful lot of people who don't care – a very good response is something like 3 or 4 per cent. But the response you get is from those who do bother. . . . Although you get only a small percentage replying, you're giving everyone the chance to comment and to be listened to. We get the more intelligent types who are interested in the county replying. The type who says, 'Roll on five o'clock, when do the pubs open?' doesn't really care.

This, however, begs a question of why the vast majority of the county's population appears 'not to care' (assuming that it even knew of this particular exercise) about the development of a strategic policy with profound implications for future housing and job prospects. The local property-owners certainly 'cared'; their response was remarkable in its unanimity:

There is a widespread feeling that the principal issue is conservation. . . . A very strong consensus has emerged from the views received that Suffolk has grown too fast in recent years. . . . There is a very strong lobby in all quarters against development in the countryside or major extensions to villages, mainly on grounds of preserving agricultural land. . . . The agricultural industry would be concerned at the possibility that new job opportunities could be a further drain on the farm work force at a time when the decline in agricultural employment shows signs of levelling out. . . . Time after time the replies have stated that conservation is the most important issue, or that the traditional character or quality of life in Suffolk must be preserved at all costs. [*Suffolk County Structure Plan: The Next Steps*, pp. 2, 3, 7, 12, 17.]

Consultation has been a bit biased towards the conservation groups. The replies we've had have been very unbalanced. The sort of people who replied kept mentioning things like 'the granary of England' and 'the quality of life'. . . . We're putting out another report incorporating these views, and we'll just have to hope that this will stir up the other side before it's too late. [County planning official.]

Far from extending democratic control, therefore, Suffolk's early experiences of public participation suggest that existing patterns of political strengths and weaknesses have been reinforced. As Wibberley notes (1975, p. 3) the vogue for public participation makes planning authorities vulnerable to the sectional pressures of well-organized environmental groups. Or, as Lowe (1975, p. 75) puts it, 'The danger is that (as at the national level) one part of the local establishment talking to another part to the exclusion of "outsiders" be considered to fulfill the needs of "public participation".' Thus the groups which are ordinarily excluded from the centres of power generally fail to respond to opportunities for participation, while more influential groups respond *en masse* and thereby reaffirm the central tenets of the non-politics ethic discussed earlier. That is, the unanimity of the property-owners' voices serves, in the absence of articulated opposition, to confirm the prevailing image of political consensus.[12]

What we are arguing, then, is that inaction, fatalism, apathy and passivity are for most members of Suffolk's working class (as well as for most of its representatives in the Labour Party) a standard and routinized response to a situation of continuing objective deprivation and political exclusion. For most of the time they neither expect nor are expected to play any part in policy-making, and when occasionally formal and pre-structured opportunities for 'participation' are offered to them in an attempt to maintain a 'healthy' and 'open' democracy, they react for the most part as they always have reacted – by doing nothing. Most people in Suffolk 'know' that politics are not for the likes of them.

We noted earlier the emphasis placed by many council members in Suffolk on informality and particularism, and the way in which the formal and potentially divisive party divisions which emerged after reorganization have been mediated and diluted by a re-emergence of personal friendships cross-cutting party caucuses. Just as this central value of 'non-political informality' has accounted in large part for the lack of concerted Labour opposition to county and district policies in Suffolk, as has been shown, so too, when applied to the relationship between council members and those to whom they are responsible, the same value produces much the same effect. Thus the stress laid by most council members on informality and personal contact when dealing with their constituents results in the effective prevention of any organized and large-scale opposition emerging to their policies from outside the council. Thus we encounter a third aspect of non-decision-making.

Of course, just as the 1974 reorganization upset established patterns of relationships *within* the county's various local authorities, so too it fundamentally altered the traditional pattern of relationship *between* councillors and those they represent. The new larger wards, for example, made it more difficult for aspiring council members to gain election on the basis of a personal vote, and this in many cases resulted in former 'Independents' donning a blue rosette in order to harness the organizational capacity of the Conservative Party in gaining election. Nevertheless, whether they ran as Independents or official party candidates, many councillors still believed that a personal following was significant if not essential:

In rural areas the individual carries more weight. If he's well known, irrespective of his politics, a local man has an advantage over a non-local man, especially in Suffolk. It's a personal following. [Labour county councillor.]

Local people know the political beliefs of independents but they vote for the individual in the smaller villages. I like to think that all groups would vote for me for what I am, rather than my political views. [Farmer and district councillor.]

I've got a pretty high standing locally – all sorts of people support me, even those who haven't got an out and out Labour Party attitude to politics. Locally it's more a case of who the bloke is, and what he's done for them. [Labour district councillor.]

In the country parishes, they choose them because of the people they are. . . . They are, and they should be, people who are known to the people who vote for them. . . . Because so-and-so is wearing a red rosette or a blue one, it doesn't really matter. [Independent district councillor.]

The particularism of a personal following is constantly reinforced by members' resistance to bureaucratic reform, and insistence on influence being exerted at a personal face-to-face level. In Mid-Suffolk, for example, members have for some time opposed any proposal for a bureaucratic 'points system' for allocating council houses, and have instead been adamant that available housing stock should be allocated on the basis of recommendations made by the particular member responsible for the ward in which the house is situated:

The onus falls on the local representative for who gets housed. He is responsible. When someone gets a house round here, I'm ninety-nine per cent responsible. If I say you're not going to get a house, you don't get one. The people you put into those houses will vote for you, and those you don't will fight you. I've got a moral conscience. I know all my bad housing cases. They are my own personal priority list. I've fought against the introduction of a points system. Those who want to operate a points system can do it, but I won't. [Labour Mid-Suffolk member.]

As the council's Housing Officer rightly observed, this system of allocation 'leads to a great deal of member involvement in housing'. But at the same time, of course, it also leads to the positive encouragement and maintenance of ties of personal dependency and loyalty on the part of disadvantaged groups. Whatever its weaknesses and its intrinsic biases (see, for example, Rex and Moore, 1967), a bureaucratic points system does at least lay down recognizable criteria for allocation which are applied more or less universally. If those with common objective interests with regard to the consumption of housing can be seen as sharing common class situations (this is itself problematic – see Haddon, 1970; Bell, 1976; Saunders 1978 – but it is a useful conceptualization in that if focuses attention upon *collective* housing interests), then a bureaucratic system of allocation is more likely to confirm the existence of these common interests than is a particularistic system. That is, when houses are distributed according to council members' subjective assessments of individual merits, then the housing question is more likely to be seen by both councillors *and* applicants as a problem to be considered at the individual and personal level. As such, problems of housing *policy* will rarely be consciously examined, while any mutual 'class' identification among those disadvantaged by housing policies is likely to be fragmented and cross-cut by each applicant's (or in this case, supplicant's) reliance on vertical ties of loyalty to the individuals, who can 'swing it for them'.

Such encouragement of particularism and individualism to the detriment of any embryonic collective consciousness is in fact common in Suffolk politics. Thus influence on a host of different questions is generally expected by council members of both parties to be exerted by the individuals concerned, and this is a major factor in explaining why pressure-group activity and organized working-class-based campaigns of protest are rare:

There is no pressure group activity at all. I don't believe in being pressurised. People go to see their ward member and stir him up. If they convince me it's sensible I'll stir things up – but I do stress *sensible* – there's no organisations. It's all done on a face-to-face personal level. [District councillor.]

The 'sensible' way of influencing council members is, it transpires, the 'friendly chat', the 'quiet aside', and so on:

In the country, it's a smaller community, and people know each other so much better. . . . You play golf with them, or you meet them at WI meetings. You know their families. [District councillor.]

The people in the country usually find out the best way of going about things. There is an informal system which is probably as important or more important, and more active besides, than the formal one. [Ex-RDC chairman.]

In the country things are done in a relaxed, feudal manner. Certain families have played a part in local affairs for years, and they still do. There's a friend of mine who gets involved, but he doesn't *belong* to anything. What he does he does with a gin and tonic in his hand. Countrymen don't form groups – they do it by influence and personal contact. [Suffolk farmer.]

Now, it is apparent that this emphasis on particularistic and informal modes of influence restricts lower-class opposition from developing in two ways. First, given that the members of the rural working class are rarely to be found playing golf, shooting pheasants, or drinking gin and tonic with those in positions of power and eminence, the quality and quantity of their contacts with leading council members may be expected to be highly restricted. In consequence, they may either attempt to use more formal and organized methods of voicing their demands – in which case they are likely to be disregarded as 'irresponsible', 'unreasonable', 'politically motivated', or whatever – or do nothing (see Dearlove, 1973; Saunders, 1975). As we have seen, most adopt the latter course.

Secondly, and more important from our present perspective, the necessity of pursuing face-to-face and personal influence directs attention away from generalized grievances and towards individual complaints. Lower-class solidarism (Parkin, 1974), that is, is constantly undermined through the operation of a political system where only individual interests are recognized. In this sense, issues become diffused into problems and collective awareness is rarely generated out of widespread complaints.

It is in relation to this second point that we may return to the central theme of the last chapter and consider the significance of community as an ideology. The non-politics ethic and the spirit of individualism and particularism in Suffolk's local government both spring from an entrenched community ideology which emphasizes common interests based upon a common area of residence. In other words, economic and social cleavages are dismissed as largely insignificant in comparison with the bonds that unite all classes in a particular geographical area:

Country people tend to get along with each other side by side – regardless of incomes – much better than people in towns; getting together is done that much more easily in the countryside. [Conservative county committee chairman.]

They make their own community here and, all right, their wages are lower, but their standards are lower – they're not fighting to keep up with the Joneses at all. You have chaps playing bowls here together, the greatest of pals on all occasions, and one of them will be a very rich farmer with a Mercedes, and the other one will be his farm labourer or a chap down the road in a tied cottage. You know, you don't get that in towns. [Independent district councillor.]

I find I have a great deal in common with the rural working class. It's the old alliance between landowners and Tory rural working class. You can't live close to people in political conflict. So you don't get much politics in rural areas. [Conservative county committee chairman and landowner.]

A sense of fellow-feeling, vertical identification, and local attachment is fostered among the less privileged by constant reminders that they are 'rural folk' living in a society dominated by an urban mass. In other words, in addition to the positive ties of localism, there are, as we have seen in Chapter 5, very strong negative reactions to urbanism and 'outsiders'. Now, we do not wish to imply that the ideology of community is a consciously evolved device by means of which a rural ruling class deliberately perpetuates its privileges while maintaining the identification of low-income groups. Far from it: it is an ideology to which many of the locally powerful are firmly and personally committed. They *believe* in the reality of *gemeinschaftlich* relationships – in the wholesome qualities of the 'organic community'. Their antipathy to urban values and the 'urban way of life' is real enough. Indeed, many respondents claimed that they felt they had more in common with rural members from the opposing party than they did with urban colleagues of their own party:

I feel closer to the rural socialists than the Ipswich Tories really. [County councillor and landowner.]

Town Tories are different from country Tories. . . . There was a marked difference between the Tory from Ipswich and those from the country right from the beginning. At the first meeting of the council, the Tory people from the sticks were so pleasant with us, on Christian name terms right away, yet the four Tories from Ipswich were cast aside. . . . Mind you, there's also this Ipswich/County thing within the Labour group as well as the Tories. [Labour county councillor.]

Community ties, therefore, are in no way cynically and self-interestedly exploited, for the antipathy to 'urbanites' and 'outsiders' is genuine. However, two qualifications need to be made. The first is that although the ideology of community is probably rarely (if ever) intentionally and deliberately manipulated *in order to* promote and strengthen cross-class solidarity and vertical identification, it nevertheless serves this function. Whenever the shortage of working-class housing (other than tied housing) is attributed to an 'invasion of weekend cottagers and second home buyers', or whenever the rigid planning policies are explained in terms of excluding any future influx of 'alien' migrants from London, then we may suggest that internal cohesion is being promoted by deflecting attention from potentially contentious internal cleavages to a real or imagined 'threat' to the 'rural community' posed by outsiders. When in 1966 a Suffolk vicar and rural district councillor maintained, 'These London people hate coming down here, and we hate having them', and suggested that the government should pay their passages to Australia rather than permit them to migrate to Suffolk (see *East Anglian Daily Times*, 4 November 1966), he was only stating explicitly what many of his colleagues often felt implicitly – that immigration into the county represented a threat to all rural people. To the extent that such arguments strike a chord of sympathy with local working-class groups, a lower-class solidarism will clearly not develop. This in our view is the case in Suffolk.

Our second qualification is that although the antipathy to 'outsiders' and 'urbanites' is felt strongly by members of all classes alike, it does not cross-cut solidarity among them in the same way, for it is rarely strong enough fundamentally to divide different sections of property-owners from each other. Unlike the situation in Banbury (Stacey, 1960), for example, where the local/newcomer split bisected both upper and lower classes, in Suffolk it represents a cleavage in the latter, but only a differentiation with the former. Whatever their attitudes towards each other during the everyday activities of life in the rural village, farmers and newcomers pursue exactly similar policies in the local politics of the area.

The sources of political conflict

We have reached a point in our argument where we have explained the ways in which conflict is avoided in Suffolk despite the perpetuation of class-biased policies by the farmers, landowners, and immigrants or urbanites who collectively control the county's political process. One possible objection to our argument, however, is that if this group is so powerful that it can institutionalize opposition and even mystify cleavages in political and economic interests, then it may be expected that no conflict would ever occur. After all, if all conflict could be avoided, how is it that some conflict does arise? Although political issues are relatively few and far between, they are not entirely absent in Suffolk politics. We are therefore left with the problem of explaining, not inaction (the problem to which we first addressed ourselves), but the emergence of conflict in a situation of pervasive political domination. We may consider three situations in which such conflict will become manifest.

The first is where a split develops within the ruling group itself. One obvious example here concerns the division between immigrants and farmers over environmental consequences of farming activity. As we have seen, many of Suffolk's *causes célèbres* over the years have concerned the antagonisms between these two groups over aerial spraying, hedge removal, ploughed-up footpaths, and so on. Nevertheless, while not wishing to underemphasize the significance of these conflicts, we would maintain that among such relatively privileged sections of Suffolk society, the local/newcomer, rural/urban divide is less *politically* significant than the horizontal division between these groups together and the rural working class. They may not like each other, but they share fundamentally common interests which lead them both to support the same political policies. As we saw earlier, it is simply not the case that a keenly environment-conscious immigrant middle class finds itself consistently at loggerheads with profit-conscious desecrating farmers over the pursuit of local political policies. The stereotype is not entirely unfounded, of course, but it is our experience that most farmers profess to be concerned with conservation, and the differences between them and the immigrants are ones of degree which will certainly not result in any significant shift in the distribution of material or political resources among the local population as a whole. Indeed, as we saw earlier in this chapter, there is as much conflict between smaller and larger farmers over the desirability of development in the more remote rural areas.

The second situation in which conflict has developed in Suffolk has been where outside agencies have attempted to intervene in local affairs. We have already seen some examples of this: the Central Electricity Generating Board proposals for a new power station at Orford Ness, and the East Anglian Regional Planners' suggestions for a new town at Eye/Diss are just two recent instances of outside bodies putting forward suggestions which have provoked considerable local opposition. Indeed, most major issues in recent years appear to have been generated in this way. The controversy which surrounded the proposed expansion of Ipswich in the mid-1960s, for example, was aroused as a result of the government's study of the future of the south-east (Ministry of Housing and Local Government, 1964) which envisaged a considerable expansion of population in the town. Similarly, a highly-publicized issue was provoked by the decision of the Ipswich Water Undertaking in the late 1960s to construct a large reservoir on agricultural and scrub land to the south of the town at Tattingstone. In both cases, outside agencies (the government and the Water Authority respectively) were seen by opponents as interfering with well-established local policies, and in both cases opposition came from an alliance of the East Suffolk County Council, the farming and landowning bodies, and preservation groups.[13]

The significance of these and other similar issues is twofold. First, it is apparent that in so far as they come to be represented as conflicts between 'locals' and 'interfering outsiders', they may provide further grounds for the perpetuation of hostility to 'urbanites' and 'outsiders' in general. 'They' are seen not to understand or care for the needs and problems of rural areas, and as such, outside intervention may paradoxically tend to strengthen local identification, and hence established power relations, within the county. The second point is that, although all of these issues received extensive publicity, and all were discussed by various of our informants as examples of the sort of conflicts which have arisen in Suffolk over the years, *none of them were spontaneously and indigenously derived*. Major issues and fundamental confrontations may thus occur between local and extra-local interests but they rarely develop within the locality itself. Clearly, no matter how powerful the local political leadership it is no match for the central government and various organs of state when they intervene in local affairs (for examples see Hampton, 1970). But in those areas where it exercises discretion, if not autonomy from the central authority, its power remains unchallenged.

The third situation where conflict may occur is where the locally powerful are content that it should. Hacker (1965, p. 135) has summarized this argument clearly: 'The élite is content to let the public blow off steam on certain questions. This is acknowledged to be necessary, for democracy must have issues to squabble about. If attention is focussed on fluoride in the water and progressivism in the schools, then eyes will be deflected from more important matters.' There has been no shortage of such 'diversionary' issues in Suffolk. In Mid-Suffolk, for example, there have been acrimonious public squabbles about issues as diverse as the appointment of school governors and the saying of prayers before council meetings. The problem of noise from jets from USAF bases in Suffolk (outsiders again) has provided a constant source of 'news' for many years, while fluoridation of the water supply is a constantly recurring 'issue' which never ceases to stir up antagonisms in the letters pages of the local press. From observation of such issues, we may suggest that the publicity and attention which they receive varies in inverse proportion to their political significance (in terms of their effect on the overall pattern of resource distribution). The more fundamental the issue, the less likely it is to manifest itself into a political conflict.[14]

It would appear therefore that an analysis of such conflicts as have occurred in Suffolk, far from casting doubt upon our assertions of the hegemony of propertied interests, only strengthens them. The situation in Suffolk seems almost analogous to that in rural Wales where 'The views of the élites tend to confirm both the existence of some stresses and tensions, and the absence of widespread and overt class hostility' (Madgwick *et al.*, 1973, p. 156). Or as one of our small farm respondents put it: 'It's the big people who get on these councils so there's no one left to pressure the council. It's their decisions, not the decisions of the small people. They pretend to give you a say, but what they say, goes.' This, in just three sentences, is how we too would summarize the situation.

Conclusions

In Chapter 4 we noted that agricultural workers are dependent upon local farmers in rural areas for both employment and housing. Moreover, the greater proportion of workers living in tied cottages on the farm, together with the de-bureaucratization of the work situation consequent upon the declining use of labour, was resulting in a situation in which workers were more likely to be brought into close, personal, face-to-face contact with their employers. In this chapter we have demonstrated how the successful pursuit of policies advantageous to farmers and landowners has ensured that these trends have proceeded largely undisturbed by local government interference. Indeed, in so far as local councils in Suffolk have signally refused to countenance industrial development in rural areas or engage in widespread council-house building, they have provided the essential infrastructure whereby the powerlessness of local agricultural workers has been maintained and a low-wage rural economy perpetuated.

The failure to provide alternative employment opportunities for local manual workers by the pursuit of conservationist planning policies has also ensured that as agricultural workers leave the land, due to the mechanization of agriculture and other reasons, so they have had to leave the villages in search of employment. They have been replaced by urban, middle-class newcomers who, as we observed in Chapter 5, have proved to be fierce protectors of the visual aspects of the English countryside and as a result something of an irritant to resident farmers. Their impact upon the local status structure has been disruptive and one consequence of their arrival has been to draw farmers and farm workers closer together in a defence of local agricultural interests against the potential threats posited by alien outsiders (Newby, 1974; 1977, Chapter VI). In this chapter, however, we have noted that whatever the subjective differences perceived by farmers and newcomers over such matters as the environmental consequences of farming practices these have had little effect upon their common pursuit of local political policies. In this sense the newcomers have not presented the threat to the local political system that the frequent skirmishes over hedgerows and footpaths might indicate. By and large the former oligarchy of farmers and landowners has experienced few difficulties in incorporating such newcomers into the prevailing political practice.

However, this constant strife over the effects of farming practice on the environment has not been without important consequences. Much of the conflict takes place on a personal basis and much of it – the consequences of zealous stubble-burning, hedgerow removal, trampled cornfields, open gates, etc. – occurs actually on the farm itself. The farm worker, therefore, directly observes much conflict in action – indeed in so far as it affects his work situation he is likely to be part of it himself. It is not surprising, then, that the farm worker shares the farmer's antipathy to such interfering outsiders. However, the farm worker is often entirely unaware that, miles away in the council chamber, representatives of both the farmer's and the newcomer's interests are busy agreeing upon political policies which are to his detriment. As far as farm workers are concerned, therefore, not only has the hegemony of local property-owners systematically denied an improvement in their life-chances, but – ironically, and in a totally unintended fashion – provided the wherewithal for the increasing identification of workers with their employers in both the work and community situation. Estranged from the alien newcomers, farm workers have increasingly recognized a common identity with local farmers. Farm workers have therefore been more ready to endorse the values and beliefs which farmers hold concerning their respective social situations. It is to an analysis of this *Weltanschauung* that we now turn.

We saw in the last chapter that an apparent consensus between classes and different interest groups in rural areas may in fact disguise an underlying and fundamental conflict of interests. This is likely to be the case where economically and politically dominant groups are in a position to impose their values, beliefs, and perceptions of the world on to subordinate and less powerful groups, and thus to influence the latter's perceptions of the legitimacy of their situation. To the extent that this occurs, gross and manifest inequalities may come to be seen by all classes as 'natural' if not desirable, and established patterns of economic privilege and political control may thus be perpetuated virtually without challenge. Clearly, class relations are most stable when they are unquestioned; the successful manipulation of lower-class perceptions and evaluations of their situation is therefore unlikely to be a highly significant factor in maintaining social and political stability. We saw an example of this in the last chapter, when we discussed the ideological significance of the concept of 'community' in rural Suffolk, and how commitment to such an ideology encourages the formation and subjective recognition of vertical ties of identification, thereby avoiding conflict between different classes. But although we have argued that high levels of 'moral density' – e.g. in the work situation of farmers and their workers, or in the encapsulated rural village – are likely to prove amenable to the maintenance of social stability there remain the problems of how far, and in what ways, the legitimating beliefs and values of dominant groups come to be transmitted to members of subordinate classes. It is our intention in this and the following chapter to pick up these loose threads in our argument, and to weave a tighter and more comprehensive picture of the ideological sources of rural stability.

Social imagery, ideology and hegemony

Ever since the publication in 1966 of David Lockwood's influential paper on variations in working-class images of society, there has been a marked and growing interest among students of social stratification with the ways in which different sections of the British working class conceive of the system in which they live, and of their relatively lowly position within it. In his original formulation of the problem, Lockwood argued that perceptions of the social order (and, derivatively, evaluations of its legitimacy and/or permanency) were strongly related to the work and community experiences of different 'types' of workers. Those, like coalminers and shipbuilders, for example, who lived in cohesive and homogeneous occupational communities and worked in large-scale heavy industry tended to subscribe to a 'them-and-us' dichotomous class model. Groups like car workers, on the other hand, had an almost entirely pecuniary model of society, while workers who were to a large extent isolated from other members of their class both at work and in their leisure hours had a view of society which approximated to the predominantly middle-class image of a graded status hierarchy. Among this latter group – the so-called 'traditional deferential' workers – were included agricultural workers, for they were customarily employed in relatively small units where they were to be found as often as not working shoulder to shoulder with their employers, while their residence in close-knit rural villages, or even in isolated cottages attached to their place of work, only served to reinforce vertical social solidarity. As we saw in Chapter 1, it was precisely this group which Newby (1977) chose to study when he came to consider the problem of the 'traditional deferential' worker in Britain.

Newby's findings, however, were in many ways disconcerting and surprising. Farm workers in Suffolk, it transpired, did not appear especially or notably 'deferential'. In terms of their responses to a battery of traditional attitude questions, designed to elicit their views on such upper-class institutions as the House of Lords and public schools, it seemed that most farm workers interviewed held no very strong or firm beliefs about the superiority or otherwise of higher status groups. Indeed, they generally appeared to care little either way. Nor did they subscribe with any unanimity or enthusiasm to the 'status hierarchy' model of society described in Lockwood's paper. Indeed, nearly 60 per cent of them thought that there were just two classes in society – a dichotomous view of the stratification system more commonly associated with coalminers and shipyard workers than with the stereotypical rustic worker. In short, Newby concluded that many farm workers (in common with at least some sections of the urban industrial working class) had no single unified and coherent image of society and the social divisions which cut through it. Instead, they held somewhat confused, incomplete, ambivalent and often internally contradictory impressions of the social order and of their place within it. Nor, he claimed, should this come as any great surprise, for it was possible to identify a number of contradictions and cross-cutting pressures which came to bear on many agricultural workers, and which clearly gave rise to contradictory and confused social imagery as a result. To take the most obvious example, farm workers experienced objective and relative material deprivation in their work and their home lives, yet at the same time they were personally and familiarly acquainted with the very men – their employers – who were responsible for paying them low wages. Thus one set of pressures led toward a radical interpretation of their situation, while another at the same time checked any such response. As we have noted in earlier chapters, the emphasis placed upon particularism by Suffolk's dominant groups serves to fragment lower-class solidarism before it has a chance to emerge.

In a useful theoretical contribution to the debate on sources of social stability, Mann (1970) has argued that lower-class groups will rarely need to develop any consistent and coherent image of their place in society, and like Newby, he has produced recent empirical evidence (on industrial workers in Peterborough – see Blackburn and Mann, 1975) to show that working-class images of society may rarely approximate to any of Lockwood's three ideal types. Unlike dominant groups in society, the working class has little to defend, to rationalize, to explain, or to justify. Thus its members may rarely feel the need to bridge or reconcile the strains and inconsistencies in their views of the social world – indeed, they may even fail to recognize that such strains exist – simply because they are not called upon to do so. Ruling-class groups, on the other hand, may consistently be obliged to produce rational and acceptable explanations of their privileged position – acceptable both to themselves (nobody wishes to see himself as undeserving) and to others. Employers of rural labour are one such group, for the close cooperation which exists in farming between employer and employee, while possibly easing the transmission of values and beliefs from the former to the latter, also presents to the latter a stark and unremitting reminder of the enormous social and material gap which exists between them. The farm worker who eats in his employer's kitchen also becomes very familiar with his employer's possessions, the like of which he could never dream of owning. Thus it becomes imperative for the ruling groups in rural society to develop a consistent and justificatory model of social reality and to transmit elements of this model to subordinate groups. It was clear, however, from Newby's evidence that farm workers did not generally subscribe to the predominantly middle-class notion of society as a graded status hierarchy. They did not, that is, embrace what Parkin (1971) has identified as the dominant value system in society. Instead they tended to *accept* their position within the social structure without morally *endorsing* it. This being the case, we may ask whether the dominant class in rural society can be said to have succeeded in imposing its ideas of legitimacy, and transmitting its beliefs about the acceptability of the social order.

Parkin (1971) argues that if a subordinate group fails to subscribe to the principal values of a dominant group, then ideological manipulation on the part of the latter appears unlikely as an explanation of social stability:

The major problem raised by the class differentiated view of the normative system is that of social control. If the subordinate class were to subscribe to a value system sharply distinguished from that of the dominant class, then the latter's normative control over the former would obviously be seriously diminished. In this situation, the dominant class would have to rely on physical coercion as a substitute for moral suasion. [p. 80.]

We would argue that the imposition of ruling-class ideas and values, even in the most encapsulated of communities and the most pater-nalistic of farms,[1] is never more than patchy, but nevertheless that such ideological manipulation as does occur is *sufficient* in most cases to counter or neutralize the effects on class imagery and class consciousness of the everyday experience of material deprivation on the part of most rural workers. That is, although the ruling ideas in rural society are not necessarily everywhere the ideas of the ruling class, they are nevertheless sufficiently reflexive of the interests of the ruling groups to maintain a minimum level of 'moral' attachment (Etzioni, 1961) on the part of less privileged sections of the population.

In order to make the point clearer, it is useful to distinguish the three related concepts of hegemony, social imagery and ideology. In part, this is to follow Lockwood (1975) who draws a distinction between class imagery and class ideology. Lockwood sees class imagery as referring to largely implicit models of the social world which derive out of our everyday experience of interaction within that world. An image of society, in other words, has a certain 'concreteness'; it is the sum of what we 'know' about the world as a direct result of our ongoing lived experiences within it. It will rarely be coherent (since it will reflect a range of often contradictory experiences) nor explicit to consciousness, and will remain for the most part subjectively unexamined and largely taken for granted – 'not in need of further analysis', as Schutz (1967, p. 74) puts it.

Lockwood contrasts social class imagery with the concept of ideology which refers to a relatively formalized and explicit system of beliefs related in some way to specific class interests. Ideologies, in other words, represent readily available explanatory systems which may be drawn upon to 'make sense of' particular social situations where taken-for-granted knowledge is, for one reason or another, problematic. We may see ideologies, then, as relatively coherent social theories which are evolved outside the individual's everyday lived experiences, but which may then come to be applied to the explanation of various aspects of those experiences. Thus conservative ideologies, for example, may derive out of various agencies of the state, or a range of institutions such as the schools, the churches and the mass media (of the kind identified by Althusser (1971) as 'ideological state apparatuses'), while radical or 'utopian' (Mannheim, 1936) ideologies may derive out of those organizations, such as radical class-based parties, which present a challenge to dominant class interests. The point is, however, that in both cases ideologies represent external systems of ascribed beliefs which come to be applied to concrete social and political situations *ex post facto* as explanations or justification.

The fact that ideologies are systems of beliefs generated externally to ongoing lived experiences does not, of course, imply that they have no relevance to these experiences. As we shall see later, the crucial point about ideology as a mode of social control is that it cannot strain credulity too far – i.e. it must be seen to be applicable to specific situations before it is accepted as a plausible explanation for them. Nevertheless, the point which Lockwood wishes to emphasize is that ideologies may vary, and even come into conflict with, aspects of social class imagery which develop in the course of everyday lived experience. It is possible, in other words, to find situations in which the cliché phrases and well-worn slogans voiced by any given group appear to bear little resemblance to, and may even seem incongruent with, its members' core images of society. As Lockwood (1975, p. 248) observes: 'There is no inherent reason why such an ideology, which is made up of fairly limited, abstract, and "ascribed" beliefs, should be identical with a social class imagery which is more diffuse and inchoate, and more spontaneously acquired by the individual's experience of his immediate work and leisure environment.' There may, therefore, be a considerable difference between what we 'know' about concrete instances, and what we 'believe' about abstract or distant phenomena, for what we 'know' derives largely out of personal lived experience and what is embedded within our consciousness, while what we 'believe' will to a large extent reflect our willingness or ability to adopt, reject, or take an ambivalent position in regard to certain ideological belief 'packages' offered us as shorthand and readily digestible accounts of the world outside our lived experience. As Scase (1974, p. 171) has observed: '. . . actors' conceptions of the class structure are shaped not only by "objective" patterns of structural relationships, but also by interpretations generated by wider social processes.'

Now such a disjuncture between image and ideology may be characteristic of any social group. Indeed, wherever a group or its individual members profess views on matters lying beyond their immediate lived experience, we may presume that such views are ideological in so far as their source lies in beliefs generated by agencies outside the group and transmitted to it. This may at times result in apparent contradictions. A good example is provided by our farmers' opinions on trade unions. At one point in our interviews with farmers we asked three successive questions on this general theme. The first was concerned with respondents' attitudes towards the agricultural workers' union and, as we saw in Chapter 4, only 15 per cent of all those interviewed were directly hostile towards the union and its activities. The second was concerned with attitudes towards trade unions generally – respondents were asked whether or not they felt that unions were 'for the working man at everyone else's expense' – and here over three-quarters of all respondents (76 per cent of the total) took a generally hostile and negative attitude towards the union movement. In the third question of the series, we asked whether the National Farmers' Union could rightly be seen as championing farmers' interests at everyone else's expense, and not surprisingly, three-quarters of all those answering the question felt that it could not (see Chapter 3).[2] Thus farmers took generally favourable views towards the NUAAW and the NFU, but were often strongly antagonistic towards unions in general. But of course, questions relating to the activities of the NUAAW and the NFU were immediately meaningful to most farmers, for most had probably discussed and considered these very issues many times (see Chapter 3), and even if they had not, most (85 per cent) at least belonged to the NFU and most probably employed men who were members of the workers' union (although many claimed that they neither knew nor cared whether their employees were union members). Few if any, however, had any first-hand experience of industrial trade unions in general. Their beliefs in regard to this question, therefore, were generated, not from their own concrete work and community experiences, but from exposure to certain ideological sets of beliefs and notions stemming from early political socialization and selectively reinforcing exposure to the mass media and its portrayals of union activities. Interestingly, although many farmers felt that *their* image as portrayed in the media was unfair and misleading, they appeared to have no such qualms regarding the images portrayed of others. Indeed, as Hyman (1972) has noted, people's antagonism towards trade unions appears to increase the less direct experience they have of them. Clearly this was so with farmers.

Although such strains and seeming contradictions between social imagery and received ideology may be found in most if not all social groups, it is clear that they are most likely to be found among those sections of the population whose lived experiences diverge most markedly from their received ideologies. Such groups will usually be found among the subordinate classes in any society, for it is there that the optimism of dominant ideologies is most strained. In other words, it is likely that the more powerful and privileged the group concerned the more congruent and complementary its ideology and social image are – the concrete life experiences of the ruling social groups will usually be in accord with their received beliefs such that the latter will come to be seen by them as 'obvious' and 'self-evident' (what Lloyd Warner (Warner *et al.*, 1963) referred to as 'of course' statements). Lower-class groups, on the other hand, are unlikely to be so sure – hence the 'ambivalence' noted by Newby, Mann and others. Working-class ambivalence, then, may be understood as a manifestation of an underlying tension between received beliefs and concrete 'knowledge' – a tension which becomes less marked among more privileged groups where received belief itself takes on the form of 'obvious' knowledge.

At this point, however, it is necessary to ask how such 'concrete knowledge' develops, and it is here that the concept of hegemony needs to be introduced. As it stands, Lockwood's analysis of social imagery as experientially grounded is inadequate. The point is that experience has to be interpreted before it can provide a basis for knowledge. As the long and protracted debates on the philosophy of science have indicated, there can be no neutral 'observation language', no way of seeing or experiencing the world which is not dependent on some prior theoretical–explanatory framework. This being the case, we have to ask which interpretative framework guides the development of 'concrete knowledge', and where is its source? In other words, while retaining the valuable distinction between ideology (as a system of formal beliefs generated externally to specific life-experiences of individuals) and imagery (as the taken-for-granted working assumptions on which social life is ordinarily based), we still face the problem of determining how such immediate experiences are mediated.

One possible answer, deriving from social phenomenology, is that meaning is intersubjectively constructed in the course of everyday life. Taken-for-granted realities are therefore accomplished by social actors jointly negotiating the meaning to be attached to their specific shared situations. Such negotiation will rarely take the form of conscious activity, for individuals routinely apply shared 'common-sense' perspectives, developed and modified over the course of previous interaction in similar situations. Individuals therefore confront a particular situation with what Schutz terms 'cookbook recipes' for understanding and predicting each other's actions. Only when such recipes are found to be inappropriate is the process of intersubjective mediation of meaning likely to be thrown up for conscious examination.

The problem with this argument, however, lies in its implicit assumption that reality, or 'concrete knowledge', is accomplished on the basis of negotiation between equal parties. Yet it is apparent that the social construction of reality itself occurs within a pre-existing political context. As Giddens (1976, p. 113) writes:

The creation of frames of meaning occurs as the mediation of practical activities, and in terms of differentials of power which actors are able to bring to bear. . . . The reflexive elaboration of frames of meaning is characteristically imbalanced in relation to the possession of power, whether this be a result of the superior linguistic or dialectical skills of one person in conversation with another; the possession of relevant types of 'technical knowledge'; the mobilization of authority or 'force', etc. 'What passes for social reality' stands in immediate relation to the distribution of power.

Quite simply, some groups enjoy a greater capacity to have their definitions of reality accepted than do other groups. In such a situation, discourse between them is, from the very outset, 'systematically distorted' (Habermas, 1976).

The fact of systematically distorted communication, however, should not lead us to conclude that social imagery is simply imposed from above. There *is* a necessary distinction to be drawn between ideologies, which *are* imposed from external sources, and imagery, which is the product of ongoing negotiation and reinterpretation within a pre-existing political framework. Thus Poulantzas (1973*b*, p. 203) argues that it is misleading to suggest that dominant views of the world are simply grafted on to the working class, for the process whereby dominant ideas are evolved involves all classes. What passes for 'experiential knowledge' is thus the product of an ongoing process of social negotiation within an asymmetrical yet reciprocal political context. More precisely, the production of social imagery is a dynamic process contained within the confines of a hegemonic system of core beliefs which constitute the ontological foundation for *both* the imposition of dominant ideologies *and* the construction of social imagery. This is what Boggs (1976, p. 39) means when he refers to the 'dualistic' character of hegemony; that 'an entire system of values, attitudes, beliefs, morality, etc.' operates both as 'a general conception of life for the masses, and as a scholastic programme or set of principles which is advanced by a sector of the intellectuals'.

The concept of hegemony, therefore, rests at the foundation of any understanding of ideology and social imagery. Hegemony constitutes the building blocks by means of which coherent sets of beliefs about the world and less coherent 'feelings' about what the world is like are realized. Hegemony is distinct from ideology because it is not formalized, and is distinct from imagery because it is not particularized. These distinctions are made most clearly by Raymond Williams (1977, pp. 109–10):

Ideology, in its normal senses, is a relatively formal and articulated system of meanings, values and beliefs of a kind that can be abstracted as a 'world view' or 'class outlook'. . . . The concept of hegemony often, in practice, resembles these definitions, but it is distinct in its refusal to equate consciousness with the articulate formal system which can be and ordinarily is abstracted as 'ideology'. . . . It is a lived system of meanings and values

– constitutive and constituting – which as they are experienced as practices appear as reciprocally confirming. It thus constitutes a sense of reality for most people in the society, a sense of absolute-because-experienced reality, beyond which it is very difficult for most members of the society to move, in most areas of their lives.

Hegemony thus appears virtually unchallengeable. Ideologies are open to debate; because they are formalized they can be dissected, criticized, and countered by alternative explanatory systems. Social imagery is an ongoing process in which modifications are constantly possible as new situations are encountered and new puzzles are thrown up for resolution. But hegemony constitutes the common-sense basis which underlies dominant ideologies, which makes alternative ideologies appear 'ridiculous', and which pervades the social construction of reality. To draw a parallel with Kuhn's arguments about scientific knowledge, we may suggest that hegemony constitutes the paradigm, ideologies the theories, and the construction of social imagery the process of 'normal science' (Kuhn, 1970). Just as in science new theories and routine practice must both address themselves to the core assumptions of the scientific community, so too in social life hegemony effectively mediates between competing ideologies and limits the scope of ongoing practical accounting procedures.[3]

It is, however, necessary to note that dominant ideologies may prove extremely adaptable in the face of changing conditions. We would thus dispute Habermas' contention that 'Traditions can retain legitimizing force only as long as they are not torn out of interpretive systems that guarantee continuity and identity' (1976, p. 71), for as we shall see in the next chapter, ideologies which developed in the earliest stages of British capitalism may still be found today, in revised form, as apparently convincing justifications for a situation which has long since superseded them. The question of whether these ideologies find a receptive audience or whether, on the contrary, they strain credulity too far as a result of a weakening of their hegemonic foundations, is an empirical question with which we shall be concerned in this and the final chapter.

Such a question, however, raises problems of methodology, and it is necessary briefly to consider these before turning to our empirical data on the farmers and farm workers. The first problem is that an analysis of hegemony cannot adequately be accomplished within a case study such as that discussed here. Hegemony is, in Gramsci's terms, a fundamental feature of 'civil society' as a whole, and is by no means confined to the relationship between individual farmers and farm workers. It is, in other words, a 'given' in our analysis. For example, while it is possible in research such as this to examine, say, the ways in which farmers and farm workers conceive of a 'fair' return on capital or a 'just' wage, it is not possible to analyse why it is that the fundamental questions of why capital has the right to *any* return, or why the farm worker is obliged to sell his labour-power, are so rarely raised. Our analysis, then, is concerned with the observable manifestations of hegemony in the form of ideologies and social imagery, but cannot go beyond this to a consideration of hegemony itself.

Secondly, the distinction between ideology and imagery, while valid at a conceptual level, is extraordinarily difficult to draw empirically. As Poulantzas (1973*b*, pp. 206–7) writes, 'Ideology is present to such an extent in all the agents' activities that it becomes indistinguishable from their lived experience'. Often (and especially in the case of the most successful ideologies), it is impossible to distinguish with any confidence what somebody 'knows' on the basis of his commonsense interpretation of his ongoing experiences, from what he believes on the basis of received wisdoms. The point is especially pertinent in a survey-based piece of social research such as this, where data are generated almost entirely out of what respondents say in answer to specified questions. If social imagery is largely taken for granted, for example, it seems unlikely that survey research will prove a very effective instrument for tapping it (Bulmer, 1975; Lockwood, 1975). Given the constraints of this method, it seems that only fragments of ideologies and hints of social imagery will come to be recorded. Nevertheless, we should still expect to find a greater degree of internal consistency and coherence among the farmers' answers than Newby found among farm workers. Our principal aim, of course, in attempting to trace farmers' ideologies and social imagery was to compare our results with those for the farm workers, and thus to arrive at some conclusions regarding the transmission of beliefs and values from one to the other. We should not merely expect farmers' responses to our questions to be more concise and less logically confused than those of their workers, therefore, for in addition we should expect to find fundamental elements common in each.

This, however, raises a third problem. Given the ambivalence of most farm workers, we should not expect anything approaching total congruence between their responses and those of their generally more coherent employers. The point is that *if* social control is maintained at least in part through the successful transmission of farmers' ideologies to their workers, this will not necessarily result in the workers' views and beliefs *corresponding* to those of the farmers. Rather it seems likely that only certain fragmented elements of the farmers' ideologies will successfully be transmitted, these being enough to check any counter-ideologies or radical meaning systems which may come to be accepted or generated among the subordinate group. This being the case, we are faced with the insoluble problem of determining the *level* at which ideological control may be said to exist. How much of farmers' ideologies must their workers accept before ideological manipulation may be asserted as an instrument of social control? Furthermore, even if we assume that a 'significant' degree of overlap can be established between the professed beliefs and values of farmers and their workers, we are faced with the problem of assessing the *causal* relation between them. As we saw in Chapter 6, causality is an essential component of power relationships. It makes no sense to see any individual or group as powerful except in relation to another party's subsequent response or lack of response. Traditional authority and deference are thus reverse sides of the same coin, linked in a causal relationship to one another.

The significance of this is twofold. First, since ideologies, if they are transmitted at all between farmers and workers, are transmitted in personal interaction on an individual level, we cannot assess ideological control except in terms of individual sets of relationships. We cannot, that is, compare sets of aggregate data – e.g. the proportions of farmers saying x compared with the proportions of farm workers – with a view to establishing causality, for this would be to fall foul of the so-called 'ecological fallacy'. We cannot, for example, argue that because our data reveal that certain facets of farmers' articulated beliefs and values coincide with those found among farm workers that individual farmers necessarily share these beliefs and values with their own employees. This being the case, we clearly cannot impute causality – for that, we must consider each individual relationship. Secondly, and following on from this point, even if a high degree of congruence is found between many different sets of farmer–worker relations, we still cannot automatically attribute causality – and hence ideological power – to individual farmers. Quite simply, it is likely that any such similarity may be the result of both parties' exposure to a common hegemonic source such as the mass media (Scase, 1974). It is only where farmers' ideologies differ from, or are not encompassed within, the dominant ideologies current in the society at large that we can suggest with any confidence that similarities with farm workers' responses may be causally explained. In other words, where the responses of *both* farmers and farm workers differ markedly from the dominant beliefs and values of the wider society, we may be justified in asserting a relationship of causal significance between them, and in looking to processes within the work and community situations of farmers and their employees to explain this causal mechanism. Thus in Chapter 6, for example, we saw how the ideology of localism and ruralism ran counter to dominant 'urban' values, and thus provided one instance of probable ideological manipulation between the traditional ruling and subordinate classes in Suffolk. In Chapter 8, on the other hand, we shall demonstrate how many of the most central and fundamental facets of farmers' ideologies can be found in one form or another in society as a whole, and in these cases, causal connections with farm workers' values and beliefs will be less clearly demonstrated. The point is, then, that in many cases, both farmers and farm workers may be expected to be subject to the same hegemonic culture, the difference being that this will tend to reaffirm the ideologies and social imagery of the former, while undermining any alternative perspectives which may develop among the latter.

Our purpose in this chapter, therefore, is rather more limited than we had once anticipated. In the main, we shall confine ourselves to an examination of how our respondents tended to view their world and their position within it, and we shall restrict our discussion of the significance of their views and beliefs for social order in the countryside to pointing to possible areas in which farmers' and farm workers' responses *may* be causally related. The material we present should therefore be taken as indicative of the social imagery and ideologies of a property-owning section of the British middle class but should not too readily be related to the ambiguities and confused imagery characteristic of agricultural workers.

Class awareness and class consciousness

To argue, as we have above, that dominant groups in British society are unlikely to experience the same degree of tension between imagery and ideology as that experienced by subordinate classes is not to argue that the ideologies and *Weltanschauungen* of dominant groups are indistinguishable. Indeed, in one respect, there is a strain between their social imagery and political ideology which would appear every bit as great, every bit as inconsistent, as that noted in relation to the 'ambivalent' working classes: namely the strain between their manifest consciousness of class identity and class interests on the one hand, and their resolute ideological refusal to accept the salience (and at times even the existence) of class differences in society on the other. We are not the first to draw attention to the paradox that those who most emphatically deny the relevance of class differences on the ideological level are also those who, in the course of their everyday lives, exhibit greatest awareness of their own class membership. Of course, it is by no means surprising that this dilemma should exist, for while class exclusivity generates its own particular benefits in terms of preserving the existing pattern of resource distribution (Parkin, 1974), the ideology of classlessness serves to deny that such exclusivity is operating, and thus to justify the consequent perpetuation of this unequal pattern. At the outset, then, we should note that dominant ideologies may no more accord with the lived experiences of dominant groups than with those of subordinate groups. The difference, however, is that dominant groups *choose to adopt them* as convenient short-hand *rationalizations* and justifications for their own position, while subordinate groups may be *obliged to accept them*, in part at least, as explanations of their relatively underprivileged position. In the everyday experience of both groups, therefore, the objective realities of a class-structured society will be manifest in a host of different ways, but whereas these will be rationalized

Table 65 *Patterns of voting of East Anglian farmers, 1964–74**

Overall voting pattern, 1964–74*	1000+ acres sample No.	1000+ acres sample %	44 parishes sample No.	44 parishes sample %	HN sample No.	HN sample %
Consistently Conservative	93	95	41	76	38	74
Consistently Labour	2	2	1	2	2	4
Consistently other	—	—	2	4	—	—
Floating between Conservative and Labour	2	2	4	7	8	16
Other	1	1	6	11	3	6
Total	98	100	54	100	51	100

* i.e. 1964, 1966, 1970 and February 1974 general elections.

P.P.P.—K

in the case of dominant groups, they will be obscured in the case of subordinate groups.

Like most sections of the British middle class, farmers exhibit extraordinary class solidarity in their behaviour, if not in their ideologies. Their voting behaviour is an obvious case in point. Among all farmers, and particularly among those with 1000 acres or more of land, Conservative voting is clearly the norm. Even at the height of Labour Party popularity in 1966, only three of our 1000 + acres sample and one of our forty-four parishes sample could bring themselves to vote Labour. Indeed, there is certainly a generalized expectation in the farming community that farmers will, almost to a man, vote for, join, and perhaps even run on behalf of the Conservative Party. The moral pressure exerted – or at least *felt* to be exerted – by such generalized expectations upon the odd deviant or recalcitrant case can be intense:

Publicly we belong to the Conservative Party. My father's Labour, and he belongs to the Conservative Party! Conservatives have got this attitude that all farmers are Conservatives. . . . They came round some time ago, so we joined. [200-acre Suffolk farmer and Liberal voter.]

It is, of course, ironic that such pressures should come to be felt by *farmers*, when so much attention has been paid by rural constituency Labour parties to the possibility that *farm workers* may feel constrained to vote against their consciences. It is also indicative of the growing strength of the Conservative Party, for as late as 1951 the Eye constituency (undoubtedly the most rural of the Suffolk seats) elected a Liberal MP.

Considering the figures given in Table 65, it seems doubtful whether any section of the manual working class in this country exhibits such solidarity in its voting behaviour as the farmers do. That 95 per cent of the 1000 + acres farmers have regularly voted Conservative over the last ten years is not perhaps surprising, but it is indicative of a degree of political commitment and cohesiveness which not even the most politicized sections of the working class could equal, and which a group such as the farm workers could come nowhere near matching.[4] Not only is this support for the Conservative cause enduring, but it is in most cases also morally committed. That is to say, most farmers are Conservatives out of sentiment as much as calculation. Indeed, Self and Storing (1962, p. 203) have noted that 'Many have certainly been persuaded that "Labour is best for agriculture", while continuing to vote Conservative'. Be that as it may, it is clear that most of our respondents were 'gut Tories', and although they were often to be heard complaining about Conservative policies, especially in relation to agriculture, the possibility of their withdrawing support from the party at election time was virtually nil.

The farmers' vote – that phenomenon which has received so much attention on the part of politicians and political commentators alike (for a summary see Bell and Newby, 1974) – is thus to all intents and purposes solid. It makes no more sense for the Labour Party to hope to woo it than it does for the Conservatives to fear losing it. Indeed, 62 per cent of the 1000 + acres farmers in our survey not only voted Conservative but belonged to the party, the equivalent figure among the farmers in the forty-four parishes being only slightly lower at 54 per cent. This solidarity behind one party can only be explained with reference to farmers' ideological commitment to Conservatism. In other words, although when a farmer votes Conservative he presumably does so partly in the anticipation that this will benefit him personally (e.g. through lower taxes, higher subsidies, or whatever), he also undoubtedly does so partly as a symbolic reaffirmation of his commitment to certain core – almost 'sacred' – beliefs and values. Most farmers are 'expressive' as well as 'instrumental' Conservatives.[5] They vote Conservative because the image they still hold of that party is that it most closely represents their fundamental beliefs regarding the sanctity of property, the inherent value of work, the freedom of the individual, the right to prosper from one's endeavours, and so on. These may be seen as the ideological elements, common to a greater or lesser degree to most farmers, which underpin their collective support for the Conservative Party at election time.

Such ideological elements became manifest many times in our interviews with farmers, but they emerged most clearly and resoundingly in response to a question which asked respondents what, if anything, they felt was wrong with Britain today. Such a broad and abstract question was, of course, an open invitation to farmers to dig deep into their ready-made repertoire of received beliefs, conventional wisdoms and ideologies, and most did so readily with little further prompting. It was evident that most farmers not only agreed that something *was* fundamentally 'wrong', but also had firm and convinced views as to what that 'something' was. Indeed, although the sorts of factors discussed by most farmers lay beyond their own lived experience, there was often a remarkable similarity in the content – and sometimes even the wording – of their replies. Take, for example, those who replied in terms of others' unwillingness to work. This was a standard response on the part of large and small farmers alike, for their belief that there were people in Britain who were 'getting something for nothing', and who were not being penalized for their laziness, clearly offended a deeply rooted 'work ethic'.

People don't want to work. They consider the country owes them a living, but no one owes them a living. [Suffolk farmer, 110 acres.]

The incentive to work isn't what it was. Unemployment benefit is too high – it should be a meagre living standard. A man that's able to work but isn't willing to should be pinched. It's too easy for the lazy bugger. [Suffolk farmer, 235 acres.]

The Welfare State has cushioned certain people and conditioned them to think they have a right to things without having to work for them. There tends to be a hard core of people who feel the world owes them a living. [Essex farmer, 1100 acres.]

No one is really prepared to work for anything. The Welfare State gives people too much. There's a loss of pride in work too. [Norfolk farmer, 1000 acres.]

Everyone wants something for nothing. . . . People don't want to work for what they've got. They want what I've got, but they forget my family had to work for it. [Cambridgeshire farmer, 1100 acres.]

People don't work hard enough. They don't want to *earn* their money. I don't mind a man having a lot of money if he *earns* it. But if he's not working hard for it, it's not right. [Norfolk farmer, 2000 acres.]

The basic problem is that we all think that we can get more out of life than we put in. The Welfare State provides a safety net so nobody really cares. This is disastrous. [Norfolk farmer, 1500 acres.]

Now not only do all these replies (and there are many more of similar sentiment) range over the same *theme* – that people are 'work-shy' – but they tend to follow the same logic and often to use the same lexicon. Note, for example, the frequent references to the 'Welfare State', to the 'world not owing people a living', and so on. Indeed, certain cliché phrases seem to reappear in farmers' responses to this question with a fascinating regularity:

The incentive to work isn't what it was. . . . You've got to have conscientious men – a fair day's work for a fair day's pay. [Suffolk farmer, 120 acres.]

It won't improve until people do an honest day's work for an honest day's pay. There's too much money wasted on social security – on those who won't work. [Suffolk farmer, 150 acres.]

There's too many want something for nothing. People won't do an honest day's work for a good day's pay. They aren't satisfied with their lot. [Suffolk farmer, 420 acres.]

No one wants to do a fair day's work for a fair day's pay. They all want something for nothing. Too many get too much for nothing. [Norfolk farmer, 1100 acres.]

We have to get back to a fair day's work for a fair day's pay. The golden goose can't indefinitely go on laying golden eggs. We will go bankrupt. [Cambridgeshire farmer, 1000 acres.]

And so on.

Needless to say, this strong and widespread concern with a balance between toil and wage is not generally directed at those who, because of accident of birth, have no financial need to work. Indeed, many of those who were most committed to the 'work-shy' explanation of the country's ills were those who had inherited their farms and their wealth from their fathers. As we shall see, they were generally able to generate satisfactory rationalizations by means of which they could condemn others for not working while justifying their own lack of need to work, but this need not concern us at the moment. Suffice it to note that the widespread use of the term 'a fair day's work for a fair day's pay' is usually directed implicitly (and sometimes explicitly) at the current 'folk devils', the overpaid and underworked, strike-prone and irresponsible car workers.

This immediately leads us to note a second point: namely that criticisms of scroungers and work-shysters were rarely, if at all, directed at the agricultural working class. As we saw in Chapter 4, farmers are generally full of admiration and respect for their employees (largely, one suspects, because they patently are not 'overpaid and underworked'), and as we shall see, many suggested to us that if the balance between toil and reward were skewed in the case of the farm workers, it was because they did not earn enough relative to the quantity and quality of the tasks they performed. Clearly, then, when farmers came to diagnose the cause of the country's ills in terms of the population's aversion to work, they did so while excepting the two groups – farmers and farm workers – with whom they were most familiar. Their comments, that is, were directed against those of whom they had *least* experience and *least* primary knowledge. Most farmers could only 'know' about 'social security dodgers', 'Welfare State scroungers', 'overpaid shirkers' and the rest from the images they have received second-hand – principally through the media. This, of course, explains the amazing congruity of the content and form of their responses – why so many, for example, drew upon the slogan 'a fair day's work for a fair day's pay'. Farmers, that is, endorse ready-made cliché explanations for particular phenomena which lie outside their everyday experience and which they learn from those national institutions which function to make such phenomena meaningful in commonsense terms. Their responses are thus ideological in source, and highly predictable in nature.[6]

This conclusion is confirmed by other varieties of response recorded in relation to the question on the cause of Britain's ills. As we saw earlier in this chapter, for example, farmers were often very hostile towards trade unions in general (although at the same time well disposed towards the NUAAW and the NFU), and this led some of them to attribute the country's ailments to the 'selfishness' and 'irresponsibility' of industrial unions (of which, of course, they had no direct concrete experience):

It's the power of the unions. It's swung too far. They're the root cause of inflation. [Essex farmer, 1200 acres.]

There have got to be more people doing what's right for the country – not for themselves. There are too many strikes. Strikes should be a last resort. The trade unions are too powerful. [Suffolk farmer, 850 acres.]

Our only problem is the unions. They're too powerful and control the workers. [Suffolk farmer, 75 acres.]

We are too democratic. We have too many troublemakers who would only be tolerated in a democracy. . . . The doctrine the unions favour would get them shot in Russia. [Suffolk farmer, 300 acres.]

Now not only do such ideologies reflect media images quite closely (see, for example, the analysis of media presentation of industrial conflict by Glasgow University Media Group (1976) and Morley (1976)), but they also commend themselves to farmers as explanations of why there should be mounting evidence of apparent lower-class dissatisfaction in Britain. In other words, by blaming trade unions, Communists or whatever farmers find it possible to maintain an image of society as a healthy organic body with workers and management pulling together for the common good. Trouble, that is, is inspired by agitators who can 'turn the workers' heads' and is certainly not endemic to the social framework as a whole. Thus, asked whether they saw the class system as essentially conflictual or consensual, nearly 80 per cent of respondents saw it as wholly or largely consensual, while around one-quarter of these added the proviso that society was generally harmonious except when strife and bitterness were 'stirred up' by agitators.

The answers we recorded blaming trade unions and their ilk for the problems currently faced in Britain raise another significant point – namely, that farmers' ideologies were by no means always entirely consistent. It is not just that they invariably managed to be anti-union in the abstract, while pro-union (in the case of the NUAAW) in the concrete, but that their answers often revealed an internal logical tension. In the case of the trade unions, for example, we were commonly told that unions were a 'good thing' in themselves, but that their activities were wrong or misguided – that unions were an essential component of a free society, but that their freedom should be curtailed. Indeed, this tension between freedom and control revealed itself in other ways, too. Thus, for example, one explanation of Britain's ills was that individual freedom was being eroded:

You get the feeling that everyone is screwing you. I like to think it's a country where you're free to be rich and free to be poor. The statute book must be bloody enormous, and each rule is an infringement of your freedom and my freedom. [Suffolk farmer, 500 acres.]

I'm an advocate of a free society. If a welder on the oil pipe line earns over a hundred pounds a week, and wants to booze it all away, O.K. But if he wants to send his kids to Eton, then that's his right. [Norfolk farm manager, 5000 acres.]

Yet one of the popular cures for Britain's ailments involved further restrictions on freedom:

What I'd like to see is national service brought back – discipline is one of the best things any man can ever have. It was a very retrograde step when national service was abandoned. [Suffolk farmer, 700 acres.]

Viewed from the outside, the workers, in inverted commas, have lost their respect for management. It's due firstly to management being weak and ineffective in some cases, and secondly to the workers being politically indoctrinated with extreme left-wing ideas. . . . With stronger discipline, everybody would be happier. [Suffolk farmer, 120 acres.]

The British are too soft. There are too many do-gooders. They abolish capital punishment and so on, and then law and order breaks down. [Suffolk farmer, 180 acres.]

The apparent contradiction here between advocacy of greater freedom and advocacy of greater restrictions on that freedom can, of course, be explained, for when farmers complain of lack of freedom, they are usually referring to the economic aspects of freedom – the freedom to be rich or poor – while their desire for more authority and discipline is pitched entirely at the political level – the need to control disruptive elements in the population. In other words, they desire fewer economic restrictions on their own businesses, but greater political restrictions on the activities of those to whom they are ideologically opposed.

This dualism is well revealed by analysis of one last set of explanations put forward for Britain's ills. Thus, one highly popular response to this question stressed the lack of incentives to people in Britain to work, get ahead, and contribute to the country's profitability:

There's no incentive for the chap who's prepared to work hard to do a decent week's work. He's clobbered by tax. At the same time, there's no disincentive for not working. [Suffolk farmer, 40 acres.]

It's a lack of incentive. The unemployable are too well looked after in comparison with earning people. There's no incentive, and no response for hard work. [Norfolk farmer, 1000 acres.]

There are no real incentives. And the taxation system is vicious. People are deprived of the desire to do well for themselves. [Cambridgeshire farmer, 1100 acres.]

We all want something for nothing. I believe in incentive, and this is lacking at whatever level. [Suffolk farmer, 1000 acres.]

It all comes down to lack of incentives. People need incentives. If they don't have them, the militants get hold of them. The unions are a force to be reckoned with precisely because people have no incentives. [Norfolk farmer, 1000 acres.]

Now it is evident that such incentives are assumed by those who champion them to be material in nature. People, that is, need more money if they are to 'pull their weight'. But against this, many farmers recoiled at the apparent 'greed' and materialism which they saw as characterizing modern Britain, and cited this as the prime cause of the country's problems:

We as a people are never satisfied. There's terrible greed and people want something for nothing. . . . History shows that a country which is immoral – and this country has become immoral – goes downhill. [Norfolk farmer, 3000 acres.]

It's discontent – there's no satisfaction, always craving for more and more. . . . There is greed and jealousy. One group gets something and then the others want it. [Suffolk farmer, 110 acres.]

People are too greedy. Everyone thinks their standard of living will go on rising, but it won't. They are misled by a false sense of values – money values have taken over. Everyone *wants* – but things like colour televisions aren't a necessity. [Suffolk farmer, 250 acres.]

So many are not content with their lot. They must have a new car, and colour television, and silly toys for the children. No one wants a true sense of values – people forget what the priorities are. [Suffolk farmer, 200 acres.]

Nobody is satisfied with their lot. Their standard of living is better, but nobody is satisfied. [Suffolk farmer, 350 acres.]

Such sentiments, clearly echoing Durkheim's concern with the 'malady of infinite aspiration' in anomic industrial society, contrast vividly with the call for greater material incentives. But as with the apparent tension between freedom and control, so too with the strain between incentive and greed: farmers, it is clear, apply their diagnoses selectively. Thus, implicit in most of the responses we have recorded is the idea that incentives are necessary for the 'haves', while self-control and moral values are necessary for the 'have-nots'. When car workers demand increased remuneration, it is greed; when business-men do so, it is to establish incentives.

Our discussion of the apparent inconsistencies in farmers' views as to what is wrong with Britain is important for, as we noted earlier, it seems to be the case that such inconsistencies are more often associated with lower-class groups in society. What our evidence suggests, on the other hand, is that a powerful, wealthy, and prestigious section of the middle and even upper class may also sub-scribe to apparently contradictory ideologies. Two points need to be noted about this. First, dominant groups can generally afford to be inconsistent. That is, for as long as the hegemonic foundation remains secure their ideologies are rarely challenged, and connections be-tween disparate parts of those ideologies are rarely suggested. It is doubtful, indeed, whether they themselves ever recognize the incon-sistencies between, say, advocacy of incentives and condemnation of greed in others. Secondly, following on from this, it can be argued that inconsistencies are inherent in dominant as well as subordinate groups' ideologies, and are even *necessary* in so far as they may then come to be applied to a wide range of different contingencies. For example, when farmers want more money for themselves, they manage to justify their claim in terms of the need for incentives, just reward for hard work, and so on. When others demand higher returns, on the other hand, their claims can be criticized and dismissed by resort to opposite ideologies; thus others are 'greedy', or do not deserve higher remuneration because they are work-shy. In this sense, farmers cannot lose. They, like other dominant groups, can manage and select their ideologies to fit their requirements in a wide range of different situations. This necessarily means that some of their ideologies will contradict each other, but for as long as nobody highlights such contradictions, their repertoire of justifications, rationalizations, and explanations remains intact. All that is necessary is that others accept their definitions. But is this the case?

We noted earlier in this chapter that Newby's study of 'deference' among agricultural workers revealed a startling lack of 'deferential' attitudes. Indeed, the picture they held of the class system was most commonly that of a two-class dichotomous model more usually associated with the more radical and traditionally class-conscious sections of the working class. Needless to say, this model does not accord with that subscribed to by the farmers. Thus, as Table 66 indicates, the farmers overwhelmingly subscribed to a multi-class model of social stratification, and there appears to be no significant relationship between the responses of the farm workers and those of their employers in the HN sample. In other words, there is no evidence of vertical congruence on this aspect of class ideology. Farm workers appear *not* to accept farmers' definitions. On the contrary, there is overwhelming evidence of a horizontal class division here between farmers and farm workers. Most farmers, in fact, appeared to subscribe to a graded status model of social stratification, entirely inconsistent with their workers' dichotomous models; 'classes' were thus often distinguished in terms of whom one would or would not interact with in specific situations. Indeed, caste-like taboos on interaction, especially on communal eating, were quite common:

I still think of the upper class as the aristocracy and the county set. Then there's the farmers, coupled with the professionals who *think* they're above us and the traders who run their own businesses. And then there's the farm workers. . . . I would quite cheerfully eat in a restaurant with any of my men, but I wouldn't ask them to a party in my house. They wouldn't enjoy it, either. [Suffolk farmer, 500 acres.]

I knew a lorry driver who met a doctor here on holiday. The doctor invited him to stay with him, but he said he couldn't possibly do it. Strange, isn't it? But I went to Scotland with my shepherd, and he was frightened to have dinner with me in the hotel, even though we were sharing the same bedroom! He was embarrassed about having dinner like that. [Norfolk farmer, 3000 acres.]

It depends what you mean by class. It's very difficult. Of course, there is a class system. Take myself – I don't mix socially with the chaps that work on the farm any more than I mix socially with Sir X. We don't dine together and that sort of thing. I go around with the ordinary farmer – the middle class. [Suffolk farmer, 1100 acres.]

I have many friends whom I would regard as being in a different class. Some I would invite to dinner and some I wouldn't. They wouldn't come if I asked them. They'd come for *tea*, but they wouldn't come for dinner. [Suffolk farmer, 250 acres.]

We aren't so class-conscious around here. I'd talk to the roadman – would *you* talk to the road-sweeper? It's more intimate. Of course, he wouldn't come to supper! [Suffolk farmer, 120 acres.]

Table 66 *Number of social classes identified by farmers and farm workers*

Number of classes	1000+ acres		44 parishes		HN		Farm workers (1972)	
	No.	%	No.	%	No.	%	No.	%
Nil/classless	3	4	5	14	7	16	10	4
Two	9	13	7	20	8	19	134	59
Three	41	59	18	52	26	60	55	24
Other	17	24	5	14	2	5	29	13
Total	70	100	35	100	43	100	228	100

As will be noted from Table 66 the majority of farmers identified three classes – working or lower, middle, and upper. Many, however, added refinements and exceptions to this basic model, and some (usually the larger farmers) described quite complex models in pains-taking details. It is worth quoting some of these:

For practical purposes, the UK is still structured into classes. . . . I personally believe that human beings have to live in a stratified society because we all know we're not equal to everybody else, and we want to belong with our equals. . . . I gradate people in terms of their level of evolution. You don't want to go around with gross people if you're above them. At a particular level, though, there are also vertical splits. For example, the leadership class is split into businessmen, teachers, politicians, and so on. It's a grid-type society – vertically separate functions and horizontally separate classes. Such a society fulfils the needs of human beings – it's a structure in which they can grow while still feeling secure. [Cambridgeshire farmer, 1000 acres.]

Everybody working here is different. It's insulting to say that everybody is the same. One's social grade – you can say there are two sorts of people – bosses/professionals and the rest – or you can divide it up into six or ten sections. . . . Others define what I am – upper middle-class, or lower upper-class or whatever. If you say you're upper-class, it means some of your relations are titled, or you're in Debrett or Burke's *Peerage*. Obviously I'm not in that. But if we have farm pupils to live in the house, then we stipulate that they should have public school backgrounds so that we aren't misunderstood. [Norfolk farmer, 1500 acres.]

There are classes, of course. Do you mean financial or social? I would say there are five classes – the aristocracy, the very rich, the professional class like civil servants, doctors and lawyers, the working-class very rich, and the working-class poor. Financially, you could say that the working-class very rich are on a par with the professional class. The aristocracy, of course, are titled. The very rich are the industrialists with liquid cash – property developers, bookmakers, spivs, etc. – the wheeler-dealers who do the country a disservice. The working-class very rich are the building workers, miners and car workers – the £100 a week men. The working-class poor are some farm workers, shop workers, labourers -- people like that. [Norfolk farmer, 1000 acres.]

Yes, there are still classes. The social standing of farmers is quite high. A sizeable farmer would rank with a solicitor and a doctor and treat them as equals – play golf with them. You could even be friends on equal terms with a Crown Court judge. I would say I was upper-middle-class. . . . The average Rotarian is middle-class. A bank manager is between middle-class and upper-middle-class. Those in small business are middle-class. . . . Above the upper-middle-class is the aristocracy. . . . The whole system is dynamic – individuals can achieve a lot. You can't break into the aristocracy, but you can get into the upper-middle-class. [Suffolk farmer, 2500 acres.]

These answers reveal not only the articulateness of many farmers, but also their detailed awareness of status differences – many of the answers are clearly reminiscent of Weber, if not Lloyd Warner. It is particularly interesting to note, however, that the complexities and graded refinements of the models tend to be applied at the level of the class of the respondent. Thus for middle-class respondents the working class is often dismissed as a largely homogeneous mass, and the upper class is usually equated with the aristocracy, while many splits and divisions are noted in and among the middle class. This is not, of course, surprising, for as Young and Willmott (1956), among others, have noted, perceptions of class differences tend to become less clearly defined the greater the social distance between the respondent and the group he is describing. Consider, for example, the response of a 5000-acre Norfolk farmer: 'There is the monarchy, the nobility, the aristocracy, the upper class – where I fit in – and the so-called middle and working classes.' Perhaps 1 per cent of the population is thus divided into four classes, while the remainder are divided into two. Similarly, a 1700-acre Norfolk farmer distinguished between 'the upper crust, the aristocrats, the wealthy, the old school tie set, the middle class, and the working class'. The complexity of class imagery thus closely reflects class position.

Although the great majority of farmers subscribed to a multi-stratified status hierarchy model of the class system, we should also note from Table 66 that a substantial minority, particularly among the smaller farmers, denied the existence of any such class system. What Goldthorpe *et al.* (1969) have referred to as the 'myth of embourgeoisement' was for some of our farmers an apparent 'fact':

I don't recognize the existence of class. There's more opportunities now than in the past. There aren't the inequalities now – not really. [Suffolk farmer, 100 acres.]

Class doesn't come into it at all with me. I'm just as much a working man as the lad who works with me. I'm very much a working man. [Suffolk farmer, 90 acres.]

There aren't classes as such. You can't categorize people. You can classify them as the type you'd wish to be friendly with or not. But it's sad to think people use the term class. At school, one was envious and respectful of those in the classes above one, but as one goes up the school, one gets less aware that there are forms below one. It's the same in life. [Norfolk farmer, 1500 acres.]

You shouldn't talk of classes. Jack can be as good as his master. I look down on no man. [Suffolk farmer, 200 acres.]

I am working-class because I work. We are all in the working class now. We all work – doctors and directors as well. [Suffolk farmer, 300 acres.]

Thus, it is not that 'everybody is middle-class now', so much as 'everybody is working-class now'. The consequences, however, are the same – namely, the denial of class differences, and emphasis on a consensual view of society.

However, many of those who asserted that they were living in a classless society, or that class was an anachronistic and redundant concept, nevertheless then went on to describe in some detail what can only be interpreted as a class-differentiated model of society. One farmer, for example, started off by telling us, 'Class is an out-dated word. There's no class barrier nowadays', but then a few minutes later continued, 'Classes will always be with us. We very much *should* have them. If everyone earned the same, we'd all do as little as possible.' This respondent was by no means unique. Clearly, though, he and others like him referred to the term 'class' in a variety of different senses. In this particular case, the first part of the answer was probably an immediate 'gut' reaction to our original question, while the second part was a more considered response to later probing. Similarly, other respondents gave very confusing answers with regard to the enumeration of social classes. Several, for example, identified just two classes, upper and lower, only to describe them-selves as 'middle'![7]

Just as we noted the existence of ambiguities and contradictions in farmers' responses to the question on what is wrong with the country, so too it seems that we must conclude that however complex or articulate, their responses to our questions on class are also frequently internally incoherent. And as with our explanation with regard to the former, it seems that these ambiguities in class percep-tions reflect the ideological sources of the responses. Thus, leaving aside for a moment those who answered the question with reference solely to the local social system in which they lived (those, for example, who confined their responses to ranking farmers, farm workers, and perhaps local traders and professional newcomers) most respondents described the class system in the *abstract*, and to do so, inevitably drew upon certain received beliefs, values, and 'knowledge' about their society at large. For most respondents, that is, the class question evoked *ideological* explanations and descrip-tions, and where different fragments of dominant ideologies were drawn upon by the same respondent (e.g. the view that class is unimportant and the view that inequality is desirable, or the view that class does not exist and the view that there are many different social classes), the answer was inevitably logically confused.

The ideological nature of farmers' responses on this question is further revealed (as with their views on what is wrong with the country) by the similarity with which they came to express themselves. Take, for example, the responses on the inevitability of class inequality. In all three samples over 80 per cent of respondents judged that inequality was inevitable and necessary (indeed, only slightly smaller proportions also saw it as 'natural' or 'desirable'):[8]

There are dozens of classes in this country – there always have been, and there always will be. I don't even think abolishing the public schools would make any difference. Look at Russia – you'll never get a one-class society. [Suffolk farmer, 650 acres.]

They do exist, and they'll always exist. Go back to when history started, and it always existed. Nobody can stop it, and if they do, I hope I'm not alive when it's done. It would be a poor thing. There's always got to be rich and poor. You'll never get equal rights, and if there were, there'd be a hell of a lot of unrest. [Cambridgeshire farmer, 1000 acres.]

It is inevitable. Even looking at communist countries, in Russia, they have a class system. Certain people are privileged because of their talents and abilities – I don't see how you'll ever alter it. You've always got to have people who'll run things. [Suffolk farmer, 500 acres.]

It's inevitable. You get it in the animal and the human world. You have it in Russia. It's desirable, too. Unless you have a boss and have incentives, you'll never get anything done. Communism is marvellous in theory, but nature's not like that. [Suffolk farmer, 2600 acres.]

There are the sit-down-and-spenders and the get-up-and-goers. The latter will always have the money. It's not necessarily desirable – but it's inevitable. [Suffolk farmer, 1000 acres.]

I go a lot by nature. The pigs aren't all level, the crops aren't all level. It's a natural thing. [Suffolk farmer, 750 acres.]

I go back to George Orwell and all pigs are equal. I'm afraid it's a fact of life. There'll always be somebody with more money and influence. It's just as a coal-miner friend of mine said – 'when communism comes, I'll have a maid like the colliery manager has'. As soon as you get a flower show, somebody will want to win it. [Suffolk farmer, 110 acres.]

It's inevitable because all countries have class, whether it's based on L.s.d. or education or breeding. Animals divide themselves up, and humans always will. [Suffolk farmer, 250 acres.]

It's in human nature to reach for the moon. We all started level with a cave and a club, but the better ones caught more dinosaurs and grew big and strong. [Suffolk farmer, 300 acres.]

As with the range of answers on what is wrong with the country, these responses reveal certain common themes – the references to 'nature' or perhaps 'human nature', the allusions to Russia and other Communist countries as the ultimate 'proof' of the resilience of class inequalities, and the resigned tone of the retort that inequality is quite simply a 'fact of life'. The most common theme, however, which, like the 'fair day's work for a fair day's pay' theme upon which we commented earlier was often repeated using the very same words in the same syntax, is that which invoked an allegory on natural inequality. Quite simply, this is the argument, repeated time and time again by our respondents, that if a certain sum of money were shared out equally among a certain number of people (the precise number varies in different accounts), then in a specified time period (again varying among respondents) the same pattern of inequality would reassert itself:

I believe in the old adage, all men are equal, but some are more equal than others. It's the old story – if all the money was shared out equally today, some people would have it all and some would have nothing by tomorrow morning. [Suffolk farmer, 120 acres.]

You'll never make everybody the same. You could give two people a pound each and say do what you can with it. With one it would all be gone, but the other would make something of his money. If you gave everybody the same opportunities, they wouldn't all take them – let's face it. [Suffolk farmer, 250 acres.]

It's natural. If you gave two people £5 each, one would end up with £10 and one with nothing. Some people are more shrewd, and save and invest and do well. [Norfolk farmer, 1200 acres.]

This levelling-out process never will work. Give the miners £5000 a year, and it will all be in the hands of the brewers by next weekend. [Essex farmer, 1000 acres.]

Again, then, we find the same ideas being expressed in the same way by large numbers of different respondents, and again we can only conclude that our questions have succeeded in tapping quite central and widely-held *ideologies* to which most farmers find it expeditious to subscribe.

What emerges clearly, then, as we consider our respondents'

replies to our questions on class and inequality, is the fact that our abstract questions provoked ideological responses. It would be a mistake to argue that because most farmers replied to the question in terms of a multi-class model, or because most claimed that class was inevitable, that these responses constitute either a considered and well-thought-out picture of their world, or a fundamental set of beliefs according to which they lived their everyday lives. Some farmers clearly were concerned with the problems raised by our questions, and some obviously had spent many hours pondering the very topics which we raised with them in interviews. But most simply do not seem to have experienced or interpreted their worlds in the terms set by our questions. Put simply, they recognize *differences* between people, but rarely identify *classes*. They do not see class in structural terms. This is not to say that our questions were not meaningful for them, but it is to recognize that, to a large extent, they were meaningful only on the ideological rather than the concrete level. They could discuss the abstract notion of class, but it rarely related to how they as individuals interacted with others of the same or different 'class'.[9] The farmers may see a graded status hierarchy, and their workers a dichotomous class model, but both seem to shelve such ideological encumbrances when involved in routine interaction at work or in the community. Each has his own appropriate ideology, but these are rarely permitted to impinge upon the stuff of everyday life.

The differences between farmers' and farm workers' responses to the class question were thus often considerable. Farmers, for example, generally saw the class system as highly fluid, and asserted that there were considerable opportunities for those at the bottom of the ladder to climb the rungs and improve themselves. Farm workers, on the other hand, usually saw the class system as rigid and closed, and few were prepared to accept that real opportunities for upward mobility existed (see Table 67). Now while these differences may in part reflect the different groups' lived experiences (e.g. the farmer who has made good, or the farm worker who has failed, despite all his efforts, to become anything other than a farm worker), it is apparent that they are in large part ideological. It is convenient for a farmer, when asked, to suggest that anybody could get where he has got, given the correct attitudes and perhaps a little luck (see below), while it is equally convenient for the farm worker to state the opposite. In neither case, however, do such perceptions of the fluidity or otherwise of the class system necessarily affect the ways in which farmers and farm workers see their world or routinely interpret their position within it, or their relationship with each other.

Table 67 *Assessments of social mobility by farmers and farm workers*

Extent of social mobility	1000+ acres		44 parishes		HN		Farm workers	
	No.	%	No.	%	No.	%	No.	%
None	—	—	1	2	1	2	85	42
A little	11	24	7	14	7	15	53	26
Some	12	27	13	27	21	44	21	10
Quite a lot	15	33	8	16	9	19	24	12
A lot	7	16	20	41	10	21	20	10
Total	45	100	49	100	48	100	203	100

Take as another example the factors identified by farmers and farm workers as determining one's class position (Table 68). The farm workers appear to have placed somewhat greater emphasis on ascriptive factors (e.g. inheritance) and, indeed, on fortuitous factors than the farmers, who tended rather to emphasize achievement-oriented factors (notably education). Thus, while education ranked as only the sixth most significant determinant among the farm workers, it was seen by the farmers as second only to inheritance. Similarly, although both farmers and farm workers recognized the importance of inheritance, this factor was emphasized far more by the latter, nearly half of them citing it compared with, for example, only one-quarter of the larger farmers. These responses are, of course, entirely consistent with the answers on opportunities for social mobility (discussed earlier) for the greater the emphasis placed on 'achievement' factors such as education and hard work, the more 'open' is society likely to be seen. Interestingly, on the other hand, the answers set out in Table 68 do not appear to be very consistent with farmers' responses to a question asked at a different point in the interviews where they were called upon to account for their own personal success in farming (Table 69).

Now, it must immediately be admitted that the factors making for success in farming may be quite different from those leading to success in the class system as a whole. As we saw in Chapter 2, for example, inheritance remains the single most significant passport to farming success, while 'achievement'-oriented factors such as formal

Table 68 Determinants of social class cited by farmers and farm workers

Determinant cited	1000 + acres sample		44 parishes sample		HN sample		Farm workers	
	% of replies (N=123)	% of respondents* (N=105)	% of replies (N=70)	% of respondents* (N=57)	% of replies (N=76)	% of respondents* (N=54)	% of replies (N=253)	% of respondents* (N=233)
Inheritance	21	25	31	37	33	44	44	48
Education	17	20	27	33	26	37	11	12
Hard work	18	21	20	25	14	20	15	17
Innate ability	11	13	11	14	7	9	7	7
Job/position	9	10	10	12	7	9	9	10
Luck	5	6	—	—	5	7	12	14
Other	19	22	1	2	8	11	2	2
Total	100	127	100	123	100	137	100	108

* This represents the percentage of respondents citing each factor. Since more than one reply could be given, the totals are more than 100 per cent.

Table 69 *Reasons given by farmers to account for their success in farming*

Determinant cited	1000+ acres sample		44 parishes sample		HN sample	
	% of replies (N=179)	% of respondents (N=105)	% of replies (N=73)	% of respondents (N=57)	% of replies (N=76)	% of respondents (N=54)
Hard work	14	23	31	39	32	44
Business skills	31	52	22	28	14	21
Commitment/ambition	23	40	10	12	13	19
Luck	13	22	14	18	13	19
Father	7	12	11	14	9	13
Feel for the land/commonsense	7	12	7	9	7	10
Education	3	5	4	5	5	7
(No achievements)	2	4	1	2	7	9
Total	100	170	100	127	100	142

educational qualifications appear rather less significant than in other occupations. Nevertheless, the differences revealed on farmers' answers in Tables 68 and 69 (notably on the role of education, but also on the importance of factors such as luck and hard work) seem to suggest that farmers have given one set of answers in relation to the *experience* of being successful, and another set in relation to their *beliefs* about success in the wider society. They have not, that is, answered the abstract class question in terms of their own concrete experience, but have rather responded in terms of how they have been led to believe others can 'make good' in urban society. This is not, of course, to suggest that the answers presented in Table 69 are in some way 'cleansed' of ideological influences, for it is likely that farmers interpreted their own success in terms of their ideological beliefs. Thus a belief that hard work brings its own rewards, for example, will tend to guide a farmer's judgement of his own earlier experiences, thus leading him perhaps to reinterpret his own biography. For example, hard work may come to be emphasized in his 'accounts' and inheritance ignored. Whatever the case, however (and, as we noted earlier, it is rarely possible to distinguish empirically between experiential image and received ideology), the important point is that, although ideology may have intruded into farmers' explanations of their own success, their concrete experience does not appear to have been drawn upon in their discussion of the determinants of the success of others. As with other elements of their answers on class, therefore, we may conclude that farmers responded to our questions almost entirely in terms of their received beliefs and ideologies, and that their answers may therefore bear little relevance to their lived experiences.

Finally on this theme, we may consider one last aspect of farmers' responses to our questions on class; namely, the criteria they cited as being significant in distinguishing different classes from one another (Table 70). What is immediately noticeable here is that, although both farmers and farm workers tended to emphasize money as the single most significant criterion of class differentiation, and although farm workers were even more likely to stress financial factors than were the farmers, both groups seem also to have been aware of rather less tangible factors which also served to distinguish the classes. Indeed, in their comments on the highest status groups in society (variously termed the 'upper class' or 'real gentlemen'), many farmers *and* farm workers agreed that money was largely irrelevant. Both groups were concerned to draw a distinction between an

Table 70 Criteria used by farmers and farm workers to distinguish different social classes

Criterion mentioned	1000+ acres sample		44 parishes sample		HN sample		Farm workers	
	% of replies (N=192)	% of respondents (N=105)	% of replies (N=90)	% of respondents (N=57)	% of replies (N=91)	% of respondents (N=54)	% of replies (N=365)	% of respondents (N=233)
Money	16	30	23	37	20	33	38	59
Birth, breeding, values	13	24	18	28	21	35	20	31
Work, job, position	23	42	17	26	11	19	14	22
Education	9	17	17	26	23	39	8	13
Life-style	15	27	19	30	20	33	7	11
Employment status	9	16	—	—	—	—	10	16
Other	15	27	6	9	5	9	4	6
Total	100	183	100	156	100	188	100	157

'upstart' middle class – the *nouveaux riches* who may have material possessions but are distinctly lacking in the traditional personal qualities found in 'top people' – and the venerated (if not always wealthy) gentry. Thus the following quotations are taken from Newby's interviews with farm workers (quoted in Newby, 1977, Chapter VII):

There's the real gentlemen, then there's the middle-class, and then there's the working-class. A gentleman has tons of money and never works, but the working man works all his life. Then you get the jumped-up ones in between. They *think* they've got a lot, but they haven't really. They're more snobs than anything else. The upper-crust will talk to you, but the middle-class feel you shouldn't be there – they'll ignore you.

The top people aren't necessarily the richest, but they've spent years learning to be top people. They're born into it. . . . A gentleman always recognises his workman. You can always tell a gentleman by the way he rubs shoulders with his workmen. He classes them as just one of themselves. Some of the middle-class, they're jumped up and happen to be snobby.

Bowing and scraping to squires is all finished. The *real* gentry treat the working man very well. It's the jumped-up man who's got up quick who looks down on him – the two cars, caravan, and boat type of people. They're jumped-up buggers who've had a bit of money – they're real bastards.

The real high class fellow is a gentleman, and he talks to you different from the jumped-up ones. With him it's all due to breeding. It goes back through the years when the old squire had all the land. It's all tradition and inheritance really – it gets passed on. A gentleman treats you well, but what I call the middle-class, those who think they're it, are real bastards. They're mostly people who've moved in, people with plenty of money. I never take any notice of people who buy two or three cottages and make them into one. It's *principles*, not money, that's definite. Some of the biggest snobs haven't got any. But titled people, you can talk to them as we talk to ourselves.

Compare these comments with the following taken from our interviews with Suffolk farmers:

Many I'd call 'gentlemen' are relatively poor. For example, they may be retired and living on a small pension – damn hard-pushed to keep a car on the road. . . . Class is intelligence, conversation, manners, your attitude to life. I'm a landed gentleman. I'm typical – public school, Trinity College, Rifle Brigade, farming, JP – there are dozens like me. . . . Douglas-Home is the best example I can think of of a gentleman. I have a high regard for him. [Suffolk landowner, 1000 acres.]

The people who hold coffee mornings see themselves as upper-crust – they won't speak to you if they think you work with your hands. But someone like Major-General X is upper-class. He's a real gentleman – he'll speak to anybody. Mr W thinks he's well up, but he's not, but he won't speak to you. [Suffolk farmer, 200 acres.]

The old-fashioned rich are a whole lot better than the newly rich. They understand more, and don't try to put it over on you. You can tell a real gentleman, because he'll talk to you like we're talking now. [Suffolk farmer, 100 acres.]

I use one pub, and I'm equally happy whoever I talk to in that pub – a company director or a farm worker. The only dangerous class is the one which thinks it's one layer higher than it is. It's still the case that it's the upper class and the working-class who don't shout about it, but there's a middle-class that shouts about being upper-class. . . . Membership of the pretentious middle-class is based on money. It's quite simple for me to buy a drink for a man who doesn't earn as much as I do. If he bought me one back I wouldn't refuse it. But the danger lies in people who want to be seen in the right places. Anybody who happens to be born into the right family tends not to have to prove it. [Suffolk farmer, 300 acres.]

The middle-class tend to be snobs. The upper class are real gentlemen – born and bred – they'll mix with anyone. It's like Lord Y said, he'd talk to a working man the same as to a farmer. Major-General X is the same – he says 'Hello, Peter' when he sees me. . . . Class isn't money – the upper crust might be as poor as mice, but they're still upper-class. You can distinguish between them and the middle-class on manners. [Suffolk farmer, 250 acres.]

Tradition and upbringing comes into it. A few social climbers think that they're better than other people. But you get a certain type who's always been in a higher social class – like squires – who are real gentlemen with a good social conscience. They'll stop and speak to anybody, even if he's sweeping the roads. They're in a class of their own, yet in manner they're classless. They're gentry – no pretences. Those who have climbed up are the worst. They pass you by – they don't want to talk to you. [Suffolk farm manager, 1100 acres.]

The similarity in answers is striking. Many farmers *and* farm workers appear to agree that it is possible and desirable to distinguish between the well-bred, well-mannered gentleman who will 'talk to any man', and the upwardly-mobile affluent and status-conscious *arriviste*. Does this, then, represent the exception to our argument in this section to the effect that class is an abstract concept viewed from different ideological perspectives by farmers and their workers?

We think not. Earlier, it will be recalled, we suggested that there is no reason to suggest that farmers and farm workers should produce essentially similar responses to questions about class, *except where they answered such questions with reference to the local, rather than the national, social system.* In other words, some respondents, in discussing the relevance of the term 'class' drew upon their lived experiences generated out of interaction in the locality. For them, the question was rather less abstract than for those who, strictly speaking, answered the question 'correctly', for they answered, not in terms of some vague and ill-defined concepts drawn from the media and other secondary sources, but in terms of their own experience of upper-class patronage and middle-class status anxiety in their own areas of residence. They answered the question on class at the national level in the same way as they answered the previous question on stratification in the village, and in consequence, their answers were more 'concrete'.

The highly significant point to emerge from this is that, as we have seen in Chapters 5 and 6, there is an alliance between the locals of whatever class against the newcomers. Put another way, there is evidence of strong vertical identification between the traditional lower and upper classes of rural society, this being expressed in such diverse forms as the image of community which they both share, or the gentlemanly ethic to which they both subscribe. This does not mean that each does not have its own class identity. What it does mean, however, is that both farmers and farm workers tend, in Giddens's terms, to be 'class aware', but not 'class conscious' (Giddens, 1973, p. 111). Furthermore, it is apparent that such ideological control as may occur between farmers and their workers is likely to operate in relation to specific rather than generalized issues. Put crudely, it is likely to concern farmers little if their workers see society in terms of two opposing classes, provided they do not then apply this abstract model to an interpretation of their own situation *vis-à-vis* their employer. This, as we shall see, they rarely do.

On low wages and high profits

We have noted in Chapter 4 that agricultural wage levels in East Anglia are among the lowest in the country, while the region's large-scale arable agriculture generates the highest returns. Farm workers as a whole are, of course, stereotypically cited as a low-income group, but the particular configuration of highly profitable farming and very

314 Social imagery and class ideology

low earnings which pertains in the eastern region clearly provides grounds enough for the workers there to be more dissatisfied than others (see Runciman, 1966). In short, a problem of control and legitimation manifestly faces the East Anglian farmer. The inequalities between him and his employees are obvious, and the more successful he is in encouraging the identification of his men with his enterprise, the more glaring are the unequal returns of the different contributors to that enterprise likely to become. It is difficult, for example, for a farmer to maintain that he and his workers are a 'team' (still less a 'family') – see Chapter 4 – when the returns are so unevenly distributed. As Newby (1975, pp. 158–9) has noted: 'One problem with the maintenance of traditional modes of control by means of face-to-face interaction is the risk of carrying the degree of identification too far, so that differentiation, and thence the legitimation of hierarchy, is denied.' It is not simply what Newby refers to as the 'familiarity-breeds-contempt' problem although this is clearly significant. But the problem of identification also concerns the visibility of the asymmetry of the relationship. The closer the farmer is to his workers, therefore, the greater are the problems he faces, both in maintaining social distance, and in justifying the relative imbalance (in both material and political terms) in the relationship.

That farmers are often well aware of the advantages to be gained from maintaining the identification and 'loyalty' of their workforce is apparent from our discussion in Chapter 4. Their sentiments regarding the desirability of close personal relations between themselves and their employees were often emotive (witness the frequent references to the farm employees as constituting a 'family', and the repeated assertion of moral responsibilities on the part of farmers as employers), but this cannot disguise the calculative element which can also be discerned in their desire to maintain work relationships at a personal level. It is instructive in this regard to consider farmers' responses to a question which asked them whether they felt they had more in common with farm workers, or with comparable businessmen in other industries outside agriculture. The answers are given in Table 71.

The farm workers interviewed by Newby, it will be noted, were almost to a man convinced that they had more in common with their employers than with other sections of the working class in industry. This is, of course, interesting in its own right given that the great majority of farm workers were quite willing to identify themselves

Table 71 *The identification of farmers and farm workers with each other and with other members of their respective classes*

Level of identification	1000+ acres No.	%	44 parishes No.	%	HN No.	%	Farm workers No.	%
Vertical	52	53	40	74	32	63	214	92
Horizontal	29	30	4	7	6	12	12	5
Ambivalent	17	17	10	19	13	25	7	3
Total	98	100	54	100	51	100	233	100

as 'working-class'. In other words, it appears that such generalized class labels have little relevance to them when it comes to interacting with their employers. But it is also interesting in that a far higher proportion of farm workers identified upwards with their employers than farmers did downwards with their workers. Thus, across the three samples, between a half (in the 1000+ acres group) and three-quarters of the farmers identified with farm workers, compared with over 90 per cent of farm workers who identified with the farmers. What do these figures mean?

We would argue that, just like the notions of 'community' and 'gentility', vertical identification represents one component of farmers' ideologies which aids the maintenance of traditional rural class relations. Farmers, that is, answered the question normatively as well as descriptively; farmers and farm workers *do and should* identify with each other against urban-industrial interests, whether they be those of large-scale enterprises or mammoth trade unions:

One is farming because one likes it, and one takes an extraordinary pride in the land – in the national heritage. So one is absolutely at one with the farm labourers. [Norfolk farmer, 1000 acres.]

Farmers are businessmen because they have to be. But if you go to the local ploughing match, you'll see the farmers and workers in together. Farmers aren't a stuck-up lot. We're all in the game together. Workers aren't just numbers on a sheet. We know their families. [Suffolk farmer, 750 acres.]

We are so near to each other. We see them at work, and talk to them, and ask if they are happy and so on, so that they feel part of the business. [Suffolk farmer, 300 acres.]

A farmer and his workers have a close relationship. They see things alike. When it rains, it rains on both of them. It's a common bond. A good farmer knows all about his workers and their families. The crop has to be got in for both their sakes. [Suffolk farmer, 500 acres.]

There's so much individuality on a farm. In a factory, you've got hundreds of employees. If a farm worker's got a problem, it's the farmer's problem. Each farm's a family really. [Suffolk farmer, 120 acres.]

It's different to businessmen in industry. The way of life has something to do with it. The set-up's different. . . . Here we all work and pull together on a partnership basis. They're as concerned as we are about the beet troubles. [Suffolk farmer, 350 acres.]

Relatively few farmers were prepared to admit that they had more in common with other businessmen than with their own employees, for to do so would be to admit of class interest and to deny the validity of the 'partnership' model of farming relationships. (This explains the anger of one of our respondents who refused to answer the question, condemning it as 'socialistic'.) Yet, as we saw in Chapter 5, few farmers counted any of their workers among their personal friends, and few interacted socially with their employees other than in highly ritualized contexts such as ploughing matches, to take one example referred to by one of the respondents quoted above. As one put it:

I feel I get on well with the men, but I wouldn't want to spend an evening with them. Our interests and education are too far apart. I should get much more pleasure talking to business friends. We have more in common. [Suffolk farmer, 1000 acres.]

Few of his colleagues were so frank. Most farmers subscribed whole-heartedly to the view that they and their employees were 'on the same side' even though socially they rarely mixed. But what is most significant of all, of course, is that their workers endorsed these sentiments even more strongly than they themselves did.

The high level of commitment of farm workers to their employers, and to the aims and objectives of their enterprises, surpassing as it does even the commitment of farmers themselves to an ideology of vertical identification, is nevertheless constantly threatened by two factors. One is the low level of agricultural workers' wages. The other is the high level of wealth and prosperity of most of the medium- and large-scale farmers. In other words, cross-cutting the identification of worker with employer is the fact, visible to both, that the worker is being poorly paid while the latter is receiving often very high returns. For the remainder of this chapter we shall consider how it is that farmers manage to explain and justify these disparities, and thus maintain the identification of their workers and the asymmetrical relationship between them.

That farm workers are among the lowest-paid sections of the working class need hardly be argued. It is ironic, for example, that when the government introduced a £6 per week wage rise ceiling in 1975, thus limiting the increases obtainable by most workers, the agricultural workers achieved their largest ever percentage rise when they gained the full £6. Nor is the value of additional benefits – food and housing, for example – of very great significance in narrowing the wages gap between agricultural and industrial workers (see Newby, 1977, Chapter III). Now given the concern expressed by most farmers for the welfare and happiness of their workers, such low wage rates are clearly a potential source of embarrassment. For most farmers, therefore, there is likely to be a strain between the aims of profit maximization on the one hand and paternal concern for the workforce on the other. Previous work on role strain in other contexts – e.g. Wray's study of the position of the foreman in industry, or Burchard's study of military chaplains (see Wray, 1948; Burchard, 1954) – has indicated a number of ways in which such strains may be managed, and there appear to be certain parallels here with the response of farmers to the low-wage problem. For example, noting the strain between pacifism or non-retaliation as central to the Christian ethic as against the *raison d'être* of the military as a war machine, Burchard found that military chaplains had resort to a variety of different rationalizations for their continuing employment by the armed forces, including the denial that any problem existed. Similarly, about one-quarter of all our respondents reconciled the strain between profit maximization and paternalism on the question of low wages by denying the validity of the premise on which it was based. In other words, they refused to accept that farm workers *were* low paid:

The cost of living in the country is lower. There are mitigating circumstances. They can grow their own food. People are more generous in the country – farmers give them potatoes and things – most farmers are like that. . . . They don't have to work on a farm – they quite enjoy it. Perhaps they're fools to do it. [Suffolk farmer, 500 acres.]

I think they get their fair share. They get rises as they come up. They never go on strike so they must be happy. [Suffolk farmer, 75 acres.]

My total wage bill has gone up 28 per cent since January this year. They earn an average of £1650 per year. They're also getting a house which is worth £400 or £500 a year. They've got no costs in travelling to work. No time lost in getting to and from work. They have a useful garden to grow produce. They can get some – not much, but some – produce cheap off the farm. They're probably effectively getting £2300 to £2400 a year. They're equally well-paid as any townsman. *And* they have the joy of living in the countryside. I'd say they were OK. [Cambridgeshire farmer, 1100 acres.]

The tied cottage is worth a lot. The same with their clothes – they don't need expensive clothes like the chap in the city. The workers are happy with their wages. Are they low paid? They're not as badly paid as the shop workers. [Suffolk farmer, 600 acres.]

Absolute balls! My son went for an interview as a hospital theatre assistant – a 50-hour week for £24. My people who do 50 hours get £32 plus a house. My stockman's in the £2000 a year bracket. It's the same in every efficient farm in the country. It's only those who are no good who are on the minimum. [Suffolk farmer, 750 acres.]

Thus, by pointing to the value of hidden benefits, and by comparing farm workers' wages with those of other even lower-paid groups, between 21 per cent (in the forty-four parishes) and 29 per cent (in the 1000+ acres sample) of our respondents managed to deny that their workers were poorly paid.

Most farmers, however, did accept that, in the terms of the question put to them, farm workers were not receiving their 'fair share' of national income in wages. Table 72 sets out the principal reasons put forward by the farmers to explain this.

Clearly, although farmers were able to draw upon a variety of explanations for their workers' low wages, the most popular by far was that of the 'cheap food policy'. Thus nearly half of all our respondents claimed specifically that they 'could not' pay their workers more while it remained government policy to keep the cost of food to the consumer down:

There was a chap on the television the other night saying that the farm workers should demand an extra £10 a week. There isn't a farmer in England who wouldn't *like* to pay it, but how can we? If the returns were adequate, no farmer would mind. [Suffolk farmer, 500 acres.]

It's become an inherent right in this country for the housewife to have cheap food. The housewife is the god. Everybody is the housewife's ally. Let them have a go at producing it. Why should the housewife be entitled to cheap food when she's very happy to pay high prices for everything else? When cars go up 15 per cent, there's never a quibble from anyone.

Table 72 Farmers' explanations for the low wages of agricultural workers

Blame attributed to:	1000+ acres sample		44 parishes sample		HN sample	
	% of replies (N=72)	% of respondents (N=59)	% of replies (N=57)	% of respondents (N=42)	% of replies (N=50)	% of respondents (N=38)
Cheap food policy	49	59	47	64	42	55
Other government policy	8	10	9	12	22	29
Farmers	10	12	12	17	12	16
Agricultural Workers' Union	10	12	5	7	2	3
Market factors	1	2	10	14	6	8
Urbanites/industrial workers	—	—	4	5	4	5
NFU	3	4	4	5	—	—
Other	19	24	9	12	12	16
Total	100	123	100	136	100	132

But put meat up 15 per cent and see what happens. The newspapers and television would be up in arms. . . . The farmworker today is a responsible man on his own with thousands of pounds' worth of equipment. If the floor-sweeper in a factory is worth £40, then the farmworker is worth eighty. But we could never afford to pay it. [Cambridgeshire farmer, 1000 acres.]

Farmworkers always have been underpaid. But then the farmer has been underpaid as well. It's the government's fault – the cheap food policy. That's the sole reason. [Suffolk farmer, 350 acres.]

The agricultural worker's skills are worth a damn sight more than any factory worker's, but the only way we can afford to pay more is if the British housewife pays more for her food. Agriculture has always lagged behind other industries. [Essex farmer, 1000 acres.]

Compared with industry, they don't get a fair wage. But when the men ask for a rise, it puts the price up, so are you prepared to pay more for your food? They deserve more. But there's a big outcry when a penny goes on the cost of living. [Suffolk farmer, 750 acres.]

The attractions of this argument for farmers are obvious. First, by blaming the cheap food policy for workers' low wage levels, they effectively deny their own responsibility as employers. Indeed, if we refer again to Table 72, it is apparent that most of the other arguments serve a similar function – if low wages are not due to the housewife, they can be blamed on the government, on other workers, on the 'urban masses', and even on the farm workers' union! This leads to the second point of attraction about the cheap food policy argument – namely that, like the community ideology discussed in the last chapter, it serves to identify 'outsiders' as a common enemy of the farmer and farm worker alike, and thus to reaffirm vertical ties of solidarity between them. The farmers, that is, argue not only that it is not their fault that their workers are poorly paid but also that, like their workers, they too suffer at the hands of a cynical government unconcerned with rural folk and the agricultural industry. Thus, farmers benevolently extol the virtues of the farm labour force, and willingly admit that the returns to labour are unfair, but, with resort to a zero-sum conception of farming returns, argue that they are prevented from following their instincts to pay more by their own meagre returns.

For the plausibility of farmers' arguments about the causes of low wages to be maintained, it is clearly necessary for them to be able to explain, justify or effectively deny their own relative wealth. Thus, if they wish to claim that they cannot pay higher wages due to their own 'meagre' returns, it becomes incumbent upon them to demonstrate their own low levels of income and lack of wealth. This is often difficult, for patently their returns are, in absolute terms at least, far from meagre, while their capital is considerable. After all, when land prices reached £1000 per acre in 1973, many of our farmers became 'paper millionaires' and the source of this wealth – their extensive land holdings – was there for all (including their workers) to see and contemplate. In the same year, the returns to arable farmers hit new records, and while the farm workers' wages may have been low, the 'cheap food policy' does not appear to have dealt too harshly with farmers' profits (see Chapter 3). How, then, do farmers rationalize this situation, to themselves, to their workers, and to outsiders?

Many, quite simply, deny that they are wealthy.[10] Sometimes they argue this in absolute terms – as one farm manager said quite seriously of his employer, 'Even his Rolls-Royce is seven or eight years old.' More often, however, they suggest that, relative to some comparable group such as company directors in industry, farmers are poorly rewarded:

My income from farming is very, very low. Farming has not given me a good standard of living. I've had to work like a Trojan to send my children to public school. [Suffolk farmer, 450 acres.]

My wealth is purely tied up in the land. It's not immediately realisable. There's a myth of wealth in agriculture. The return as an investment – 1½ per cent – is terrible. The return on working capital is still lower than you'd get from stocks and shares or the Building Society. The bigger the farmer, the bigger his overdraft. [Cambridgeshire farmer, 1100 acres.]

The more sophisticated of these answers do not so much deny the existence of personal wealth as deny that it is significant. Two reasons are commonly put forward in support of such a contention. The first relates back to the ideology of 'excessive materialism', discussed earlier. Some farmers, that is, suggested that people are too concerned with the distribution of material possessions – that they would be better occupied contemplating other questions:

There's no need to justify it. The important thing is that people shouldn't think about money. [Norfolk farmer, 1000 acres.]

The distribution of wealth is of no interest to anybody. What we need is the maximum happiness. The same size bank account doesn't have anything to do with happiness. [Suffolk farmer, 750 acres.]

The second, which we shall consider in greater detail in Chapter 8, suggests that landed property is in essence no different from any other form of property, and is thus no more problematic in political terms than other people's ownership of, say, houses, cars, or other consumer items. Whatever the particular form taken by such arguments, however, the result is always to deny the validity or applicability of any attack on the level of farming profits or the contemporary pattern of landownership.

We shall consider the theoretical significance of this in the next chapter. Suffice it to note at present that nearly half of all our respondents denied they were wealthy, sometimes by comparing themselves with groups even wealthier than they were, or by denying the significance of wealth inequalities, or by equating their ownership of land – i.e. *wealth-producing capital* – with the more easily justified and clearly more widespread ownership of consumer items (see Table 73). Clearly there is no better defence of material privilege than the effective denial of its existence or its significance. And such denials do seem to be effective. Thus, when Newby asked his sample of farm workers whether they felt that farmers were taking more than their 'fair share' of farm income in profits, only 38 per cent agreed, while 40 per cent disagreed, and the remainder were uncertain. It must be counted something of an achievement to live in the style to which many of our farmers were accustomed, to pay one's labour force at levels which farmers themselves recognize as inadequate, and yet to have four workers in ten explicitly defending one's right to one's high returns while another two in ten are not prepared to attack them. As we argued earlier, it is at this applied level that ideological control by farmers may best be seen to operate. It is instructive to note, for example, that while one prevailing image of farmers in the public mind is that they are rich and 'feather-bedded' (an image of which they themselves are well aware – see Chapter 5), less than one in four of their workers seem to think this, despite their physical proximity to all the outward and visible signs of wealth. The fact that most farm workers see society in terms of a conflict between 'them and us' pales into insignificance when less than a quarter are prepared to criticize the level of their employers' profits.

Of course, the denial of wealth is not the only justification by means of which farmers and landowners defend their position, as Table 73 indicates. There is a variety of ideological justifications to which farmers commonly resort in defence of their levels of wealth and profitability. Indeed, as we shall see in Chapter 8, it is possible

Table 73 *Farmers' justifications of their wealth*

Justification given	1000+ acres sample		44 parishes sample		HN sample	
	% of replies (N=173)	% of respondents (N=78)	% of replies (N=78)	% of respondents (N=47)	% of replies (N=81)	% of respondents (N=50)
Money not everything/denial of wealth	24	43	29	49	31	50
Hard work	25	46	21	34	20	32
Responsibility/socially useful	22	41	15	26	14	22
Risks/incentives	12	21	10	17	7	12
Natural inequality	5	9	13	21	10	16
Stewardship	4	7	1	2	5	8
Already highly taxed	2	4	5	9	2	4
Difficult to justify	5	8	—	—	7	12
Other	1	3	6	10	4	6
Total	100	182	100	168	100	162

to trace the history of many components of their ideologies back hundreds of years. Unlike their other ideological beliefs examined earlier in this chapter, moreover, farmers' justifications of their own personal wealth, and their corresponding explanation of their employees' poor wage levels, are highly significant at the *structural* level. That is, they are not merely beliefs and attitudes to be exchanged in pub conversations and interviews; they are, rather, explanations of the concrete world in which farmers and their workers interact, and as such they have a considerable influence on the stability of that world. In the next chapter we shall describe these ideologies in detail and we shall examine the effects which they have on the maintenance of stable class and power relationships, both in the work situation, and in the wider local social system. We shall, that is, relate our discussion in this chapter to what has gone before in order to come to a fuller understanding of the dynamics of class inequality in a highly structured and dense network of social relations. Specifically, we shall argue that certain components of farmers' ideologies have entered the stock of commonsense wisdoms of many farm workers (and, indeed, of other local groups) so that notions such as stewardship, responsibility, or whatever, as well as explanations of low wages couched in terms of the 'cheap food policy', have taken on a certain facticity, and have become embedded as central elements of lower-class social imagery.

8 Property, paternalism and power

One of the main conclusions to have emerged from our consideration of the ideologies and social imagery of many farmers and landowners in East Anglia concerns the plurality of justifications and explanations upon which they customarily draw to defend or assert their economic, social, and political privileges. Clearly, there is no 'ruling-class ideology' as such in rural areas, but rather a cluster of often unrelated and sometimes conflicting dominant belief systems, each of which is logically more applicable to some situations than to others. The fact that such unrelated and occasionally inconsistent ideologies are traditionally applied so unproblematically and with so little resistance from economically disadvantaged groups is, we have seen, testimony not to the inherent validity or logic of the beliefs themselves, but rather to the ability of dominant groups in rural areas to make their definitions of reality the authoritative ones. As Berger and Luckmann (1967, pp. 126–7) vividly put it: 'The success of particular conceptual machineries is related to the power possessed by those who operate them. . . . He who has the bigger stick has the better chance of imposing his definitions of reality.'

The repertoire of major justificatory ideologies in common usage on the part of those farmers and landowners whom we interviewed has already been set out in Table 73. There we saw that, in addition to the fairly common attempt to represent the ownership of large areas of productive land as economically insignificant, farmers and landowners had resort to a variety of other ideologies by which their wealth could be defended. It is to a detailed consideration of these that we turn first.

Justifications of landownership

It is useful to consider the plurality of ideologies surrounding landownership in terms of a fourfold classification involving what may be termed 'capitalistic', 'collectivistic', 'altruistic', and 'individualistic' justifications. In the case of all four categories, it is worth noting, first, that the form which the particular justifications take in relation to ownership of land is mirrored to a large extent in urban-industrial contexts in relation to the ownership of other forms of productive capitalist property. As we shall see later in the chapter, agricultural landowners seem to differ little from other owners of productive capital in the ways in which they choose to represent the character of their property to non-owning groups, and for this reason we feel that it is possible to extrapolate from a particular discussion of one property-owning section of British society to a consideration of other groups in other sectors of the economy (e.g. industrialists, financiers, private urban landlords, and so on). Secondly, it is also apparent that the origins of many of the ideologies which surround the private ownership of land and which are in current usage by contemporary landowners can be traced back centuries through the political philosophy of the seventeenth and eighteenth centuries to the time of Thomas Aquinas and beyond. As Schlatter (1951, p. 55) observes: 'Almost every justification of private property which has been popular in modern times was anticipated by the pamphleteers and political philosophers of those centuries when princes, popes, parliaments and peasants were waging wars to determine what classes should rule modern society, and what particular form of property should be the instrument of domination.' In other words, the ideological forms surrounding landownership today are, in Veblen's terms, 'in arrears' or 'archaic' (see Veblen, 1923, p. 43). They should not be seen as the creations of those who hold the land today, but rather as the contemporary manifestations of particular ideological themes which were generated in one historical context and have been expropriated and adapted to fit another. This is clearly noticeable in the case of the 'capitalistic' and 'collectivistic' categories of ideological justification which, as we shall see, owe much to the diverse philosophies of natural rights and utilitarianism advanced by Locke and Hume respectively and to which we drew attention in Chapter 1. Clearly these and other amenable theories of property have long since entered the stock of knowledge of British society, and have been transmitted in their essence down generations and across social classes to reappear in the twentieth century as 'obvious' statements about and explanations of private ownership of capital. It would seem that many landowners and others who may never have heard of Hume nor read the works of Locke nevertheless owe a debt of gratitude to these philosophers when they unknowingly resurrect their theories to 'explain' a contemporary situation which these writers could never have envisaged.

John Locke's legacy is seen most clearly in that category of ideologies which we have termed '*capitalistic*'. As we indicated in Chapter 1, Locke argued that private property ownership was a function of two natural rights of man: the right to take from the environment what is necessary to human life and sustenance, and the right to claim exclusivity over that part of the environment upon which one has expended labour, provided it is then put to good use. Although it seems to be the case that Locke's argument was directed rather to man in an original state of nature than to men living in a society where patterns of property ownership have long since been established, it nevertheless served at the time as an admirable justification by means of which landowners, merchants and others could defend their privileges (see Tawney, 1966, p. 256). The three criteria of a 'naturally just' distribution of property – need, expenditure of labour, and creative use – could be and were easily equated with desire, entrepreneurship, and investment/accumulation respectively, and as such provided a neat 'elective affinity' with the realities of an inequitable distribution of private property and a gross exploitation of propertyless labour.[1] In other words Locke's philosophy provided a moral theory of capitalism, and it is hardly surprising that its attraction to owners of capital should have proved so strong, both in the past and today.

The stress on the expenditure of labour is one facet of natural right philosophy which survives to this day in many landowners' and farmers' justifications of their property. As can be seen from Table 73, well over one-third of all respondents argued that their wealth, represented by the land they owned and the variable capital they controlled, was clearly justified as the equitable return for years of hard work. Sometimes such arguments were advanced very forcibly:

I feel under no obligation. We've lived on a bloody shoestring. Our work collectively has made this a farm. You take the rewards in your own life for your own efforts. Reward for efforts – it's in the Bible. [Suffolk farmer, 120 acres.]

When I started on 47 acres I had two fags a day – I couldn't afford more. I worked 16 hours a day. A chap who works hard and uses his head, why should he redistribute that to the lazy bugger? If a chap likes to work, he should have money for what he likes. [Suffolk farmer, 650 acres.]

I have made my wealth by hard work and so I am entitled to it. . . . I don't approve of people making money at property games. [Norfolk farmer, 1100 acres.]

I didn't start with a lot of inherited wealth like some of the owner-occupiers. I have a level of income related to my own efforts. I want to hang on to what I have made. I suppose I can't really justify having so much more than my workers – I just have the ability to do better. [Suffolk farmer, 750 acres.]

What is interesting here is that many of those who mentioned hard work as a justification for their wealth had inherited their land and farm businesses. Indeed, there was no significant correlation between the use of a 'work' justification and respondents' career histories – against all our initial expectations, we found that those who had inherited their land and their enterprises were just as likely to defend their wealth as being a just reward for hard work as were those who had become established largely through their own efforts. Two points may be noted about this. First, it is clearly the case that the ideological justification of wealth having entered a taken-for-granted 'stock of meaning', to use Berger and Luckmann's phrase, becomes very flexible. It becomes socially available to all who may care to make use of it – including those whose wealth was simply handed on to them by the fortunes of primogeniture.[2] Secondly, it is also the case that other components of a 'capitalistic' ethic are available to landowners and farmers. Thus, for example, we saw in Table 73 that between 12 per cent (in the HN sample) and 21 per cent (in the 1000 + acres sample) of our respondents justified their wealth by pointing to the risks they had taken as a result of financial incentives. We considered this ideology of risk/incentive in some detail in Chapter 7, and would only add here that even where a farmer or landowner feels he cannot appeal to the sweat on his brow to justify his wealth, he can equally well appeal to some parallel ideology such as the risks (real or imaginary) which he bears. Many, of course, appeal to both.

The logical problems encountered by present-day landowners in attempting to justify their wealth according to a criterion of hard work reflect the problems encountered by their predecessors three hundred years ago. Thus in Locke's original formulation of natural rights theory, it soon became apparent that his criterion for a naturally just distribution of property could be interpreted unfavourably in relation to those members of the landowning class who patently did not mix their labour with nature. As Tawney (1920) noted, natural rights theory can be seen to condemn more than it justifies. As a conceptual tool for justifying economic realities natural rights theory was – and remains – ideologically useful but by itself not always adequate. So it was that a new and different philosophy arose in response to its weaknesses: this was utilitarianism.

The utilitarian theory of philosophers such as Mill and Bentham was based upon the premise that rules of justice are conventional. In other words, the principal rules which establish individuals' title to property (present possession, first possession, long possession, accession and succession) are seen to derive out of men's experience and to ensure the promotion of the greatest happiness. Put crudely, if things were not the way they are, they would be different; and they are not different because they represent the best available system of arrangements. Thus the contemporary system of property ownership was justified, not through any appeal to men's natural rights, but simply on the grounds of its very existence in that form. Utilitarianism clearly provided little ground for argument, and succeeded in arriving at much the same conclusion as natural rights theory while avoiding the complicating issue of expenditure of labour. As Plamenatz (1963, p. 311) observes: 'The beginnings of the two theories are poles apart, but the conclusion is the same: blessed are those that have wealth because everyone is the better off for not disturbing them in the enjoyment of it.'

Perhaps the most obvious example of the application by farmers and landowners in our sample of an ideology deriving from utilitarian philosophy concerns the allegory on natural inequality to which we referred in Chapter 7. By this, it will be recalled, we mean that category of justificatory statements which seek to legitimate unequal wealth by reference to its inevitability. As we saw in Chapter 7 (and as Table 73 indicates) a significant proportion of farmers and landowners argued – often in much the same terms and phrases – that even if wealth were redistributed, the current pattern of distribution would only reassert itself, and that the current pattern was therefore justifiable. The intellectual pedigree of this argument can clearly be traced back to Hume, and since we have already considered it in the last chapter, we need dwell no more on it here.

The legacy of utilitarianism extends beyond this belief in 'natural' inequality, however, for that body of philosophy can be understood as the antecedent of the second category of ideologies outlined above, namely '*collectivistic*' justifications. Collectivistic justifications, while recognizing the existence of privilege, defend it in terms of the benefits which are generated among non-property-owning groups. Thus, as Table 73 shows, between 22 per cent (in the HN sample) and 41 per cent (in the 1000+ acres sample) of our respondents justified their wealth by stressing that they used it 'wisely' and 'responsibly' to good effect. Again, the link with utilitarianism is clear, for property is justified by means of an argument which sees those who do not own it as benefiting almost as much as those that do.

Collectivistic justifications in fact take two forms, each of which tends to be used by different types of farmers and landowners. The first, emphasized mainly by traditional 'gentleman farmers', points to the socially recognized 'duties' of *noblesse oblige* which they see as entailed in the ownership of a large estate:

I don't have to justify myself. I owe a debt to society to be in the fortunate position I am – if it is a fortunate position. I carry a lot of responsibility and worries. As it says in the Bible, 'to whom is given, much is expected'. [Norfolk farmer, 3000 acres.]

I feel that the wealth I've got, as long as I play an active part in serving the community in agriculture and socially, that's the best way of redistributing wealth. It's better than giving people money – we're a nation of spongers. [Norfolk farmer, 1000 acres.]

I have tried to do the right thing by my men and give them decent homes. You feel a responsibility in that direction. We don't have profit-sharing, but we do look after them and pay above the minimum rates. I also try and do what I can for the area in general in public work. [Cambridgeshire farmer, 1000 acres.]

It is incumbent upon me to look after those who are dependent upon me. It is my job to look after them. . . . This is socially desirable. I was brought up to see this as my duty. [Cambridgeshire farmer, 3500 acres.]

One owes a lot to the community – it sounds pompous – to one's men who produce the wealth. We give them a good deal. I was drawn into local government out of a sense of responsibility. One must give as well as take. That's how I would justify my position. [Suffolk farmer, 2500 acres.]

It is worth noting here that the obligations to which these landowners refer are social, not legal, in character. As we shall see in the next section of this chapter, the law has long since shed its interest in who owns the land and, to a large extent, in how they use it, so that these rather paternalistic justifications inevitably rest upon landowners' voluntary activities in relation to their workers' welfare and community involvement.

In contrast, the second variant of 'collectivist' justifications points not to any voluntary commitment on the part of the farmer/landowner, but rather to the 'inevitable' effects which flow from the fact of landownership and agricultural enterprise – namely, the generating of employment and wages in the locality.[3] Predictably, this second form of 'collectivist' justification is used typically by those we have termed agri-businessmen:

I believe that while the rich are rich, the poor have a good standard of living. But when the rich are poor, God help the poor. If it wasn't for people like me who take risks, and thereby feed people, employ people, service industry, provide fodder for the workforce everything would come to a grinding halt. [Norfolk farmer, 1200 acres.]

I do feel that if it weren't for people like us, others wouldn't get jobs round here. If our profit was less, we'd have to cut out a man. How are you to employ people if someone doesn't have a bit more than others? If farmers could make more profit, there wouldn't be so much unemployment in country areas. [Suffolk farmer, 1100 acres.]

What is so seldom quoted is that the standard of living of the majority is assured by the minority who employ them. You must pay people who have the responsibility for the standard of living of the majority. [Suffolk farmer, 1000 acres.]

I feel I provide good salaries for those under me. Unless I see a reward, how can they? [Essex farmer, 1000 acres.]

I know of no one round here who suffers because I earn more. . . . I have to provide a living for others. They have no worries or responsibilities. I have to have the worry, and I have to do well if they are to have a decent living. So it's only right that I should be paid for providing others with a living. [Suffolk farmer, 650 acres.]

I am really the person responsible for that slice of capital upon which an awful lot of people are dependent for their living. And I'm not inefficient with it. [Essex farmer, 1000 acres.]

Whether the specific argument takes the form of a paternalistic conception of social responsibility, or a rational conception of the generation of employment, the overall message of 'collectivistic' justifications is clear – wealth is justifiable because others may benefit indirectly from it.

The third category of justifications which can be identified from the responses of our sample of farmers may be termed *'altruistic'* ideologies. While collectivistic ideologies stress the dispersal of the benefits of ownership among non-owners, altruistic ideologies tend rather to emphasize the lack of personal benefit accruing to owners. Altruistic ideologies, that is, see the land not so much as a factor of production to be used in pursuit of profit, but rather as part of a wider national heritage which the landowner sees it as his duty to protect. Land, it is argued, is essentially a communal resource, while the landowner is represented as little more than a caretaker (albeit an unusually prestigious one) or a 'steward'. This ideology of steward-ship, whose origins clearly lie in what Marx termed 'the aristocratic conditions of landownership', stresses continuity, and has at its heart the idea that the task of the landowner *qua* custodian is to hold the land 'in trust' for the nation, and in the meantime to improve it before handing it on to the next generation of 'stewards'. It is an ideology which is familiar in the philosophy of Burke, a belief that private ownership, as a recent CLA document put it, 'rests upon the benefits which private landowners have given in the past, and will continue to give if allowed, towards the stewardship of the country-side. . . . Long-term landowners can give rather than take from their land. It is an ongoing life that transcends the generations, and it gives a sense of lifetime stewardship as opposed to personal ownership' (CLA, 1975, p. 1).

Marx catches the essence of stewardship well when he writes (1964, pp. 100–1): 'The lord of an entailed estate, the first born son, belongs to the land. It inherits him. . . . There still exists the sem-blance of a more intimate connection between the proprietor and the land than that of mere material wealth. The estate is individualised with its lord. . . . It appears as the inorganic body of its lord.' Stewardship, in short, is an ideology firmly embedded in the econ-omic and social structure of pre-capitalist society. More than any of the other three categories of ideologies discussed here, it confirms Veblen's assertion regarding the 'archaic' nature of contemporary justifications.

As Table 73 indicates, only eleven of our respondents used an ideology of stewardship to justify their wealth. Not surprisingly, given the core value of continuity in the stewardship ideology, ten of these had inherited their land from their fathers, and most could trace a family connection with the land back hundreds of years. Despite the relatively small numbers citing this particular justifica-tion, however, it is apparent that the stewardship ideology is quite widely held among traditional landowners. Our discussion of the environmental question in Chapters 5 and 6, for example, shows how the concept of stewardship, involving as it does the notion of guarding a traditional landscape on behalf of others rather than exploiting the land in the pursuit of profit, is commonly evoked by landowners (and, indeed, the new immigrant middle class) in their concern to preserve the English countryside. As we saw it is an ideology which serves to rally the support of all those who profess their concern with the countryside and the 'nation's heritage', and which can be used to great political effect. To take just one example, the response of the landed interest in Britain to wealth tax and land nationalization proposals has often been couched in these very terms. As a correspondent in the *East Anglian Daily Times* (29 December 1973) put it:

The farmer who owns his land puts more effort into it, he cherishes the soil for its abundant power to produce crops, and he will not overtax that power with bad rotations. He thinks more deeply about the new permanent features such as buildings or skyline views, the planting of trees which he will never see grow to maturity, and all the long term aspects of good husbandry . . . land nationalization would destroy a part of what is England.

In many ways, the stewardship ideology bears distinct similarities to those ideologies discussed at the end of Chapter 7 which sought to deny the existence or significance of land as a source of personal wealth, for the notion of the landowner as steward emphasizes his unwillingness or 'inability' to sell, and thus his 'forfeit' of the usual rights of property ownership. But the stewardship ideology goes beyond this, for it does not simply represent the landowner as custodian – a 'non-owner' holding the land in trust for future generations and for the country as a whole – but at the same time stresses the 'selflessness' and 'altruism' entailed in this task:

Inherited wealth is difficult to justify, but it is obligated family wealth. It has a basic social inequity in it. So you have to look after it well. My wealth is not spendable. [Cambridgeshire farmer, 1500 acres.]

My family has farmed this area for over 300 years. . . . Basically I am a churchman, and I have a feeling of stewardship. One is conscious of the need to discharge adequately one's duty. One has been given a great deal to be responsible for, so I must do things well. [Norfolk farmer, 2000 acres.]

The England that is attractive is the estate England. Not the hard-up owner-occupier or tenant. It's our national heritage that you see when you go shooting – land that's been in the same family for a long time, and this does something for the soul of *homo sapiens*. You don't have to justify this – you are proud of yourself, what you've done, and what your family's done. It should go on for ever. [Norfolk farmer, 3000 acres.]

A landowner feels it's more in trust for the next generation. You're not out for a quick return. [Suffolk farmer, 1000 acres.]

The fourth category of justifications – *'individualistic'* ideologies – has already been briefly mentioned in Chapter 7. These ideologies take the form of attempts by farmers to justify their ownership of land by equating it with other people's ownership of other forms of property which are generally taken as being unquestionably justifiable. 'Individualistic' ideologies, that is, rest upon the fact that certain types of property which, following Lafargue (n.d.), we may term 'property of personal appropriation' (PPA), are widely distributed in modern Britain. Such property of personal appropriation includes items such as clothing, furnishings, cars, etc. – items over which there appears to be a broad consensus of values regarding the desirability of private and individual ownership. This fourth category of ideologies thus seeks to achieve legitimacy for the private ownership of productive land by asserting its similarity to PPA:

It's human instinct that once you've got something, you hang on to it. It's like your motor car – you'd take a dim view if someone said they were taking it away. [Suffolk farmer, 250 acres.]

Everyone wants to own their own property – it's fundamental. [Suffolk farmer, 450 acres.]

The love of the land and gardens, the wildlife and beauty of our countryside, is in the blood. . . . If more people had a small piece of garden to cultivate, the world would be happier and healthier. [Suffolk farmer, 750 acres.]

It's the same as owning your own house. It gives you a certain status – you have a stake in the country. . . . 'Scratch an Englishman', they say. [Norfolk farmer, 1000 acres.]

In including land as one type of PPA, these respondents stressed the intimate and personal attachment which they felt to their property – just as the home-owner glows with a sense of pride about his house, and the car-owner jealously cossets his car, so these farmers emphasize an emotional tie with their land. To this extent, 'individualistic' ideologies have much in common with 'altruistic' ones, the difference being that the latter stress the role of safeguarding property on behalf of others, while the former emphasize personal exclusivity – 'I don't envy your house, so you should not covet my thousand acres'. This difference is clearly revealed in questions relating to public access rights – while the landowner who embraces an 'altruistic' ideology may cite the public's use of his land as a justification of his ownership of it, the landowner who endorses an 'individualistic' ideology is more likely to deny such rights of access on the grounds that they violate his ownership of a *personal* piece of property. As one respondent put it: 'Some people have got nice flowers in their garden – they wouldn't want me poking about. Property's property, and land is land. It's the same thing.' Of course, given that these ideologies are almost infinitely malleable, it is quite possible for landowners to resort to an 'altruistic' ideology when justifying their landed wealth, and an 'individualistic' one when dealing with access issues. As we have noted before, these ideologies are the servants of those who use them, not vice versa, and the occasion of their use will most likely reflect the demands of any given situation.[4]

Types of property

In order to assess and more fully appreciate the practical use of the four categories of justificatory ideologies we have outlined, and in particular the relation of these ideologies with material class relations, it is necessary to consider in some detail the concept of property as it applies in modern capitalist society. First, we should note that the legal concept of property refers not to any inherent quality of objects *per se*, but rather to the legally defined rights which attach to such objects in any given society. Property, then, may loosely be defined for the purposes of our discussion as the authoritatively defined relationship between individuals and the objects of their environment. It follows from this that the notion of property will vary according to the particular society in question, and that qualitatively similar 'objects' may come to be regarded – in law and in custom – in any society in diverse ways. In advanced capitalist society, the principal rights which may be identified in relation to the legal concept of property are those relating to control, benefit and disposal (alienation). That is to say, property ownership involves the expectation of exclusivity in relation to the control over, derived benefits from, and dispersal of the object in question – an expectation which may be established through the application of legal sanctions if deemed necessary. This is not to argue that all forms of property ownership in advanced capitalist society necessarily involve the exercise of all three of these rights of exclusivity; entailed property, for example, may not be alienated through sale. But as Benn and Peters (1959) point out, where all three rights do not apply, it is because a specific exception or qualification has been made through the application of legal process.

Property rights of exclusivity in modern capitalist society are defined in law by universalistic rather than particularistic criteria. In other words, the law relating to property is unconcerned with the particular identity of the owner and, usually, with the purpose to which his property is put. As Renner (1949, p. 90) observes:

Property as a legal institution is indifferent towards subject (*persona*) and object (*res*). *De jure* it only regulates detention without being concerned with the identity of the *persona* or the type of the goods. The law protects possession, the power to dispose of the *res*. A system of private law is content to know that material wealth is firmly held by the individuals, it does not care what use they make of it or who they are.

We have already seen two major implications of this for the ideo-logical justification of landownership. The first is that since all forms of private property are equally recognized in, and subsumed under, the law, it is not difficult to argue that all forms are therefore quali-tatively similar. As our respondent quoted earlier put it, 'property is property'. This being the case, and given that everybody owns something (i.e. everybody enjoys some rights of exclusivity over some item of property), it may be claimed that we all have some vested interest in the *status quo*; that in a 'property-owning democracy' the distribution of property gives rise to a fundamental commensur-ability rather than conflict of interests, differences being only those of degree. Similarly, if 'property is property', then it becomes that much easier for landowners to resort to the 'individualistic' ideology dis-cussed above, and successfully to represent their ownership of land as nothing more than one example of ownership of PPA (we shall return to this later).

The second major implication of a legally disinterested conception of property is that the law does not recognize personal obligation. Provided the legal boundaries surrounding the ownership of property are not transgressed, the law is not generally interested in how that property is used[5] – on whether it is used to the benefit of other non-owners or not. Now we have seen that the ownership of land may come to be associated by landowners (and by others less directly associated with it) with the necessary discharge of socially sanctioned customary obligations, and that these obligations – summarized in the notion of *noblesse oblige* – are today sometimes cited as justifications for the continuation of the current system of landownership (see the discussion of 'collectivistic' ideologies above). However, it is clearly the case that the law is concerned, not with obligations, but with rights. Indeed, the only significant legal obligations regarding property ownership today fall, not on the owner, but on the non-owner – those who do not own land are obliged not to trespass, but those who do are not obliged to distribute the benefits. As Mac-Pherson (1973) points out, the rise of a capitalist market gave rise to a legal conception of property rights unfettered by the necessary performance of any social function. 'Property' and 'private property' thus came to be synonymous.

In relation to the concept of property in a modern capitalist society, therefore, it makes little sense to draw the traditional dichotomy of rights against obligations. Rather, we should distinguish between rights specified in law, and uses permitted by law. Thus as Giddens (1973, p. 102) writes:

The rights of property and of the sale of labour are rights of the alienation or disposal of goods ('commodities' in the Marxian sense) which underpin the system of power, not in spite of, but because of the fact that they are specified in terms of freedom of economic exchange. The operation of market relationships obviously pre-supposes the existence of normative agreements (ultimately sanctioned by the state) which define the general conditions governing the formation of contractual ties, etc.; but these norms merely specify the boundaries of the framework.

In other words, while legally constituted property rights are concerned with specifying the boundaries on access or exclusivity, they are not concerned with specifying when or how the various control, benefit and alienation functions are achieved, except within very broad regulatory limits. *Access* is stipulated by law, while *use* or *function* is left virtually unfettered. The law is thus prescriptive with regard to exclusivity rights but permissive with regard to property functions.

We are now in a position to construct one dimension of a typology of property in advanced capitalist society, for the function in use of any given property right of exclusivity may range on a continuum between outright accumulation and absolute subsistence. That is, property may be used as a factor of production and reproduction, or it may be used up in consumption (i.e. it does not reproduce itself). As with most continua, these polar types are 'ideal', and most empirical examples of property use will fall somewhere between them. For example, owner-occupied housing is clearly used more for the function of consumption than for production and reproduction, yet inflation of land values will endow it with an accumulative potential (Saunders, 1978). Furthermore, the function of housing within a capitalist economy involves a highly significant secondary reproductive function. As Berle (1959, p. 28) notes:

> The workman's house is his shelter and his home; he enjoys it and consumes it gradually; his automobile is an enjoyable adjunct to his life, and he consumes that. But without house and transport, no labour force would be available to run any plant in the US. Provision for this type of consumption is therefore (at least partly) required capital expenditure.

Housing, therefore, is an essential component in the reproduction of labour power in capitalist society (Castells, 1976). Nevertheless, its function is clearly less directly accumulative than that of, say, the factory to which the householder goes to work.

The distinction we are drawing between the two ideal types of property function may be summarized, with reference to Lafargue (n.d.) as the distinction between capital and PPA.[6] While capital is related to the process of production and involves the expropriation of surplus value, PPA is related to the static conditions of consumption. The essential differences between the two concern a difference in disposal (production against consumption), benefit (profit against usufruct), and control (user against manager).

If function provides us with one dimension for a typology of property in capitalist society, the degree to which access is widely or narrowly defined (i.e. the degree of exclusivity) provides us with another. Here, again, it is possible to construct a continuum between two polar types – in this case private or narrowly defined against public or widely defined rights of access – although again it is necessary to remember that these are two abstract points on a continuum, and not simple dichotomies. In advanced capitalist society, many forms of property are neither wholly public nor wholly private since the three defining rights of property – control, benefit, and alienation – are often divided. As regards productive property, for example, it is clear that rights of control are often narrowly concentrated in management, while rights of benefit may be relatively widely dispersed among holders of company stock. Similarly with certain types of property as consumption, such as local authority housing, rights of benefit may be held by the current occupier, while rights of control, and certainly rights of alienation, are vested in the public authority concerned.

We have, therefore, two continua by means of which different types of property may be identified, one relating to function, and one to access. By combining them, we arrive at a fourfold typology (Fig. 9).

		Degree of exclusivity	
		High	Low
Degree of accumulative potential	High	Individual means of production (1)	Collective means of production (3)
	Low	Individual means of consumption (2)	Collective means of consumption (4)

Figure 9 *A typology of property in capitalist society*[7]

Table 74 *Property and property ideologies*

Type of property (see Fig. 9)	Example from contemporary landownership	Affinitive ideology	Example of contemporary justification
1. Individual means of production	Privately-owned farm, hiring full-time, non-family labour	Capitalistic	'Hard work' 'Risk'
2. Individual means of consumption	Family farm	Individualistic	'PPA'
3. Collective means of production	Publicly-owned productive land (e.g. Forestry Commission)	Collectivistic	'Creates employment for workers' *'Noblesse oblige'*
4. Collective means of consumption	Publicly-owned recreation land (e.g. parks, etc.)	Altruistic	'Stewardship'

The individual means of production (type 1) necessarily includes both constant capital (e.g. land, buildings, machinery and so on) and variable capital (i.e. contracted labour power). Thus to take an example from agriculture, we would maintain that for a farm to be included in box 1 (i.e. to designate it as of high accumulative potential), it must make use of full-time non-family hired labour (see Poulantzas, 1973*a*; Bell and Newby, 1974). The family farm, even though it may produce in and for a capitalist market, cannot realistically be included in box 1, since the family farmer uses and owns his 'means of production' more as a means of maintaining himself and his immediate dependents (i.e. in an essentially static fashion) than as a means of capital accumulation through the expropriation of surplus labour power. Extraction of surplus value is thus a necessary condition of individual means of production.

Type 2 – individual means of consumption – corresponds to what we have termed PPA, and is characterized by consumer commodities ranging from clothing to housing. Types 3 and 4, by contrast, represent types of property which are less characteristic of *laissez-faire* capitalism in that a growth in their significance is usually regarded as an encroachment upon the sanctity of the first two types. Thus box 3 – collective means of production – generally refers in advanced capitalist societies to state ownership of productive means, although other forms of socialized production (e.g. syndicalism) could equally be included, while type 4 – collective means of consumption – refers to property such as hospitals, roads, schools and so on controlled by the state on behalf of its individual members. The growth of type 4 in particular is often associated with the rise in the concept of 'citizenship' – e.g. in relation to the development of public welfare which may itself be conceived as a form of type 4 property.

This fourfold typology may also be applied with reference to four distinguishable types of agricultural landed property as in Table 74. Thus type 1 is represented by the privately owned capitalist farm, type 2 by the family or subsistence farm, type 3 by institutionally owned productive land such as Forestry Commission holdings, and type 4 by publicly owned recreational land such as municipal parks, nature reserves, and so on. Other patterns of landownership (e.g. land owned by quasi-non-governmental organizations such as the National Trust) are rather more difficult to place in any one category (e.g. National Trust land would appear to involve both public and private ownership rights) but this only reflects the fact that the dimensions of the typology are continua rather than dichotomies. What is clearly unproblematic, however, is the location in the typology of most of the farms which were included in our survey, for although some of the smaller farms in the forty-four parishes sample may be allocated to box 2 on account of their lack of full-time non-family hired labour, all of the others belong without doubt to box 1. In other words, the type of landed property which our respondents sought to justify in interviews with us was that represented by type 1

– individual means of production, or, more simply, capital (non-capitalist farmers were not asked wealth justification questions, so all our answers were given by farmers whose holdings were of this type).

Having said this, it was clearly also the case that many of our respondents used justifications which had less of an elective affinity with the nature of type 1 property than with one or other of the other three types shown in Table 74. Thus we saw earlier that the answers to our questions on wealth justification elicited four typical categories of reply, only one of which – 'capitalistic' ideologies (stressing elements deriving out of natural right philosophy such as hard work and risk) – was essentially applicable to the type of property which was being discussed. The other three – 'collectivistic', 'altruistic', and 'individualistic' – may rather be seen as relating to the other three forms of property identified in the typology – i.e. collective means of production, collective means of consumption, and individual means of consumption respectively. *In short, our respondents commonly sought to justify their private ownership of the means of production by representing it variously as either non-private, or non-productive, or both, and by drawing upon the apposite ideology to reinforce their position.*

Take, for example, the way productive property comes to be represented as PPA (i.e. type 2) through the use of an *ideology of individualism.* As we saw earlier, the principle of private ownership of the means of consumption such as clothing or housing is firmly established in British society largely because we can all claim title to some form of PPA. As Marshall (1963) observes, it is virtually impossible *not* to own some private means of consumption. This is a significant point, for it follows that there are some forms of property which are so widespread that they can only be considered virtually irrelevant to any system of social stratification (except, that is, on the ideological level). Clearly, however, the pattern of landownership which we have considered in this book is very different – few of us can lay claim to any more than a few square yards of freehold, and the large capitalist farm can by no stretch of logic be equated with that. Over half of all privately owned agricultural land in England and Wales is in the hands of something like 0·4 per cent of the population, while in East Anglia the concentration of ownership is even denser. As Veblen (1964, p. 52) argues, the small family farmer may validly defend his property in terms of what we have labelled an 'individualistic' ideology, but for the large capitalist producer to do so is surely an example of mystification:

It is not unusual to defend private property in land and other natural resources on the plea that the cultivator must have unhampered use of the land which is the raw material of his work. In the main, as things have turned out in recent times, this plea is petty-foggery and subterfuge. It is not the small farmer's holding that needs apology or defence.

What we are arguing, therefore, is that the assumption that if *any* form of property is justifiable then so too are *all* forms, represents an ideological position which can only be maintained for as long as the very real differences between productive and consumption property remain blurred. As Kahn-Freund writes:

The property concept can ultimately serve the political function of creating the illusion that factual situations are identical because they happen to be reflected in the same legal institution. [Introduction to Renner, 1949, p. 36.]

Or as Benn and Peters (1959, p. 160) put it:

It is tempting to assume that what applies to individual, applies equally to private corporative proprietorship, and to utilise arguments appropriate to personal goods to defend individual control of capital goods. Food, clothes, houses, pictures, and books are clearly in a different category from railway trucks, coal mines, and factories, and it would be strange if arguments relevant to forms of control for the one were applicable to the other ... the claims that the opportunity to acquire property satisfies a deep-rooted acquisitive instinct, or provides an incentive to effort, or provides a firm basis for the family, may all be cogent when applied to personal goods, but are relatively weaker when applied to capital goods ... to treat them on the same terms as personal goods is to ignore important differences which may weigh heavily on the other side.

Whereas 'individualistic' ideologies are used by landowners in such a way that the distinction between ownership of private means of production and ownership of private means of consumption becomes confused, so 'collectivistic' ideologies serve, intentionally or otherwise, to confuse rights over private means of production with those relating to collective means of production. 'Collectivistic' ideologies, it will be recalled, seek to justify landownership by pointing to the real or imagined benefits which accrue to non-owners, whether through the charitable interpretation of *noblesse oblige*, or through the operation of market factors in generating employment. The main point to be made here, of course, is that even if such benefits are distributed among non-owners, they in no way constitute property rights as such. In the case of the receipt of charity, the distribution of benefits may to some extent be sanctioned by custom, but we have seen that any legal obligations which may once have attached to estate ownership have long since disappeared. Indeed, the socially sanctioned response to the receipt of charity is very different from that which usually follows from the receipt of one's rights, for the recipient generally shows gratitude as a sign of his recognition that such benefits need not have been distributed to him. As Newby (1975) points out, the gift relationship is a very significant mechanism for maintaining social deference and thus for securing legitimacy for prevailing ownership relations in the eyes of non-owners. In the case of those benefits which are derived from the generation of wages rather than the distribution of charity, it is apparent that the recipients do have rights, but only in so far as they enter a contractual relationship whereby they give up their rights over their labour power. In other words, their entitlement to benefit derives not from their relation to the means of production *per se*, but rather from an entirely separate contractual agreement involving their alienation of their labour power which is then used to generate further benefits for the property owner. Indeed, far from landownership benefiting those who are employed to work the land, it is apparent that it is their alienated labour power which benefits those who own the land.[8]

It is not just that 'collectivistic' ideologies make a false assertion with regard to the distribution of benefits, however, for it is also clearly the case that they ignore entirely the other two components of ownership – namely control and alienation. As we saw in Chapter 4, the hierarchical organization of farming allows little formal control to employees (and even where attempts are made by relatively enlightened farmers to 'involve' their employees in the running of the farm, it is evident that this in no way represents a redistribution of rights of control – control is 'granted' on the owner's terms and can always be rescinded, modified, or ignored at will). Rights over the disposal of the land are, needless to say, even more jealously guarded. In short, 'collectivistic' ideologies, like 'individualistic' ones, totally misrepresent and obscure the true nature of ownership rights.

If 'individualistic' ideologies are based on the fallacious assumption that landownership is akin to consumption-type property, and 'collectivistic' ideologies are based on the equally fallacious argument that landownership is widely beneficial, then *'altruistic' ideologies* are doubly fallacious for they are furthest removed from the realities of private ownership of the means of production, stressing as they do *both* the 'non-productive' *and* 'public' character of such ownership. The archetype of altruistic ideologies is that which we identified earlier as the notion of 'stewardship' – the idea that 'the owner of an estate for the time being was steward of a trust for unborn generations, and temporary recipient of the fruits of his forebears' endeavours' (Thompson, 1963, p. 5). As we have already suggested, the notion of stewardship is clearly anachronistic. Belonging as it does to the pre-capitalist period, it is in many ways inherently the weakest and most vulnerable of the ideologies we have discussed, for the realities of capitalist enterprise would seem to contradict its validity with embarrassing vividness.

Evidence of such contradictions has been presented in earlier chapters, although perhaps the best example concerns the strain, discussed in Chapters 5 and 6, between the stewardship ideology as it comes to be applied in relation to environmental conservation, and the necessity to rationalize the farming enterprise in order to maintain profitability. Thus we saw that landowners in East Anglia were able to pursue a policy of excluding potential competitors for cheap labour and of maintaining their own material and environmental advantages – all with the active support of the immigrant middle class – by resorting to a stewardship ideology which was frequently belied by their actions in removing hedgerows, refusing rights of access, and so on – all of which antagonized their middle-class allies. That these strains and contradictions are, on the whole, so effectively managed (i.e. that they generally fail to expose the mystifying nature of 'altruistic' ideologies, and thus avoid any challenge to ownership rights on the part of non-property-owning groups) is testimony to the power which landowners have, both in the work situation and in the community at large. The political significance of the ideologies we have been discussing is thus in the final analysis contingent upon the prior distribution of power in the rural social structure.

Ideologies of property: their structural significance

So far in this chapter we have described the various ideologies of landownership at the individual level, and although some of the structural implications of such ideologies will be apparent from the preceding discussion, it is obviously incumbent upon us to address this problem directly. For, as we stated at the beginning of Chapter 7, the ideologies which farmers and landowners espouse are not purely a matter of personal whim or psychological idiosyncrasy but have important implications, if not purpose, in stabilizing a hierarchical social structure. We should emphasize, however, that we are not advocating an idealist *explanation* of this social structure, but offering an account of how, in a rural area and in an industry like agriculture where the most salient principle of stratification is property owner-ship (rather than, say, income), an inegalitarian structure is legiti-mated with reference to such ideologies. If we concentrate on ideologies of property, rather than on other legitimating ideologies which we have described in this book (see, for example, Chapters 4, 5 and 6), it is because we believe the rights associated with property to be such a taken-for-granted (and hence hegemonic) aspect of the social structure and to be fundamental in both shaping the system of rural social stratification and prompting a good deal of the political activity in which farmers and landowners engage.

We firmly believe, then, that we must begin our examination of the structural implications of these ideologies of property at the point of production. It is here that farmers make their profits by first extracting and then retaining a proportion of the value of their workers' labour power. Their right to do so is sanctified in the law relating to property and hence guaranteed by the coercive power of the state in the unlikely and infrequent occasions that it might be called upon to protect the farmer's property rights. It hardly needs be added, however, that the role of property is in reality considerably more complex than this grossly over-simplified Marxian model suggests. For while the law relating to property clearly sanctifies the right of the farmer to expropriate a surplus, the legitimacy of this expropriation, and in particular the *rate* of expropriation, is a matter not so much of the law but of prevailing ideas of social justice to which farmers on the one hand and farm workers on the other sub-scribe. Thus a consideration of the political economy of agriculture – i.e. the process of surplus expropriation and distribution and the legitimation of this process – leads the analysis in two opposite, though complementary, directions. First, because the relationship between farmers and workers is (compared with most other indus-tries) a close, personal one, we must consider the process of legitima-tion mostly in terms of direct, personal contact in both the work and community situations; with a social structure, in other words, which is essentially local in its nature. Secondly, however, we are forced to consider matters which lie far beyond the farm gate, namely the nature of the law relating to property rights, the role of the state in shaping those rights and hence the activity of farmers and land-owners (or their representatives) in influencing the intervention of the state in a manner beneficial to their interests.

Earlier in this book we have paid particular attention to the manner in which the relationship between farmer and farm worker is stabilized by examining the transmission of legitimating ideologies in both the work situation (Chapter 4) and the local community (Chapter 5). We have emphasized the fact that because most farmers live adjacent to the workplace the gap in income and life-style generated by the property relationships between employer and employee is a very visible one. By no means all the justifications of these unequal rewards which farmers feel obliged to make from time to time concern property *per se*. As we saw in Chapter 4 employers' attempts to define the work situation in a generally harmonious and cooperative fashion extend beyond the narrower definition of property relationships but encompass the totality of the agricultural workers' experiences. This does not imply that farmers are always successful in their attempts to create such 'greedy institutions' out of their farms and the immediate locality, for the organization of the farm and the composition of the local community may render it impossible entirely to deny access to other, more potentially disruptive and antagonistic interpretations. (Bell and Newby, 1973; Newby, 1977, Chapter VII). However, the desire of agricultural employers to promote such stability does draw them into the kind of paternalistic social relationships which we examined in Chapters 4 and 5.

Ideologies of property clearly represent an important aspect of the series of values which employers try to transmit in these situations. Indeed, they may be regarded as the most fundamental aspect of these values, both in a sociological sense, but more pertinently in an everyday practical sense by the farmers themselves. Were, for example, agricultural workers suddenly to question the property rights of farmers – their right to hire and fire labour, their right to control, benefit from and alienate their means of production, including the land itself, etc. – then there is little doubt that the farmer would be unable to continue in business. In an instinctive recognition of this, therefore, most farmers, however much they may consult their workers over such matters as the organization of the work and the timing of various activities, insist on 'drawing the line' at the invasion of such rights. It is, after all, *their* farm, they would stoutly maintain, and they therefore ultimately have the right to do whatever they wish with it. It must be added that this discussion is somewhat hypothetical since these rights are only very rarely challenged, least of all by agricultural workers. For the entitlement of the farmer to control his farm in whatever way he sees fit is merely an expression of the most pervasive and most taken-for-granted of all ideologies of property in contemporary British society – the 'individualistic' ideology of PPA. This private ownership of the farm by the farmer is regarded as merely an extension of the rights accruing to the ownership of any private possessions. Once the farm is defined in this way then *ipso facto* the farmer is accepted as having similar rights over how his property is to be used and disposed of. In this case the farmer is claiming no more and no less than any other owner of property – including the farm worker himself. He is merely drawing upon a readily available, widespread and generally accepted notion of property rights which is in no way specific to agriculture. (See Newby, 1977, Chapter VII; Rose *et al.*, 1976.)

This exemplifies a very obvious point, but one which must never-theless be constantly borne in mind in the discussion which follows: namely that it is impossible entirely to divorce the ideologies with regard to property rights and property in agriculture from those which are present in society generally. While they are given a specific content by the peculiarities of agricultural production – and par-ticularly by the nature of the social system which is supported by it – they essentially correspond to similar ideologies of property found elsewhere in British society.[9] This particularly applies to the ideology of PPA, which is the most pervasive and on that account the most 'obvious' and self-evident. Marshall's dictum again applies: it is difficult for anyone *not* to follow the apparent logic of the argument. The hegemony of this ideology is so complete that there is virtually no access to any alternative definitions of the farm which would deny the applicability of the ideology of PPA. Hence comments from farm workers like 'It's the farmer's farm – it's up to him how he runs it' (Newby, 1977, p. 372), express what is regarded as a self-evident truth which no farm workers would have the ability, or even the desire, to challenge.

Within the particularistic social system which characterizes most farms and rural communities, however, farmers do not defend their property rights solely on such abstract grounds as PPA. A second argument employed by farmers is the utilitarian notion that private property results in the greatest good of all. Given the often pater-nalistic relationship between farmers and farm workers which we examined in Chapter 4, it would be surprising if farmers did not extend such paternalism to include the supposed distribution of benefits which accrue from property ownership. The farmer's ownership of extensive property thus enables him to 'look after' his workers by creating employment for them, by providing them with decent housing, by allowing a generous source of perquisites and so on. In the face-to-face work situation characteristic of most farms, where the employer is a personally familiar figure, and given that most farms are personal or family proprietorships, this argument seems more plausible than in large industrial corporations. Thus on the farm it is often the farmer's wealth rather than the farm worker's labour which seems to be creating employment. The greater the farmer's wealth then the greater is the implied benefit to the farm workers (Bourne, 1912, pp. 104–5; Rose *et al.*, 1976, p. 717). Here a 'collectivistic' justification is being offered of the legitimacy of individual forms of property ownership. As when adopting the ideology of PPA, an available, if somewhat logically inappropriate, ideology is being employed to defend, legitimate and hence stabilize a highly inegalitarian distribution of property.

It is largely the attempts by farmers and landowners to maintain these property relationships which draws them into political activity outside the farm. In Chapter 6, for example, we examined the role of the agricultural interest in local politics in Suffolk and in Chapter 3 we considered the political activity of farmers and landowners at the national level, particularly through the activities of pressure groups like the NFU and the CLA. Both locally and nationally politics provides an arena in which farmers and landowners may expound their legitimating ideologies, particularly in response to what are perceived as external threats to the existing pattern of property relationships. Additionally, however, such political activity is put to more positive purpose – by providing the wherewithal for continued profitability and stable management. In each case farmers and landowners have felt the need to be active in the wider society beyond the work situation in order to obtain some degree of control over the social and economic context which surrounds the point of production. What is significant from our present perspective is that such political activity has involved the promotion of those ideologies of property ownership that we have described above.

In Chapters 5 and 6, for example, we indicated the extent to which the local social structure facilitates the transmission of dominant definitions of the situation, including ideologies of property, to the propertyless. In addition, however, we indicated how the control of local politics in rural areas also enabled a degree of control to be obtained over local labour markets and hence the context within which workers are allocated to the work situation. This was achieved partly through the control of scarce local resources – most notably the local housing stock, both tied and rented – but also through the control of local planning consent which tended to deny access to potential competitors for labour. An economic domination of the work situation is thus matched by a wider domination of the local labour market through the control of local politics. Such control was not, however, expressed in terms of dominance but in terms of 'service' to the local community and more specifically through an ideology of stewardship with regard to property. That is, just as in the work situation farmers and landowners would prefer to be thought of as 'looking after' their workers, so this was reflected in a similar interpretation of their role in the local community and even with regard to their own property. The ideology of stewardship was constantly used to fend off the threat of industrial intrusion in the countryside, an argument which was highly successful since it corresponded to the preservationist zeal of the other major political grouping in rural areas – the ex-urbanite middle class. As we pointed out in Chapter 6, such preservationist sentiments unfortunately tend to rebound on the economic activities of farmers when their ideology of stewardship is taken at face value; for the changes in farming practice wrought by economic necessity often produce vehement local conflict over the preservation of the rural landscape. It is also interesting to note that farmers typically fend off *these* attacks by resorting to a defence in terms of the ideology of PPA (see p. 216 above).

We have tried to show that, both in the work situation and in the local political context, those with landed property share a coherent repertoire of justificatory ideologies, any of which may be drawn upon when necessary to 'explain' their privileges. In the course of everyday life, however, such ideologies rarely need to be made explicit, for, as we have shown, the privileges are seldom questioned and the domination rarely challenged. When, in response to a perceived threat or challenge, such ideologies are drawn upon, they are generally sufficient to reinforce the legitimacy of the *status quo*. Indeed, having resort to a battery of different justifications – individualistic, collectivistic, altruistic, as well as purely capitalistic – farmers and landowners have more than one explanation available. Moreover, as we have demonstrated on several occasions, the definitions of reality which they put forward are all too often not only the dominant ones, but more often the only ones.

Indeed the perceived threats to existing property relationships come not so much from the local level, but nationally from politically unsympathetic governments and certain nationally based organizations such as trade unions, consumer groups and the environmental lobby. The major farming organizations, like the NFU and CLA, were formed precisely to counter the threat posed by organizations such as these, though now their role is as much promotional as defensive, as we saw in Chapter 3. The economics of food production have been highly politicized since the passing of the Corn Production Act in 1916, and today the NFU is, whatever the *de jure* technicalities of the situation, involved in continual bargaining with the government of the day in order to direct state intervention in agriculture so as to affect the market for various farm products in a way which it sees as being most beneficial to its members' interests. In certain important respects the 'market' for farm produce has become politically negotiable, first in Whitehall and then in Brussels, just as the market for labour has become nationally negotiable, at least in its major parameters, between the NFU and the NUAAW. In other words, because many of the conditions which determine the rate of agricultural profitability are now determined nationally, so farmers have mobilized themselves – very successfully, it might be added – to defend their interests at the national level.

A similar pattern may be observed regarding the ownership of agricultural land. Since the nineteenth century the private ownership of land has been under sporadic political attack, such ownership having become something of a symbol of social and political privilege. The major attack on private landownership has taken place through the fiscal policies of the state, the most recent (as was indicated in Chapter 3) being the institution of Capital Transfer Tax and Wealth Tax. However, in other respects successive Town and Country Planning Acts have also fettered the freedom of private landowners to do whatever they wish with their own property. Once again these external threats have resulted in a remarkable degree of political mobilization on the part of landowners, the success of which we discussed in Chapter 3. As we indicated in that chapter the CLA's recent attempts to prevent the introduction of Capital Transfer Tax and Wealth Tax were conducted almost entirely in terms of the ideologies of property which we have outlined. This serves to demonstrate that the property relationships which enable a surplus to be extracted at the point of production can only be guaranteed by farmers and landowners engaging in activities which take them far away from their holdings. It is in pursuit of this guarantee that much of the political activity of our respondents can be explained.

Similarly our analysis of rural class relations has taken us far away from the forty-four parishes in East Suffolk in which it began. We are only too aware that our statement on the nature and significance of property relationships, and the ideologies which are associated with them, can only be regarded as a preliminary and undoubtedly inadequate analysis. Nevertheless we intend to pursue this problem further, since it obviously has a much wider relevance than that of farming in East Anglia. Indeed the strength of these ideologies is in the very fact that they are so widespread and so 'obvious' in commonsense terms. To allude to the rhetoric in which these ideologies are frequently expressed, the householder would indeed object to people trampling through his garden and the car-owner would feel aggrieved if the ownership of his car were threatened by fiscal measures. We *do* all claim the right to determine how our personal possessions shall be used. Thus once the premises on which these ideologies are based are accepted (i.e. that all forms of property ownership are essentially the same, or that it is possible to benefit from property without owning it, or to own property without benefiting from it), then the internal logic of the arguments is unassailable. It is in the almost entirely unquestioned nature of these premises that there is reflected an ideology of property which is truly hegemonic. Clearly if we are to understand the sources of stability in the stratification systems of advanced capitalist societies then much more attention will have to be devoted to the institution of property and its ideological supports.

Notes to chapters

Chapter 1: Introduction

1 The following pages represent a highly condensed version of a complex argument which is elaborated more fully in Newby, 1975, 1976.

2 Of course, this is an idealized picture which overstates some points and ignores others to give a view of a 'natural' system of landed social stratification. Caird himself was aware of the faults of the system, and especially the lack of business acumen among landowners, or an appropriate background for administering their estates when compared with those in the highest positions in industry (see Caird, 1878, pp. 102-4).

Chapter 2: Of farming and farmers

1 For those who are not entirely familiar with farming terminology, arable farming refers generally to the growing of cash crops and especially cereals, but also sugar beet and other root crops, potatoes, onions, carrots, beans, peas, etc. Farms of the arable type may simply rotate such crops so as to maintain soil fertility – here, for example, lies the importance of crops like oilseed rape, potatoes and sugar beet which allow the recovery of the land after cereals have been grown on it while being themselves profitable cash crops. For a picture of a typical year's work on an arable farm in East Anglia see Newby (1977).

2 All measurements of size in the classification statistics refer to business size, i.e. are calculated in standard-man-days. In some ways this is a more precise measure of the size of a farm business than acreage of crops and grass. Although one might expect that the larger the acreage of a holding then the larger the business, this is not universally the case. Some enterprises on very small acreages can, in fact, be very large businesses. This is the case, for example, with

intensive livestock holdings. In 1974 there were 1319 holdings in England and Wales of less than 5 acres of crops and grass but with a standard labour requirement of 1200+ smds. A holding with that requirement would be classified by the Ministry of Agriculture as 'large'. At the other extreme there were 558 holdings in excess of 150 acres of crops and grass which had a requirement of less than 275 smds, i.e. were 'part-time holdings'. Because of the greater precision of figures based on standard labour requirement we should ideally have drawn our samples on this basis, but this proved impossible (see Appendix I).

3   These statistics are of relatively recent origin. As the Ministry's statistical handling techniques have improved so these statistics have become more detailed. This means, however, that we cannot provide a complete range of statistics down to 1945.

4   Interestingly, this fact is also more pronounced in the east than nationally (with the exception of Suffolk). It is particularly the case in Cambridgeshire where it is almost certainly due to Fen farming patterns, but it is also true of Essex and Norfolk. There are historical reasons why this should be the case. Land tenure patterns have persisted so that, for example, Norfolk has long had more than average numbers of both very large and very small holdings; equally Suffolk has been unusual compared with the other three counties in respect of land tenure and size of holdings (see below, Chapter 3). However, it is also undoubtedly the case that a holding of about 50 acres in one of the eastern counties is a very different proposition economically from 50 acres of hill land in Wales. With the exception of the Brecklands of South Norfolk, North Suffolk, soil types are generally good in the east and a 50-acre holding is more likely to be a full-time one. We would therefore expect that, even though there are a more than average number of holdings of less than 50 acres in three of the eastern counties, there would be fewer than average part-time holdings. This is in fact the case, as we see below.

5   The smaller average size in Cambridgeshire is largely a reflection of farming activity in the Fens, especially the Isle of Ely, where an extremely fertile soil allows high production and yields on relatively small pieces of land. When we examine the overall distribution of full-time to part-time holdings we again find Cambridgeshire contains rather fewer full-time holdings than the norm for the eastern counties. While 61 per cent of holdings in Essex and 60 per cent in Norfolk are full-time, the figure for Cambridgeshire is 56 per cent.

Suffolk, which has a higher average holding size, also has a higher proportion of full-time holdings at 68 per cent.

6   Newby has described this in more detail in an article entitled 'In the Field: Reflections on the Study of Suffolk Farm Workers', in Bell and Newby (1977).

7   The later sample was unproblematic but the forty-four parishes sample had to be divested of all part-time holdings. In this way an original sample of 202 holdings was reduced to 96. Details of the final samples, and response rates, are given below:

Sample	Number	Respondents	Response rate %
1000+ acres	155	105	67·7
44 parishes	96	57	59·4
HN	48*	40	83·3
Total	299	198†	66·2

* The rest of Newby's original sample was drawn in the random forty-four parishes sample and later added back into the HN sample for analysis. See text.

† There was some overlap between the samples and so the figures in this column equate with the number of interviews conducted, i.e. 198. See text.

A word is necessary here on the way in which we analysed our data and the overlap between samples. The 1000+ acres sample had one respondent in common with the forty-four parishes sample and so data for this interview were analysed for both samples. In addition three respondents were common to all three samples and the same procedure was followed.

In the case of the HN sample, as originally constituted (N=48 – see above), it was simply those of Newby's original sample who did not appear in the random forty-four parishes sample. In analysis, of course, it had to be reconstituted in its original form (N=71 minus non-respondents). In the end we had fourteen respondents who were interviewed in the forty-four parishes sample and who had also been part of Newby's original sample. These had to be added to the forty interviewed as part of the HN sample. Consequently from a total of 198 respondents we obtained 216 data records, viz.:

(1) 1000+ acres sample (N=105)
(2) 44 parishes sample (N=57)   } (N=216)
(3) HN   (N=40+14=54)
(4) Total interviewed   (N=198)

Our total overlap is, therefore, 216 − 198 = 18 and it is made up of the four respondents who were common to the samples discussed above and the fourteen of Newby's original sample who were included in the forty-four parishes sample. For the most part, however, we will be concerned with the two random samples – the 1000 + acres and the forty-four parishes – and data will be presented in tables for each of these samples. We have described our experiences in handling this methodology in Newby *et al.* (1975).

8   Taken together the cumulative effects of educational experience seemed to have a practical effect upon our research. The generally better-educated and, perhaps, more sophisticated respondents in the 1000 + acres sample were more ready to accept the researchers and their project at face value; they were less suspicious of our motives and undoubtedly regarded us as people essentially like themselves and who could therefore communicate their view of the world and the realities of large-scale farming to a wider, non-agricultural audience. Of course, these comments would apply with equal force to some of those in the forty-four parishes sample, but there was here a greater reluctance to answer some of our questions and generally less of an acceptance that the kind of research we were undertaking was worthwhile. See Newby *et al.* (1975).

9   Of the ninety-three wives of respondents for whom we have details in the 1000 + acres sample, twenty-six, or 28 per cent, had had some kind of employment since marriage. In several cases this did not take them out of the home since they were employed as a secretary of the family farming company, but three wives had their own businesses unconnected with the family farm. Altogether twenty-one of the twenty-six worked full-time and exclusively in non-manual occupations, ranging from secretaries to doctors. In the forty-four parishes sample twelve of the wives had been employed since marriage, eight of them in full-time jobs. These included three employers in their own right, seven intermediate or junior non-manual and two unskilled workers.

Chapter 3: Market situations

1   We do not represent the marketing options so far discussed as the *only* ones open to the farmer. They are, rather, basic strategies. It is quite possible for farmers deliberately to aim for premium prices, for example, by growing high quality crops which command a better price, or by growing crops for seed, and so on. Equally, mar-

keting varies considerably according to the type of produce under consideration.

2   In itself the fact that there has been no recent survey of land-ownership is interesting. Consequently a great deal of intelligent guesswork is necessary whenever landownership is discussed. The last complete survey of landownership in Britain was made in the 1870s (see Chapter 1) and there is some opposition by landowners to any idea that a survey should be undertaken today. Consequently even the Country Landowners' Association, when discussing the issue of landownership, is operating in the dark. For example, the following quotation is taken from a recent CLA discussion paper by a working party on landownership:

The Working Party discussed whether a comprehensive survey of the existing structure of landownership carried out by M.A.F.F. would be of assistance. After consultation it was decided that a survey by the Govern-ment would not assist the Working Party. . . . However, in the absence of reliable information on ownership of land but in the light of comprehensive statistics on land occupation it has been possible to make various com-ments. [See The Country Landowners' Association, 'The Future of Land-ownership – A CLA Discussion Paper', February 1976, para. 8, p. 2.]

This quotation is, we feel, somewhat tongue-in-cheek. Apart from the fact that land occupation statistics are somewhat dubious (see Rose *et al.*, 1977) sources in the Ministry of Agriculture and the CLA independently informed us of the CLA's reluctance to have an official investigation of landownership carried out by the Ministry.

It should be emphasized that this chapter is based upon events and information up until the autumn of 1976. However, it is worth mentioning that in 1977 the Minister agreed to set up a Committee of Inquiry into landownership under Lord Northfield. This was pre-cipitated by increasing concern over foreign and institutional interest in land purchases, but how wide-ranging this inquiry will turn out to be, and whether it will lead to the gathering of comprehensive details of landownership in Britain, remains to be seen at the time of writing.

3   Clery (1975, p. 46) estimates the figure for city institutions to be 400000 acres. The figure given by Gibbs and Harrison is for the UK rather than England and Wales. Our impression is that Clery's figure is an overestimate but that Gibbs' and Harrison's estimate is certainly now an underestimate. City ownership of land will be discussed in more detail later in this chapter. It is, perhaps, worth pointing out that the top ten landowners in Britain include only one

private individual, the rest being institutional and ranging from the Scottish Department to the Church Commissioners (see *Sunday Times*, 2 February 1975, p. 11).

4   While only 56 per cent of land is classified as owner-occupied, it is nevertheless the case that some of the traditional private land-owners, possibly a majority of them, farm some of their land and equally some of the land owned by financial institutions is farmed by the owners. Moreover some land which appears as rented in official statistics is in fact owned. On this last point see Rose *et al.* (1977) and below.

5   Statistics on land prices are not without their problems. Several sets of statistics are produced from various sources, including the Ministry of Agriculture, and all have their advantages and dis-advantages. For a short discussion of land price statistics see *Farmland Market*, No. 6, July 1976, p. 17. Because the figures produced by *Farmland Market* are based on auction sales, and therefore reflect the open market in land more closely, we shall largely use these figures, wherever possible, in our analysis of recent trends in the market.

6   The National Farmers' Union made its own analysis of factors influencing land prices. See Appendix A of the NFU's written sub-mission to the Select Committee on the Wealth Tax, *Final Report*, (HMSO, London, 1976), vol. III, p. 934.

7   The reference to roll-over money relates to the influence of governmental action upon the land market. During the course of the 1970–4 Conservative government, the Chancellor of the Exchequer, Anthony Barber, was persuaded to allow landowners who sold land at development prices to avoid the resulting Capital Gains Tax provided that the money thereby made was reinvested in agriculture within a three-year period. Hence a number of farmers and land-owners found that their windfall gains had to be quickly reinvested and they did not always care how much they paid for land when it meant avoiding CGT. Equally the bizarre 'death bed' arrangements were made by wealthy people who, by purchasing farmland with their liquid assets, could claim the 45 per cent agricultural abatement under the terms of estate duty. Perfectly legal transactions by farming and non-farming individuals had as important an effect on the land market as anything the City institutions did, yet it was the institu-tions who were seen as the villains in the land market by most farmers, especially as they are not subject to CTT or Wealth Tax.

In an article in *Farmers' Weekly* it was reported that: 'On the land which agriculture loses to development, the capital gains tax roll-over relief and estate duty concessions have left £1000 million each year urgently seeking land.' See Alasdair MacGregor, 'This inflated isle . . . ', *Farmers' Weekly*, 28 December 1973, p. 46. MacGregor observes that if farmland is sold for £10 000 an acre for development and the farmer is prepared to pay £1000 per acre for more land to avoid CGT, then the 50 000 acres lost to development represents 500 000 acres required by farmers who have sold development land each year. 'An area the size of the Isle of Wight is being sold; the money is trying to buy an area almost as big as Hampshire' (ibid., p. 46). If this is the case, then farmers themselves must largely be responsible for land price fluctuations for it is a rare year when 500 000 acres of land appears on the market for sale. However, only one week later, the NFU's fortnightly journal, *British Farmer and Stockbreeder*, commenting on a report by the NFU's land prices panel, stated: 'The panel's conclusions, however, fairly reflect the general farming opinion by viewing with concern the number of investment syndicates and similar bodies investing in agricultural land, although the effect of these activities on future farm structure in this country is likely to be greater than their influence on land prices, in the panel's view' (*British Farmer and Stockbreeder*, 5 January 1974, p. 7). The above comment again indicates the general concern about ownership, i.e. 'farm structure'.

The CLA's land price survey, based on figures collected from 150 chartered surveyors in all parts of England and Wales, shows that of reported sales of over a quarter of a million acres since January 1973 about 18·4 per cent was purchased by institutions (see *Farmland Market*, nos. 3–6, 1975 and 1976, CLA Table 4). But the CLA's figures may not be representative. Indeed at the height of the land price boom in late 1973 when the CLA reported that over one-third of all land purchases were accounted for by City institutions, a report for *Farmers' Weekly* had this to say:

. . . over the whole country there is certainly no strong evidence that City money is going into anything like this proportion of total acreage sold.

It follows from this, and from the fact that outside investors are largely interested only in tenanted land, that their influence on prices has not been great. The spectacular increases have occurred in the value of land with vacant possession. Here the biggest culprits have been farmers with roll-over money to spend, death-duty purchasers and the odd speculator. [Campbell, 1973, pp. 68–9.]

We shall return briefly to the subject of taxation – especially CTT

360 Notes to pages 85-7

and Wealth Tax – when we consider the NFU and CLA as pressure groups and their campaign to have the Labour government's taxation proposals modified. Accounts of the impact of CTT on agriculture can be found in *Farmland Market*, nos. 2–6, and in Harrison (ed., 1976).

8 For similar comments see Sir Michael Culme-Seymour's reported statements in *Farmers' Weekly*, 27 December 1974, p. 40; the Foreword to the *Report of the Working Party on Business Organisation in Agriculture*, Country Landowners' Association (London, 1974), p. 1; Lord Davidson's evidence for the CLA in the Select Committee on the Wealth Tax, *Final Report* (HMSO, London, 1976), vol. III, pp. 781–2; and the submission of the NFU, ibid., p. 930.

The similarity of these comments, not only with one another, but with those of our respondents, is quite striking.

9 For example the following exchange is taken from the evidence given by the CLA to the Select Committee (op. cit., p. 783):

Q. May I ask you . . . have you an idea of the number of farmers plus landowners that would come within the scope of this [wealth] tax?

A. . . . The calculations are around about 30000 occupiers would come within the scope.

Q. You say 30000 . . . I believe the Inland Revenue puts 100000 as being the top number of people within the country that will come within the scope, and the farming community, I assume is about one per cent, or at the most 2 per cent of the total population of this country.

Chairman It just confirms the town people's belief that all the wealthy people live out in the country.

Q. Well, that might be so.

A. I do not think that any of us would describe it as wealth. I think we should describe it as capital invested on which we have to make a living . . . 80 per cent of capital is invested in illiquid assets which have been recently inflated out of all proportion to their productive value [i.e. land].

10 Similar sentiments can be found in the evidence of the CLA and NFU to the Select Committee on the Wealth Tax. See ibid., pp. 765–87 and 927–69.

11 Two of the most feared institutions are Property Growth Assurance and Fountain Farming. For details of PGA see: David Campbell, 'The New Landlords', *Farmers' Weekly*, 9 November 1973, pp. 68–75; 'We're Not a Bunch of City Tycoons', *Farmers'*

Weekly, 25 May 1973, p. 63; 'Institutions Return as Land Prices Rise', *Farmers' Weekly*, 22 August 1975, p. 51; 'A Stake in Land at £10 a Month', *Farmers' Weekly*, 5 April 1974, p. 55; 'City Land Buyer Back in Market', *Farmers' Weekly*, 13 August 1976, p. 51; Lorana Sullivan, 'Why the City is Going Back to the Farm', *Sunday Times*, 2 May 1976, p. 54; Peter Wormell, 'The Landlord in the Bowler', *Big Farm Management*, August 1974, pp. 50–3; P. Hutley, quoted in the *Essex County Standard*, 27 April 1973.

And on Fountain Farming see: Anthony Rosen, 'Increased Land Prices – Their Implications on the Future Structure of Agriculture', unpublished paper presented to the Rank Hovis McDougall Hampshire Harvest Review, 6 November 1973; Anthony Rosen, 'Who Will Own Britain', *Farmland Market*, No. 3, January 1975, pp. 9–11; David Campbell, op. cit., 1973; P. Wormell, op. cit., 1974.

12 Under the provisions of the old Estate Duty, anyone who gave his estate away and then survived for seven years could thereby enable his heirs to evade the tax entirely. If he did die in the interim, the rate of tax depended on how long he had survived after the transfer. Rosen (1973, p. 2) has made the following comments:

However, it is not, fortunately, my brief to explain to those poor millionaires, the owner-occupiers, how they should so arrange their affairs to enable the traditional nepotism of owner-occupation to continue unabated. . . . Suffice to say that Estate Duty is still a voluntary tax and there are only four reasons for paying it –
1. If you believe the Government can spend your money better than you can.
2. A bad accountant.
3. A sudden early demise.
4. If you do not trust your relatives.

13 The CLA in particular has publicized its views with great energy. While accepting that agriculture must bear its share of capital taxation 'to exact a high tax rate on functional capital, or money tied up in a business [can] only do grave harm to the business and the national economy' (Barker, 1976, p. 47). CLA investment surveys show cut-backs on large estates because of the threat of capital taxation and the need to build up reserves to pay taxes. After the recent purchase by British Airways Pension Fund of a 1500-acre estate for £2 million, a disgruntled owner-occupier wrote to *Farmers' Weekly* with a typical lament about pension funds not being subject to CTT and so being the likely future owners of the land – but owners who

will contribute nothing to rural society (*Farmers' Weekly*, 7 May 1976, pp. 39–40).

But the fact remains that with land yielding a steady 5 to 6 per cent gross per annum, institutions regard it as a good long-term investment, especially as rents are keeping pace with inflation. A recent article in the *Sunday Times* concluded:

The financial institutions' agricultural holdings seem destined to increase in coming years. For the past year or so, few top quality farms have come on the market because of indecision caused by legislation. . . . But, as Britain's various taxes on accumulated wealth start to bite, the only British investors who will be able to buy the country's large, good and efficient farms will be the institutions. Small wonder that many are aiming to make farmland as much as 15 % of their property portfolios and that their managers are learning more about farming by doing it themselves. [Sullivan, *Sunday Times*, 2 May 1976, p. 54.]

14   East Anglia covers not only Essex, Suffolk, Norfolk and Cambridgeshire but Bedfordshire, Hertfordshire and Holland (Lincolnshire). This survey must have one of the most unusual opening sentences of any study to come out of Cambridge University:

Ownership of one kind or another is perhaps the most common of human aspirations. A feeling of substance induced by sufficient acres is enjoyed by the traditional landowner, and it is also good to realise how dear to the heart of man is his own small plot, which, like Naboth's vineyard, becomes part of his life and is therefore invaluable. The morale of landownership, however, is not the aim of this study. [University of Cambridge, 1947, p. 4.]

15   The figures quoted are taken from the Appendix of the Cambridge study (University of Cambridge, 1947, pp. 28–32). We have amalgamated East with West Suffolk, and Cambridgeshire with the Soke of Peterborough to allow comparison with the present situation.

16   We have discussed this issue in greater detail elsewhere (Rose *et al.*, 1977) and so we shall repeat only the central arguments here.

17   We have not included Essex in this analysis since our sample was taken from only part of the county. However, it is interesting to note that *de facto* ownership among our Essex sample was 97 per cent. This compares with the figure of 63·6 per cent in the official statistics for the whole country (see Table 26). It should be noted that the figures on which Tables 27 and 28 are based are recalculations of similar statistics which originally appeared in Rose *et al.*, 1977.

18   Certain comments need to be made on these tables. In the case of Table 27 the *de jure* figures for our sample in Cambridgeshire and Norfolk appear to under-represent holdings in the wholly owned category and over-represent those in the 'over 50 per cent' rented category. This distortion is particularly great for Cambridgeshire and may well be due to the fact that the average size of holdings in our sample for that county was almost 1000 acres more than the average for all holdings of over 1000 acres. Table 28 produces a similar result in terms of owned and rented land in Cambridgeshire, i.e. an under-representation of owned land. However, here we also encounter the same problem for Suffolk, presumably due to the fact, as Table 25 would indicate, that we had in that sample five large over 50 per cent rented holdings *de jure* and *de facto*. But whatever the problems of our sample the difference between the figures on a *de jure* as against *de facto* basis is remarkable.

We have been careful to contact respondents to check the accuracy of our figures and they have confirmed our argument. As holdings become larger and companies and trusts are formed, land tenure arrangements become more complex and the Ministry statistics become a fiction. Unfortunately we can only draw a meaningful comparison between farms in our sample and Ministry statistics for holdings of over 1000 acres since our sample of 1000+ acres farms was a 1 in 2 random one based on MAFF lists. The forty-four parishes is an area where owner-occupation is relatively high even according to the official statistics which we were able to examine at parish level.

19   Harrison records similar observations in a recent publication and notes that he had anticipated this problem since there were: ' . . . advantages which accrued in the past under the old Estate Duty legislation, from having estates valued on a subject-to-tenancy basis, as distinct from the much higher assessments of those valued on an owner-occupier basis' (Harrison, 1975, p. 33). It was certainly the case in our experience that the complex land tenure arrangements to be found on large holdings were basically designed to avoid a greater tax burden, especially, as Harrison notes, Estate Duty.

For the distinction between conceptual and technical instruments in the production of official statistics see Hindess (1973). We have discussed here only the conceptual weaknesses of land tenure statistics; the technical weaknesses are analysed in Rose *et al.*, 1977.

20   Of course some of the land which is owned is subject to mortgage, but for both samples two-thirds of respondents were

outright owners of their land. In the 1000 + acres sample 12 per cent, and in the forty-four parishes 25 per cent, had land which was wholly or mainly mortgaged – in most cases through the Agricultural Mortgage Corporation. Given the high rates of capital inheritance (see Table 11 above) it is hardly surprising that few farmers have had to borrow capital to buy land.

21   For example Nix maintains that a farmer buying land in the late 1960s could afford to borrow up to 50 per cent of the purchase price, whereas today he could not service a loan of more than 25 per cent of purchase price. See John Nix, 'The Economic Value of Agricultural Land', *Farmland Market*, no. 5, January 1976, pp. 16–19. However, Nix also acknowledges that a farmer already owning a considerable amount of land can borrow more since he can spread the cost of the borrowing.

22   The CLA is primarily concerned with matters of landownership and especially taxation as it affects landowners. It therefore tends to put most of its bargaining efforts into negotiations with the Treasury.

23   Indeed it seems sometimes that the NFU is so used to special treatment from governments that when its arguments fall on deaf ears they become quite offended. For example, the following appeared in the *East Anglian Daily Times* on 30 November 1973: 'Farmers' pleas to the Government to expand agriculture are being treated as if they were pay challenges from mineworkers or railwaymen, the director-general of the National Farms' Union . . . said last night. . . . In backing the farmers to invest more in food production, the Government would not be giving way to the demands of another pressure group.'

24   Cf. the data presented by Wilson (1978).

25   The history of the CLA and its changing role are discussed in Self and Storing, 1962, Chapter 8.

26   The information in this and the following three paragraphs is based largely on A. Hunt, 'Agriculture and the Market', in Edwards and Rogers (eds., 1974).

27   For a detailed account of the operation and history of marketing boards see Giddings (1974).

28   After which consideration we decided to ask a very general initial question on marketing which we found, by trial and error in piloting, to act as the most reliable producer of the information we required. The question was 'How sensitive are you to changes in the market for various farming products?' and we followed this with a

question concerning any innovations made by the farmer in the management or husbandry of his farm.

The problem with the initial question was, it was always realized, how to systematize for analytical purposes the variety of answers we received. In the end the interviewer, on the basis of his observations and overall perceptions of each respondent, coded market sensitivity as being one of four possible categories: (1) Very high (2) Quite high (3) Quite low (4) Very low. We are almost tempted to put an exclamation mark here. Obviously these were highly subjective categories but they were based on such things as the overall impression gained from the total interview; our direct observations – for example market charts on the wall of the office filled out each day; marketing information piled on a respondent's desk and so on; the kind of capital investment programmes, if any, undertaken by the farmer; willingness to try out new crops and new varieties, e.g. oilseed rape, Maris Huntsman wheat; and general evidence of the diligence of the farmer in trying to find the most profitable outlet for his produce or to farm the most profitable crops, e.g. wheat for seed to obtain a premium price.

29   For a case study of such an operation see Anthony Collins, 'Contract growing for the big food chains', *Big Farm Management*, November 1974, pp. 63–7. See also the three articles on marketing by David Chance, 'Focus on wheat marketing', 'Juggling is not marketing' and 'Planning our marketing' in *Big Farm Management*, November 1975, pp. 1–3, December 1975, pp. 85–6, and January 1976, pp. 103–5.

Chapter 4: The work situation

1   A more precise comparison is offered by the replies given to the question by those farmers who were the employers of the workers interviewed by Newby, i.e. the HN sample. Among these 37·0 per cent had thought of leaving farming and 25·5 per cent would choose a different occupation if they had their lives over again.

2   Hence among the HN sample it was believed that specialized workers could only be hired 'with great difficulty' by 42·3 per cent of the farmers interviewed, compared with only 11·3 per cent believing that general workers were equally difficult to find. See Newby, 1977, p. 164.

3   In this chapter we are concerned only with those values and beliefs which pertain to the work situation itself. Clearly these are

underpinned by much wider social values – most notably an almost complete hegemony of the ideology of private property – which we shall explore further in Chapters 7 and 8.

4   We in fact coded the replies to this question. Among the 1000+ acres sample, 68·0 per cent felt that relations had changed, and of this 68·0 per cent, 89·5 per cent felt that they had improved. Thus overall less than 10 per cent felt that labour relations had deteriorated. Among the forty-four parishes sample, 65·8 per cent felt they had changed, 94·7 per cent of whom believed they had improved; in the HN sample, 66·7 per cent regarded them as having changed, of whom 87·0 per cent thought they had improved.

5   Two levels of hierarchy indicate that the enterprise consists solely of a farmer and his workers; three levels implies an intermediary – e.g. farmer–manager–worker; four levels implies two intermediaries – e.g. farmer–manager–foreman–worker; and so on.

6   In an earlier paper (Bell and Newby, 1974) this cell was labelled 'hobby farmer'. While gentleman farmers do indeed tend to treat their farming activities as something akin to a hobby – e.g. the emphasis on sport and the primacy of maintaining a distinctive lifestyle – the use of the term 'hobby' implies a part-time activity. Our respondents were not all full-time farmers so that the use of the term 'hobby' here we do not regard as inappropriate. However, it should be apparent that our typology applies only to full-time farmers and that clearly other variables would need to be incorporated if it were to be extended to part-time farmers in addition. (On the latter, see Gasson, 1966c.)

7   Because of their hostility to any form of abstract activity and their extreme devotion to practical, manual labour we suspect that they may be over-represented in our refusal rate. Active managerials tend not only to be 'busy', but hostile to any activity not obviously and demonstrably connected with agricultural husbandry including answering a lot of questions from inquiring academics.

8   In order not to contaminate the data with information obtained about farm *managers*, these have been eliminated from the analysis, together with all part-time farmers.

Chapter 5: Status situation and the local community

1   Not surprisingly, there was a strong association between a farmer's self-conception as a squire and his disposition towards involvement in local affairs. Thus, 94 per cent of those who described

themselves as squires (compared with 52 per cent of those who did not) held at least one position of responsibility locally. It is also worth noting, in the light of our discussion in Chapter 3 of the historical pattern of landownership in the region, that all of those who claimed to be squires resided in the two most easterly counties – Norfolk and Suffolk – where the traditions of the great estates have always been strongest, and where the decline of landed influence and wealth has probably proceeded most slowly.

2   Farmers employing no hired workers have been excluded. The questions from which these data were computed were slightly different. We asked our respondents, 'How involved do you feel in the life of your employees outside the course of work?' and coded the replies according to the categories given in this table. Later we asked, 'Would you say that your wife felt equally involved? For example, does she: (1) Visit the wife of a worker who is ill, or who has just had a baby? (2) Give occasional presents to employees' children at Christmas or on birthdays? (3) Help out in the home of an employee who has some kind of domestic crisis?' We have coded an affirmative reply to all three questions as 'very involved' and a negative reply to all three as 'not at all involved'. We have coded affirmative replies to either (1) and/or (3) or (2) and/or (3) as 'quite involved' and to (1) and/or (2) only as 'not much involved'.

3   We were particularly interested whether they were farmers or not and so collected more specific data when the friends they nominated were farmers. Not all farmers actually nominated four friends – and in the analysis that follows we have 'summed' the friends, i.e. we are describing a universe that equals $n \times$ number of friends nominated and further, it should be noted that it was not always possible to collect full information for all or any of the friends so nominated.

Chapter 6: The rural power structure

1   Under the 1888 Act (despite pressure from the Justices in the east of the county) Suffolk was divided into two administrative counties – East and West. According to Whitfield (1970), this represented a considerable victory for the Hervey family who succeeded in gaining this concession when the Bill went to the Lords. Ipswich, meanwhile, became an independent county borough. The forty-four parishes selected for our study of farmers (see Chapter 2) were situated entirely in East Suffolk.

2   Questionnaires asking for information on sex, age, occupation, education, length of residence, party affiliation (if any), positions of responsibility within the council (e.g. committee chairmanships), and affiliation to other statutory or voluntary organizations in the region, were sent in batches to the clerks of all county, rural district, urban district and borough councils in Norfolk, Suffolk, Cambridgeshire and non-metropolitan Essex. Clerks were requested to distribute them among their members, and then to collect and return all those which were completed. Six clerks refused to cooperate with our request, while a further nine failed to respond in any way, despite further requests. This left us with an eventual sample of eighty-three authorities – five counties, fifteen boroughs, twenty-seven urban districts and thirty-six rural districts. The response rate from these different authorities varied widely on a range between 3 and 100 per cent, the mean response rate by type of council being: county, 55 per cent; urban district, 49 per cent; rural district 39 per cent; borough 37 per cent. A total of 1124 council members responded to the survey. Obviously such relatively low response rates pose problems for the reliability of the survey's findings, although where the characteristics of the respondents could be compared with those of the total sample, there appeared to be no significant bias generated by disproportionate responses. For example, 80 per cent of our respondents were male and this accorded with the sex distribution of the total sample. In addition, in five 'control' authorities where the occupational character of the total memberships was already known, there does not appear to have been any systematic bias in the types of members responding to the survey. In relation to the proportion of farmers replying, for example, farmers were over-represented relative to their numbers in two cases (by margins of 11 per cent and 14 per cent), under-represented in one (by a margin of 17 per cent), and were proportionately represented among respondents in the other two.

3   It is perhaps worth speculating whether the over-representation of farmers in such positions is a reflection of their occupational status, or of some intervening variable(s) co-varying with this status. For example, there is a strong correlation in many local authorities in this country between occupancy of leading positions and factors such as sex, age, length of residence, length of service, and type of school attended. But in our survey farmers were themselves found to be disproportionately male, old, traditional residents, long-servers, and the products of a public-school education. However even when

we controlled for the effects of these factors, farmers were still found to be over-represented among council and committee chairmen to a significant degree. Thus, not only were farmers found to hold many key positions in East Anglian local authorities, but it also appears that they did so in large part because they were farmers. The occupation of farmer would thus seem to serve as a positive factor in attaining potentially powerful positions within local authorities. As we shall see, this still appears the case even after the 1974 reorganization.

It should also be noted that there was a tendency for larger farmers to hold more chairmanships relative to their numbers than smaller farmers. Taking employed labour force as the criterion of size, we found that while 73 per cent of farmers on local authorities employed some labour, 78 per cent of those who held chairmanships did so.

4 Of the five Suffolk MPs elected at the October 1974 election, only one (the Labour Member for Ipswich, Ken Weetch) has, or has had, no agricultural interest. Of the others, Sir Harwood Harrison at Eye is joint-owner of a 350-acre farm in Northamptonshire, and previously farmed 650 acres in Essex; Eldon Griffiths at Bury St Edmunds used to farm a 500-strong pig unit in Sussex; Keith Stainton at Sudbury and Woodbridge is chairman and managing director of Burton, Son, and Sanders Ltd, a food manufacturing and distributing company; and James Prior, MP for Lowestoft, farms 370 acres in Suffolk and is former Minister of Agriculture in the 1970–4 Conservative government (Roth, 1975). In the case of the Eye constituency (which covers the area of Suffolk around the forty-four parishes), a new candidate with no agricultural connections (John Selwyn Gummer) has somewhat surprisingly been selected to replace Sir Harwood Harrison, who is due to retire at the end of the current parliament. This may to some extent reflect a decline in the strength of farmers in the constituency party, and a corresponding increase in the significance of professionals and others, many of whom may be urban immigrants. As a party officer, himself a farmer, mused when discussing the candidature, 'I always thought we wanted a farmer to represent this constituency – it seems a natural thing. . . . But rural constituencies are beginning to realize that if they're going to have a voice, they must have a professional MP.' However, the significance of newcomers in the constituency Conservative parties, while increasing, has by no means eclipsed that of local farmers and landowners, and an extraordinarily high proportion of the farming population continues to belong to and participate in the party. No fewer

than 111 of our 198 farmer respondents, for example, were Conservative Party members, and 16 per cent of these held formal party office. We shall consider the political beliefs and commitments of our respondents in more detail in the next chapter.

We should also note, this time with regard to farmers on parish councils, that although smaller farmers are found at this level of local government, they are rarely found at higher levels. In our survey, 41 per cent of those who employed no labour and 37 per cent of those with less than 150 acres, sat on parish councils, but at district level these figures fell to 0 and 2 per cent, while none of the smaller farmers had county council seats. Among those employing at least one man or occupying at least 150 acres, on the other hand, 18 per cent of both had served on district councils, and 9 and 8 per cent respectively on county councils. Indeed, although we do not have adequate statistical evidence to back up our assertion, we would argue that there are also significant differences in the type of farmer found at district and county levels. That is, farmers on county councils, though not necessarily larger than those on the districts (79 per cent of farmers at county level were found to employ labour, compared with 75 per cent at district level), tend to be more traditional high-status landowners, while those on the districts are more entrepreneurial and expansionist working farmers or agribusinessmen. As one county councillor and landowner put it, those on the county councils 'are more upper-class, wouldn't you say? . . . Wealthy people with a good education and a broad vision.' This distinction is, as we shall see, of considerable significance. Suffice it to say here, however, that our data generally confirm Bracey's observation that farmers who become involved in local government are usually 'well-to-do' (Bracey, 1959), although our farmers' willingness to participate in parish affairs is, it seems, somewhat unusual (see Bracey, 1959, p. 44).

5   This assumption of equivalence between the self-interest of the landowner and the public interest, coupled with the obvious contempt with which landowners often regard a supposedly ignorant urban populace, is neatly revealed in a speech made at a 1958 Council for the Preservation of Rural England meeting by Sir Clough Williams Ellis, and approvingly repeated in a recent Suffolk Preservation Society newsletter (Winter 1973–4, no. 7, p. 8):

We have to face it that we are and ever shall be a minority movement, there can be no dictating or attempted bossing around, only steadfast pressure on our fellows and those who govern us in what we deem the right direction. We must without false modesty accept this responsibility for we *do* know more than most because we care more, and have therefore thought, read, discussed, seen, and understood more, which is the answer to those neutrals who shrug off any responsibility for what happens and say, 'It's just a matter of taste'.

Thus, there is no cause for debate on the pros and cons of conservation, and those who believe otherwise merely reveal their ignorance of the issue. It is the *duty* of those who 'realize' this to ensure that their views are accepted by planners and other governmental agencies. Little wonder, then, that Eversley describes the environmental movement in this country as 'élitist', and dismisses its leaders as 'self-appointed arbiters of taste'.

6   At this time, of course, the town of Ipswich was not administratively part of East Suffolk, although much of the southern part of the county lay within its commuter belt. Central and northern Suffolk, however, lay out of reach of Ipswich for most people, and while a number of former East Suffolk councillors have told us that the reason the county council did not enter into an overspill agreement with London was that it already had sufficient employment facilities at Ipswich, this cannot fully explain why schemes were not developed in the more northerly towns. We would argue, of course, that the problem to be explained is not so much why East Suffolk did not enter overspill agreements, as why West Suffolk did. Both authorities, after all, were to a large extent dominated by conservationist landowners. We are still not entirely certain as to why this difference in policy occurred, but there do seem to have been at least two major reasons.

The first was that the members in West Suffolk, recognizing that they had even less industry than East Suffolk, anticipated some degree of compulsion from central government if they did not agree to some overspill development:

West Suffolk had to decide whether to assist the government by taking overspill, or whether to resist. As we were nearer to London than either East Suffolk or Norfolk, we felt it would be imposed upon us if we didn't negotiate a scheme. East Suffolk, on the other hand, reckoned that they were less likely to have a scheme imposed upon them because they were further from London. West Suffolk was almost too underpopulated. [ex-West Suffolk committee chairman and large landowner.]

The two County Councils took diametrically opposed views of how to help London and find jobs in Suffolk for future generations. We believed in controlled expansion where we wanted it, rather than having the government force it on us. [ex-West Suffolk committee chairman and large landowner.]

The second major factor concerned the relative strength of the council officers in the old East and West authorities. In West Suffolk the officers – and especially the Chief Planning Officer – were strong, relatively progressive, and determined, while in East Suffolk they were somewhat weaker and more conservative:

West Suffolk, before the overspill agreement, was ruled more by the gentry than even East Suffolk was. Yet West Suffolk went in for London overspill. The only reason that I can think of is a difference in the outlook of the officers. . . . We had a planning officer who was very much in favour of retaining the olde worlde charm and over the last decade, councillors and officers have wanted to preserve the rural character. [ex-East Suffolk Labour member.]

In West, you had X, and he got through all the development at Haverhill, Mildenhall, and elsewhere. He dominated the planning committee. . . . But in East, we've always had rather weak and subdued Chief Planning Officers, and what with the Lords and Sirs and whatnot on the planning committee, the committee has effectively controlled planning. Consequently, there's been virtually no development at all in East Suffolk, because they're protecting the landowners' interests. As is so often the case in rural areas, the difference has been due to different personalities. [County council planning official.]

This, of course, raises the question of why West Suffolk appointed stronger officers, and this is a question which we cannot answer. We should, however, note that the strength of the officers in West Suffolk was not confined to issues of planning, for that authority took a number of decisions during the 1960s (notably the introduction of comprehensive schooling and the development of higher public spending on various social services) which East Suffolk did not take, and in many cases these reflected the influence of the officers (as well as a recognition on the part of the members that the new towns to which they had committed themselves needed certain provisions which necessitated higher levels of spending).

Predictably, the differences between East and West were thrown into sharp relief by the 1974 reorganization, notably in relation to attempts to 'equalize' standards of social services provision throughout the new Suffolk area.

7 See the *East Anglian Daily Times*, 3 December 1975. This

particular issue is interesting, not only because it reveals that members are not sufficiently concerned with the environment to spend additional money on it, but also because it points to the significance of the concept of 'political responsibility' (see later). Furthermore, it is apparent in this issue that low expenditure policies remain favoured by most members, even against environmental protection policies. As we shall see, maintenance of a low rate is a fundamental article of faith in Suffolk politics, and this produces a number of adverse consequences for the less privileged sections of the county's population.

8 Housing is almost entirely a district council responsibility, although county council planning policies severely restrict district council autonomy. It is, for example, an obvious hindrance to the construction of local authority houses in rural areas to have to conform with the old East Suffolk policy that 'Only single or semi-detached dwellings would be appropriate and the highest standards of design and materials would be desired' (East Suffolk County Council, *Policy for the Classification of Towns and Villages*, 1973, p. 7) and that, 'It will not be satisfactory simply to pack closely together traditional semi-detached dwellings under the guise of economy in building land' (East Suffolk County Council, *Planning Information Handbook*, 1970, p. 26). Houses built to these specifications are usually privately developed and expensively priced. Furthermore, prior to the 1974 reorganization, the county council operated a classification of settlements scheme which made any new development in rural areas very difficult. A new strategic plan is currently being developed which may prove somewhat more flexible (although, as we shall see, public comment has tended overwhelmingly to endorse a system of rigid restrictions), but until this is completed, the old policy continues to be applied.

9 We would not argue with Parsons's contention that it is erfectly possible for more than one party to a power relationship to benefit from a given exercise of power – his attack on the 'zero-sum' conception of power found in the work of Mills (1956) and others is, in our view, quite justified. As Barry (1965), for example, has shown, a general term such as the public interest may thus be meaningful in some situations, for all may benefit to a greater or lesser extent from certain types of decisions. However, as Giddens (1968) points out, Parsons overemphasizes the extent of consensus in power relationships, and his arguments seem not to admit of the possibility of conflict (even the sight of troops on the streets is, for Parsons, a

'legitimate' exercise in restoring trust in situations of 'power defla-
tion').

As regards the possibility of legitimacy being manipulated by
superordinate groups, we should note two points. First, not only
have pluralist theorists (e.g. Wolfinger, 1971) criticized the notions
of 'mobilization of bias' and 'false consciousness' which such an
argument necessarily implies, but even Bachrach and Baratz have in
their later work suggested that, 'the presumption must be that there
is a consensus on the prevailing allocation of values' where there is
no evidence of a conflict of subjectively recognized goals (1970,
p. 49). This is, of course, an assumption which neither Lukes (1974)
nor ourselves are prepared to make. Secondly, it is worth referring
to Mann's work on working-class consciousness where he argues
that ruling groups in society are generally more likely to develop a
coherent set of ideologies and *Weltanschauungen* with which to
explain and (if necessary) justify their privileged position in the
world, while subordinate groups generally have more ambivalent
world views in which working-class values are intermingled with
those of dominant groups to which they are constantly exposed
(Mann, 1970). If this is the case, then we should expect a locally
oriented rural working class to be even more susceptible to the ideas
and values of local propertied interests than are working-class
groups in more urban occupational communities (Merton, 1957;
Bulmer, 1975), and thus more likely to attribute at least some degree
of legitimacy to the power of those above them (Newby, 1977). We
shall consider this argument more fully in the next chapter.

10   This letter was written in response to a number of comments
made by a fellow Labour councillor and reported in the press a few
days earlier. The theme of these comments had been an attack on the
prevailing idea that party politics had no place in local government,
and a corresponding assertion that Labour councillors should pursue
socialist policies (see the *Suffolk Mercury*, 28 December 1973). In her
letter, however, the councillor quoted here sought to dissociate
herself entirely from these comments: 'Mr L., like anyone else, has
a right to express his opinions, but I wish to make it clear that I have
no desire to be associated with them. . . . I trust that your discerning
readers are capable of drawing their own conclusions about opinions
expressed by Mr L.' This, it should be remembered, was in response
to the comments of a member of her own party! Such a curious
desire to be associated with the 'independents' on the council against
a Labour colleague is, however, by no means unique to this letter-

writer, for Councillor L. was something of a 'folk devil' in Suffolk's local government circles, and many Labour councillors found his full-blooded socialism too embarrassing to identify with. When one subscribes to a consensus ideology, it is uncomfortable to be constantly reminded of political differences. As a result, attempts were made to isolate Councillor L. and others like him: 'In this interview [with the local press] I said one or two things about other members. When I went to the next meeting of the Policy and Resources committee, they all stared at me. We got through the agenda, and they announced a special item – a vote of censure on me from S. [a Conservative]. R. – the chairman of the committee – hadn't even told me this was coming up. . . . Any chairman should have warned me to give me a chance to defend myself, let alone a chairman from my own party.' Similarly in the county council Labour group, the relatively radical group leader from Ipswich elected in 1974 has recently been replaced by the old East Suffolk group leader – a figure on the right of the Party, and a firm believer in consensus politics at the local level. This change can only be indicative of a growing accommodation of the county Labour group to the 'keep politics out of local government' ethic.

11   At times we found such arguments hardly credible. One Conservative member, for example, living in a residentially exclusive, low density area, in a house standing in 32 acres of ground, told us:

Expenditure has been approved for far fewer houses than are planned, one of the real problems being lack of available land. For instance, we need four acres of land near here but the only available site is not suitable for intensive development. However, I think we could find the land because we've got some council houses with quite large gardens abutting a children's playground. We could take the playground, and some off each of the gardens, and build there.

But the seemingly obvious bias revealed in this statement is never systematically attacked by the Labour group, for agreement is always comforting, and attacks at this level would obviously prove somewhat uncomfortable for all concerned. Thus a potential issue is avoided by the Labour members choosing to attribute credence to policies and statements which at times strain credibility.

12   There is a parallel here with Madgwick's findings in his study of rural politics in Wales where the farming interest was found to be the sole organized (and thus politically articulate) voice – 'No other

class is coherent enough to operate as a group' (1973, p. 156). The situation is not entirely analogous, however, for as we have seen, farmers and landowners in Suffolk constitute only part (albeit a highly significant and powerful part) of a wider property-owning class, other sections of which (e.g. high-status newcomers) have proved themselves equally, if not more, coherent in the pursuit and defence of their interests.

13   In the case of the Ipswich expansion issue, this opposition was successful, while in the case of the reservoir it was not. The Ipswich issue in particular provides a clear example of the community of interest which exists between county councillors and preservation and agricultural groups. Thus a report commissioned by the Department of the Environment strongly favoured development to the west of Ipswich, and this plan was supported by the Ipswich Borough Council. The county council, however, joined with the NFU and CLA in opposing any large-scale development in principle, and in suggesting that if expansion had to come, it should be to the east on poor-quality agricultural land. Their opposition led to the Minister's asking for the original firm of planning consultants to reconsider their earlier proposals. This they did, but in 1967 only reaffirmed their view that development should be to the west. The county council however, remained unconvinced, and commissioned a second report from another firm of planning consultants. This, too, reported favourably on development to the west. Indeed, it concluded that only one factor out of ten considered pointed to an easterly development, and that was the saving in agricultural land (Lichfield and Chapman, 1970). Although the matter was finally resolved in 1969 when the government withdrew its proposals for any development at Ipswich largely as a result of financial strictures and reduced population estimates, this issue demonstrates the degree of significance accorded agricultural landed interests by the county council. This was reaffirmed in interviews with representatives of the farming and environmental organizations in Suffolk who claimed that their task was considerably harder when dealing with outside statutory bodies than it was when dealing with the county council:

We have great battles with the Eastern Road Construction Unit to get early consultation on road building schemes. . . . Certainly, it's the national bodies like the ERCU that we have most trouble with. [CLA official.]

We have ready access to planning officers nowadays, and one man from the county planning department attends all our committee meetings to advise us. . . . We find our greatest problems, however, came from statutory authorities like the CEGB. [Preservation society official.]

14   We should also note here that should fundamental articles of ruling-class policy or ideology be seriously challenged by opposition from within the county, such challenges are likely to be either minimally reported by the local press, or reported in a negative context. There have been some examples of this in recent years in relation to press treatment and coverage of county and district council Labour attacks on various Conservative policies. At the county level, for example, some of the more left-wing Labour members complained bitterly that their attacks on majority group policy were under-reported:

We just don't get reported. Our very moderate Labour group on the County Council has been described as a 'mad minority from Ipswich', 'wild and irresponsible', all because we dare to raise politics. . . . I've got up and spoken on the rates issue time and again, but I don't get two lines of reporting. You can write it out for them [reporters] and they still won't put it in. I recently came out with a long spiel on rates, redundancies, the lot, and I got one line in the *East Anglian*. . . . We need publicity from stirring it in the council. But in the *East Anglian* they write for their readers – the county squires. I've always considered publicity as crucial if we're going to get anywhere.

Now this does not necessarily imply that a conscious and deliberate policy of censorship is being followed by the local press. The point is rather that the *East Anglian Daily Times* group of newspapers enjoys a local monopoly in Suffolk, so that what it considers 'news' and worthy of comment is all that ever comes to be reported. We may not, therefore, disbelieve the local reporter who told us:

It's not a deliberate bias – it's a question of space. There's no intentional political bias on the *East Anglian*. The thing that determines these things is purely the space available. . . . Sometimes interesting things get said in debates, but then I'm told I've only got half a column, so I can only report what was decided, and have to leave out what was said.

But clearly, space is made available for what is considered at editorial level to be important. From a Conservative perspective (and there can be no doubt that the *East Anglian Daily Times* has a right-wing editorial position), Labour opposition in full council meetings may be interpreted as 'histrionics', 'irresponsible' or whatever and therefore unworthy of inclusion. For whatever the reason, however, the lack of publicity accorded to the few opponents of majority group policies who have been outspoken serves to dilute the significance of their attacks. Opposition is clearly futile, if nobody gets to hear it. In this sense, the editorial policy of the local press provides the final piece in the jigsaw of the local political system which we have been putting together in this chapter, for it functions as a failsafe device which ensures that, in the rare event of fundamental opposition being articulated against local ruling-class policies, it will be effectively smothered through lack of reportage.

Chapter 7: Social imagery and class ideology

1   Newby found that farm workers holding graded hierarchy models of society tended to be found in 'paternalistic' rather than 'bureaucratic' farms, and in encapsulated or farm-centred community situations. In both cases, of course, they may be expected to interact more closely and frequently with their employers and thus, it would seem, to be more susceptible to the latter's values, ideologies, and situational definitions.

2   As we saw in Chapter 3, we also asked whether respondents felt that the NFU was 'sufficiently militant'. Our choice of phrase here was deliberate, for we suspected that the term 'militancy' would evoke a strong negative ideological reaction on the part of most farmers who would most likely associate it with industrial unions rather than with their own organization. In other words, we anticipated that this question, like the three previous questions on trade unions, would highlight the tension between ideological beliefs and social imagery. Thus as we saw in Chapter 3, many farmers reacted against the use of the word 'militancy', and many, indeed, went to some pains to point out that the NFU was 'not really a trade union' – a response which may be interpreted as an attempt to reconcile ideological belief and concrete 'knowledge' in the light of these being thrown into sharp relief by this line of questioning.

3   The analogy with Kuhn's work can be carried further than this, however, for it is clear that paradigms in science and hegemony in social life are not total in their scope. Revolutions occur in science, just as they do in society. Kuhn explains scientific revolutions as occurring at the point where normal science can no longer adequately cope with the puzzles it is encountering. There then follows what is akin to a '*Gestalt* switch' in which both normal science and established theories are abandoned in favour of an entirely new and incommensurable perspective; the world, quite simply, appears

differently than it did before. Applying Kuhn's insights to our present concern with hegemony, it is apparent that a whole system of beliefs, theories and commonsense understandings may, with only relatively minor amendments in the face of continuing anomalies, prove extraordinarily resistant to material changes and to competing ideologies. This is reflected in the frustrated comment by Horkheimer and Adorno (1973, p. 203) that 'It requires only a small effort of mind to throw off this all-powerful and at the same time empty illusion; but to make this effort seems to be the most difficult thing of all'. Yet at the same time, it is apparent that hegemony may break down as individuals are confronted with more and more inconsistencies. If this occurs, then old ideologies and social imagery lose their supports, and new ideologies may come to be adopted (always assuming that they are available – hence Gramsci's emphasis on the importance of developing counter-hegemonic ideologies in the parties of the left).

It is beyond the scope of this book to consider how such a 'legitimation crisis' may occur in societies such as Britain. This is a key theme of a future work on which the present authors are engaged.

4 Unfortunately, Newby did not collect data on the voting behaviour of his farm worker sample, although there is substantial evidence from various voting studies to suggest that the rural working class in general, and agricultural workers in particular, are even less solidaristic in their support for the Labour Party than is the working class as a whole. (It should be remembered that something like one-third of British manual workers vote Conservative.)

5 As we have already argued, there is unlikely to be any noticeable strain between the calculative and ideological components of farmers' voting behaviour for, as in other areas, what they believe in is generally congruent with what is in their own individual interests. That is, the pursuit of their own self-interest (in this case, by voting for a right-wing party), is at the same time the pursuit of deeply-felt beliefs and sentiments. As Parkin (1974) notes, when a dominant group acts in concert (e.g. when 95 per cent of the members vote for the same party), such action rarely conflicts with individual interests within the group. Collectivism only tends to conflict with individual interests among lower-class groups. Farmers, then, are in the happy position of being able to pursue their own 'rugged individuality' while at the same time maintaining their commitment to a common class ideology and identity.

6 It is possible to draw a parallel here between farmers' responses

to broad and abstract questions such as 'What is wrong with the country?', and Bernstein's work on linguistic codes (Bernstein, 1973). We would not suggest, of course, that our farmers used what Bernstein identifies as a 'restricted code', for most were articulate in the extreme. Nevertheless, Bernstein argues that predictability is an essential characteristic of a restricted code, for that code is used in familiar situations to convey meanings, large parts of which are often taken for granted by both parties to the interaction. Thus detailed thought is rarely called for, for communication is accomplished through the use of shorthand phrases, and even manual gestures. We would argue that for many farmers, the question 'What is wrong with the country?' evokes little original abstract thought, but rather stimulates a 'restricted' response in terms of short-hand packaged ideologies indicated by the popular use of particular phrases and slogans.

7   Most farmers in fact described themselves as 'middle-class' whatever the model they put forward to describe the class system as a whole. Indeed, just as the farm workers interviewed by Newby (1972) tended to have a realistic view of their objective class situation (70 per cent of them saw themselves as 'working-class'), so too the farmers appeared to have few illusions regarding their place in society. Taking the three samples, between 51 per cent (in the forty-four parishes) and 58 per cent (in the 1000+ acres sample) described themselves as 'middle-class' – indeed, among the latter, a further 8 per cent described themselves as 'upper-class' (quite realistically). Between 13 per cent (in the 1000+ acres sample) and 25 per cent (in the forty-four parishes) stated that they were 'classless' or 'ordinary', while only between 8 per cent and 10 per cent in all three samples called themselves 'working-class'. It should be emphasized, however, that although most farmers generally described themselves as 'middle-class' in our interviews, they often did so diffidently, and there is no reason to suppose that such a self-conception in any way forms a relevant identity for them in their everyday lives. Indeed, as we shall see, it is doubtful whether such class terminology has much salience for many farmers outside of our formal interview.

8   The proportions seeing class as 'necessary' were 82 per cent in the forty-four parishes sample, 83 per cent in the 1000+ acres sample, and 86 per cent in the HN sample. Interestingly, although very high, these proportions are slightly lower than the proportion of farm workers in Newby's study who saw class as 'necessary' – a staggeringly high 91 per cent. Seventy-nine per cent of the 1000+

acres sample, 67 per cent of the forty-four parishes sample, and 66 per cent of the HN sample also saw class inequality as 'natural' or 'desirable', the comparable figure among the farm workers being somewhat lower at 52 per cent. Thus farm workers were more inclined to see class divisions as inevitable, but less inclined to see this as desirable.

9 It was noticeable in many interviews that the class question became somewhat obtrusive – it simply did not 'fit in' with the context of the remainder of the questionnaire, most of which was concerned with the everyday experiences generated within farming. It was not that farmers were not prepared to answer the question, or that they could not answer it (although some could not), but that we gained the impression that many of them were somewhat unclear about why we should wish to ask it. For this reason, many of the responses to the class question are incomplete. That is to say, we do not have a complete inventory of each respondent's views on self-rated class, extent of social mobility, criteria and determinants of class membership, and so on. We 'probed' in each case, of course, but insistent probing on such an abstract topic proved difficult, while farmers' spontaneous answers were often perhaps more valid than a series of utterances coaxed from them. The tables which follow in the text, therefore, are often based on a relatively small proportion of each sample.

10 Some farmers in our sample, of course, clearly were *not* wealthy, but the question on wealth justification was not asked of the family and small-scale farmers. The point is that many of the obviously wealthy and successful farmers denied their wealth, or at least denied its significance.

Chapter 8: Property, paternalism and power

1 The similarities between Locke's philosophy and Calvin's theology in terms of their 'elective affinity' with the spirit of capitalism are notable. Weber's celebrated analysis of the latter in his *The Protestant Ethic and the Spirit of Capitalism* (1930) emphasizes the very same ideological components of Calvinism – the expenditure of labour and productivity of use – as we have emphasized in relation to Locke. However, it is important to note that, as far as Locke's philosophy is concerned, we would agree with Tawney (and others) that his ideas were a systematized *reflection* of ideologies which were already present – though perhaps underdeveloped – among dominant

property-owning groups. Much the same argument may, of course, be advanced in relation to Calvin's philosophy (e.g. see Samuelson, 1964) although Weber's theory in regard to the enabling capacity of a Puritan ethic *vis-à-vis* the rise of capitalism is inconsistent with such an interpretation.

2   Although we found no correlation between inheritance and the use of 'work' justifications, there was a correlation between inheritance and explanations of success in farming. In other words, while the *justification* of wealth seems to pay scant regard to such matters as whether the wealth was inherited, the *explanation* of it, while still to a large extent ideological, nevertheless does reflect to some extent the 'objective' situation. Thus, we divided farmers' *explanations* of their success into two categories; the first we may term 'achievement factors' (such as hard work, commitment, ambition, business sense, and so on), the second, 'fortuitous factors' (e.g. luck, quality of father and so on). As predicted, we found that those who had inherited their land were more likely to mention fortuitous factors than those who had not. Sixty-two per cent of inheritors mentioned achievement factors compared with 76 per cent of non-inheritors, while 32 per cent of inheritors mentioned fortuitous factors, compared with 19 per cent of non-inheritors.

What these results appear to indicate is that, although explanations of why respondents were wealthy were clearly far from 'objective', they nevertheless bore rather more resemblance to the actual situation than did their justifications. It would appear, then, that while Berger and Luckmann (1967) are undoubtedly correct in pointing out that the dominance achieved by definitions of reality reflect the power available to those who hold them, nevertheless these definitions are to some extent contextually restrained. It is difficult, that is, for a group to explain its wealth in terms of its own efforts when this is patently not the case, and thus other explanations have to be sought. Ideologies may be amenable to those who use them, but even the most powerful groups must take care that they do not strain credulity *too* far.

3   This latter form of 'collectivistic' ideology perhaps owes as much to the Scottish political economists as to the English utilitarian philosophers. It is exemplified, for example, by the following extract taken from Adam Smith's *Wealth of Nations* (cited by Weber, 1930, p. 212): 'It is not from the benevolence of the butcher, the brewer, or the baker that we expect our dinner, but from their regard to their own interest. We address ourselves, not to their humanity,

but to their self-love; and never talk to them of our own necessities, but of their advantages.' Such essentially aggressive justifications of private property ownership may perhaps more properly be understood as variants of 'capitalistic' rather than 'collectivistic' ideologies, although we choose to include them under the latter category since, like resort to justifications couched in terms of *noblesse oblige*, their effect is more to point to the benefits which accrue to others than to highlight the benefits enjoyed by the property-owners themselves.

4 An immediate objection to our argument may be that if ideologies are contextually situated, the interview situation may be expected to give rise only to those ideologies which farmers deem appropriate when dealing with 'outsiders' (in our case, university interviewers). However, we would first point to complementary illustrative material, cited in Chapter 3, and gathered from sources other than our interviews, which seems to confirm the validity of our four-fold classification set out here – e.g. the response of the NFU and CLA to wealth tax proposals. Secondly, we would again state that most landowners are undoubtedly familiar with most of the ideologies discussed in this chapter, and while in everyday situations they may need to refer only to particular ideologies in particular contexts, it seems likely that the extraordinary context of a formal interview led them to delve into a wider range of ideologies in response to some broad direct and implicitly threatening questions.

5 There are a few exceptions to this. For example, Kahn-Freund, in his introduction to Renner (1949), cites the power of the state in Britain to dispossess farmers who do not use their land productively. However, the rarity of such occurrences seems only to lend weight to the argument that the law is not generally interested in the use to which property is put, although increasing state regulation of property use (e.g. in the case of urban rented housing) may be increasing in certain contexts.

6 Lafargue actually developed a trichotomy of property types, his third category being the instruments of labour (i.e. tools). As he himself recognized, however, property in the form of instruments of labour comes, with the development of capitalism, to be alienated from the labour which uses it, and to be subsumed under capital. Thus:

So long as petty manual industry prevails, the free producer is the proprietor of his instruments of labour. . . . There remain many vestiges of this private property in the instrument of labour, but they are fast disappearing. In all the industries which have been seized on by machinery, the individual implement has been torn out of the worker's hand and replaced by the machine tool – a collective instrument of labour which can no longer be the property of the producer. Capitalism divests man of his personal property, the tool. . . . [Lafargue, n.d., p. 9.]

In developing a typology of property in capitalist society, we are therefore justified in contrasting capital, including instruments of labour, with PPA.

7   The typology presented here represents a modified version of that initially presented by us in a paper published in the *Sociological Review* (Rose *et al.*, 1976). In that paper, we presented what we termed a typology of property 'rights', but on reflection it is clear that this was misleading since the horizontal axis is itself a dimension referring to rights of access (i.e. rights over control, benefit and alienation), in contrast to the vertical dimension which refers to function. Initially, for example, we designated box 1 'personal rights of production' *per se*, since the law in capitalist society is largely disinterested in whether property is used for production or consumption. Rights refer only to access, not to use. Thus we now prefer to present the typology as a framework for distinguishing different types of property rather than different types of property rights, and the labels appended to each of the four boxes have been amended accordingly. It is important to emphasize, however, that the four boxes represent ideal types, and also that there is still nothing inherent in objects such as houses, farms or whatever which places them in any of the four categories. Each type, that is, is distinguished from each other not on any essential characteristic, but according to the relation between exclusivity and use in any given typical context.

8   As Marx (1968, p. 87) observed:

To say that the most favourable condition for wage labour is the most rapid possible growth of productive capital is only to say that the more rapidly the working-class increases and enlarges the power that is hostile to it, the wealth that does not belong to it, and that rules over it, the more favourable will be the conditions under which it is allowed to labour anew at increasing bourgeois wealth, at enlarging the power of capital, content with forging for itself the golden chains by which the bourgeoisie drags it in its chain.

9   The specific way in which the elision of PPA and capital may be accomplished may, however, vary in different contexts. To take just one example, ownership rights in relation to industrial capital are often justified with reference to the division which is deemed to

have arisen between ownership and control, not through representing productive property as PPA, but rather through representing PPA as productive capital. Thus the argument is often advanced by industrialists and commentators (including academics) alike that rights of ownership of the individual means of production in capitalist society have become diffused, both directly among holders of joint stock (of whom there are, of course, relatively few), and indirectly among that sizeable proportion of the population which has money invested in institutions such as pension funds and insurance companies which themselves invest in company stock. The fallacy of this argument has been capably exposed by Nichols (1969), Miliband (1969), and others on many occasions. As Berle (1959) points out, the *de jure* 'owners' of such indirect stock are in fact totally divorced from it – their pension funds or insurance companies invest their money in they know not what, and pay them out on maturity from they know not whence. To speak of such 'proxy owners' as enjoying 'property rights' beyond those of benefit is itself a doubtful proposition, but to go beyond this and argue that such arrangements constitute a widespread distribution of productive capital is clearly a total nonsense. Far from constituting capitalistic property, the average investment in life insurance cover or a pension fund is, from the viewpoint of the investor, merely one variant of the personal means of consumption (PPA):

As certain portions for consumption are needed over different periods of different length, the workers must provide funds of reserve out of their earnings. . . . Thus they assume the legal character mask of owners, creditors and the rest. Yet the economic significance of this type of property is only that it provides a reserve fund for the subject, a fund of reserve for the purpose of consumption. . . . For the legal owners, this kind of property is and remains only a fund for the purpose of consumption which is temporarily deposited; it exercises the function of capital only in the hands of the capitalist. [Renner, 1949, pp. 234–6.]

To argue, then, that such property is itself capitalistic in the hands of its varied 'owners' is to misrepresent its function-in-use for them. Such an argument, however, has a significant ideological character, for it implicitly justifies a *de facto* accumulation of economic power in a few hands by its *de jure* dispersal among many. For our present purposes, therefore, we should note that the ideological confusion of these two types of property may be a common ideological tool in the justification of ownership of the individual means of production in agriculture *and* in other industries. Certainly we feel that our findings derived from a somewhat limited analysis of landowning in rural East Anglia have much wider implications which could repay further analysis in other contexts.

The parallels between agricultural and industrial capital in relation to 'individualistic' ideologies of PPA are also apparent in relation to the other ideologies – collectivistic and altruistic – which we have discussed. Workers' participation as an ideology provides one obvious example, while the argument that nationalized industry is in some way 'owned' by those who work in it (with the corollary that it is therefore irrational for them to take industrial action in pursuit of higher wages) is another. Again, we would suggest that the framework advanced in this chapter for analysing ideologies and types of property may fruitfully be applied in other areas of research.

Bibliography

ALTHUSSER, Louis (1971), 'Ideology and Ideological State Apparatuses', in his *Lenin and Philosophy and Other Essays*, London: New Left Books.

AMBROSE, Peter (1974), *The Quiet Revolution*, London: Chatto and Windus for Sussex University Press.

ARENSBERG, C. A., and KIMBALL, S. T. (1968), *Family and Community in Ireland*, 2nd ed., Cambridge, Mass.: Harvard University Press.

ARNOLD-BAKER, C. (1958), *Parish Administration*, London: Methuen.

ASHTON, J., and CRACKNELL, B. E. (1961), 'Agricultural Holdings and Farm Business Structure in England and Wales', *Journal of Agricultural Economics*, vol. 14, pp. 472–506.

ASHTON, J., and ROGERS, S. J., (eds.) (1971), *Economic Change and Agriculture*, Edinburgh: Oliver and Boyd.

ATKINSON, A. B. (1974), *Unequal Shares*, London: Allen Lane.

ATTWOOD, E. A. (1963), 'The Origins of State Support for British Agriculture', *Manchester School*, vol. 31, 2, May, pp. 129–48.

BACHRACH, P., and BARATZ, M. S. (1970), 'The Two Faces of Power', in their *Power and Poverty*, New York: Oxford University Press.

BAIN, G. S. (1970), *The Growth of White-Collar Unionism*, Oxford: Clarendon Press.

BARKER, Alan (1976), 'Socialist Peer Rejects State Land Takeover', *Farmers' Weekly*, 4 June 1976, p. 47.

BARRY, Brian (1965), *Political Argument*, London: Routledge and Kegan Paul.

BATEMAN, John (1883), *The Great Landowners of Great Britain and Ireland*, Leicester: Leicester University Press (reprinted 1971).

BEALEY, F., BLONDEL, J., and McCANN, W. (1965), *Constituency Politics: A Study of Newcastle-Under-Lyme*, London: Faber and Faber.

388 *Bibliography*

BECHHOFER, Frank, and ELLIOTT, Brian (1968), 'An Approach to the Study of Shopkeepers in the Class Structure', *European Journal of Sociology*, vol. 9, pp. 180–202.

BECHHOFER, Frank, ELLIOTT, Brian, RUSHFORTH, Monica, and BLAND, Richard (1974), 'The Petits Bourgeois in the Class Structure', in F. Parkin (ed.) (1974).

BELL, Colin (1968), *Middle Class Families*, London: Routledge and Kegan Paul.

BELL, Colin (1976), 'Towards a Political Economy of Housing', in E. L. Wheelwright and K. Buckley (eds.), *Essays in the Political Economy of Australian Capitalism*, Sydney: ANZ.

BELL, Colin, and NEWBY, Howard (1971), *Community Studies*, London: Allen and Unwin.

BELL, Colin, and NEWBY, Howard (1973), 'The Sources of Variation in Agricultural Workers' Images of Society', *Sociological Review*, vol. 21, No. 2, pp. 229–53.

BELL, Colin, and NEWBY, Howard (1974), 'Capitalist Farmers in the Class Structure', *Sociologia Ruralis*, vol. 14, No. 1/2, pp. 86–107.

BELL, Colin, and NEWBY, Howard (1976), 'Community, Communion, Class and Community Action: the Social Sources of the New Urban Politics', in D. Herbert and R. Johnson (eds.), *Social Areas in Cities*, vol. 2, London: Wiley, pp. 189–208.

BELL, Colin, and NEWBY, Howard (eds.) (1977), *Doing Sociological Research*, London: Allen and Unwin.

BENN, S. I., and PETERS, R. (1959), *Social Principles and the Democratic State*, London: Allen and Unwin.

BENYON, V. H., and HARRISON, J. E. (1962), *The Political Significance of the Agricultural Vote*, Newton Abbot: University of Exeter, Department of Agricultural Economics.

BERESFORD, T. (1975), *We Plough the Fields*, Harmondsworth: Penguin Books.

BERGER, P., and LUCKMANN, T. (1967), *The Social Construction of Reality*, London: Allen Lane.

BERLE, A., Jnr (1959), *Power Without Property*, London: Sidgwick and Jackson.

BERNSTEIN, B. (1973), *Class Codes and Control*, vol. 1, London: Routledge and Kegan Paul.

BEST, G. (1971), *Mid-Victorian Britain, 1851–75*, London: Weidenfeld and Nicolson.

BEST, R., and COPPOCK, J. T. (1962), *The Changing Use of Land in Britain*, London: Faber.

BIRCH, A. A. (1960), *Small Town Politics*, Oxford: Oxford University Press.

BLACK, M. (1968), 'Agricultural Labour in an Expanding Economy', *Journal of Agricultural Economics*, vol. 19, No. 1, pp. 59–76.

BLACKBURN, R. M. (1967), *Union Character and Social Class*, London: Batsford.

BLACKBURN, R., and MANN, M. (1975), 'Ideology in the Non-Skilled Working Class', in M. Bulmer (ed.) (1975), pp. 131–60.

BLYTHE, Ronald (1969), *Akenfield*, London: Allen Lane.

BOGGS, C. (1976), *Gramsci's Marxism*, London: Pluto Press.

BOURNE, G. (1912), *Change in the Village*, London: Duckworth.

BRACEY, Howard (1959), *English Rural Life*, London: Routledge and Kegan Paul.

BRITTON, D. K. (1974), 'The Structure of Agriculture', in A. Edwards and A. Rogers (eds.) (1974), pp. 21–38.

BUCKLEY, W. (1967), *Sociology and Modern Systems Theory*, Englewood Cliffs: Prentice Hall.

BULMER, M. (ed.) (1975), *Working Class Images of Society*, London: Routledge and Kegan Paul.

BULPITT, J. (1967), *Party Politics in English Local Government*, London: Longman.

BURCHARD, W. (1954), 'Role Conflicts of Military Chaplains', *American Sociological Review*, vol. 19, pp. 528–35.

BURNHAM, James (1941), *The Managerial Revolution*, New York: Day.

BYRNE, Nicholas (1975), 'Agricultural Investment: A Guide to Performance (1945–1974)', *Farmland Market*, No. 4, July, pp. 9–12.

CAIRD, James (1851), *English Agriculture in 1850–51*, London: Cass (reprinted 1966).

CAIRD, James (1878), *The Landed Interest and the Supply of Food*, London: Cass (reprinted 1968).

CAMPBELL, David (1973), 'The New Landlords', *Farmers' Weekly*, 9 November 1973, pp. 68–75.

CARR-SAUNDERS, A. M., and WILSON, P. R. (1964), *The Professions*, London: Cass.

CASTELLS, M. (1976), 'Advanced Capitalism, Collective Consumption and Urban Contradictions: New Sources of Inequality and New Models for Change', in L. N. Lindberg *et al.* (eds.), *Stress and Contradiction in Modern Capitalism*, Lexington, Mass.: D. C. Heath, pp. 175–97.

CHILD, J. (1969), *The Business Enterprise in Modern Industrial Society*, London: Collier-Macmillan.

CLEGG, S. (1975), *Power, Rule and Domination*, London: Routledge and Kegan Paul.

CLERY, Peter (1975), *Farming Finance*, Ipswich: Farming Press Ltd.

CLIVE, A. F. L. (1966), 'The Outlook on the Agricultural Landowner in the United Kingdom', *Chartered Surveyor*, vol. 98, No. 9, pp. 470–2.

COLEMAN, D. C. (1973), 'Gentlemen and Players', *Economic History Review*, vol. 26, No. 1, pp. 92–116.

CONNELL, J. (1974), 'The Metropolitan Village: Spatial and Social Processes in Discontinuous Suburbs', in J. H. Johnson (ed.), *The Geography of Suburban Growth*, London: Wiley.

CONVERSE, P. E. (1965), 'The Nature of Belief Systems in Mass Publics', in D. E. Apter (ed.), *Ideology and Discontent*, Glencoe, Ill.: Free Press, pp. 206–61.

COPPOCK, J. T. (1964), *An Agricultural Atlas of England and Wales*, London: Faber.

COPPOCK, J. T. (1971), *An Agricultural Geography of Great Britain*, London: Bell.

COSER, Lewis (1974), *Greedy Institutions*, New York: Free Press.

COTGROVE, S. (1976), 'Environmentalism and Utopia', *Sociological Review*, vol. 24, No. 1, February, pp. 23–42.

COUNTRY LANDOWNERS' ASSOCIATION (1974), 'Constraints on Business Organisation in Agriculture. Report of an Independent Working Party – Chairman, Viscount Davidson', London: CLA.

COUNTRY LANDOWNERS' ASSOCIATION: (1975), *Your Land*, London: CLA.

COUNTRY LANDOWNERS' ASSOCIATION (1976), 'The Future of Land-ownership – A CLA Discussion Paper', London: CLA.

COWLING, K., METCALF, D., and RAYNER, A. (1970), *Resource Structure of Agriculture: an Economic Analysis*, Oxford: Pergamon.

CRENSON, M. (1971), *The Unpolitics of Air Pollution*, Baltimore: Johns Hopkins Press.

CREWE, I. (ed.) (1974), *Élites in Western Democracy*, London: Croom Helm.

CROUCH, Colin (1974), 'The Ideology of a Managerial Élite: the National Board for Prices and Incomes, 1965–1970', in I. Crewe (ed.) (1974).

CULLINGWORTH, J. B. (1973), *Problems of an Urban Society*, vol. 1, *The Social Framework of Planning*, London: Allen and Unwin.

DAHL, Robert (1961), *Who Governs?* New Haven: Yale University Press.

DAVIDOFF, Leonore (1974), 'Mastered for Life: Servant, Wife and Mother in Victorian England', *Journal of Social History*, vol. 7, No. 4, pp. 405–28.

DAVIDOFF, Leonore, L'ESPERANCE, Jean, and NEWBY, Howard (1976), 'Landscapes with Figures: Home and Community in Victorian England', in Juliet Mitchell and Ann Oakley (eds.), *The Rights and Wrongs of Women*, Harmondsworth: Penguin Books, pp. 139–75.

DAY, Graham, and FITTON, Martin (1975), 'Religion and Social Status in Rural Wales: "Buchedd" and its Lessons for Concepts of Stratification in Community Studies', *Sociological Review*, vol. 23, No. 4, pp. 867–92.

DEARLOVE, J. (1973), *The Politics of Policy in Local Government*, London: Cambridge University Press.

DOE/MAFF (1975), *Abolition of the Tied Cottage System in Agriculture: Consultative Document*, London: HMSO.

DONALDSON, J. G. S., and DONALDSON, F. (1972), *Farming in Britain Today*, Harmondsworth: Penguin Books.

ECONOMIC DEVELOPMENT COMMITTEE FOR THE AGRICULTURE INDUSTRY (1968), *The Import-Saving Role of Agriculture*, London: HMSO.

ECONOMIC DEVELOPMENT COMMITTEE FOR THE AGRICULTURE INDUSTRY (1972), *Agricultural Manpower*, London: HMSO.

EDWARDS, A., and ROGERS, A. (eds.) (1974), *Agricultural Resources*, London: Faber.

ELLIOTT, Brian, and McCRONE, David (1975), 'Landlords in Edinburgh: Some Preliminary Findings', *Sociological Review*, vol. 23, No. 3, pp. 539–62.

EMMETT, I. (1971), 'The Social Filter in the Leisure Field', *Recreation News Supplement*, No. 4, July, pp. 7–8.

ETZIONI, A. (1961), *A Comparative Analysis of Complex Organizations*, New York: Free Press.

EVERSLEY, David (1974), 'Conservation for the Minority?', *Built Environment*, vol. 3, January, pp. 14–15.

FINER, S. E. (1955/6), 'The Political Power of Private Capital', *Sociological Review*, vol. 3, No. 4, pp. 279–94; vol. 4, No. 1, pp. 5–30.

FRANKENBERG, R. (1965), *Communities in Britain*, Harmondsworth: Penguin Books.

GASSON, Ruth (1966a), 'The Challenge to British Farming 1960–1970', *Westminster Bank Review*, May, pp. 32–41.

GASSON, Ruth (1966b), 'The Changing Location of Intensive Crop sin England and Wales', *Geography*, vol. 51, No. 1, pp. 16–28.

GASSON, Ruth (1966c), *Occupational Immobility of Small Farmers*, Cambridge: University of Cambridge, Department of Land Economy, Occasional Paper No. 13.

GASSON, Ruth (1974), 'Resources in Agriculture: Labour', in A. Edwards and A. Rogers (eds.) (1974), pp. 107–34.

GAVIN, W. (1967), *Ninety Years of Family Farming*, London: Hutchinson.

GENOVESE, E. D. (1971), *In Red and Black*, London: Allen Lane.

GENOVESE, E. D. (1974), *Roll Jordan Roll*, New York: Pantheon.

GERTH, H. H., and MILLS, C. W. (1948), *From Max Weber*, London: Routledge and Kegan Paul.

GIBBS, Richard, and HARRISON, Alan (1974), 'Landownership by Public and Semi-Public Bodies in Great Britain', Miscellaneous Study 56, revised edition, University of Reading, Department of Agricultural Economics and Management.

GIDDENS, Anthony (1968), 'Power in the Recent Writings of Talcott Parsons', *Sociology*, vol. 2, pp. 257–72.

GIDDENS, Anthony (1973), *The Class Structure of the Advanced Societies*, London: Hutchinson.

GIDDENS, Anthony (1974), 'Preface' to P. Stanworth and A. Giddens (eds.), *Elites and Power in British Society*, London: Cambridge University Press.

GIDDENS, Anthony (1976), *New Rules of Sociological Method*, London: Hutchinson.

GIDDINGS, P. J. (1974), *Marketing Boards and Ministers*, Westmead: Saxon House, D. C. Heath.

GLASGOW UNIVERSITY MEDIA GROUP (1976), *Bad News*, London: Routledge and Kegan Paul.

GOFFMAN, Erving (1969), *The Presentation of Self in Everyday Life*, London: Allen Lane.

GOFFMAN, Erving (1973), 'The Nature of Deference and Demeanour', in his *Interaction Ritual*, Harmondsworth: Penguin Books, pp. 47–96.

GOLDTHORPE, J., LOCKWOOD, D., BECHHOFER, F., PLATT, J. (1969), *The Affluent Worker in the Class Structure*, London: Cambridge University Press.

GOULDNER, Alvin (1970), *The Coming Crisis of Western Sociology*, London: Heinemann.

GRANT, W. (1971), 'Local Councils, Conflict and Rules of the Game', *British Journal of Political Science*, vol. 1, pp. 253–5.

GRAY, John (1975), *On the Contestability of Social and Political Concepts*, University of Essex, Department of Government, mimeo.

GREEN, Daniel (1975), *Politics of Food*, London: Cremonesi.

GUTTSMAN, W. L. (1969), *The British Political Elite*, London: MacGibbon and Kee.

HABERMAS, J. (1976), *Legitimation Crisis*, London: Heinemann.

HACKER, A. (1965), 'Power To Do What?', in I. Horowitz, *The New Sociology: Essays in Social Science and Social Theory in Honour of C. Wright Mills*, London: Oxford University Press.

HADDON, R. F. (1970), 'A Minority in a Welfare State Society: the Location of West Indians in the London Housing Market', *New Atlantis*, vol. 2, pp. 80–133.

HAMILTON, Willie (1975), *My Queen and I*, London: Quartet Books.

HAMPTON, W. (1970), *Democracy and Community: A Study of Politics in Sheffield*, London: Oxford University Press.

HARRIS, Nigel (1971), *Beliefs in Society*, Harmondsworth: Penguin Books.

HARRISON, Alan (1965), 'Some Features of Farm Business Structures', *Journal of Agricultural Economics*, vol. 16, No. 3, pp. 330–54.

HARRISON, Alan (1972), *The Financial Structure of Farm Business*, Reading: University of Reading, Department of Agricultural Economics and Management, Miscellaneous Study 53.

HARRISON, Alan (1973), 'Financing Farming Change', *Journal of Farm Management*, vol. 2, No. 7, Winter, pp. 354–61.

HARRISON, Alan (1975), *Farmers and Farm Businesses in England*, University of Reading, Department of Agricultural Economics and Management, Miscellaneous Study 62.

HARRISON, Alan (ed.) (1976), *Farming, The Land and Changing Capital Taxation*, Reading: University of Reading, Department of Agricultural Economics and Management.

HERFINDAHL, O. (1965), 'What is Conservation?', in I. Burton and R. Kates, *Readings in Resource Management and Conservation*, London: University of Chicago Press, pp. 229–36.

HEWITT, Christopher J. (1973), 'Elites and the Distribution of Power in British Society', in P. Stanworth and A. Giddens (eds.) (1973).

HILL, Berkeley (1976), 'Land Mess', *The Guardian*, 2 April.

HINDESS, Barry, *The Use of Official Statistics in Sociology*, London: Macmillan.

HOBSBAWM, E. J. (1969), *Industry and Empire*, Harmondsworth: Penguin Books.

HOBSBAWM, E. J., and RUDÉ, G. (1971), *Captain Swing*, London: Lawrence and Wishart.

HORKHEIMER, M., and ADORNO, T. (1973), *Aspects of Sociology*, London: Heinemann.

HOUSE OF COMMONS (1976), *Select Committee on The Wealth Tax: Final Report* (3 vols.), London: HMSO.

HOWARTH, Richard W. (1969), 'The Political Strength of British Agriculture', *Political Studies*, vol. 17, pp. 458–69.

HUNT, A. (1974), 'Agriculture and the Market', in Edwards and Rogers (eds.) (1974), pp. 39–60.

HYMAN, R. (1972), *Strikes*, London: Fontana.

INGHAM, G. K. (1970), *Size of Industrial Organisation and Worker Behaviour*, Cambridge: Cambridge University Press.

IRVING, Barry, and HILGENDORF, Linden (1975), *Tied Cottages in British Agriculture*, London: Tavistock Institute for Human Relations.

JACKSON, J. A. (ed.) (1970), *Professions and Professionalisation*, Cambridge: Cambridge University Press.

JENKINS, D. (1971), *The Agricultural Community in South-West Wales at the Turn of the Twentieth Century*, Cardiff: University of Wales Press.

JOHNSON, R. (1973), 'The Nationalisation of English Rural Politics: Norfolk S.W. 1945–70', *Parliamentary Affairs*, vol. 26, pp. 1–33.

JOHNSON, T. J. (1972), *Professions and Power*, London: Macmillan.

JORDAN, Z. (1972), *Karl Marx*, London: Nelson.

KUHN, T. S. (1970), *The Structure of Scientific Revolutions*, 2nd ed., London: University of Chicago Press.

LAFARGUE, P. (n.d.), *Evolution of Property from Savagery to Civilisation*, Calcutta: Sreekali Prakasalaya.

LANE, T., and ROBERTS, K. (1971), *Strike at Pilkington's*, London: Fontana.

LAW, Sylvia (1974), 'Leisure and Recreation: Problems and Prospects', *Planning Outlook*, vol. 12.

LEE, J. M. (1963), *Social Leaders and Public Persons*, Oxford: Oxford University Press.

LEHMAN, E. (1969), 'Toward a Macrosociology of Power', *American Sociological Review*, vol. 34, pp. 453–65.

LEMON, Anthony (1975), 'Post-war Industrial Growth in East Anglian Small Towns: A Study of Migrant Firms 1945–70', School of Geography, University of Oxford, Research Paper No. 12.

LICHFIELD, N., and CHAPMAN, H. (1970), 'Cost Benefit Analysis in Urban Expansion: A Case Study, Ipswich', *Urban Studies*, vol. 7, 1970, pp. 156–79.

LITTLEJOHN, James (1963), *Westrigg*, London: Routledge and Kegan Paul.

LOCKE, J. (1960), *Second Treatise on Government*, ed. P. Laslett, Cambridge: Cambridge University Press.

LOCKWOOD, David (1958), *The Blackcoated Worker*, London: Allen and Unwin.

LOCKWOOD, David (1966), 'Sources of Variation in Working-Class Images of Society', *Sociological Review*, vol. 14, pp. 249–67.

LOCKWOOD, David (1975), 'In Search of the Traditional Workər', in M. Bulmer (ed.) (1975), pp. 239–50.

LOWE, P. D. (1975), 'The Environmental Lobby: A Survey', *Built Environment Quarterly*, vol. II, pp. 73–6, 158–61, 235–8.

LUKES, Steven (1974), *Power: A Radical View*, London: Macmillan.

MACGREGOR, Alasdair (1973), 'This Inflated Isle', *Farmers' Weekly*, 28 December 1973, p. 46.

MACPHERSON, C. B. (1973), *Democratic Theory: Essays in Retrieval*, Oxford: Clarendon Press.

MADGWICK, P., *et al.* (1973), *The Politics of Rural Wales*, London: Hutchinson.

MAFF (annually), *Agricultural Statistics: England and Wales*, London: HMSO.

MAFF (annually), *Farm Classification in England and Wales*, London: HMSO.

MAFF (1966), *A Century of Agricultural Statistics*, London: HMSO.

MAFF (1970), *The Changing Structure of Agriculture*, London: HMSO.

MAFF (1975), *Farming From Our Own Resources*, London: HMSO.

MANN, M. (1970), 'The Social Cohesion of Liberal Democracy', *American Sociological Review*, vol. 35, pp. 423–39.

MANNHEIM, K. (1936), *Ideology and Utopia*, London: Kegan Paul.

MARCUSE, Herbert (1976), 'Repressive Tolerance', in Connerton, P. (ed.), *Critical Sociology*, Harmondsworth: Penguin.

MARSHALL, T. H. (1963), *Sociology at the Crossroads*, London: Heinemann.

MARSHALL, T. H. (1965), 'Citizenship and Social Class', in his *Class, Citizenship and Social Development*, New York: Anchor.

MARTIN, R. (1971), 'The Concept of Power: A Critical Defence', *British Journal of Sociology*, vol. 22, pp. 240–56.

MARTIN, R., and FRYER, R. H. (1973), *Redundancy and Paternalist Capitalism*, London: Allen and Unwin.

MARX, Karl (1964), *The Economic and Philosophic Manuscripts of 1844* (ed. D. J. Struik), New York: International Publishers.

MARX, Karl (1968), 'Wage Labour and Capital', in Marx, K., and Engels, F., *Selected Works* (single volume), London: Lawrence and Wishart.

MATHIESEN, T. (1974), *The Politics of Abolition*, London: Martin Robertson.

MERTON, Robert (1957), 'Patterns of Influence: Local and Cosmopolitan Influentials', in his *Social Theory and Social Structure*, Glencoe: Free Press, pp. 441–74.

MILIBAND, Ralph (1969), *The State in Capitalist Society*, London: Weidenfeld and Nicolson.

MILL, J. S. (1848), *Principles of Political Economy*, vol. 2, Boston: Beacon Books.

MILLS, C. Wright (1956), *The Power Elite*, New York: Oxford University Press.

MINISTRY OF HOUSING AND LOCAL GOVERNMENT (1964), *The South East Study 1961–1981*, London: HMSO.

MITCHELL, G. D. (1951), 'The Parish Council and the Rural Community', *Public Administration*, vol. 29, pp. 393–401.

MOORHOUSE, H. F., and CHAMBERLAIN, C. (1974), 'Lower Class Attitudes Towards the British Political System', *Sociological Review*, vol. 22, No. 4, pp. 503–26.

MORLEY, D. (1976), 'Industrial Conflict and the Mass Media', *Sociological Review*, vol. 24, pp. 245–69.

MOSS, L., and PARKER, S. (1967), *The Local Government Councillor*, London: HMSO.

NALSON, J. S. (1968), *Mobility of Farm Families*, Manchester: Manchester University Press.

NAPOLITAN, L., and BROWN, C. J. (1963), 'A Type of Farming Classification of Agricultural Holdings in England and Wales According to Enterprise Patterns', *Journal of Agricultural Economics*, vol. 15, pp. 595–616.

NATIONAL FARMERS UNION (1976), *Annual Report*, London: NFU.

NEWBY, Howard (1972a), 'The Low Earnings of Agricultural Workers: A Sociological Approach', *Journal of Agricultural Economics*, vol. 23, No. 1, January, pp. 15–24.

NEWBY, Howard (1972b), 'Agricultural Workers in the Class Structure', *Sociological Review*, vol. 20, No. 3, pp. 413–39.

NEWBY, Howard (1974), 'The Changing Sociological Environment of the Farm', *Journal of Farm Management*, vol. 2, No. 9, pp. 474–87.

NEWBY, Howard (1975), 'The Deferential Dialectic', *Comparative Studies in Society and History*, vol. 17, No. 2, pp. 139–64.

NEWBY, Howard (1976), 'Paternalism and Capitalism', in R. Scase (ed.), *Industrial Society: Class Cleavage and Control*, London: Allen and Unwin, pp. 59–73.

NEWBY, Howard (1977), *The Deferential Worker*, London: Allen Lane.

NEWBY, Howard (ed.), *International Perspectives in Rural Sociology: Change and Continuity in the Rural World*, London: Wiley.

NEWBY, Howard, ROSE, David, SAUNDERS, Peter, and BELL, Colin (1975), 'Field Work', in C. Le Vay (ed.), *The Design and Interpretation of Questionnaires*, Aberystwyth: University College, Aberystwyth, Department of Agricultural Economics, pp. 45–73.

NICHOLS, Theo (1969), *Ownership, Control and Ideology*, London: Allen and Unwin.

NISBET, Robert (1966), *The Sociological Tradition*, London: Heinemann.

PAHL, J., and PAHL, R. E. (1972), *Managers and their Wives*, London: Allen Lane.

PAHL, R. E. (1965), *Urbs in Rure*, London: Weidenfeld and Nicolson.

PAHL, R. E. (1968), 'The Rural–Urban Continuum', in his *Readings in Urban Sociology*, Oxford: Pergamon, pp. 263–305.

PAHL, R. E., and WINKLER, J. T. (1973), 'The Economic Elite: Theory and Practice', in P. Stanworth and A. Giddens (eds.) (1973).

PARKIN, Frank (1967), *Middle Class Radicalism*, Manchester: Manchester University Press.

PARKIN, Frank (1971), *Class Inequality and Political Order*, London: MacGibbon and Kee.

PARKIN, F. (1974), 'Strategies of Social Closure in Class Formation', in his *The Social Analysis of Class Structure*, London: Tavistock, pp. 1–18.

PARRY, G., and MORRISS, P. (1974), 'When is a Decision Not a Decision?', in I. Crewe (ed.), *British Political Sociology Yearbook*, vol. 1, *Élites in Western Democracy*, London: Croom Helm, pp. 317–36.

PARSONS, Talcott (1966), *Societies: Evolutionary and Comparative Perspectives*, Englewood Cliffs, N.J.: McGraw-Hill.

PENNOCK, J. Roland (1959), 'The Political Power of British Agriculture', *Political Studies*, vol. 7, pp. 291–6.

PERKIN, Harold (1969), *The Origins of British Society 1780–1880*, London: Routledge and Kegan Paul.

PERKIN, Harold (1973), 'Land Reform and Class Conflict in Victorian Britain', in J. Butt and I. Y. Clark (eds.), *The Victorians and Social Protest*, Newton Abbot: David and Charles, pp. 177–217.

PERROTT, Ray (1968), *The Aristocrats*, London: Weidenfeld and Nicolson.

PERRY, P. J. (1974), *British Agriculture, 1875–1914*, London: Methuen.

PETTIGREW, A. (1972), 'Information Control as a Power Resource', *Sociology*, vol. 6, pp. 187–204.

PLAMENATZ, J. (1963), *Man and Society*, vol. 1, London: Longman.

PLATT, J. (1971), 'Variations in Answers to Different Questions on Perceptions of Class', *Sociological Review*, vol. 19, No. 3, pp. 409–18.

PLOWMAN, D. E. G., MINCHINTON, W. E., and STACEY, M. (1962), 'Local Social Status in England and Wales', *Sociological Review*, vol. 10, No. 2, pp. 161–202.

PLUMB, H. (1971), *Address* to the Royal Society of Arts, 28 April.

POULANTZAS, Nicos (1973a), 'On Social Classes', *New Left Review*, No. 78, pp. 27–54.

POULANTZAS, Nicos (1973*b*), *Political Power and Social Classes*, London: New Left Books.

POULANTZAS, Nicos (1975), *Classes in Contemporary Capitalism*, London: New Left Books.

PRANDY, K. (1965), *Professional Employees: A Study of Scientists and Engineers*, London: Faber.

REES, Alwyn (1950), *Life in a Welsh Countryside*, Cardiff: University of Wales Press.

RENNER, K. (1949), *The Institutions of Private Law and their Social Functions*, London: Routledge and Kegan Paul.

REX, John, and MOORE, Robert (1967), *Race, Community and Conflict*, Oxford: Oxford University Press.

ROBERTS, K., COOK, F. G., CLARK, S. C., and SEMEONOFF, E. (1977), *The Fragmentary Class Structure*, London: Heinemann.

ROGERS, Alan (1974), 'The Pattern of Farming', in A. Edwards and A. Rogers (eds.) (1974), pp. 181–212.

ROSE, David, SAUNDERS, Peter, NEWBY, Howard, and BELL, Colin (1976), 'Ideologies of Property: A Case Study', *Sociological Review*, vol. 24, No. 4, December, pp. 699–731.

ROSE, David, NEWBY, Howard, SAUNDERS, Peter, and BELL, Colin (1977), 'Land Tenure and Official Statistics', *Journal of Agricultural Economics*, vol. 28, No. 1, January, pp. 67–75.

ROSEN, Anthony (1973), 'Increased Land Prices – Their Implications on the Future Structure of Agriculture', R.H.M. *Hampshire Harvest Review*, September.

ROSEN, Anthony (1975), 'Who Will Own Britain?', *Farmland Market*, No. 3, January, pp. 9–11.

ROTH, Andrew (1973), 'The Business Background of MPs', in John Urry and Wakeford (eds.), *Power in Britain*, London: Heinemann.

ROTH, Andrew (1975), *The MP's Chart*, London: Parliamentary Profiles.

RUNCIMAN, W. G. (1966), *Relative Deprivation and Social Justice*, London: Routledge and Kegan Paul.

SAMPSON, A. (1971), *The New Anatomy of Britain*, London: Harrap.

SAMUELSON, K. (1964), *Religion and Economic Action*, London: Heinemann.

SAUNDERS, Peter (1977), 'They Make the Rules', *Policy and Politics*, vol. 4, 1975, pp. 31–58.

SAUNDERS, Peter (1978), 'Domestic Property and Social Class', *International Journal of Urban and Regional Research*, vol. 2., no. 2.

SAUNDERS, Peter, NEWBY, Howard, BELL, Colin, and ROSE, David (1978), 'Rural Community and Rural Community Power', in H. Newby (ed.) (1978).

SCASE, R. (1974), 'Conceptions of the Class Structure and Political Ideology: Some Observations on Attitudes in England and Sweden', in F. Parkin, *The Social Analysis of Class Structure*, London: Tavistock, pp. 149–78.

SCHLATTER, R. (1951), *Private Property – The History of an Idea*, London: Allen and Unwin.

SCHUTZ, A. (1967), *The Phenomenology of the Social World*, Evanston, Illinois: Northwestern University Press.

SCOTT, J. (1974), *Exploitation in Rural Class Relations: A Victim's Perspective*, New York: The Asia Society.

SELF, P., and STORING, H. (1962), *The State and the Farmer*, London: Allen and Unwin.

SMELLIE, K. (1968), *A History of Local Government*, 4th edn, London: Allen and Unwin.

STACEY, Margaret (1960), *Tradition and Change*, Oxford: Oxford University Press.

STACEY, Margaret, BATSTONE, Eric, BELL, Colin, and MURCOTT, Anne (1975), *Power, Persistence and Change*, London: Routledge and Kegan Paul.

STANWORTH, P., and GIDDENS, A. (1975) (eds.), *Elites and Power in British Society*, Cambridge: Cambridge University Press.

STEIN, M. (1964), *The Eclipse of Community*, New York: Harper Row.

STINCHCOMBE, A. (1962), 'Agricultural Enterprise and Rural Class Relations', *American Journal of Sociology*, vol. 67, No. 2, pp. 169–76.

STREET, A. G. (1937), *Farming England*, London: Batsford.

STURMEY, S. G. (1955), 'Owner Farming in England and Wales', *Manchester School*, vol. 23, pp. 245–68.

SUFFOLK COUNTY COUNCIL (1974/5), *County Planning Statistics*, Ipswich: Suffolk County Council Planning Department.

SULLIVAN, Lorana (1976), 'Why the City is Going Back to the Farm', *Sunday Times*, 2 May 1976, p. 54.

TABB, W. (1972), 'Alternative Futures and Distributional Planning', *Journal of the American Institute of Planners*, vol. 35, pp. 25–32.

TAWNEY, R. H. (1920), *The Sickness of an Acquisitive Society*, London: Allen and Unwin.

TAWNEY, R. H. (1966), *Religion and the Rise of Capitalism*, Harmondsworth: Penguin Books.

THOMPSON, F. M. L. (1963), *English Landed Society in the Nineteenth Century*, London: Routledge and Kegan Paul.

UNIVERSITY OF CAMBRIDGE (1947), *Landownership in the Eastern Counties*, Cambridge: University of Cambridge, Farm Economics Branch.

VEBLEN, T. (1923), *Absentee Ownership and Business Enterprise in Modern Times*, New York: Sentry Press.

VIDICH, A., and BENSMAN, J. (1958), *Small Town in Mass Society*, New York: Anchor.

WARNER, W. L., LOW, J., LUNT, P., and SROLE, L. (1963), *Yankee City*, New Haven, Conn.: Yale University Press.

WATSON, W. (1964), 'Social Mobility and Social Class in Industrial Communities', in M. Gluckman (ed.), *Closed Systems and Open Minds*, Edinburgh: Oliver and Boyd.

WATT, Hew (1975), 'Stop Exploiting the Land', *Farmland Market*, No. 3, January, pp. 12–13.

WEBER, Max (1930), *The Protestant Ethic and the Spirit of Capitalism*, London: Allen and Unwin.

WEBER, Max (1964), *The Theory of Social and Economic Organization*, Glencoe, Ill.: Free Press.

WEBER, Max (1968), *Economy and Society* (ed. Roth and Wittich), New York: Bedminster Press.

WESTERGAARD, John (1974), 'Some Aspects of the Study of Modern British Society', in J. Rex, *Approaches to Sociology*, London: Routledge and Kegan Paul, pp. 12–38.

WESTERGAARD, John, and RESLER, Henrietta (1975), *Class in a Capitalist Society*, London: Heinemann.

WHITFIELD, G. K. (1970), *The Evolution of Local Government Authorities and Areas in Suffolk 1555–1894*, University of Kent M.A. thesis.

WIBBERLEY, Gerald (1975), 'Rural Resource Development in Britain and Environmental Concern', *Journal of Agricultural Economics*, vol. 27, no. 1, pp. 1–16.

WILKINSON, R. H. (1970), 'The Gentlemanly Ideal and the Maintenance of a Political Elite', in P. W. Musgrove (ed.), *Sociology, History and Education*, London: Methuen, pp. 126–42.

WILLIAMS, Raymond (1973), *The Country and the City*, London: Chatto and Windus.

WILLIAMS, Raymond (1977), *Marxism and Literature*, Oxford: Oxford University Press.

WILLIAMS, W. M. (1956), *The Sociology of an English Village*, London: Routledge and Kegan Paul.

WILLIAMS, W. M. (1964), *A West Country Village: Ashworthy*, London: Routledge and Kegan Paul.

WILSON, G. (1978), 'Farmers' Organisations in Advanced Industrial Societies', in H. Newby (ed.) (1978).

WINKLER, J. T. (1976), 'Corporatism', *European Journal of Sociology*, vol. 17, No. 1, pp. 100–36.

WOLFINGER, R. (1971), 'Nondecisions and the Study of Local Politics', *American Political Science Review*, vol. 65, pp. 1063–80.

WORMELL, Peter (1974), 'The Landlord in the Bowler', *Big Farm Management*, August, pp. 50–3.

WORMELL, Peter (1976), 'University Survey Analyses East Anglian Farmers', *East Anglian Daily Times*, 31 July 1976, p. 5.

WRAY, D. (1948), 'Marginal Men of Industry: the Foremen', *American Journal of Sociology*, vol. 54, pp. 298–301.

YOUNG, M., and WILLMOTT, P. (1956), 'Social Grading by Manual Workers', *British Journal of Sociology*, vol. 7, pp. 337–45.

Appendix 1

Of methods and samples

In Chapter 2 we gave brief details concerning our methodology. In this appendix we wish to concentrate discussion mainly on the way in which we obtained our sample. As far as interviewing respondents was concerned, however, all interviews were conducted by the authors between July 1974 and March 1975, after a few pilot interviews in Essex in the spring of 1974. Newby re-interviewed most of the HN sample, Bell interviewed the Essex farmers in the 1000 + acres sample, Rose interviewed most of the rest of the 1000 + acres sample and Saunders most of the forty-four parishes sample. However, in order that all the authors should have a complete picture, each interviewed some respondents from each sample.

The drawing of the samples eventually proved relatively unproblematic, but we had initially anticipated certain problems in this regard. This was because the only adequate sampling frame for farmers is held by the Ministry of Agriculture which conducts an annual census of all farms in England and Wales. We required at minimum the names and addresses of all farmers in the forty-four parishes and all farmers in Cambridgeshire, Essex, Norfolk and Suffolk with holdings of over 1000 acres.[1] From previous experience we knew that the Ministry, although empowered to release this kind of information if 'in the public interest', were extremely reluctant to do so (see Newby, 1977). Nevertheless we approached its Academic Liaison Officer and, as a result of discussions, it was agreed that our request for sampling frames would be considered. We were equally sensitized to one other potential problem which Newby had encountered in his previous research. It is not only necessary to persuade the Ministry to provide a sampling frame, but politic to inform the NFU and CLA of this type of research and seek their cooperation in addition. We were only too aware that failure to do this could jeopardize our whole research. Consequently, we approached both organizations and explained our intentions.

The subsequent discussions with the NFU and CLA produced a

satisfactory response and within days we were able to obtain all the information we required from the Ministry's Census and Surveys Branch.

Consequently, the main potential problem – an adequate sampling frame – was solved. It remained only to remove from the lists with which we were provided any names or companies which appeared more than once.[2] We then proceeded to draw a one-in-two random sample of holdings of over 1000 acres and a one-in-three stratified random sample, by acreage size groups, in the forty-four parishes. The former sample was relatively unproblematic but the latter had then to be divested of all part-time holdings. Tables 75, 76 and 77 give the necessary details of our two random samples. In the case of the forty-four parishes sample, Table 76 represents only an initial 'crude' selection. We decided that any farmer contacted who was not employed full-time on his holding would not be interviewed, and the sample was to be adjusted on assumptions of randomness. Moreover, included in the first sample of 154 farms were eighteen of Newby's original sample. The rest of his original sample were then added as the HN sample to be re-interviewed. The final forty-four parishes sample is represented in Table 77. A comparison with Table 76 shows that sixty-one of the 'crude' sample were dropped, mainly because they were part-time holdings but a few because of multiple holdings not immediately identifiable from Ministry lists. Details of the final samples are given in note 7 of Chapter 2 (see above, p. 355).

The questionnaire

The questionnaire we used is reproduced as Appendix 2. We always intended that this should not be a completely closed instrument and so we gave ample opportunity for our respondents to discuss matters in an open-ended way, despite the later coding and data analysis problems. We attempted to steer the delicate and uneasy course between the collection of 'hard' data and a more unstructured approach amenable to *verstehen*.[3]

Finally we wish to deal with our method of making initial contact. When piloting we had merely sent a letter explaining very generally what we were doing and enclosing a pre-paid card on which respondents could indicate whether or not they would cooperate. This made it much too easy for our respondents to refuse and our response rate was only about 30 per cent. Consequently, we modified our procedure, retaining the letter but adding an explanatory and, we hoped, seductive leaflet. This consisted mainly of an article by the agricultural correspondent of *The Times*, written shortly after Bell and Newby had been awarded the SSRC grant, and which was complimentary to the idea behind the project. Moreover, this kind of public relations exercise was made all the more necessary since our research began during a period of severe student unrest at the University of Essex which was fully (if not accurately) reported in the media. Rather than enclosing a pre-paid card, we stated in our letter that we would telephone to arrange an interview. This enabled farmers to discuss with us more fully our aims, and made it less easy for them to refuse.

Table 75   *The 1000 + acres sample*

	Farms	Samples	Interviewed	Refused
Cambridgeshire	50	27	18	9
Essex	41	20	15	5
Norfolk	135	69	46	23
Suffolk	84	39	26	13
Total	310	155	105	50

Response rate: 67·75 per cent.

Table 76   *The original forty-four parishes sample*

Size-group (acres)	Farms	Sample
0–4¾	88	29
5–14¾	77	25
15–19¾	15	5
20–29¾	30	10
30–49¾	32	11
50–99¾	59	19
100–149¾	40	13
150–299¾	61	20
300–499¾	41	13
500–699¾	13	4
700–999¾	8	3
1000+	5	2
Total	469	154

Table 77   *The final forty-four parishes sample*

Size-group (acres)	Sample	Interviewed	Refused/not contacted
0–4¾	1	1	0
5–14¾	7	1	6
15–19¾	0	0	0
20–29¾	7	3	4
30–49¾	9	3	6
50–99¾	18	11	7
100–149¾	12	11	1
150–299¾	19	13	6
300–499¾	11	7	4
500–699¾	4	2	2
700–999¾	3	3	0
1000+	2	2	0
Total	93	57	36

Response rate: 61·3 per cent.

Note: Except where stated all correlations in this book are significant at the level $p < ·01$.

Notes

1   We decided upon the lower limit of 1000 acres as a result of (a) an examination of county agricultural statistics, (b) the desire, within our given resources, to have an initial sample of approximately 150 farms to represent the capitalist organized business farms in East Anglia, and (c) to ensure all respondents employed non-family labour. Although size of business in terms of standard-man-days would have been a preferable basis on which to have drawn this sample than acreage, our anticipation of problems in drawing the sample forced us to abandon such criteria. (In the event, even the Ministry could not have provided a sample on this basis, as we were later informed.)

2   Again this was a problem of which previous research had made us aware. The Ministry samples 'holdings', but many farmers have more than one building and consequently there is the 'double count' or 'multiple holdings' problem referred to by, for example, Harrison (1964, 1975) by which a farmer's name or company appears

more than once in Ministry lists. Equally, of course, this meant that any farmer whose total holdings were in excess of 100 acres but who had no individual holding of this size would not appear in the 1000+ acres sample.

3   For a fuller discussion see Newby *et al.* (1975).

Appendix 2
Farmers' questionnaire

Before I begin I just want to emphasize one or two things about the questions I am going to ask you. Firstly, it almost goes without saying that if there are any particular questions which you don't wish to answer then you are at perfect liberty to do so. Secondly, all the replies are, of course, *entirely confidential*. What happens to them afterwards is that we take all the replies off the completed questionnaire and combine them in the form of statistical tables, so that we can say so many said this and so many said that – so I can give you an assurance of complete confidentiality. Perhaps we can begin, then.

1. First of all, could you tell me the acreage of this holding?
2. And what type of farm is it?

   1. Dairy
   2. Livestock
   3. Poultry
   4. Pigs
   5. Arable

   6. Predominantly vegetable
   7. Predominantly fruit
   8. Horticulture
   9. Mixed
   10. Part-time

   Now I want to ask a few questions about your life up to now.
3. Firstly, were you brought up on this farm?

   1. Yes   0. No

   If no, where were you brought up?
4. Where were you born?
5. What year was that?
6. What type of secondary education did you have?
7. How old were you when you left full-time education?

   1. Under 14
   2. 14
   3. 15
   4. 16

   5. 17
   6. 18
   7. 18+
   8. DK/NA
8. Have you passed any of the following?

   1. School Certificate
   2. GCE 'O' Levels
   3. GCE 'A' Levels

9. Have you served an apprenticeship or studied for any other qualifications in agriculture?

   Yes   No

   If yes
   1. Apprenticeship   4. Nat. Cert.
   2. City and Guilds Stage 1   5. Nat. or Coll. Dip.
      or UEI, UCLI or UYI   6. Univ. Degree
   3. City and Guilds Stage 2   0. None
      and/or 3

10. I'd like to know about all the jobs you have had up to now. We'll start with the first job you ever had and work up to the present, including any military service. If you have only ever been a farmer I should like you to tell me all the details of your farming career.

    What was your first job?
    Where was that?
    (How big a farm? Did you own it?)
    How long were you there?
    Why did you leave?
    Where did you go? etc.

11. IF ANY NON-AGRICULTURAL JOB(S):
    Casting your mind back over all these jobs you have had, including your present one, which have you liked best?
    IF NOT FARMING:
    Why do you say that?

12. Do you have any other business interests apart from your farm?
    1. Yes   0. No
    What are they?
    How significant are these other interests to you?
    (PROMPT: moneywise, emotionally, etc.)

13. Could you please estimate the typical time spent on the following activities?
    First of all, office work – on average how many hours per day do you spend on routine paperwork, telephone calls, personal callers, planning and so on?
    Secondly, supervision of the men on the farm, NOT counting time actually spent *working* with them.
    And how many hours in a week do you spend actually working alongside your men?
    On average what are the total number of hours on work associated with your farm?

14. Are you married?
       1. Yes   0. No

    If married, obtain number and sex of children, age, number working, jobs if not on farm (for married daughters get husband's occupation).

    Has your wife had a job?
       1. Yes   0. No

    If yes, what is/was it?
    (Note if full- or part-time)
    If no, what did she do before marriage?

15. Does your family take an interest in farm affairs?
       1. Yes   0. No

    If yes, can you give me an idea of their involvement in the following tasks?

    First your wife: (Go through tasks in turn asking after each one: Does he/she . . . regularly, occasionally, rarely, never? Then repeat for each relative.)
    a. Answers phone, deals with callers, runs farm errands.
    b. Does office paper work.
    c. Gives workers their orders.
    d. Works on the land.
    e. Makes future farm policies.

16. Can you give me some details about the types of jobs held by your close relatives? First your father. What job does he do? (Take note of D.K.s. If anyone is deceased, retired or unemployed ask for last normal job. Go through persons listed below.)

    Repeat for: Brother 1
                   Brother 2
                   Brother 3
                   Brother 4
                  *Sister 1
                   Sister 2
                   Sister 3
                   Sister 4
                   Wife's father
                  *(If sisters married obtain occupation of husbands.)

17. Can you think of four men with whom you are friendly and tell me what jobs they have? You can include relations, neighbours, people you work with or anyone else with whom you are

friendly. (Check for job, firm/industry, residence, whether relative and acreage if farmer.)

Do the four know each other?

18. You said earlier that you farm .... acres.

How many acres do you rent, and how many do you own? And do you let out land to anyone else?

If no land owned move to B.

A   Let's discuss the land you own, first,

Is your land fully owned or do you have a mortgage or similar arrangement?

1. Fully owned   4. Lease back
2. Mortgaged through AMC   5. Other (specify)
3. Other mortgage

If all land owned (non rented)

Do you think owning as well as farming the land confers any particular outlook on life – say if you compare yourself with a tenant farmer, do you see yourself as significantly different in any way?

B   Now I should like to refer to the land you rent.

First of all, what about the landlord – is he a private landlord, an institution, or what?

1. Private landlord (farmer)   5. National Trust
2. Private landlord   6. Bank/Insurance Co.
   (non-farmer)   (specify)
3. Church Commissioners   7. Other institution (specify)
4. Oxbridge College

FOR EACH LANDLORD

(a) How do you get on with your landlord(s)?

(b) How often do you see your landlord?

(c) Do you think it's a good thing that you see him that often?

(d) Why do you say this?

(e) Do you ever meet your landlord socially?

If yes,

(f) Where do you meet him?

What are the terms of your lease(s)?

(PROMPT – restrictions on crop rotation, length of time etc.)

Have you heard of any tenants who have had problems with their landlords in this part of the country?

1. Yes   0. No

If yes, can you give me brief details?

Have you had any particular problems with your landlord(s) or agents recently?

1. Yes   0. No

If yes, could you tell me about it please?

If all land rented, do you think that renting rather than owning the land confers any particular outlook on life – say if you compare yourself with an owner-occupier, do you see yourself as significantly different in any way?

C   IF SOME LAND LET OUT

You let out . . . . acres. How many tenants does that involve?

    (a) How do you get on with your tenant(s)?

    (b) How often do you see him/them?

    (c) Do you think it's a good thing that you see him that often?

    (d) Why do you say this?

    (e) Do you ever meet your tenant(s) socially?

        If yes,

    (f) Where?

D   IF SOME LAND RENTED AND SOME OWNED

What do you think of yourself as – a tenant, an owner-occupier (or a landlord)?

If self rates tenant

Do you think that renting rather than owning the land confers any particular outlook on life – say if you compare yourself with an owner-occupier, do you see yourself as significantly different in any way?

If self rates owner or landlord

Do you think owning as well as farming the land confers any particular outlook on life – say if you compare yourself with a tenant farmer, do you see yourself as significantly different in any way?

FOR TENANTS AND OWNER-OCCUPIERS

19. What are the advantages of being a . . . . as opposed to a . . . . would you say?

And what are the disadvantages?

Would you rather be a . . . . than a . . . . ? Why?

20. IF NOT INHERITED FROM FATHER

One of the things we are particularly interested in is how people come into farming. Can you tell me what made you become a farmer in the first place? Was there any particular event that led up to it, had you always wanted to, or what?

21. Do you think that the inflation in the price of agricultural land since 1970 has been harmful or beneficial to the farming industry?
    1. Harmful   2. Beneficial
    Why?
    (PROBE: on obstacles to entry into farming.)

22. IF NOT INHERITED FROM FATHER
    How did you come by the capital to start in farming?

23. Are you the sole owner of your farm or are you in partnership?
    1. Sole owner   2. Partnership
    If partnership: Who are you in partnership with?
    (Get names and relationship)
    Is your business a limited company?
    1. Yes   0. No
    If yes, how are the shares divided?

24. How sensitive are you to changes in the market for various farming products?
    Since you began farming here, have you introduced any innovations in the management and/or husbandry of the farm which you think are important?
    1. Yes   0. No
    If yes, can you tell me about them? And why you made them? Was this in response to changes in the market?

25. Quite a few farmers these days sign contracts with companies like Bird's Eye or Walls or Ross Foods. Are you contracted to produce for companies like these?
    1. Yes   0. No
    If no, have you ever seriously considered doing so?
    1. Yes   0. No
    If yes, why haven't you then?
    If no, why not?
    If yes, which company(ies)?
    Some farmers occasionally say that companies like ....
    exert too much control over their own farming practices. Would you agree with them?

26. A great deal has been written in the farming press recently about farms being bought by City institutions – insurance companies, finance houses and so on. Do you think this trend is beneficial to the farming industry?

       1. Yes   0. No

       Why?

27. Do you think the men who own big business have too much power in this country?

       1. Yes   0. No

       Why do you say that?

       (PROMPT: Ford, ICI, Fisons, Shell, etc.)

28. Some people say that in farming bigger means better. Do you agree?

       1. Yes   0. No

       Why/why not?

       (PROBE: for ideas about good farmer and whether other farmers in general have this view. Attempt to obtain examples of 'good' farmers.)

29. If the opportunity arose to expand the size of your farm, would you do so?

       1. Yes   0. No

       If yes, Why?

       What is the ultimate size for an efficient farm like yours?

30. Roughly what is the amount of annual turnover of this farm? Can you give me an estimate of your profit margin before tax on your turnover?

       Do you know your profit per acre?

31. How do you feel about your present level of income? Are you:

       1. Completely satisfied   3. A little dissatisfied

       2. Quite satisfied   4. Very dissatisfied

       If dissatisfied, And who do you blame for this state of affairs?

32. In the recent election campaign a great deal was talked on all sides about the unfair distribution of income in our country. It's not only trade unionists who say this, but also many leading industrialists and others not connected with the Labour Party. Now you are better off than many people, have you ever felt the need to justify this to yourself in any way?

       1. Yes   0. No

       Could you explain a little bit about this please?

       How would you account for your achievements in farming?

33. In the past *two* years, have you made use of the following sources of advice on farming? Could you please rank the three most important in terms of assisting you in planning and running the farm?

       1. Commercial representatives

2. ADAS
3. University staff
4. Fieldmen (Bird's Eye/BSC, etc.)
5. NFU staff
6. Farm recording agencies
7. Bank managers and accountants
8. Private consultants
9. Estate or land agents
10. Relatives
11. Neighbours not related
12. Farmers' discussion groups, farm walks – demonstrations
13. Evening lectures, conferences
14. Visits to agricultural research centres and agricultural shows
15. Farming programmes on radio and television
16. Farming press
17. Local and national newspapers (specify)

34. IF NO WORKERS, GO TO QUESTION 42
    Could you tell me how many workers, including members of your family, you employ on this holding full-time?
    Men   Women
    And what kinds of jobs do they do? PROBE for managers and foremen.
    How many of them are members of your family?
    How many full-time partners and directors?
    How many regular part-time workers, including family?
    What kind of jobs do they do?
    How many are family?
    How many part-time partners and directors?

35. Do you work alongside your employees?
    1. Regularly   3. Rarely
    2. Occasionally   4. Never

36. When you have an applicant for a job on your farm, what qualities in him do you look for?
    Do you think the possession of formal qualifications make a man a better farm worker?
    1. Yes   0. No
    Why is this?

37. Would you say employer/employee relations have changed in any significant way since you began farming?
    1. Yes   0. No

If yes, could you explain in what way they have changed? And why?

If no, why has there been no change in farming when everywhere else there has?

(PROBE for 'team' or 'family' metaphors without introducing these terms directly.)

38. How involved do you feel in the life of your employees outside the course of work?
     1. Very involved   3. Not much involved
     2. Involved   4. Not at all involved
     Can you explain what you mean by .... involved?
     Do you ever see your workers off the farm?
     1. Yes   0. No
     If yes, whereabouts?
     Would you say that your wife felt equally involved? For example does she:
     1. Visit the wife of a worker who is ill, or who has just had a baby?
     2. Give occasional presents to employees' children?
     3. Help out in the home of an employee who has some kind of domestic crisis?

39. What, in your experience, is the best way to handle workers on a farm?

40. Can you tell me how many workers have quit their job on the farm?
     1. Over the last year
     2. Over the last five years

41. Do you have any tied or service cottages for your employees?
     1. Yes   0. No
     The tied cottage system is one of the most controversial topics in farming as far as the NUAAW is concerned, and, of course, *Farmers' Weekly* recently carried out a survey about it. Could you give me your views on the system? Have you ever had to resort to legal action to remove a tied cottage tenant?
     1. Yes   0. No
     If yes, could you tell me about it?

42. Some people say that farm workers do not get their fair share of national income in wages. Do you agree?
     1. Yes   0. No
     If yes, whose fault is that?
     If no, so you would say farm workers' pay is fair?

43. Would you say that farmers have more in common with farm workers than with businessmen in industry?
    1. Yes   0. No
    Why do you say that?
44. Generally what is your attitude to the farm workers' union?
45. Do you think that trade unions are for the working man at everyone else's expense?
    1. Yes   0. No
    Why do you say that?
    What would you say if I said that the NFU is for the farmers at everyone else's expense?
46. Do you belong to the NFU?
    1. Yes   0. No
    If no, go to question 47.
    If yes, when did you join the NFU?
    Why did you join?
    Which branch do you attend?
    How often do you attend meetings? Would you say you went?
        Regularly   Rarely
        Occasionally   Never
    When did you last go to one?
    If never or rarely, why don't you bother much with branch meetings?
    Have you ever held any official post in the NFU?
    1. Yes   0. No
    If yes, which one(s)?
    How often do you talk to fellow farmers about NFU matters?
    1. Very often   3. Now and then
    2. A good deal   4. Hardly ever
    Would you say the NFU adequately represents the interests of farmers at (a) local and (b) national level?
    1. Yes   0. No
    Why do you say that?
47. FOR NON-NFU MEMBERS
    Have you ever been a member of the NFU?
    1. Yes   0. No
    If yes, why did you leave?
    If no, do you have any serious objections to joining the NFU?
    1. Yes   0. No
    If yes, why is this?
    (PROBE for instrumental *v.* ideological reason.)
    If no, is it just that you never bothered to join, then?

48. Would you say that the NFU is run for all sections of the farming industry or do they favour any particular section?

    1. Run for all   2. Particular

    If particular, please specify.

    Do you think the NFU is sufficiently militant?

    1. Yes   0. No

    If no, what sort of militant action do you think the NFU should take?

49. Are you a member of the CLA?

    1. Yes   0. No

    If no, go to question 50.

    If yes, when did you join?

    Why did you join?

    How often do you attend meetings?

    Regularly   Rarely

    Occasionally   Never

    If rarely or never, why?

    Do you think the CLA adequately represents the interests of landowners at (a) local and (b) national level?

    1. Yes   0. No

    Why do you say that?

50. FOR NON-CLA MEMBERS

    Have you ever been a member of the CLA?

    1. Yes   0. No

    If yes, why did you leave?

    If no, do you have any serious objections to joining the CLA?

    1. Yes   0. No

    If yes, why is this?

    (PROBE for instrumental *v.* ideological reason.)

    If no, is it just that you never bothered to join, then?

51. Do you belong to any other agricultural societies, clubs or associations? (PROMPT: RASE, BFS, local farmers' clubs.)

    Now I would like to ask you a few questions about life here in . . . .

52. Now you have lived here since . . . .?

    How interested are you in what goes on in . . . .?

    1. Very interested   3. Little interested

    2. Fairly interested   4. Not at all interested

53. Do you belong to any clubs or associations? (For each ask if any official position held and how often attended – regularly, occasionally, rarely, never.)

54. Do you belong to any religious organization?
    If yes, ask if any official position held and regularity of attendance.
55. Do you or your wife hold any positions of responsibility locally?
    Check list (specify at each point)
    1. JP (specify bench)
    2. Area Health Authorities
    3. School/college governor
    4. Water/Drainage Board
    5. Village Hall committee
    6. Charity trustees
    7. Regional Planning Board
    8. Valuation panel
    9. Youth Employment Committee
    10. Clerk to parish council
56. Some people say that with all the changes in the countryside there has been a loss of community in the rural village. Is this so, do you think?
    1. Yes   0. No
    Why? (PROBE for attitudes to newcomers.)
    What do you mean by community?
57. Traditionally, say in the 19th century, many villages were run by squire, parson and schoolteacher, and, of course, 'squire' was also a landowner and farmer. Do any farmers still behave like squires?
58. What sort of view do you think people in general have of farmers?
    Why do you think they have this view?
    What about here in the village? What sort of view do you think other people have of farmers?
    What is it that decides social standing of different people here do you think?
    What about nationally?
59. People often talk about there being different classes in this country.
    What do you think?
    CHECK FOR
    1. Number of social classes
    2. Terminology
    3. Major factors determining class position

4. Position respondent sees himself as holding
5. Explanations of why individuals hold the class position they do
6. Assessment of extent of upward mobility – hard work
7. View of necessity and desirability of system
8. Degree of class conflict or harmony
9. Leadership characteristics

60. You only have to open a newspaper or listen to the news nowadays to see something wrong somewhere. What do you think is wrong with the country today?
    Why do you say that?

61. How interested are you in national politics?
    1. Very interested   3. Not particularly interested
    2. Quite interested   4. Not at all interested

62. Would you mind telling me how you voted in the last four general elections?

63. Do you belong to any political party?
    1. Yes   0. No
    If yes, which?
    1. Con   3. Lib
    2. Lab   4. Other
    Do you hold office in the party?
    1. Yes   0. No
    If yes, what office?
    How long have you held office?
    If no, have you ever held office in the party?
    1. Yes   0. No
    If yes, what office
    When was this? How long for?
    Now I would like to ask you some questions about local government.

64. Firstly, are you, or have you ever been, a member of any parish, district, or county council?
    1. Yes   0. No
    If yes, get names of councils, dates of service.
    If *not* a member of any old or new district or county council in 1974 proceed to question 68.
    If currently a member of district or county council, or if a member of old authority until April 1974, proceed to question 74.

65. To what extent do you believe you are personally affected by decisions taken by the local and county councils?
Why do you say this?
66. Generally speaking, would you say that the local and county councils take much notice of what farmers want in making their decisions?
    1. Yes   0. No
Is there any particular reason why you say this?
(PROBE – Do farmers have more say than other people?)
67. So if you wanted to make your views known to the council in the hope of influencing it, how would you go about it?
68. FOR FARMERS IN EAST SUFFOLK ONLY
In your experience, are there any organizations or groups in this area which seem to be fairly successful in affecting the outcome of local issues in which they take an interest?
    1. Yes   0. No
If yes, who?
Why do you say this?
(PROBE – What have they done in the past? What do you know about them? What about the NFU?)
69. FOR FARMERS IN EAST SUFFOLK ONLY
What about individuals who tend to be fairly influential locally? Can you think of anybody who takes an active interest in local affairs and who tends to get involved in local issues?
    1. Yes   0. No
If yes, who?
Why do you say this?
(PROBE – What have they done in the past? What do you know about them?)
70. Do you think that the kind of local issues that concern you as a farmer are of equal concern to other local people?
    1. Yes   0. No
If yes, can you give me an example?
PROMPT – What about town dwellers?
    local industry?
    amenity societies?
    farm workers?
If no, do you think, therefore, that the issues that concern you as a farmer conflict with those of other local people?
    1. Yes   0. No
If yes, whose interests conflict with those of the farmers?

Who generally prevails?

71. Recently there has been some national concern over the effects of farming practices on the environment. What do you think about this?

72. Are you concerned by any local activities by preservation or amenity societies?

(PROBE – footpaths, hedges stubble burning, preservation generally.)

What has been *your* practice in the last decade in removing hedgerows (or other 'traditional features of the rural landscape')?

73. Finally, looking back over your life as a farmer, have you ever thought of giving it all up and leaving farming?

   1. Yes   0. No

If yes, have you done anything about it?
Why have you thought of leaving?
So why do you remain a farmer?

74. Can you tell me what aspects of the farming occupation you most value?

And what do you like least?

75. If you could go back and start life all over again would you choose a different occupation?

   1. Yes   0. No

Why do you say that?

Appendix 3
The 'Community Power' study

In Chapter 6 we discuss the role of farmers and landowners in local government in Suffolk. We investigated their activities at all three levels of local government (parish, district and county councils) with particular emphasis on the forty-four parishes. This involved the former rural districts of Blyth, Deben, Hartismere and Gipping and the district councils (since 1974) of Mid-Suffolk and Suffolk Coastal, in which the forty-four parishes were included. We also examined a number of issues on the former East Suffolk County Council and the new Suffolk County Council, formed in 1974. In our investigation of local politics we used a number of techniques, viz.:

1. A search of local newspapers since 1960 in order to examine the history of decision-making in Suffolk over this period. We also monitored all local newspapers in East Suffolk between 1973 and 1976. From this search we were able to assess the nature and extent of local political conflict and to select issues for further analysis in interviews (see below).

2. A postal questionnaire survey of all local councillors in East Anglia, as described in detail in Chapter 6, note 2.

3. Data were also gained from our main survey of farmers – see Questions 64–70, Appendix 2.

4. The major method of data collection, however, was a series of unstructured interviews conducted with local councillors, local government officers and other individuals involved in local politics (for example, instituting constituency party officials, journalists, pressure-group officials, etc.) in Suffolk. Eventually fifty such interviews were completed between April 1974 and February 1976. Although not pre-structured we did use an *aide mémoire* as follows:

    (1) Council memberships and chairmanships if any.
    (2) Why became a councillor – approached/political/service.
    (3) Role of chairmen and chief officers.
    (4) Allocation to committees, selection of chairmen.

(5) Party groups – whips, pre-council meetings, etc.
Did respondent stand as Ind? How ind are Inds?
Why did (didn't) party politics evolve after reorganization.
What have been the consequences, where are areas of disagreement?
(6) Any local issues?
Why was Ipswich expansion stopped – role of farming lobby.
Why was Sizewell welcomed?
Tattingstone, restrictions on housing development, concessionary bus fares, fluoridation, comprehensive education.
(7) Why are there so few issues?
Consensus/the public interest/are there conflicts of interests?
What about development/overspill (why not in East Suffolk?)
Rigid planning restrictions.
Agriculture *v.* preservation.
Rehousing tied cottage tenants, weekend cottages (improvement grants).
Low rates – why so few houses built.
Why relatively low welfare expenditure.
(Labour respondents – why haven't you pressed on this?)
(8) Conflict since reorganization – between East and West at county level.
Between urban and rural at district level.
Between district and county.
(9) Relations with local organizations and individuals, preservation societies.
NFU.
Individual electors – farmers.
Formal consultations/informal grapevine/no contact.
How can/should those with a grievance go about expressing it, and what effect will this have?
What affects re-election chances – party affiliation, individual reputation? How significant is the agricultural vote?
Why were so many returned unopposed in past? Why such low turnout at elections?
(10) Role conflict between private interests and duties as councillor?
Why so many farmers on councils? Is this significant?

(Press hard on this with ex-Hartismere respondents.)
(11) Parish councils – power before and after reorganization.
Relation with higher local authorities.
Relation with local organizations (amenity, community councils).
What sort of people on PCs? How are they recruited and why?
(12) Occupation and length of residence of respondent.
Organizational memberships of respondent.
Other positions of responsibility (school managers, area health councils, JP, water boards, etc.). How appointed? What do duties entail? What is significance of the body, etc.?

Index

paternalism, 26–31, 170–89
  passim, 241
Pennock, J. R., 40
Perkin, H., 32, 34, 112
Perrott, R., 226
Perry, P. J., 34
Pettigrew, A., 228
Plamenetz, J., 329
Plowman, D., *et al.*, 208
Plumb, H., 15
Poor Law Amendment Act 1834,
  222–3
Poor Relief Act 1601, 222
Poulantzas, N., 17, 20, 284, 286,
  339
power: in local communities,
  227–9, 253–75 *passim*;
  legitimacy, community and,
  253–5; non-decision-making
  and, 254–71; and 'objective
  interests', 243–8; pluralist
  theories of, 253–5, 262–3
Prandy, K., 18
property: ideologies of, 25, 105,
  255, 325–51 *passim*; and
  political domination, 248–71;
  and political philosophy, 22–5,
  325–35 *passim*; and property
  relationships, 20–6; types of,
  335–44
Property Growth Assurance
  Company, 87

Rees, A. D., 16, 183
Renner, K., 336, 383, 385
research design, 58–9, 403–25
Return of Owners of Land, the,
  35, 95
Rex, J., and Moore, R., 267
Roberts, K., *et al.*, 18
Rogers, A., 47, 50
Rose, D., *et al.*, 22, 75, 98–9,
  347–8, 357–8, 362–3, 384
Rosen, A., 13, 86, 361
Roth, A., 40, 369

Runciman, W. G., 314
rural housing market, 194, 251–4;
  see also housing; local
  government
rural labour market, 146–89
  passim, 245, 254

sampling, *see* research design
Sampson, A., 123
Samuelsson, K., 382
Saunders, P., 258, 269
Saunders, P., *et al.*, 75, 227
Scase, R., 281, 287
Schlatter, R., 22, 23, 326
Schutz, A., 280
Scott, J., 28
Self, P., and Storing, H., 40,
  120–3, 127, 130, 290, 364
'size effect', 172, 180
Smellie, K. B., 222
Smith, Adam, 24, 382–3
social class, *see* class
social status, *see* status
squirearchy, 196–200, 221–6
Stacey, M., 28
Stacey, M., *et al.*, 28
Stanworth, P., and Giddens, A., 20
status; attributional *versus*
  interactional, 208; local
  system of, 195–200, 206–7,
  312–13
Stein, M., 222
Stinchcombe, A., 26, 76
Sturmey, S. G., 35, 37
Suffolk Coastal DC: farmers'
  representation on, 232–3;
  housing policy, 251; party
  politics in, 256–61;
Suffolk County Council:
  budgetary policy, 249–50;
  farmers' representation on,
  232–3; party politics in, 256–61;
  planning policies, 233–48
  passim, 264–5; public
  expenditure cuts by, 250